Lecture Notes in Computer Science 12154

More information about this series at http://www.springer.com/series/7408

Jonathan P. Bowen · Zhiming Liu ·
Zili Zhang (Eds.)

Engineering Trustworthy Software Systems

5th International School, SETSS 2019
Chongqing, China, April 21–27, 2019
Tutorial Lectures

 Springer

Editors
Jonathan P. Bowen 🆔
Southwest University
Chongqing, China

Zhiming Liu 🆔
Southwest University
Chongqing, China

Zili Zhang
Southwest University
Chongqing, China

ISSN 0302-9743   ISSN 1611-3349 (electronic)
Lecture Notes in Computer Science
ISBN 978-3-030-55088-2   ISBN 978-3-030-55089-9 (eBook)
https://doi.org/10.1007/978-3-030-55089-9

LNCS Sublibrary: SL2 – Programming and Software Engineering

This Springer imprint is published by the registered company Springer Nature Switzerland AG
The registered company address is: Gewerbestrasse 11, 6330 Cham, Switzerland

Preface

The 5th School on Engineering Trustworthy Software Systems (SETSS 2019) was held during April 21–27, 2019, at Southwest University, Chongqing, China. It was aimed at PhD and Master students in particular, from around China and elsewhere, as well as being suitable for university researchers and industry software engineers. This volume contains tutorial papers related to a selection of the lecture courses and evening seminars delivered at the School.

SETSS 2019 was organized by the School of Computer and Information Science, in particular the Centre for Research and Innovation in Software Engineering (RISE), at Southwest University, providing lectures on leading-edge research in methods and tools for use in computer system engineering. The School aimed to enable participants to learn about state-of-the-art software engineering methods and technology advances from experts in the field.

The opening session was chaired by Prof. Guoqiang Xiao, Dean of the School of Computer and Information Science. A welcome speech was delivered by the Vice President of Southwest University, Prof. Yanqiang Cui, followed by an introductory briefing for SETSS 2019 by Prof. Zhiming Liu. The session finished with a photograph of participants at the School (see page xiii).

The following lecture courses (each consisting of six, or for Yu Guo three, hour-long lecture sessions, with breaks) were delivered during the School, chaired by Zhiming Liu and Shmuel Tyszberowicz:

- Manfred Broy: "Modeling Cyber Physical Systems: Requirements, Interface Specifications and Architectures in a Concurrent World"
- Lei Bu: "From Bounded Reachability Analysis of Linear Hybrid Automata to Verification of Industrial CPS and IoT"
- Yu Guo: "Blockchain Based Protocols for Perfectly Fair Exchange"
- Joost-Pieter Katoen: "Principles of Probabilistic Programming"
- Kim G. Larsen: "From Timed Automata to Stochastic Hybrid Games Model Checking, Synthesis, Refinement, Performance Analysis and Machine Learning"
- Grigore Roşu: "$\mathbb{K}$—A Semantic Framework for Programming Languages and Formal Analysis Tools"

In addition, there were two two-hour evening seminars chaired by Bin Gu:

- Yu Jiang: "Empirical Evaluation of Fuzzing Techniques and Some Potential Enhancements"
- Zhiming Liu: "Software Architecture Modelling – Master Complexity and Enable Healthy Evolution"

Three hour-long workshop sessions by Bin Gu, Zhibin Yang, and Bingqing Xu, were chaired by Zhiming Liu. These additional seminars and workshops complemented the longer lecture courses.

Courses

"Modeling Cyber Physical Systems: Requirements, Interface Specifications and Architectures in a Concurrent World"

Lecturer: Prof. Dr. Manfred Broy, Technical University of Munich, Germany

Biography: Manfred Broy's research is in software and systems engineering both in theoretical and practical aspects. This includes system models, specification and refinement of system and software components, specification techniques, development methods, and verification. He is leading a research group working in a number of industrial projects that apply mathematically based techniques to combine practical approaches to software engineering with mathematical rigor. His main topics are requirements engineering, software and system architectures, componentware, software development processes, software evolution, and software quality. The CASE tool AutoFocus was developed in his group. One of Manfred Broy's main themes is the role of software in a networked world. As a member of acatech under his leadership the study Agenda Cyber-Physical Systems was created for the Federal Ministry of Research to comprehensively investigate the next stage of global networking through the combination of cyberspace and embedded systems in all their implications and potential. Since January 2016, Professor Broy has been the founding president of the Bavarian Center for Digitization. There he is working on the topics of digital transformation and digital innovation.

Overview: Systems such as cyber-physical systems exist and act in a distributed concurrent world where space and time are most important issues. This is in contrast to concurrency as it appears in computer systems, operating systems, and programming languages. When modeling systems that are closely related to their physical operational context, we need models that allow us to express aspects of the physical world such as time, interaction, concurrency, and distribution. The lectures presented a number of models capable of capturing a model-based way such as types of systems as a basis for writing requirements and finally systems specifications.

"From Bounded Reachability Analysis of Linear Hybrid Automata to Verification of Industrial CPS and IoT"

Lecturer: Prof. Lei Bu, Nanjing University, China

Biography: Lei Bu is currently a professor at the Department of Computer Science and Technology, Nanjing University, China. He received his bachelor and PhD degree in Computer Science from Nanjing University in 2004 and 2010, respectively. He has been visiting scholars in institutes like Carnegie Mellon University, Microsoft Research Asia, and so on. His main research interests include model checking, hybrid systems, and cyber-physical systems. He has published more than 50 papers in leading journals and conferences like TC, TPDS, TCPS, RTSS, CAV, DATE, VMCAI, and so on. He has won awards under the Chinese Computer Federation young talent development program and the Microsoft Research Asia Star Track young faculty program.

Overview: Safety assurance of real-time safety-critical systems is a very important problem. Hybrid automata (HA) is the natural modeling language for real-time systems with both discrete and continuous state changes. However, as the behavior of HA is too complex, the state-of-the-art techniques cannot scale up to industrial level cases. In this series of lectures, I gave a brief introduction of HA and presented an overview of our specific path-oriented methods for complexity controlling in the bounded verification of linear hybrid automata (LHA). I also showed how our methods and tools are adapted and deployed in the verification of industrial CPS and smart home IoT systems.

"Blockchain Based Protocols for Perfectly Fair Exchange"

Lecturer: Dr. Yu Guo, SETBIT Labs, China

Biography: Dr. Yu Guo is the Founder/CEO of SETBIT Labs, a startup focusing on blockchain technology and blockchain security. He graduated from the University of Science and Technology of China (USTC) and received his PhD degree in 2007. He was an associate professor in USTC between 2007–2016, working on formal verification, system software, and computer security. His research interests include programming languages, formal verification, system software, cryptography, and computer security. He worked in a Fintech company as a technical vice president for two years, owning more than 30 patents about blockchain infrastructure. He founded SETBIT Labs in 2018, which reported numerous vulnerabilities in smart contracts and attacking events on blockchains, leading the research of smart contract verification, smart contract analysis, and cryptographic protocols.

Overview: Online commerce traditionally needs trusted third parties (TTP) to solve the deadlock where the buyer is willing to do the payment prior to receiving the goods, while the seller won't send the data until the buyer pays. The TTP withholds the payment until the buyer confirms the goods. However, TTPs tend to be a centralized entity to guarantee the trust, which inevitably increase risks of both privacy leaking and functional failure. Reducing the dependence on TTPs while keeping fairness has been a classic open problem for decades. The perfect fairness, ensuring neither party of the buyer and seller cannot take any advantage over the other, helps to build trustless online trading system that can be highly effective. Participants are able to exchange digitalized goods (or data) without concerns about mistrust. The lectures presents recently-proposed protocols. They use state-of-the-art cryptographic schemes to achieve fair exchange of data by means of blockchain techniques. The lectures covered blockchains, security protocols, and cryptography, showing thriving research results from blockchain communities.

"Principles of Probabilistic Programming"

Lecturer: Prof. Joost-Pieter Katoen, RWTH Aachen University, Germany and University of Twente, The Netherlands

Biography: Prof. Joost-Pieter Katoen is a Distinguished Professor with RWTH Aachen University, Aachen, Germany, and holds a part-time professorship at the University of Twente, Enschede, The Netherlands. He is a member of Academia Europaea (since

2013) and received a honorary doctorate degree from Aalborg University, Aalborg, Denmark in 2017. He has been visiting professor at, among others, the University of Oxford, IST Austria, and Macquarie University in Sydney. His research interests include formal methods, model checking, concurrency theory, and probabilistic computation. In 2018, he received an ERC Advanced Research Grant to continue his work on foundations of probabilistic programming. Joost-Pieter Katoen has co-authored more than 200 conference papers, 75 journal papers, and the book on *Principles of Model Checking* (2008). His work has received about 20,000 citations. Prof. Katoen is the Chairman of the Steering Committee of TACAS, and Steering Committee member of the conferences CONCUR, QEST, and FORMATS. He is also member of the IFIP Working Groups 1.8 (Concurrency Theory) and 2.2 (Programming Concepts).

Overview: Probabilistic programming combines probability theory, statistics, and – most importantly from a modeling point of view – programming languages. They allow modeling of a much larger class of models in a rather succinct manner. The full potential of modern probabilistic programming languages comes from automating the process of inferring unobserved variables in the model conditioned on observed data. As some researchers put it: The goal of probabilistic programming is to enable probabilistic modeling and machine learning to be accessible to the working programmer. Probabilistic programs steer autonomous robots, are at the heart of security mechanisms, encompass randomised algorithms, and are used in AI to infer statistical conclusions about huge amounts of uncertain data. In this series of lectures, I introduced the main concepts of probabilistic programming and discussed how classical program verification a la Dijkstra can be used to answer questions such as: Do these programs compute what one expects them to do? Do they terminate at all? With what probability? How much resources do they consume? Applications to Bayesian networks showed how insightful information about analyzing such networks can be obtained in a fully automated manner by using program verification.

"From Timed Automata to Stochastic Hybrid Games Model Checking, Synthesis, Refinement, Performance Analysis and Machine Learning"

Lecturer: Prof. Kim G. Larsen, Aalborg University, Denmark

Biography: Kim G. Larsen is a professor in the Department of Computer Science at Aalborg University within the Distributed and Embedded Systems Unit and director of the ICT-competence center CISS, Center for Embedded Software Systems. In 2015, he won an ERC Advanced Grant with the project LASSO for learning, analysis, synthesis, and optimization of cyber-physical systems. He is also director of the Sino-Danish Basic Research Center IDEA4CPS, the Danish Innovation Network InfinIT, as well as the newly founded innovation research center DiCyPS: Data Intensive Cyber Physical Systems. Larsen is prime investigator of the tool UPPAAL and co-founder of the company UP4ALL International. In 2013 he was the recipient of the CAV Award for his work on UPPAAL as "the foremost model checker for real-time Systems." Larsen became Honorary Doctor (Honoris causa) at Uppsala

University, Sweden, in 1999. In 2007, he became Knight of the Order of the Dannebrog. In 2007, he became Honorary Doctor (Honoris causa) at ENS Cachan, France. In 2012, he became Honary Member of Academia Europaea. Since 2016, he has been appointed INRIA International Chair for a five-year period. He has also won the prestigious industrial Grundfos Award 2016, and has been appointed Distinguished Professor of Northeastern University under the Chinese *Recruitment Program of Foreign Experts* in 2018.

Overview: Timed automata and games and their priced extensions have emerged as useful formalisms for modeling real-time and energy-aware systems as found in several embedded and cyber-physical systems. During the last 20 years the real-time model checker UPPAAL has been developed allowing for efficient verification of hard timing constraints of timed automata. Moreover a number of significant branches exists, e.g. UPPAAL CORA providing efficient support for optimization, UPPAAL TIGA allowing for automatic synthesis of strategies for given safety and liveness objectives, and ECDAR supports refinement and compositional development of real-time systems. Also the branch UPPAAL SMC, provides a highly scalable new engine supporting (distributed) statistical model checking of stochastic hybrid automata. Most recently, the new branch UPPAAL STRATEGO supporting safe and optimal strategies for stochastic hybrid games by combining symbolic methods with machine learning. The lectures reviewed and provided demonstrations of the various branches of UPPAAL, the corresponding modeling formalisms as well as sketched the symbolic or statistical algorithms applied. The focus was on applications of the tools suite to a range of real-time and cyber-physical examples including schedulability and performance evaluation of mixed criticality systems, modeling and analysis of biological systems, energy-aware wireless sensor networks, smart grids and smart houses, and intelligent traffic.

"𝕂—A Semantic Framework for Programming Languages and Formal Analysis Tools"

Lecturer: Prof. Grigore Roşu, University of Illinois at Urbana-Champaign, USA

Biography: Grigore Roşu is a professor in the Department of Computer Science at the University of Illinois at Urbana-Champaign (UIUC), where he leads the Formal Systems Laboratory (FSL), and the founder and president of Runtime Verification, Inc (RV). His research interests encompass both theoretical foundations and system development in the areas of formal methods, software engineering, and programming languages. Before joining UIUC in 2002, he was a research scientist at NASA Ames. He obtained his PhD at the University of California at San Diego in 2000. He was presented the CAREER Award by the NSF, the Dean's Award for Excellence in research by the College of Engineering at UIUC in 2014, and the Outstanding Junior Award by the Computer Science Department at UIUC in 2005. He won the ASE IEEE/ACM Most Influential Paper Award in 2016 (for an ASE 2001 paper) and the RV Test of Time Award (for an RV 2001 paper) for papers that helped shape the runtime verification field, the ACM SIGSOFT Distinguished Paper Awards at ASE 2008, ASE 2016, and OOPSLA 2016, and the Best Software Science Paper Award at ETAPS 2002. He was ranked a UIUC excellent teacher in Spring 2013, Fall 2012, Spring 2008, and Fall 2004.

Overview: K is a rewrite-based executable semantic framework in which programming languages, type systems, and formal analysis tools can be defined using configurations, computations, and rules. Configurations organize the state in units called cells, which are labeled and can be nested. Computations carry computational meaning as special nested list structures sequentializing computational tasks, such as fragments of program. Computations extend the original language abstract syntax. K (rewrite) rules make it explicit which parts of the term they read-only, write-only, read-write, or do not care about. This makes K suitable for defining truly concurrent languages even in the presence of sharing. Computations are like any other terms in a rewriting environment: they can be matched, moved from one place to another, modified, or deleted. This makes K suitable for defining control-intensive features such as abrupt termination, exceptions or call/cc. Several real languages have been defined in K, such as C (ISO C11 standard), Java (1.4), JavaScript (ES5), Python, Scheme, Verilog, the Ethereum VM, and dozens of prototypical or classroom ones. The ISO C11 semantics and a fast LLVM backend for K power RV-Match (https://runtimeverification.com/match), one of the most advanced commercial automated analysis tools for C. The EVM semantics and a general-purpose Haskell backend for K power a program verifier for Ethereum smart contracts used by several blockchain companies. The lessons taught attendees how to define a language or a type system in K, and then how to automatically obtain an executable model of the defined language or system which is amenable to formal analysis. Major real language semantics defined in K was also discussed, as well as commercial formal analysis tools based on them, such as the the RV-Match ISO C11 undefinedness checker (https://runtimeverification.com/match/).

From the presentations, a record of the School has been distilled in the chapters within this volume as follows:

- Manfred Broy: "Seamless Model-Based System Development: Foundations"
- Lei Bu, Jiawan Wang, Yuming Wu, and Xuandong Li: "From Bounded Reachability Analysis of Linear Hybrid Automata to Verification of Industrial CPS and IoT"
- Marcin Szymczak and Joost-Pieter Katoen: "Weakest Preexpectation Semantics for Bayesian Inference: Conditioning, Continuous Distributions and Divergence"
- Xiaohong Chen and Grigore Roşu: "𝕂—A Semantic Framework for Programming Languages and Formal Analysis"
- Zhiming Liu, Jonathan P. Bowen, Bo Liu, Shmuel Tyszberowicz, and Tingting Zhang: "Software Abstractions and Human-Cyber-Physical Systems Architecture Modelling"

For further online information on SETSS 2019, see: http://www.swu-rise.net.cn/SETSS2019.

SETSS 2019 was supported by IFIP Working Group 2.3 on Programming Methodology. The aim of WG 2.3 is to increase programmers' ability to compose programs which fits very well with the themes of SETSS.

We would like to thank the lecturers and their co-authors for their professional commitment and effort, the reviewers for their help in improving the papers in this volume, the strong support of Southwest University, and the enthusiastic work of the local organization team, without which SETSS 2019 and these proceedings would not have been possible. Thank you to Bo Liu for providing the photograph and information. Finally, we are grateful for the support of Alfred Hofmann and Anna Kramer of Springer *Lecture Notes in Computer Science* (LNCS) in the publication of this volume.

May 2020

Jonathan P. Bowen
Zhiming Liu
Zili Zhang

Group photograph at SETSS 2019.
Seated front row, left to right:
Weiwei Chen (Professor), Yongjun Jin (Professor, SWU),
Zili Zhang (Professor, SWU), Grigore Roşu (SETSS lecturer),
Yanqiang Cui (Vice President, SWU), Lei Bu (SETSS lecturer),
Guogiang Xiao (Dean, SWU), Zuoxun Liu (Professor, SWU),
Zhiming Liu (SETSS organizer), Shmuel Tyazberwicz (SETSS organizer).

Organization

School Chairs

Zili Zhang	Southwest University, China
Guoquiang Xiao	Southwest University, China

Academic Instructors

Jonathan P. Bowen	RISE, Southwest University, China, and London South Bank University, UK
Zhiming Liu	RISE, Southwest University, China

Organization Committee

Bo Liu (Chair)	RISE, Southwest University, China
Huazhen Liang	RISE, Southwest University, China
Shmuel Tyszberowicz	RISE, Southwest University, China, and Tel Aviv University, Israel
Qing Wang	RISE, Southwest University, China
Xia Zeng	RISE, Southwest University, China
Hengjun Zhao	RISE, Southwest University, China

School Academic Committee

Michael Butler	University of Southampton, UK
Yixiang Chen	East China Normal University, China
Zhi Jin	Peking University, China
Zhiming Liu	RISE, Southwest University, China
Cong Tian	Xi'Dian University, China
Ji Wang	National University of Defence Science and Technology, China
Yi Wang	Uppsala University, Sweden, and Northeast University, China
Jim Woodcock	University of York, UK
Jianhua Zhao	Nanjing University, China

Paper Reviewers

Jonathan P. Bowen	RISE, Southwest University, China, and London South Bank University, UK
Manfred Broy	Technical University of Munich, Germany
Lei Bu	Nanjing University, China

Joost-Pieter Katoen   RWTH Aachen University, Germany,
                                   and University of Twente, The Netherlands
Meng Sun   Peking University, China
Andrea Turrini   Institute of Software, Chinese Academy of Sciences,
                                   China
Shmuel Tyszberowicz   RISE, Southwest University, China, and Tel Aviv
                                   University, Israel
Zhibin Yang   Nanjing University of Aeronautics and Astronautics,
                                   China

Contents

Seamless Model-Based System Development: Foundations
(*Extended Abstract*)

Manfred Broy$^{(\boxtimes)}$ (iD)

Institut für Informatik, Technische Universität München, 80290 Munich, Germany
broy@in.tum.de
http://www.broy.informatik.tu-muenchen.de

Abstract. This is an extended abstract which gives an overview and sufficient references to work on model-based development of cyber-physical systems, both to its formal and scientific foundations as well as to more methodological issues including requirements engineering and architecture. Key concepts are interface behaviour and modular composition to support the modelling of the interaction between systems and their context, between subsystems, and between subservices as part of feature interactions. A logical framework is described for specification, implementation, refinement, and verification.

Keywords: Model based software and systems development · Interface · Architecture · Refinement · Design · Contracts · Assumptions · Commitments · System specification

1 Overview

Model-based development [21, 27, 28, 37, 42] addresses the development of software and software-intensive systems based on a set of carefully selected modelling concepts [30, 38], addresses the key stages of development such as requirements engineering [9, 22], architecture design [40, 41], implementation, code generation [1], and verification [32]. Seamless model-based development means that for each of the different phases of development, appropriate models are available and that these models are semantically well-founded and in a precise semantic relationship to each other [7, 38]. The development process could be understood as a step-by-step process, working out these models, with a clear idea of how the models of the next phase can be derived from the models of the previous phase and with unambiguous relationships between those models given.

Of course, model-based development needs an appropriate set of modelling concepts [38]. These modelling concepts must have a clean and proper foundation [5, 23, 25]. That can be achieved by giving a set of mathematical constructions, which can serve as models [9]. These models should be constructed in a way that they support all steps of development from requirements to architecture to implementation, up to integration and verification. This requires appropriate models for each phase the development and in each phase the models must address different aspects such as functionality (in terms of

© Springer Nature Switzerland AG 2020
J. P. Bowen et al. (Eds.): SETSS 2019, LNCS 12154, pp. 1–9, 2020.
https://doi.org/10.1007/978-3-030-55089-9_1

interfaces), data models, models of interaction and composition, models of operational behaviour, and models of verification, such as test models and specification models. In addition, quality models are needed that cover all relevant attributes and concepts of quality.

Then one needs a clear understanding how these models fit together and can be understood as refinement of each other. This requires as a foundation what is called semantic coherence, which means that these models semantically fit together [21]. An example would be that one has a clear understanding: how state models correspond to an interface model [32], how an architecture can be abstracted into an interface model [42], or how state machine models for the components of an architecture can be composed and understood as a description of a large state machine [23].

Such a set of models is the basis for an artefact model, if one has a clear knowledge how to integrate and relate them. In an artefact model [38], we collect – as in a meta-model – all the different modelling techniques available in terms of a development model such that it becomes clear which models must be produced during the development and how they are related. Such an artefact model is the basis for tool-based development [1]. In a tool, a concrete instance of the artefact model is worked out in terms of a data model where the tool must support the database creation of all these models and also the handling of the relationship of these models.

In the end, such an approach means that software development or the development of software-intensive systems is done by working out the instance of the artefact model supported by a tool following the modelling concepts and showing how these different models are related and that they are in the appropriate refinement relation, which needs a well-understood number of verification activities.

A special question is the use of quality models, which can be considered as part of the artefact model and there, in particular, as part of the requirement models where the expected quality attributes are listed and related to the other models of the system.

Such an approach to software and system modelling is called *seamless*, if all models and all development steps are in a tight relationship with a clear understanding how they benefit from each other. The models themselves must support classical principles of system design such as encapsulation, interface, abstraction, information hiding, refinement and modular composition [10]. This supports system evolution and systematic reuse.

2 On Systems, Their Interfaces and Properties

We use the term *system* in a specific way. We address discrete systems, more precisely discrete models of real-time system [26, 31] with input and output [27]. For us, a system is an entity that shows some specific behaviour by interacting with its operational context. A system has a boundary, which determines what is inside and what is outside the system. Inside the system, there is an encapsulated internal structure. The set of actions and events [34] that may occur in the interaction of the system with its operational context at its border determines the syntactic ("static") interface of the system. At its interface, a system shows a specific *interface behaviour*.

We distinguish between:

- the *syntactic interface* of a system that describes which actions may be executed at the interface and which kind of data, signals, and messages are exchanged by these actions across the system border,
- the *semantic interface* (also called *interface behaviour*), which describes the behaviour evolving over the system border by the interaction between the system and its operational context in terms of the specific data, signals, and messages exchanged in the process of interaction by input or output actions according to the syntactic interface.

For specifying predicates there are further general properties that we expect. We require that system behaviours fulfil properties such as causality and realizability that are required for a specification to be implementable (see [18, 35]). However, not all interface assertions guarantee these properties. Nevertheless, in such a case these properties can be added schematically to system specifications.

2.1 Architecture

When looking at software families and product lines, architecture becomes significant, because it determines the possibilities and options of quality, evolution, changeability, variability, and reusability [11]. What we need is an appropriate architectural modelling framework, sufficiently abstract with the required expressive power that supports modularity. With this in mind, it is a key issue to work with appropriate methodology offering a calculus for the design of architectures. This includes a number of ingredients:

From the behavioural point of view, we distinguish between [40, 41]:

- A key concept of systems as well as subsystems, also called components, as building blocks of architectures: This means that we must determine what the concept of a subsystem is and, in particular, what the concept of an interface and interface behaviour is. Interfaces are the most significant concept for architectures. Subsystems are composed and connected via their interfaces.
- The second ingredient is modular composition. We must be able to compose subsystems and decompose systems via their interfaces resulting in interfaces of the composite system. Composition should reflect parallel execution and real time.
- This requires that interfaces of subsystems can be structured into a family of sub-interfaces, which then are the basis for the composition of subsystems, more precisely the composition of sub-interfaces of subsystems with other sub-interfaces of subsystems. For this, we need a syntactic notion of interface and a notion of interface behaviour.
- In addition, we are interested in options to specify properties of interface behaviours in detail. This includes the structuring of interfaces into sub-interfaces and capturing their relationships by so-called modes formalizing feature interactions.
- Moreover, we must be able to deal with interface types and auxiliary system types. Such concepts allow us to introduce a notion of subsystems and their types, called system classes as in object-oriented programs, and these can also be used to introduce types of interfaces, with assumptions about the interfaces of auxiliary systems

with which systems are composed. Finally, it supports the instantiation of system components in a dynamic way.

- For capturing the systematic development of specifications into implementations we use the concept of refinement of systems and their interfaces, which also provides a basis of inheritance.

A key is our ability to specify properties of subsystems [33] in terms of their interfaces and to compose interface specifications in a modular way.

2.2 Structuring Architecture – Future Reference Architecture

Architecture of systems and also of software systems is about structuring systems. There are many different aspects of structuring systems and therefore of designing their architecture. Examples are *functional feature architectures* or of a *functional service architectures* [42]. Another very basic concept of architecture is the decomposition of a larger system into a number of subsystems that are composed and provide this way the behaviour of the overall system. We speak of a *subsystem architecture* or of a *component architecture* (see [42]).

This shows that architecture addresses on one hand the structuring of the functionality of systems into smaller elements called functional features and on the other hand the decomposition of systems into a set of components, with a description how these elements are connected and behave in relationship to each other. A key concept of architecture is the notion of component and interface. An interface shows at the border of a system how the system interacts with its operational context.

Following ideas of platform-dependent and platform-independent views onto software systems and the ideas of interface specification, an architecture is structured basically by the three following views.

Functional Feature Architecture: Here we describe for (software) systems their functionalities (also called functional features or services [8]) that are offered by a software system to the outside world. Today, since software systems like smartphones or cars offer a large number of features described by services, it is important to structure these services into an architecture of services and to describe both their interface behaviour, which is the functionality provided to the outside, as well as their mutual relationships, which defines their functional dependencies, often called feature interactions. Therefore, we need description techniques capturing both interface behaviours, their structuring, and their dependencies (see [19, 22]). In addition, specifications of interfaces might also rely on assumptions about their context.

In addition to functional feature architecture, the sensors and actuators, as well as the human machine interaction defining the physical access to the functional service, must be designed. We do not consider such questions of human machine interaction or of communication with sensors or actuators but underline the relevance of this topic. We concentrate on the logics of interaction which includes humans, sensors and actuators.

Platform-Independent Component Architecture (Logical Subsystem Architecture): To realize software systems, we structure and decompose them into a set of components. From the viewpoint of architecture, these components must be described by their roles, captured by the services they offer in terms of their interfaces and their interface behaviour. Such component architectures are often defined by layered architectures. The description of their components should be independent of the choice of an execution platform but, nevertheless, by the interfaces we must be able to specify parallel behaviour, real-time, and also probabilistic behaviour (see [12, 29]).

Logical subsystem architectures including architectural patterns such as service-oriented architectures are execution platform independent [16]. They consist of the following ingredients:

- a set of elements, called subsystems or components, each equipped with (a set of) interfaces
- an architectural structure connecting these interfaces

This shows that a key issue in architectural design is the specification and structuring of interfaces including their interface behaviour and the description of their architectural structure.

Platform-Dependent Software and Hardware Architecture: In the end, the abstract system described in terms of the functional service architecture and the platform-independent component architecture should be implemented on a well-chosen hardware execution platform. This means, we must define the deployment of software and its scheduling. Here, it is important that the components of the component-oriented architectures are independent deployable units that are related to their environments only by their interfaces.

For all these architectural views, we need an appropriate concept of interface, of interface behaviour specification, and of system composition in terms of interfaces as well as techniques to specify interfaces.

Finally, we must be able to describe the operational context of software systems and assumptions about its behaviour [39]. Obviously, the operational context can be seen as a system on its own and its behaviour can be captured in terms of interfaces, again. A well understood way to describe the properties of the operational context that are relevant for the systems are assumptions in terms of interface assertions for the operational context [39]. Therefore, the core of the whole approach according to its foundations is an approach to describe interfaces and the concept of composition including assumptions formulated by interface assertions.

2.3 Interfaces

As can be seen from the description of architectures and their concepts, interfaces are a key issue. In our terminology, an interface consists both of a syntactic interface and an interface behaviour. Interfaces are used to describe the functions, features, and services of sub-components. Interfaces are used to describe the overall functionality of systems and their structuring into sub-services that again can be described by interfaces. This shows that the notion of interface is essential in architectural design. In fact, interfaces occur everywhere, in the functional service architecture, in the logical subsystems or components architecture, and in the technical architecture as well [5].

There are several ways to describe interfaces. Specifying interfaces is informally or formally done by interface assertions, by interaction diagrams, and by abstract state machines. Interface assertions can be formulated quite formally or rather informally. We refer to a fully formalized notion of interface and interface behaviour that is powerful enough to support interface specification by interface assertions and that is modular for parallel composition. Although fully formalized, the concept of interface assertion can nevertheless be used in an informal or as well as in a semiformal way [14].

2.4 Formal Foundations

A milestone for the scientific foundation of model-based development and also for modelling concurrent distributed interactive systems is a book on FOCUS [1], based on the idea of introducing a timed model which at the same time covers in a more abstract version non-timed systems [4]. A lot of theoretical work is based on that providing a rich theory and also a mathematical foundation of software engineering models [5]. In particular, it provides a coherent semantic model where state-based systems and architectures are included as well as interface models. The key are the models of interfaces divided into notations of syntactic interface and interface behaviour. As it turns out, interfaces are a key to the development.

The approach also deals with services and layered architecture [15, 17]. The key is a multi-view modelling of software systems in coherent semantic framework which supports the seamless development [9]. One of the key ideas is the notion of causality [20] as a basis for quite a number of specification and verification techniques [12]. In addition, the notion of modularity, encapsulation and information hiding is one of the basis for methodological approach [5]. The approach also includes more pragmatic description techniques, such as state transition diagrams and message sequence charts [6, 14].

One emphasis is on layered architectures and all their details [39]. Also, the theoretical side is carefully investigated, in particular, describing how the approach, which develops a notation of realizability, is related to classical concepts of computability from a more practical side [18].

In addition to classical notations of architecture, functional architectures, also called feature architectures, are introduced which give a framework for the functional behaviour of systems seen from the perspective of requirements engineering. One of the key issues is a logical basis. All models that are described are embedded in a coherent logical calculus [13, 22].

A key issue is how these more formal foundations are good for dealing with software and systems engineering approaches [5]. An interesting question is how those behaviour models are related to control theory [27].

The goal of the approach is a scientific foundation of model-based development with a clear relation to engineering tasks. Some work is also devoted to relating the general approach to classical questions in dealing with cyber-physical systems, such as traceability and functional safety [30].

Pragmatic techniques are investigated too, such as tables [33]. It is also demonstrated how the approach relates to process-oriented models [36]. All the work is shown to be implementable by specific tools such as the experimental tool AutoFOCUS [1–3].

A special approach are assumption commitment techniques [24] that both support layers and layered architectures as well as treatment of systems, which need some particular context assumptions [39].

This extensive formal framework has also served as the basis for a number of consortia projects supported by the German BMBF (Bundesministerium für Bildung und Forschung), which had the goal to make the whole approach more practical and to deal with a number of important engineering aspects [37, 42].

References

1. AutoFocus3 website: https://af3.fortiss.org
2. Aravantinos, S., Voss, S., Teufl, F., Hölzl, B., Schätz, B.: AutoFOCUS 3: tooling concepts for seamless, model-based development of embedded systems. Model Based Archit. Constr. Embed. Syst. (ACES-MB) **1508**, 19–26 (2015)
3. Böhm, W., Junker, M., Vogelsang, A., Teufl, S., Pinger, R., Rahn, K.: A formal systems engineering approach in practice: an experience report. In: SER&IPs, pp. 34–41 (2014)
4. Broy, M., Stølen, K.: Specification and Development of Interactive Systems: Focus on Streams, Interfaces, and Refinement. Springer, New York (2001). https://doi.org/10.1007/978-1-4613-0091-5
5. Broy, M.: Toward a mathematical foundation of software engineering methods. IEEE Trans. Softw. Eng. **27**(1), 42–57 (2001)
6. Broy, M.: From states to histories: relating states and history views onto systems. In: Hoare, C.A.R., Broy, M., Steinbrüggen, R. (eds.): Engineering Theories of Software Construction. Springer NATO ASI Series, Series F: Computer and System Sciences, vol. 180, pp. 149–186. IOS Press (2001)
7. Broy, M.: Hierarchies of models for embedded systems. In: 1st ACM and IEEE Conference on Formal Methods and Models for Co-Design, pp. 183–190. IEEE Computer Society (2003)
8. Broy, M.: Service-oriented systems engineering: modeling services and layered architectures. In: König, H., Heiner, M., Wolisz, A. (eds.) FORTE 2003. LNCS, vol. 2767, pp. 48–61. Springer, Heidelberg (2003). https://doi.org/10.1007/978-3-540-39979-7_4
9. Broy, M.: Multi-view modeling of software systems. In: Keynote. Satellite Workshop on Formal Aspects of Component Software, 8–9 September, Pisa, Italy FM2003 (2003)
10. Broy, M.: Unifying models and engineering theories of composed software systems. In: Broy, M., Pizka, M. (eds.): Models, Algebra and Logic of Engineering Software, Marktoberdorf Summer School 2002. Springer NATO ASI Series, Series F: Computer and System Sciences, vol. 191 (2002)
11. Broy, M.: Architecture driven modeling in software development. In: Proceedings of the 9th International Conference on Engineering of Complex Computer Systems. Florence 2004, pp. 3–14. IEEE Computer Society (2004)
12. Broy, M.: Time, abstraction, causality, and modularity in interactive systems. In: FESCA 2004. Workshop at ETAPS 2004, pp. 1–8 (2004)
13. Broy, M.: A functional calculus for specification and verification of nondeterministic interactive systems. In: Dershowitz, N. (ed.) Verification: Theory and Practice. LNCS, vol. 2772, pp. 161–181. Springer, Heidelberg (2003). https://doi.org/10.1007/978-3-540-39910-0_7
14. Broy, M.: The semantic and methodological essence of message sequence charts. Sci. Comput. Program. **54**(2–3), 213–256 (2004)

15. Herzberg, D., Broy, M.: Modeling layered distributed communication systems. Formal Aspects Comput. **17**(1), 1–18 (2005)
16. Broy, M.: Service-oriented systems engineering: specification and design of services and layered architectures. In: Broy, M., Grünbauer, J., Harel, D., Hoare, T. (eds.) Engineering Theories of Software Intensive Systems. NSS, vol. 195, pp. 47–81. Springer, Dordrecht (2005). https://doi.org/10.1007/1-4020-3532-2_2
17. Broy, M., Krüger, I., Meisinger, M.: A formal model of services. ACM Trans. Softw. Eng. Methodol. 16(1) (2007)
18. Broy, M.: Interaction and realizability. In: van Leeuwen, J., Italiano, G., van der Hoek, W., Meinel, C., Sack, H., Plášil, F. (eds.) SOFSEM 2007. LNCS, vol. 4362, pp. 29–50. Springer, Heidelberg (2007). https://doi.org/10.1007/978-3-540-69507-3_3
19. Broy, M.: Two sides of structuring multi-functional software systems: function hierarchy and component architecture. In: Kim, H.K., Tanaka, J., Malloy, B., Lee, R., Wu, C., Baik, D.K. (eds.) Proceedings 5th ACIS International Conference on Software Engineering Research, Management & Applications (SERA2007), 20–22 August, pp. 3–10. IEEE Computer Society (2007)
20. Broy, M.: Relating time and causality in interactive distributed systems. In: Broy, M., Sitou, W., Hoare, C.A.R. (eds.): Engineering Methods and Tools for Software Safety and Security, NATO Science for Peace and Security Systems, D: Information and Communication Security, vol. 22, pp. 75–130. IOS Press (2009)
21. Broy, M.: Seamless model driven systems engineering based on formal models. In: Breitman, K., Cavalcanti, A. (eds.) ICFEM 2009. LNCS, vol. 5885, pp. 1–19. Springer, Heidelberg (2009). https://doi.org/10.1007/978-3-642-10373-5_1
22. Broy, M.: Multifunctional software systems: structured modeling and specification of functional requirements. Sci. Comput. Program. **75**, 1193–1214 (2010)
23. Broy, M.: A logical basis for component-oriented software and systems engineering. Comput. J. **53**(10), 1758–1782 (2010)
24. Broy, M.: Towards a theory of architectural contracts: – schemes and patterns of assumption/promise based system specification. In: Broy, M., Leuxner, Ch., Hoare, C.A.R. (eds.): Software and Systems Safety – Specification and Verification. NATO Science for Peace and Security Series – D: Information and Communication Security, vol. 30, pp. 33–87. IOS Press (2011)
25. Broy, M.: Can practitioners neglect theory and theoreticians neglect practice? Computer **44**(10), 19–24 (2011)
26. Broy, M.: Software and system modeling: structured multi-view modeling, specification, design and implementation. In: Hinchey, M., Coyle, L. (eds.) Conquering Complexity, pp. 309–372. Springer, London (2012). https://doi.org/10.1007/978-1-4471-2297-5_14
27. Broy, M.: System behaviour models with discrete and dense time. In: Chakraborty, S., Eberspächer, J. (eds.) Advances in Real-Time Systems, pp. 3–25. Springer, Berlin, Heidelberg (2012). https://doi.org/10.1007/978-3-642-24349-3_1
28. Broy, M.: Introduction to the SPES modeling framework/outlook. In: Pohl, K., Hönninger, H., Achatz, R., Broy, M. (eds.) Model-Based Engineering of Embedded Systems: The SPES 2020 Methodology, pp. 31–49. Springer, Heidelberg (2012). https://doi.org/10.1007/978-3-642-346 14-9. pp. 251-254
29. Broy, M.: System behaviour models with discrete and dense time. In: Chakraborty, S., Eberspächer, J. (eds.) Advances in Real-Time Systems. Springer, Berlin, Heidelberg (2012). https://doi.org/10.1007/978-3-642-24349-3_1
30. Broy, M.: A logical approach to systems engineering artifacts and traceability: from requirements to functional and architectural views. In: Broy, M., Peled, D., Kalus, G., (eds.): Engineering Dependable Software Systems, pp. 1–48. IOS Press (2013)
31. Broy, M.: A model of dynamic systems. In: Bensalem, S., Lakhneck, Y., Legay, A. (eds.) ETAPS 2014. LNCS, vol. 8415, pp. 39–53. Springer, Heidelberg (2014). https://doi.org/10.1007/978-3-642-54848-2_3

32. Broy, M.: Verifying of interface assertions for infinite state Mealy machines. J. Comput. Syst. Sci. **80**(7), 1298–1322 (2014)
33. Broy, M.: Pragmatic formal specification of system properties by tables. In: De Nicola, R., Hennicker, R. (eds.) Software, Services, and Systems. LNCS, vol. 8950, pp. 329–354. Springer, Cham (2015). https://doi.org/10.1007/978-3-319-15545-6_21
34. Broy, M.: From actions, transactions and processes to services. In: Dependable Software Systems Engineering, Reihe the NATO Science for Peace and Security Series D: Information and Communication Security, vol. 40, pp. 42–78 (2015)
35. Broy, M.: Computability and realizability for interactive computations. Inf. Comput. **241**(April), 277–301 (2015)
36. Broy, M.: From actions, transactions, and processes to services. In: Kordon, F., Moldt, D. (eds.) PETRI NETS 2016. LNCS, vol. 9698, pp. 13–19. Springer, Cham (2016). https://doi.org/10.1007/978-3-319-39086-4_2
37. Broy, M., Pohl, K., Daembkes, H., Hönninger, H.: Advanced Model-Based Engineering of Embedded Systems. Extensions of the SPES 2020 Methodology. Springer International Publishing, Cham (2016). https://doi.org/10.1007/978-3-642-34614-9
38. Broy, M.: A logical approach to systems engineering artifacts: semantic relationships and dependencies beyond traceability – from requirements to functional and architectural views. Softw. Syst. Model. **17**, 365–393 (2016)
39. Broy, Manfred: Theory and methodology of assumption/commitment based system interface specification and architectural contracts. Formal Methods Syst. Des. **52**(1/2018), 33–87 (2017). https://doi.org/10.1007/s10703-017-0304-9
40. Broy, M.: The leading role of software and systems architecture in the age of digitization. The Essence of Software Engineering, pp. 1–23. Springer, Cham (2018). https://doi.org/10.1007/978-3-319-73897-0_1
41. Broy, M.: On architecture specification. In: Tjoa, A., Bellatreche, L., Biffl, S., van Leeuwen, J., Wiedermann, J. (eds.) SOFSEM 2018. LNCS, vol. 10706, pp. 19–39. Springer, Cham (2018). https://doi.org/10.1007/978-3-319-73117-9_2
42. Pohl, K., Hönninger, H., Achatz, R., Broy, M. (eds.): Model-Based Engineering of Embedded Systems. The SPES 2020 Methodology. Springer, London (2012)

From Bounded Reachability Analysis of Linear Hybrid Automata to Verification of Industrial CPS and IoT

Lei Bu$^{(\boxtimes)}$ ⓘ, Jiawan Wang, Yuming Wu, and Xuandong Li

State Key Laboratory for Novel Software Technology,
Department of Computer Science and Technology, Nanjing University,
Nanjing 210023, Jiangsu, People's Republic of China
bulei@nju.edu.cn

Abstract. Hybrid Automata are a well-known framework used to model hybrid systems, containing both discrete and continuous dynamic behavior. However, reachability analysis of hybrid automata is difficult. Existing work does not scale well to the size of practical problems. This paper gives a review of how we handle the verification of hybrid systems in a path-oriented way. First, we propose a path-oriented bounded reachability analysis method to control the complexity of verification of linear hybrid automata. As we only check the reachability of one path at a time, the resulted state space for each computation is limited and hence can be solved efficiently. Then, we present an infeasible constraint guided path-pruning method to tailor the search space, a shallow synchronization semantics to handle compositional behavior, and a method based on linear temporal logic (LTL) to extend the bounded model checking (BMC) result to an unbounded state space. Such methods and tools are implemented in a tool, BACH, and have been used as the underlying decision procedure of our verification of cyber-physical systems (CPS) and Internet of Things (IoT).

1 Introduction

Cyber-Physical Systems (CPS), combining communication, computation, and control (3C), focus on the complex interdependencies and integration between the cyber-world and the physical world [23]. CPS widely occur at safety critical areas of modern society, including fields like aerospace, automotive, civil infrastructure, energy, healthcare, manufacturing, and transportation. Thus, safety assurance of CPS is an important topic which attracts lots of research attention.

Model checking [14] is a widely studied method for checking whether a system meets some given specifications and have been used in the safety assurance of various systems including hardware design, software code, and so on. Typically, a formal model of the system is built first so that various model checking methods

---

This paper follows the lecture notes presented by the first author at the School on Engineering Trustworthy Software Systems (SETSS) in year 2019.

J. P. Bowen et al. (Eds.): SETSS 2019, LNCS 12154, pp. 10–43, 2020.
https://doi.org/10.1007/978-3-030-55089-9_2

can be applied on the models. Hybrid Automata (HA) [20] is the classical modeling language for CPS with both discrete and continuous behaviors. However, model checking for hybrid automata is difficult, and the classical reachability problem for linear hybrid automata (LHA), a subclass of hybrid automata, has been proven undecidable [22].

Expensive polyhedral computation based model checking techniques are first used for LHA symbolic reachability analysis in the tool HyTech [2, 21]. The tool Checkmate [13] and d/dt [3] compute the overapproximations of reachable sets in HA also by polyhedral representations. A more scalable model checking technique with representations of polyhedra and support functions are implemented in the tool PHAVer [17] and SpaceEx [18]. However, due to the high complexity of the computation, it is still hard for existing LHA model checkers to scale well to the problems of practical interest.

To handle the above problem, we proposed a specific path-oriented method to enumerate potential paths in the step bound, and check them one by one to accomplish the bounded model checking [5] of LHA, for both single linear hybrid automaton (LHA) and compositional LHA network. We utilizing SAT solvers for candidate path enumeration and LP (Linear Programming) techniques to checking each candidate path. An IIS (Irreducible Infeasible Subset)-based path tailoring technique is also proposed to increase the efficiency of our method. And, a new shallow synchronization semantic is introduced to encode the compositional behavior succinctly. Furthermore, we also extend our bounded reachability analysis method to unbounded proof results under certain conditions.

The above techniques are all implemented into a toolset, BACH. Which gives nice support for graphical modeling, reachability verification, and online runtime verification of hybrid and CPS systems. BACH outperforms state-of-the-art tools on the well-recognized benchmarks. Now, BACH is publicly available online and has attracted hundreds of registered users globally.

Thanks to the above efficient methods and tools, we have proposed online verification of CPS and modeling-verification-fixing framework of event-driven IoT system. Successful case studies are conducted on train control system and home automation system respectively. All these applications show the efficiency and effectiveness of our path-oriented reachability analysis method.

The structure of the rest of this tutorial paper is organized as follows. We give formal definition of LHA and compositional LHA in Sect. 2. Our path-oriented bounded reachability analysis method, including the IIS acceleration technique, is shown in Sects. 3, 4 and 5. Online verification of runtime CPS and verification of the IoT in a home scenario are given in Sect. 6 and Sect. 7 respectively. We conclude in Sect. 8.

This tutorial paper makes no novel contributions. It is meant to give the students attending the SETSS 2019 Spring School and others an overview of our work on the bounded reachability analysis of linear hybrid automata and their application in complex CPS and IoT systems [6–12, 24, 29–31, 33].

2 Preliminaries

In this section, we give the formal definition of linear hybrid automata and the composition of them. We also define the reachability specifications on linear hybrid automata.

2.1 Linear Hybrid Automata

Definition 1. *A linear hybrid automaton (LHA) H is a tuple $H = (X, \Sigma, V, V_0, E, \alpha, \beta, \gamma)$, where*

- *X is a finite set of real-valued variables; Σ is a finite set of event labels; V is a finite set of locations; $V_0 \subseteq V$ is the set of initial locations.*
- *E is a finite set of transition relations. Elements in E are in the form of $(v, \sigma, \phi, \psi, v')$, where v, v' are locations in V, $\sigma \in \Sigma$ is an event label, ϕ is a set of transition guards of the form $a \leq \Sigma_{i=0}^{l} c_i x_i \leq b$ ($x_i \in X$) and ψ is a set of reset actions of the form $x := d$ ($x \in X$), where a, b, c_i and d are real numbers and a, b may be ∞.*
- *α is a labeling function mapping each location in V to its invariant which is a set of variable constraints of the form $a \leq \sum_{i=0}^{l} c_i x_i \leq b$ ($x_i \in X$), where a, b and c_i are real numbers and a, b may be ∞.*
- *β is a labeling function mapping each location in V to a set of flow conditions which are in the form of $\dot{x} = [a, b]$ ($x \in X$) where a, b are real numbers and $a \leq b$. For any location $v \in V$, for any variable $x \in X$, there exists one and only one flow condition $\dot{x} = [a, b] \in \beta(v)$.*
- *γ is a labeling function mapping each location in V_0 to a set of initial conditions which are in the form of $x = a$ ($x \in X$), where a is a real number. For any $v \in V_0$, for any $x \in X$, there exists at most one initial condition $x = a \in \gamma(v)$.*

We use *path segment* to represent the evolution of an LHA from location to location. For an LHA $H = (X, \Sigma, V, V_0, E, \alpha, \beta, \gamma)$, a path segment is a sequence of locations of the form $\langle v_0 \rangle \xrightarrow[\sigma_0]{\phi_0, \psi_0} \langle v_1 \rangle \xrightarrow[\sigma_1]{\phi_1, \psi_1} \cdots \xrightarrow[\sigma_{n-1}]{\phi_{n-1}, \psi_{n-1}} \langle v_n \rangle$, which satisfies $(v_i, \sigma_i, \phi_i, \psi_i, v_{i+1}) \in E$ for each $i (0 \leq i < n)$. A *path* in H is a path segment starting from an initial location in V_0. For a path in H of the form $\langle v_0 \rangle \xrightarrow[\sigma_0]{\phi_0, \psi_0} \langle v_1 \rangle \xrightarrow[\sigma_1]{\phi_1, \psi_1} \cdots \xrightarrow[\sigma_{n-1}]{\phi_{n-1}, \psi_{n-1}} \langle v_n \rangle$, by assigning each location v_i with a time delay stamp δ_i, we get a *timed sequence* of the form $\langle {v_0 \atop \delta_0} \rangle \xrightarrow[\sigma_0]{\phi_0, \psi_0} \langle {v_1 \atop \delta_1} \rangle \xrightarrow[\sigma_1]{\phi_1, \psi_1} \cdots \xrightarrow[\sigma_{n-1}]{\phi_{n-1}, \psi_{n-1}} \langle {v_n \atop \delta_n} \rangle$, where δ_i $(0 < i \leq n)$ is a nonnegative real number. This time sequence represents a behavior of H such that the system starts from the initial location v_0, stays there for δ_0 time units, then jumps to v_1 and stays at v_1 for δ_1 time units, and so on.

The behavior of an LHA consists of continuous and discrete evolvements and can be informally described as follows. The automaton starts at one of its initial locations, with some variables initialized according to the initial conditions of this location. By continuous evolvement, the values of all variables change continuously as time progresses, according to the flow condition associated with the current location. By discrete evolvement, the system change its current location from v to v' instantaneously, provided that there is a transition relation $(v, \sigma, \phi, \psi, v')$ from v to v', whose all transition guards in ϕ are satisfied by the current value of the variables. With the location changed by a transition $(v, \sigma, \phi, \psi, v')$, some variables are reset to new values according to the reset actions in ψ.

Given a timed sequence ω of the form $\langle {v_0 \atop \delta_0} \rangle \xrightarrow[\sigma_0]{\phi_0, \psi_0} \langle {v_1 \atop \delta_1} \rangle \xrightarrow[\sigma_1]{\phi_1, \psi_1} \cdots \xrightarrow[\sigma_{n-1}]{\phi_{n-1}, \psi_{n-1}}$
$\langle {v_n \atop \delta_n} \rangle$ in an LHA H, we use $\lambda_i(x)$ to represent the value of x when the automaton reaches the location v_i along with ω, and $\zeta_i(x)$ to represent the value of x when the automaton has stayed at v_i for delay $\delta_i(x)$ $(x \in X, 0 \le i \le n)$. It follows that $\lambda_{i+1}(x) = \begin{cases} d & \text{if } (x := d) \in \psi_i \\ \zeta_i(x) & \text{otherwise} \end{cases}$ $(0 \le i < n)$. We give formal definition of the behavior in an LHA below.

Definition 2. *Given an LHA $H = (X, \Sigma, V, V_0, E, \alpha, \beta, \gamma)$, a timed sequence of the form $\langle {v_0 \atop \delta_0} \rangle \xrightarrow[\sigma_0]{\phi_0, \psi_0} \langle {v_1 \atop \delta_1} \rangle \xrightarrow[\sigma_1]{\phi_1, \psi_1} \cdots \xrightarrow[\sigma_{n-1}]{\phi_{n-1}, \psi_{n-1}} \langle {v_n \atop \delta_n} \rangle$ represents a behavior of H if and only if the following conditions are satisfied:*

- *$\langle v_0 \rangle \xrightarrow[\sigma_0]{\phi_0, \psi_0} \langle v_1 \rangle \xrightarrow[\sigma_1]{\phi_1, \psi_1} \cdots \xrightarrow[\sigma_{n-1}]{\phi_{n-1}, \psi_{n-1}} \langle v_n \rangle$ is a path;*
- *each variable $x \in X$ evolves according to its flow condition in each location v_i $(0 \le i \le n)$, i.e., $u_i \delta_i \le \zeta_i(x) - \lambda_i(x) \le u'_i \delta_i$, where $\dot{x} = [u_i, u'_i] \in \beta(v_i)$;*
- *the transition guards in each ϕ_i $(0 \le i < n)$ are satisfied, i.e., for each transition guard $a \le \sum_{k=0}^{l} c_k x_k \le b$ in ϕ_i, $a \le \sum_{k=0}^{l} c_k \zeta_i(x_k) \le b$;*
- *the location invariant of each location v_i $(0 \le i \le n)$ is satisfied, i.e., at the time the automaton reaches and leaves v_i, each variable constraint $a \le \sum_{k=0}^{l} c_k x_k \le b$ in $\alpha(v_i)$ is satisfied, i.e., $a \le \sum_{k=0}^{l} c_k \lambda_i(x_k) \le b$ and $a \le \sum_{k=0}^{l} c_k \zeta_i(x_k) \le b$*

We now define the reachability of locations, the feasibility of paths and the satisfiability of reachability specifications in an LHA.

Definition 3. *Given an LHA $H = (X, \Sigma, V, V_0, E, \alpha, \beta, \gamma)$, we say a path $\rho = \langle v_0 \rangle \xrightarrow[\sigma_0]{\phi_0, \psi_0} \langle v_1 \rangle \xrightarrow[\sigma_1]{\phi_1, \psi_1} \cdots \xrightarrow[\sigma_{n-1}]{\phi_{n-1}, \psi_{n-1}} \langle v_n \rangle$ is feasible and the location v_n is reachable along ρ, if and only if there exists a timed sequence $\omega = \langle {v_0 \atop \delta_0} \rangle \xrightarrow[\sigma_0]{\phi_0, \psi_0}$
$\langle {v_1 \atop \delta_1} \rangle \xrightarrow[\sigma_1]{\phi_1, \psi_1} \cdots \xrightarrow[\sigma_{n-1}]{\phi_{n-1}, \psi_{n-1}} \langle {v_n \atop \delta_n} \rangle$, such that ω is a behavior of H.*

In an LHA $H = (X, \Sigma, V, V_0, E, \alpha, \beta, \gamma)$, a reachability specification, denoted as $\mathcal{R}(v, \varphi)$, consists of a location v in H and a set φ of variable constraints of the form $a \le \sum_{i=0}^{l} c_i x_i \le b$ $(x_i \in X)$, where a, b and c_i are real numbers and a, b may be ∞.

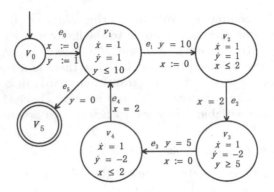

Fig. 1. Water-level monitor system

Definition 4. *Given an LHA $H = (X, \Sigma, V, V_0, E, \alpha, \beta, \gamma)$ and a reachability specification $\mathcal{R}(v, \varphi)$, a behavior of H of the form $\langle {v_0 \atop \delta_0} \rangle \xrightarrow[\sigma_0]{\phi_0, \psi_0} \langle {v_1 \atop \delta_1} \rangle \xrightarrow[\sigma_1]{\phi_1, \psi_1}$*
$\cdots \xrightarrow[\sigma_{n-1}]{\phi_{n-1}, \psi_{n-1}} \langle {v_n \atop \delta_n} \rangle$ satisfies $\mathcal{R}(v, \varphi)$, if and only if $v_n = v$ and each constraint in φ is satisfied when the automaton has stayed in the last location v_n for delay δ_n, i.e., for each variable constraint $a \le \sum_{k=0}^{l} c_k x_k \le b$ in φ, $a \le \sum_{k=0}^{l} c_k \zeta_n(x_k) \le b$.

$\mathcal{R}(v, \varphi)$ is *satisfiable* by a *witness behavior* ω if and only if ω satisfies $\mathcal{R}(v, \varphi)$; $\mathcal{R}(v, \varphi)$ is *satisfiable* along a path ρ if and only if there exists a witness behavior along ρ. An LHA H *satisfies* a reachability specification $\mathcal{R}(v, \varphi)$ if and only if there exists a witness behavior of it.

For example, Fig. 1 is the LHA model of a water level monitor system, where the location v_0 denotes the initial mode of the monitor, the variable x is for timing and the variable y denotes the water level. To check whether the water tank will be empty in the future, we need to check whether the location v_5 is reachable, or check whether there exists a witness behavior satisfying the reachability specification $\mathcal{R}(v_5, \emptyset)$.

Definition 5. *Given an LHA $H_1 = (X_1, \Sigma_1, V_1, V_{0_1}, E_1, \alpha_1, \beta_1, \gamma_1)$ and an LHA $H_2 = (X_2, \Sigma_2, V_2, V_{0_2}, E_2, \alpha_2, \beta_2, \gamma_2)$, where $X_1 \cap X_2 = \emptyset$, the composition of H_1 and H_2, denoted as $H_1 \| H_2$, is an LHA $H = (X, \Sigma, V, V_0, E, \alpha, \beta, \gamma)$ where*

- $X = X_1 \cup X_2$
- $\Sigma = \Sigma_1 \cup \Sigma_2$
- $V = V_1 \times V_2$
- $V_0 = V_{0_1} \times V_{0_2}$
- E *is defined as follows:*

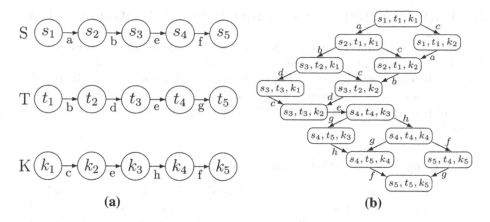

Fig. 2. The state space of the example CLHA

- *for $\sigma \in \Sigma_1 \cap \Sigma_2$, for every $(v_1, \sigma, \phi_1, \psi_1, v_1')$ in E_1 and every $(v_2, \sigma, \phi_2, \psi_2, v_2')$ in E_2, $((v_1, v_2), \sigma, \phi_1 \cup \phi_2, \psi_1 \cup \psi_2, (v_1', v_2')) \in E$.*
- *for $\sigma \in \Sigma_1 \backslash \Sigma_2$, for every $(v, \sigma, \phi, \psi, v')$ in E_1 and every v_2 in V_2, $((v, v_2), \sigma, \phi, \psi, (v', v_2)) \in E$.*
- *for $\sigma \in \Sigma_2 \backslash \Sigma_1$, for every $(v, \sigma, \phi, \psi, v')$ in E_2 and every v_1 in V_1, $((v_1, v), \sigma, \phi, \psi, (v_1, v')) \in E$.*

- $\alpha((v_1, v_2)) = \alpha_1(v_1) \cup \alpha_2(v_2)$
- $\beta((v_1, v_2)) = \beta_1(v_1) \cup \beta_2(v_2)$
- $\gamma((v_1, v_2)) = \gamma_1(v_1) \cup \gamma_2(v_2)$

For all $m > 2$, the composition of LHA(CLHA) $H_1, H_2, \cdots, H_m$, denoted as $H_1 \| H_2 \| \cdots \| H_m$, is an LHA defined recursively as $H_1 \| H_2 \| \cdots \| H_m = H_1 \| H'$ where $H' = H_2 \| H_3 \| \cdots \| H_m$.

Let $N = H_1 \| H_2 \| \cdots \| H_m$ be a CLHA where $H_i = (X_i, \Sigma_i, V_i, V_{0i}, E_i, \alpha_i, \beta_i, \gamma_i)(1 \leq i \leq m)$ and ρ be a path in N of the form $\langle v_0 \rangle \xrightarrow[\sigma_0]{\phi_0, \psi_0} \langle v_1 \rangle \xrightarrow[\sigma_1]{\phi_1, \psi_1} \cdots \xrightarrow[\sigma_{n-1}]{\phi_{n-1}, \psi_{n-1}} \langle v_n \rangle$, which satisfies $v_i = (v_{i1}, v_{i2}, \cdots, v_{im})(0 \leq i \leq n)$ where $v_{ik} \in V_k(1 \leq k \leq m)$. For any $k(1 \leq k \leq m)$, we construct the sequence ρ_k from ρ as follows: replace any v_i with $v_{ik}(0 \leq i \leq n)$, and for any $\xrightarrow[\sigma_{i-1}]{\phi_{i-1}, \psi_{i-1}} \langle v_{ik} \rangle (1 \leq i \leq n)$, if $(v_{i-1k}, \sigma_{i-1}, \phi, \psi, v_{ik}) \in E_k$, then replace it with $\xrightarrow[\sigma_{i-1}]{\phi, \psi} (1 \leq i \leq n)\langle v_{ik} \rangle$, otherwise remove it. It follows that ρ_k is a path in H_k. We say that ρ_k is the projection of ρ on H_k. Intuitively, ρ_k is the execution trace of N on H_k when N runs along ρ.

For example, Fig. 2.a gives a simple system consisting of three automata S, T and K which synchronize with each other by label b, e and f and their composition. The state space of the resulting automata is still large from Fig. 2.b even if these three subsystems are simple.

3   Path-Oriented Bounded Reachability Analysis of LHA

Now, we perform bounded reachability analysis on a single linear hybrid automaton. First, we present a framework to check the reachability of an LHA along paths of bounded length. Then, we show how to check a specific path in an LHA by linear programming. Finally, we leverage irreducible infeasible set (IIS) to perform path pruning and to improve the efficiency of this bounded reachability analysis method.

3.1   Framework of Path-Oriented Checking

Under our path-oriented framework for bounded reachability analysis of an LHA, we enumerate and check all bounded candidate paths one by one. Given an LHA H, an integer k representing the maximum length of paths, and a reachability specification $\mathcal{R}(v_t, \varphi)$ of H, bounded candidate paths in H are paths whose last location is v and have lengths no longer than k. For each enumerated path ρ, we check whether there exists a behavior along ρ satisfying $\mathcal{R}(v_t, \varphi)$. Once a satisfiable behavior is found, we return it as a witness; otherwise, we enumerate and check the next path. Since the number of bounded candidate paths in H is finite, this BMC method is terminable.

We provide two ways to enumerate all bounded candidate paths: one way is to traverse the graph structure of an LHA by depth first search (DFS); other way is to encode the path generation problem into a SAT problem and solve it by a SAT solver.

DFS-Based Path Enumeration: We first obtain the graph structure of an LHA in the discrete level. Given an LHA $H = (X, \Sigma, V, V_0, E, \alpha, \beta, \gamma)$, the graph structure of H is a tuple $G = (V, N)$, where V is a set of nodes and N is a set of edges whose elements are of the form (v, v'), where $v, v' \in V$ and there exists σ, ϕ, ψ, such that $(v, \sigma, \phi, \psi, v') \in E$ in H. Then, we traverse the graph structure $G = (V, N)$ to generate bounded candidate paths by DFS. Given a reachability specification $\mathcal{R}(v_t, \varphi)$ and a path bound k, for each location in V_0, we perform DFS from it; once the length of the current path is longer than k, we backtrack and continue the DFS. If the current path arrives at the target location v_t, it would be generated as a bounded candidate path.

For example, in the illustrative LHA H given in Fig. 1 with the reachability specification $\mathcal{R}(v_5, \emptyset)$, we perform DFS on the graph structure of H from the unique initial location v_0, to generate candidate paths to the target location v_5. When given the length bound of paths in H is 10, we generate a bounded candidate path $\rho_0 = v_0 \rightarrow v_1 \rightarrow v_2 \rightarrow v_3 \rightarrow v_4 \rightarrow v_1 \rightarrow v_5$ first, then $\rho_1 = v_0 \rightarrow v_1 \rightarrow v_2 \rightarrow v_3 \rightarrow v_4 \rightarrow v_1 \rightarrow v_2 \rightarrow v_3 \rightarrow v_4 \rightarrow v_1 \rightarrow v_5$, and finally we backtrack to the first v_1 in ρ_1 and generate the last bounded candidate path $\rho_2 = v_1 \rightarrow v_5$.

SAT-Based Path Enumeration: We first encode the bounded candidate path generation problem of an LHA into a SAT problem. Then, we utilize a SAT solver to seek its truth assignments, which are then decoded and mapped back to candidate paths.

Table 1. SAT encoding of candidate paths of length at most 2 in the water-level LHA

$\mathcal{P}^2$	$INIT \wedge TARGET \wedge NEXT \wedge EXCLUDE$
$INIT$	v_0^0
$TARGET$	$v_5^0 \vee v_5^1 \vee v_5^2$
$NEXT$	$\bigwedge_{i=0,1}((v_0^i \to v_1^{i+1}) \wedge (v_1^i \to v_2^{i+1} \vee v_5^{i+1}) \wedge (v_2^i \to v_3^{i+1})$
	$\wedge(v_3^i \to v_4^{i+1}) \wedge (v_4^i \to v_1^{i+1}))$
$EXCLUDE$	$\bigwedge_{i=0,1,2} \bigwedge_{j \in [0,5]} (v_j^i \to \bigwedge_{k \in [0,5] \wedge k \neq j} \neg v_k^i)$

We now introduce how to encode the candidate paths from the initial location v_i to the target location v_t of length no longer than k into a propositional formula set. This propositional formula set consists of four kinds of clauses: initial clauses, target clauses, next clauses and exclude clauses. We define these four kinds of clauses below:

$$
\begin{aligned}
INIT &:= \quad (loc = v_i) \\
TARGET &:= \quad (loc = v_t) \\
NEXT &:= \bigwedge_{q \in V} (loc = q \to \bigvee_{(q,\sigma,\phi,\psi,q') \in E} loc' = q') \\
EXCLUDE &:= \bigwedge_{q \in V} (loc = q \to \bigwedge_{q' \in V \wedge q \neq q'} loc \neq q')
\end{aligned}
\tag{1}
$$

In the above clauses, the discrete variable loc denotes the current location, and the discrete variable loc' denotes the next location. For each clause $\mathcal{C}$, we use $\mathcal{C}^i$ to represent that the current location is the ith location in a path. Thus, we can denote '$loc = v_j$' in $\mathcal{C}^i$ by assigning a boolean variables $v_j^i \to \top$. We encode the final propositional formula set for bounded candidate paths of length no longer than k as $\mathcal{P}^k$, where

$$
\mathcal{P}^k := INIT^0 \wedge \bigwedge_{0 \leq i \leq k-1} NEXT^i \wedge \bigwedge_{0 \leq i \leq k} EXCLUDE^i \wedge (\bigvee_{0 \leq i \leq k} TARGET^i)
\tag{2}
$$

There exists truth assignments of $\mathcal{P}^k$ if and only if there exists bounded candidate paths of length no longer than k. Take the illustrative LHA H given in Fig. 1 with the reachability specification $\mathcal{R}(v_5, \emptyset)$ as an example. When we generate candidate paths with a length bound of 2, the SAT encoding, $\mathcal{P}^2$, is shown in Table 1. We can achieve an unique truth assignment of $\mathcal{P}^2$, where 'True' is assigned to three boolean variables: v_0^0, v_1^1, and v_5^2. Intuitively, we can decode this truth assignment back into a path $\rho = v_1 \to v_5$, which is the only candidate path with a length bound of 2 in the illustrative LHA in Fig. 1.

3.2   Path-Oriented Encoding and Checking

Now we show how to check the feasibility of candidate paths by linear programming (LP). By reformulating Definition 2, 3 and 4, we encode the satisfiability problem of reachability specifications along candidate paths into the feasibility problem of groups of linear constraints. Given an LHA $H = (X, \Sigma, V, V_0, E, \alpha, \beta, \gamma)$ with a reachability specification $\mathcal{R}(v, \varphi)$ and a candidate path $\rho = \langle v_0 \rangle \xrightarrow[\sigma_0]{\phi_0, \psi_0} \langle v_1 \rangle \xrightarrow[\sigma_1]{\phi_1, \psi_1} \cdots \xrightarrow[\sigma_{n-1}]{\phi_{n-1}, \psi_{n-1}} \langle v_n \rangle$ in it, the encoded group of linear constraints for $\mathcal{R}(v, \varphi)$ to be satisfiable along ρ is denoted as $\Theta(\rho, \mathcal{R}(v, \varphi))$.

$$
\begin{aligned}
\Theta(\rho, \mathcal{R}(v, \varphi)) = & \bigwedge_{i \in [0,n]} \bigwedge_{\dot{x} = [u_i, u_i'] \in \beta(v_i)} u_i \delta_i \le \zeta_i(x) - \lambda_i(x) \le u_i' \delta_i \\
& \bigwedge_{a \le \sum_{k=0}^{l} c_k x_k \le b \in \cup_{i \in [0,n)} \phi_i} a \le \sum_{k=0}^{l} c_k \zeta_i(x_k) \le b \\
& \bigwedge_{a \le \sum_{k=0}^{l} c_k x_k \le b \in \cup_{i \in [0,n]} \alpha(v_i)} (a \le \sum_{k=0}^{l} c_k \lambda_i(x_k) \le b \wedge a \le \sum_{k=0}^{l} c_k \zeta_i(x_k) \le b) \\
& \bigwedge_{a \le \sum_{k=0}^{l} c_k x_k \le b \in \varphi} a \le \sum_{k=0}^{l} c_k \zeta_n(x_k) \le b
\end{aligned}
$$
(3)

$\Theta(\rho, \mathcal{R}(v, \varphi))$ are linear constraints on variables δ_i, $\lambda_i(x)$, and $\zeta_i(x)$. Here, as defined in Sect. 2.1, δ_i denotes the time that H stays in v_i and $\lambda_i(x)$, $\zeta_i(x)$ denote the values of the variable x when H reaches and leaves v_i. Flow conditions, transition guards, location invariants in the LHA and constraints in the reachability specification are considered respectively in $\Theta(\rho, \mathcal{R}(v, \varphi))$.

The feasibility problem of the linear constraints $\Theta(\rho, \mathcal{R}(v, \varphi))$ can be analyzed by state-of-art LP solvers efficiently. If there exists any solution for the linear constraints $\Theta(\rho, \mathcal{R}(v, \varphi))$, then the reachability specification $\mathcal{R}(v, \varphi)$ is satisfiable by at least one behavior along the path ρ; otherwise, it is not. By the above efficient linear constraints encoding and solving, we accomplish the checking of candidate paths.

3.3   IIS-Based Path Pruning

Under our path-oriented framework, if the number of enumerated candidate paths is large, the linear programming process to check all these candidate paths could be time-consuming. Luckily, by analyzing the information gathered from the checked candidate paths, some paths can be pruned during the generation of new candidate paths, reducing the number of paths to be checked and improving the efficiency of our path-oriented method. The information we gather for each path ρ during the LP of its constraint set $\Theta(\rho, \mathcal{R}(v, \varphi))$ is an irreducible infeasible set of $\Theta(\rho, \mathcal{R}(v, \varphi))$.

An irreducible infeasible set (IIS) is a minimal set of inconsistent constraints of a given infeasible constraint set. Then IIS of linear constraints can be achieved efficiently by LP solvers. We give the formal definition of IIS below.

Definition 6. *Given an unsatisfiable set of constraints Θ, an IIS of Θ is a subset Θ', where*

- $\Theta' \subseteq \Theta$
- Θ' *is unsatisfiable*
- $\underset{\Theta'' \subset \Theta'}{\forall} \Theta''$ *is satisfiable*

If a path ρ is proved to be infeasible, we can obtain its IIS by an LP solver and locate its infeasible path segment by mapping the IIS back. Since all constraints in $\Theta(\rho, \mathcal{R}(v, \varphi))$ (Eq. 3) is generated based on syntax elements of locations and transitions in the LHA, we can bind each constraint in the IIS with a source location or a source transition. Therefore, each IIS can be mapped back to a path segment in ρ straightforwardly.

Given an infeasible path segment, we can conclude that any path with this path segment is also infeasible. The negation of an infeasible path segment is encoded into a propositional formula set, which are then combined with the original propositional formula set for bounded candidate path generation. Therefore, the propositional formula set for path generation is updated iteratively and the total number of candidate paths generated from it is reduced largely.

The pseudocode of the IIS-based path-oriented framework is shown in Algorithm 1. The initial SAT encoding of bounded candidate paths $\mathcal{P}^k$ is shown in line 1 and the enumeration of bounded candidate paths is shown in line 4–8, where the truth assignment $\mathcal{B}$ of $\mathcal{P}^k$ is solved by a SAT solver in line 4 and the candidate path ρ is decoded from $\mathcal{B}$ in line 8. The checking of each candidate path ρ is shown in line 8–9, where the constraint $\Theta(\rho, \mathcal{R}(v, \varphi))$ for witness behaviors along ρ is encoded in line 8 and checked by an LP solver in line 9. Once checked feasible, we return the reachable result; and once checked infeasible, the IIS of $\Theta(\rho, \mathcal{R}(v, \varphi))$ is stored in the variable *IIS*. The IIS-based path pruning is shown in line 14–16. We decode the corresponding infeasible path segment ρ' of *IIS* in line 14. The negation of the infeasible path segment ρ' is encoded into a propositional formula set $\mathcal{P}^k_{IIS}$ in line 15. The SAT encoding of bounded candidate paths $\mathcal{P}^k$ is updated in line 16 then, so that the following enumerated candidate paths can be generated from a new propositional formula set with less truth assignments.

For example, in the illustrative LHA H given in Fig. 1 with the reachability specification $\mathcal{R}(v_5, \emptyset)$ and the bound of path length 100, the path $\rho = v_0 \xrightarrow{e_0} v_1 \xrightarrow{e_1} v_2 \xrightarrow{e_2} v_3 \xrightarrow{e_3} v_4 \xrightarrow{e_4} v_1 \xrightarrow{e_5} v_5$ is enumerated and checked by an LP solver. The LP solver returns an infeasible feedback with the IIS set of $\Theta(\rho, \mathcal{R}(v_5, \emptyset))$ as

---

Algorithm 1. Path-oriented IIS-based Framework for the Bounded Reachability Analysis of LHA

Input: An LHA H, a reachability specification $\mathcal{R}(v, \varphi)$, a path bound k
Output: T if $\mathcal{R}(v, \varphi)$ is satisfiable, F if not
1: **function** BACH_IIS($H, \mathcal{R}(v, \varphi), k$)
2:     $\mathcal{P}^k \leftarrow$ SAT encoding of candidate paths of bound k
3:     **while** True **do**
4:         $\mathcal{B} \leftarrow$ a truth assignment of $\mathcal{P}^k$ solved by a SAT solver
5:         **if** $\mathcal{B} = \emptyset$ **then**   ▷ $\mathcal{P}^k$ is unsatisfiable
6:             **return** F
7:         **end if**
8:         $\rho \leftarrow$ a candidate path decoded from $\mathcal{B}$
9:         $\Theta(\rho, \mathcal{R}(v, \varphi)) \leftarrow$ the constraint for witness behaviors along ρ
10:         $IIS \leftarrow$ the IIS of $\Theta(\rho, \mathcal{R}(v, \varphi))$ solved by an LP solver
11:         **if** $IIS = \emptyset$ **then**   ▷ $\Theta(\rho, \mathcal{R}(v, \varphi))$ is feasible
12:             **return** T
13:         **else**   ▷ $\Theta(\rho, \mathcal{R}(v, \varphi))$ is infeasible
14:             $\rho' \to$ the infeasible path segment of ρ decoded from IIS
15:             $\mathcal{P}^k_{IIS} \leftarrow$ SAT encoding of the negation of ρ'
16:             $\mathcal{P}^k \to \mathcal{P}^k \wedge \mathcal{P}^k_{IIS}$
17:         **end if**
18:     **end while**
19: **end function**

$$IIS \;=\; \delta_{v_1^2} \geq 0 \qquad\qquad\qquad \text{▷ constraint for delaying time on } v_1^2$$

$$\wedge\, \zeta_{v_4}(x) - \lambda_{v_4}(x) = \delta_{v_4} \qquad\qquad \text{▷ flow condition on } v_4$$

$$\wedge\, \zeta_{v_4}(y) - \lambda_{v_4}(y) = -2\delta_{v_4} \qquad\qquad \text{▷ flow condition on } v_4$$

$$\wedge\, \zeta_{v_1^2}(y) - \lambda_{v_1^2}(y) = \delta_{v_1^2} \qquad\qquad \text{▷ flow condition on } v_1^2$$

$$\wedge\, \lambda_{v_4}(x) = 0 \wedge \lambda_{v_4}(y) = 5 \qquad\qquad \text{▷ reset actions on } e_3$$

$$\wedge\, \lambda_{v_1^2}(y) = \zeta_{v_4}(y) \qquad\qquad \text{▷ no reset actions for } y \text{ on } e_4$$

$$\wedge\, \zeta_{v_4}(x) = 2 \qquad\qquad\qquad \text{▷ guard condition on } e_4$$

$$\wedge\, \zeta_{v_1^2}(y) = 0 \qquad\qquad\qquad \text{▷ guard condition on } e_5$$

Constraints in IIS[1] is mapped back to locations v_4, v_1^2 and transitions e_3, e_4, e_5. Thus, IIS is decoded accordingly as the shortest infeasible path segment $\rho' = v_3 \xrightarrow{e_3} v_4 \xrightarrow{e_4} v_1 \xrightarrow{e_5} v_5$. The negation of ρ' is then encoded as $\mathcal{P}^k_{IIS} = \bigwedge_{0 \leq i \leq k-len+1} (v_3^i \wedge v_4^{i+1} \wedge v_1^{i+2} \to \neg v_5^{i+3})$, where k is the path bound 100 and len is the length of ρ'. The SAT problem for the generation of next candidate paths is updated accordingly, so that any path with ρ' will not be enumerated later. By deploying IIS-based path pruning, the total number of enumerated candidate paths is reduced from 25 to 2. Considering that the 23 paths that do not need to be checked by LP solvers any more are mostly paths

---

[1] v_1^2 denotes the second occurrence of the location v_1 (the 6th location) in the path ρ.

of long lengths, the effect of IIS-based path pruning in time-consuming is even more promising.

4   Path-Oriented BMC of Composition LHA

In this section, we review how we perform path-oriented bounded reachability verification on the composition of LHA.

4.1   SAT-Based Path Enumeration Under Interleaving Semantic

First, we enumerate path sets by classical interleaving/step semantic based SAT encoding and solving. For each component of CLHA, we encode the propositional formula set for bounded candidate paths of length no longer than k as $\mathcal{P}^k$. Similarly, we define four kinds of clauses for a composition of LHA H and $\mathcal{P}^k$ below:

$$INIT := \bigvee_{v_i \in V_0} (loc^0 = v_i)$$

$$TARGET^i := (loc^i = v_t)$$

$$NEXT^i := \bigwedge_{q \in V} ((loc^i = q) \rightarrow ((tran^i = S \wedge loc^{i+1} = q)$$

$$\bigvee_{t=(q,\sigma,\phi,\psi,q') \in E} (tran^i = \sigma \wedge loc^{i+1} = q')))$$

$$EXCLUDE^i := \bigwedge_{q,q' \in V \wedge q \neq q'} \neg(loc^i = q \wedge loc^i = q') \tag{4}$$

$$\wedge \bigwedge_{\sigma,\sigma' \in \Sigma \wedge \sigma \neq \sigma'} \neg(tran^i = \sigma \wedge tran^i = \sigma')$$

$$\wedge \bigwedge_{\sigma \in \Sigma} \neg(tran^i = \sigma \wedge tran^i = S)$$

$$\mathcal{P}^k := INIT^0 \wedge \bigwedge_{0 \leq i \leq k-1} NEXT^i \wedge \bigwedge_{0 \leq i \leq k} EXCLUDE^i \wedge (\bigvee_{0 \leq i \leq k} TARGET^i)$$

For CLHA, in addition to encoding the bounded candidate path generation problem of each LHA into a SAT problem, several clauses of synchronization constraints are also required to be satisfied.

$$\mathcal{P}_N^k := \bigwedge_{1 \leq j \leq n} \mathcal{P}_{H_j}^k \wedge SYNC_N^k \tag{5}$$

We use interleaving/step synchronization semantics here. It requires that every shared label occur at the same position in the path. Therefore S clause is introduced, which denotes a stutter transition that jumping to the location itself

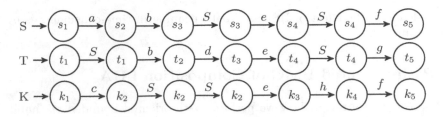

Fig. 3. A path set under interleaving semantic of the CLHA in Fig. 2

without any guards or variable change. Then, we ask all the components must fire the shard label transition in the same step.

$$SYNC_N^k := \bigwedge_{1 \le j < h \le n} \bigwedge_{0 \le i \le k} \bigwedge_{\sigma \in \Sigma_j \cap \Sigma_h} (tran_j^i = \sigma \leftrightarrow tran_h^i = \sigma)$$

$$\wedge \bigvee_{0 \le i \le k} \bigwedge_{0 \le j \le n} TARGET_j^i \qquad (6)$$

We can obtain a candidate path set of length no longer than k by solving above formulas. For example, Fig. 3 is a path set under interleaving/step semantics of Fig. 2.

4.2   Shallow Synchronization Semantic-Guided Path Set Checking

We can definitely encode the constraints of the path set using classical interleaving/step semantic as presented in the last section. For example, Fig. 3 is a potential path set under the interleaving/step semantic of Fig. 2. However, as there are many different places that we can put the stutter transition for synchronization, the number of potential path set under interleaving/step semantic is large, c.f. Fig. 2.b.

In stead, here we propose the *shallow synchronization semantic* to encode each path and the corresponding synchronization constraints separately. Unlike classical interleaving/step semantic, our shallow synchronization semantic does not require that each path to fire a discrete transition or a stutter transition while other paths do so. It only requires each path fire the corresponding shared label on the same time.

Definition 7. *Let $N = H_1 \| H_2 \| \cdots \| H_m$ be a CLHA, $P = \{\rho_1, \rho_2, \cdots, \rho_m\}$ be a path set, where ρ_i is a finite path in $H_i (1 \le i \le m)$, and $\mathcal{R}(v, \varphi)$ be a reachability specification. P satisfies $\mathcal{R}(v, \varphi)$ under shallow synchronization semantic if and only if there is a path ρ of N satisfies the following condition:*

- *the projection of ρ on H_i is $\rho_i (1 \le i \le m)$,*
- *there is a behavior of N which satisfies $\mathcal{R}(v, \varphi)$.*

Definition 8. *Let* $N = H_1 || H_2 || \cdots || H_m$ *be a CLHA, where* $H_i = (X_i, \Sigma_i, V_i, V_{0_i}, E_i, \alpha_i, \beta_i, \gamma_i)(1 \leq i \leq m)$. *A trail* τ *of* N *is of the form* $(\omega_1, \omega_2, \cdots, \omega_m)$ *where each* $\omega_i(1 \leq i \leq m)$ *is a behavior of the form* $\langle {v_{i0} \atop \delta_{i0}} \rangle \xrightarrow[\sigma_{i0}]{\phi_{i0},\psi_{i0}} \langle {v_{i1} \atop \delta_{i1}} \rangle \xrightarrow[\sigma_{i1}]{\phi_{i1},\psi_{i1}} \cdots \xrightarrow[\sigma_{in-1}]{\phi_{in-1},\psi_{in-1}} \langle {v_{in} \atop \delta_{in}} \rangle$, *and satisfies the shallow synchronization constraint, i.e. for any* $k, j(1 \leq k, j \leq m)$

- $\delta_{k0} + \delta_{k1} + \cdots + \delta_{kn_k} = \delta_{j0} + \delta_{j1} + \cdots + \delta_{jn_j}$
- *for any* $\sigma_{kp}(0 \leq p \leq n_k)$ *which is the dth occurrence in* ω_k *of the elements in* $\Sigma_k \cap \Sigma_j$, *there is* $\sigma_{jq}(0 \leq q \leq n_j)$, *which is the dth occurrence in* ω_j *of the elements in* $\Sigma_k \cap \Sigma_j$, *such that* $\sigma_{jq} = \sigma_{kp}$ *and* $\delta_{k0} + \delta_{k1} + \cdots + \delta_{kp} = \delta_{j0} + \delta_{j1} + \cdots + \delta_{jq}$.

In general, the problem of checking a path set under shallow synchronization semantic for a reachability specification could be solved by traversing the corresponding behavior of CLHA and checking if the reachability is satisfied. According to Definition 8, given a CLHA $N = H_1 || H_2 || \cdots || H_m$ with a reachability specification $\mathcal{R}(v, \varphi)$ and a candidate path set under shallow synchronization semantic $P = \{\rho_1, \rho_2, \cdots, \rho_m\}$ where $\rho_i = \langle v_{i0} \rangle \xrightarrow[\sigma_{i0}]{\phi_{i0},\psi_{i0}} \langle v_{i1} \rangle \xrightarrow[\sigma_{i1}]{\phi_{i1},\psi_{i1}} \cdots \xrightarrow[\sigma_{in-1}]{\phi_{in-1},\psi_{in-1}} \langle v_{in} \rangle$, the encoded set of linear constraints for a path set is denoted as $\Theta(P, \mathcal{R}(v, \varphi))$, and the formal definition is at below.

$$\Theta(P, \mathcal{R}(v, \varphi)) = \bigwedge_{1 \leq i \leq m} \Theta(\rho_i, \mathcal{R}(v, \varphi))$$

$$\wedge \bigwedge_{0 \leq i < j \leq n} \left(\sum_{x=0}^{n_i} \delta_{ix} = \sum_{y=0}^{n_j} \delta_{jy} \right) \tag{7}$$

$$\wedge \bigwedge_{0 \leq i < j \leq n} \bigwedge_{d} \left(\sum_{x=0}^{Occ(p_i,d,\Sigma_i \cap \Sigma_j)} \delta_{ix} = \sum_{y=0}^{Occ(p_j,d,\Sigma_i \cap \Sigma_j)} \delta_{jy} \right)$$

Flow conditions, transition guards, location invariants in the LHA and constraints in the reachability specification are considered respectively in $\Theta(\rho, \mathcal{R}(v, \varphi))$ and synchronization constraints are considered in the latter part. $Occ(p_i, d, \Sigma_i \cap \Sigma_j)$ denotes the position of the label that is dth occurrence in p_i of the set $\Sigma_i \cap \Sigma_j$. The feasibility of a path set under shallow synchronization semantic can be analyzed by solving the feasibility problem of $\Theta(P, \mathcal{R}(v, \varphi))$ with LP solver efficiently.

For example, Fig. 4 is a path set under shallow synchronization semantic, in the encoding we can see no stutter transition is introduced. Clearly, the number of all potential path sets under shallow synchronization semantic is much fewer than path sets under interleaving semantic.

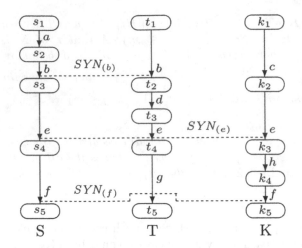

Fig. 4. A path set under shallow synchronization semantic of the CLHA in Fig. 2

4.3 Shallow Synchronization Semantic-Guided Bounded Model Checking

In this section, we perform shallow synchronization semantic path-oriented bounded model checking for CLHA.

According to the framework of path-oriented checking, we enumerate path sets under shallow synchronization semantic first. With some minor changes, the DFS-guided and SAT-based path enumeration methods for single LHA are also feasible for the composition of LHA.

SLS-DFS-Based Path Enumeration: SLS-DFS stands for shared label sequence guided depth first search. The main idea of this DFS method is, given an arbitrary path set, if the projection of each path on their shared labels, i.e. shared label sequence, are not consistent with each other, this path set cannot compose a legal behavior of the whole system. This algorithm only uses simple DFS on the first automata, and all other automata depth-first traverse paths according to maintained paths of the traversed automata to ensure the current traversed path is consistent with others in the shared label sequence. Based on this algorithm, we can enumerate the path set that conform to the synchronization constraint on the graph structure of the composition of linear hybrid automata.

SMT-Based Path Enumeration: We encode the propositional formula set for shallow synchronization semantic similarly with interleaving synchronization semantic but there is no stutter transitions. In order to count shared events, which is beyond the ability of SAT solver, we choose SMT solver to obtain a feasible solution.

Similarly, we encode bounded candidate path generation problem of each LHA into a SAT problem $\mathcal{P}^k$.

$$INIT := \bigvee_{v_i \in V_0} (loc^0 = v_i)$$

$$TARGET^i := (loc^i = v_t) \wedge \bigwedge_{i \le j \le k} \bigwedge_{\sigma \in \Sigma} tran^j \ne \sigma$$

$$NEXT^i := ((loc^i = v_t) \rightarrow (\bigwedge_{i \le j \le k} \bigwedge_{\sigma \in \Sigma} tran^j \ne \sigma) \vee \bigvee_{t=(v_t,\sigma,\phi,\psi,q') \in E}$$

$$(tran^i = \sigma \wedge loc^{i+1} = q')) \wedge \bigwedge_{q \in V - \{v_t\}} ((loc^i = q) \rightarrow$$ \hfill (8)

$$\bigvee_{t=(q,\sigma,\phi,\psi,q') \in E} (tran^i = \sigma \wedge loc^{i+1} = q'))$$

$$EXCLUDE^i := \bigwedge_{q,q' \in V \wedge q \ne q'} \neg(loc^i = q \wedge loc^i = q')$$

$$\wedge \bigwedge_{\sigma,\sigma' \in \Sigma \wedge \sigma \ne \sigma'} \neg(tran^i = \sigma \wedge tran^i = \sigma')$$

$$\mathcal{P}^k := INIT^0 \wedge \bigwedge_{0 \le i \le k-1} NEXT^i \wedge \bigwedge_{0 \le i \le k} EXCLUDE^i \wedge (\bigvee_{0 \le i \le k} TARGET^i)$$

Then we encode shallow synchronization semantic into a SMT problem $SYNC_N^k$ in Eq. 9. We count each shared event and associate it with an abstract time to ensure that they occur for the same number of times and have the same order in each automaton.

In Eq. 9, Σ_{share} denotes the set of shared event. t_j^i denotes the time when the ith transition occurs in ρ_j. $occtime_{g,\sigma}$ denotes the time of the gth occurrence of shared event σ. $count_{\sigma,j}^k$ denotes the number of occurences of shared event σ before the ith transition in ρ_j. $finalcount_\sigma$ denotes the total number of occurences of shared event σ in a path. $SYNCSTEP_j^i$ denotes if there is a gth occurence of a shared event σ occurs at ith step in H_j, the local time of H_j is $occtime_{g,\sigma}$. $COUNTERINIT$ and $COUNTERSTEP$ descibe the change of shared event counters. $FINALSYNC$ descibes the final value of shared event counters. $TIIMESYNC$ denotes that every transition should occur before the next one.

$$SYNCSTEP_j^i := \bigwedge_{\sigma \in \Sigma_{share}} ((tran_j^i = \sigma) \rightarrow \bigwedge_{0 \le g \le i} ((count_{\sigma,j}^i = g) \rightarrow (t_j^i = occtime_{g,\sigma})))$$

$$COUNTERSTEP_j^i := \bigwedge_{\sigma \in \Sigma_{share}} ((tran_j^i = \sigma) \rightarrow (count_{\sigma,j}^{i+1} = count_{\sigma,j}^i + 1))$$

$$\wedge ((tran_j^i \ne \sigma) \rightarrow (count_{\sigma,j}^{i+1} = count_{\sigma,j}^i))$$

$$COUNTERINIT_j := \bigwedge_{\sigma \in \Sigma_{share}} (count_{\sigma,j}^0 = 0)$$ \hfill (9)

$$FINALSYNC_j := \bigwedge_{\sigma \in \Sigma_{share}} (count_{\sigma,j}^k = finalcount_\sigma)$$

$$TIMESYNC_j := \bigwedge_{0 < i \le k} (t_j^{i-1} < t_j^i)$$

$$SYNC_N^k := \bigwedge_{1 \le j \le n} (\bigwedge_{0 \le i \le k} SYNCSTEP_j^i \wedge \bigwedge_{0 \le i \le k} COUNTERSTEP_j^i$$

$$\wedge\ COUNTERINIT_j \wedge FINALSYNC_j \wedge TIMESYNC_j)$$

From the above, for CLHA N, the SMT problem to find candidate path set under shallow synchronization semantic $\mathcal{P}_N^k$ is as below:

$$\mathcal{P}_N^k := \bigwedge_{1 \leq j \leq n} \mathcal{P}_{H_j}^k \wedge SYNC_N^k \tag{10}$$

After obtain a candidate path set under shallow synchronization semantic, we can check its feasibility by solving the corresponding problem as encoded in Sect. 4.2.

Compositional IIS: The irreducible infeasible set(IIS) still works in the reachability analysis of CLHA. If a path set is proved to be infeasible, we can locate infeasible path segment set by IIS. We bind each constraints in $\Theta(P, \mathcal{R}(v, \varphi))$ with a location or a transition in the corresponding path. So we can map constraints in IIS back to a path segment for each path. These path segments make up an infeasible path segment set. Any path sets containing this path segment set do not satisfy the reachability specification.

The procedure of the IIS-accelerated path-oriented framework can be extended from Algorithm 1. Every time a candidate path set is found to be infeasible, we decode the corresponding path segment set from the IIS constraint and add its negation to the propositional formula set for searching of next potential bounded candidate paths. So we can reduce the number of paths to be checked and improve the efficiency of our method.

5   From Bounded Analysis to Unbounded Proof

In this section, we propose a sound but not complete unbounded proof method for the reachability of LHA from bounded analysis.

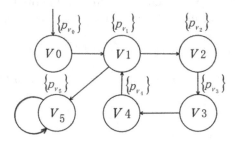

Fig. 5. DTS model of water-level monitor system

In the path-oriented bounded reachability analysis, once a IIS is found, a path segment of LHA under verification will be blocked. After several infeasible path segments are found, there may be no path left that reach the target location. For example, the detected IIS path segments in Fig. 1 are $v_0 \xrightarrow{e_0} v_1 \xrightarrow{e_5} v_5$ and

$v_3 \xrightarrow{e_3} v_4 \xrightarrow{e_4} v_1 \xrightarrow{e_5} v_5$ and the target location is v_5. It is apparent that v_5 can not be satisfied in this situation, no matter what the bound is.

We can see that if there does not exist any path to reach the target location without going through certain infeasible path segments, the reachability specification is not satisfied in the complete unbounded state space.

To simplify the problem, we transform the LHA $H = (X, \Sigma, V, V_0, E, \alpha, \beta, \gamma)$ and reachability specification $\mathcal{R}(v_t, \varphi)$ to an LHA with a bad location (the location that should not be reachable) $H' = (X, \Sigma, V \cup v_{bad}, V_0, v_{bad}, E \cup e', \alpha, \beta, \gamma)$, where v_{bad} is a new location, e' is a transition from v_t to v_{bad} with guard φ. Specially, if φ is $\emptyset$, we regard v_t as the bad location.

Then, we propose to extend the graph structure of the LHA into a transition system.

Definition 9. *Given an LHA with a bad location* $H = (X, \Sigma, V, V_0, v_{bad}, E, \alpha, \beta, \gamma)$, *the related transition system (DTS) of its graph structure* $T = (G, AP, L)$:

- $G = (V, V_0, v_{bad}, \Sigma, E')$ *is an extension to the (labeled) location graph, where*

• $E' \subseteq V \times \Sigma \times V$ *is a finite set of (labeled) transitions.* $E' = E \cup e$, *where* e *is a self-loop starting and ending in location* v_{bad};

- *AP is the atomic proposition set in* T. *For each* $v_i \in V$, *there exists an atomic proposition* $p_{v_i} \in AP$.
- $L : V \to 2^{AP}$ *is a labeling function. For each* $v_i \in V$, $L(v_i) = \{p_{v_i}\}$.

For example, the DTS modeling the water-lever monitor system in Fig. 1 is shown in Fig. 5.

We use linear temporal logic (LTL), a powerful temporal logic for describing system behaviors, to describe the property that whether there exists a path to reach the target location without containing any previously detected IIS path segment. First, we need to represent the IIS path segment in LTL. For a given path segment $\rho = v_i \to v_{i+1} \to \cdots \to v_j$, the LTL formula is

$$IIS_\rho = p_{v_i} \ \& \ X \ p_{v_{i+1}} \ \& \cdots \& \ \underbrace{X \ X \ \cdots X}_{j-i} \ p_{v_j} \qquad (11)$$

Any path without containing such IIS path segment satisfies $G(\neg IIS_\rho)$. Then we represent the property that there exists a path to reach the target location as $F \ p_{v_t}$.

All in all, given a IIS path segment set $\{\rho_1, \rho_2, \cdots, \rho_n\}$, the LTL formula

$$\neg((G(\bigwedge_{1 \le i \le n} \neg IIS_{\rho_i})) \wedge F \ p_{v_t}) \qquad (12)$$

is true when v_t is not reachable in the complete state space.

According this encoding method, we can write the LTL formula for the automaton in Fig. 1 as

$$\neg((G(\neg(p_{v_0} \ \& \ X \ p_{v_1} \ \& \ X \ X \ p_{v_5}) \wedge \neg(p_{v_3} \ \& \ X \ p_{v_4} \ \& \ X \ X \ p_{v_5}))) \wedge F \ p_{v_5})$$

The workflow of the whole unbounded proof procedure is shown in Fig. 6. Given an LHA model and a bound k, we first conduct the path-oriented BMC procedure in Sect. 3. All IIS path segments are recorded for the following unbounded proof. The checker will report reachable if BMC find a feasible path. Otherwise, the unbounded proof procedure will be performed. An LTL checker will check whether the LTL specification encoded by all IIS path segments is true on the related DTS of the LHA model. If yes, the target location is unreachable completely, else, a k-bounded unreachable conclusion will be reported.

Above procedure conducts the LTL verification after the BMC procedure is finished. In order to integrate the BMC and proof procedure tightly and reduce the overhead incurred by repeated LTL model checking, we proposed to construct a Büchi automata corresponding the LTL specification incrementally during BMC verification. In this case, if the so-far collected IIS paths can derive the unreachable argument already, it can stop the whole checking process as soon as the LTL specification becomes satisfied. Please refer to [31] for the detail.

6   Online Hybrid Automata Checking of CPS

The model checking of hybrid systems has been widely applied in guaranteeing the safety of CPS. Conventionally, complete hybrid automata models of CPS are built first, together with safety rules or targets expressed formally as specifications of models; then, these specifications are verified by hybrid system model checking methods. All these modelling and verification processes are conducted *offline* and before the systems run in real world. This conventional offline model checking of CPS has been proved to be successful in some fields or applications of CPS, such as in the computer aided design of digital hardware.

However, existing offline hybrid system model checking methods are not capable enough in many other applications of CPS, generally for two reasons:

- The large number of variables of highly complex and nondeterministic real-world systems and the checking of systems' long-run behaviors required by the offline verification all lead to state explosion during model checking;
- CPS behavior is highly dynamic, some parameters of the hybrid automaton model cannot be accurately predicted offline. This makes the classical offline modeling and state space computation infeasible.

To address the above challenges, instead of the conventional offline model checking of time-unbounded (i.e., infinite horizon, a.k.a., long run) future behaviors, we propose the *online* hybrid system model checking of time-bounded (i.e., finite horizon, a.k.a., short run) future behaviors. Different from the offline model checking of CPS, online model checking is performed during the runtime of CPS. Better online model with controlled complexity, to some extent, can be described and predicted based on the systems' running logs. The corresponding state space of verification is greatly reduced due to online fixed system variables/parameters and time-bounded system behaviors.

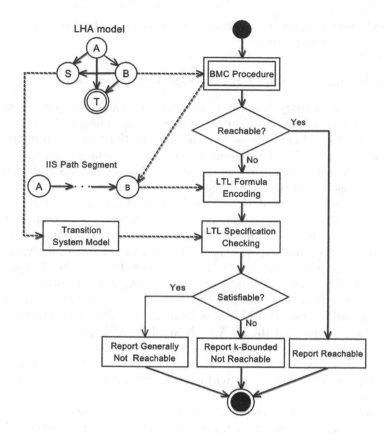

Fig. 6. Workflow of the LTL-based unbounded proof

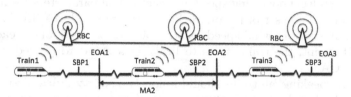

Fig. 7. Communication-based train control systems

Hybrid automata model checkers are then applied in the verification of these online models. We show the possibility of applying LHA reachability analysis method in the online model checking of CPS in two cases. Note that the online modeling and verification of CPS are required to be fast enough so that the online models and verification results are still effective when we achieve them. In the next section, we introduce a typical CPS, a *communication-based train control system* (Fig. 7), and show how we design reachability specifications, build online models and perform online verification of time-bounded short-run behaviors on these models below respectively.

6.1   Motivating Example: CBTC Train Control System

In today's railway industry, train control system plays an important role in guaranteeing the safety of trainsâ and preventing collisions among trains on the same or different tracks and in the same or opposite directions [26]. Communications Based Train Control (CBTC) system is one kind of train control system that makes use of the telecommunications among the ground systems and the trains' onboard systems for the traffic management and infrastructure control.

From each train's onboard system to the ground systems, runtime states of each train is sent periodically. From the ground systems to each train's onboard system, control parameters, including Movement Authority (MA) and Safe Braking Distance (SBD), are sent so that all trains can run accordingly [27]. MA denotes the farthest distance that the train is allowed to run ahead, and we call the end point of the MA as End-of-Authority (EOA). SBD denotes the farthest distance that the train is allowed to run without braking, and we call its end point as the SBD point. The MA of a train should always be larger then its SBD, and the distance that the EOA is ahead of the SBD point is the minimum distance for the train to stop completely in theory. When two trains A and B are running along the same track in the same direction with A running ahead of B, the EOA of B should not be within some given Rear Safe Distance (RSD) from the rear of A.

We studied the CBTC system of a typical urban railway system in China, where the ground systems try to update all trains' MAs/EOAs every 500 ms. Normally, once an updated MA/EOA is received by a train, its onboard system will compute its legal operating speed and the control parameters for its engine, by considering a large set of factors including the received MA/EOA, states of the train/track, current wind speed/weather and so on. And, once reaching the current SBD point, the train starts to brake in a standard procedure to stop before the EOA.

Generally speaking, all trains should follow two **safety rules**: first, if a train has received its MA/EOA, it must stop completely before exceeding its EOA by standard brake; second, if a train has not received MA/EOA signals for 5 s, it must brake emergently and should never collide into the train running ahead of it by emergent brake. The safety of the CBTC systems is guaranteed by checking these two safety rules, and the second one is the top concern.

System Modeling and Verification. For the *offline* verification of CBTC, ground systems and dozens of trains on a single track need to be considered together, as a large composition of hybrid systems. However, the number of hybrid systems in this composition is uncertain and can change dynamically. We consider n trains running on the track and m ground systems that communicate and control them. The hybrid automata model for trains and ground systems

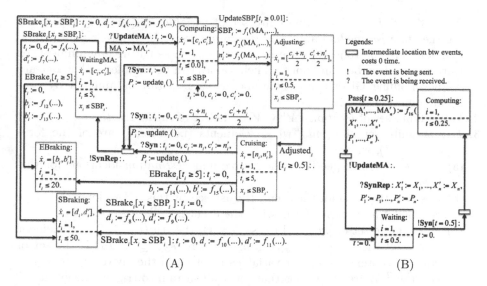

Fig. 8. Offline compositional hybrid automata model for CBTC (Note some details are omitted for simplicity.): (A) model for A train; (B) model for the ground system

are shown in Fig. 8.A and Fig. 8.B respectively. For each hybrid system, its control function is nonlinear. Each hybrid system's external environment parameters (such as wind speed, train mass) and control input parameters (such as MA/EOA) are also nondeterministic and changeable. However, there is no good way to predict these numerical values *offline*. To give one example, the onboard system can only specify a range of speed that the train has to comply with. The exact train speed $\dot{x}$ at each time instance is affected by numerous factors, such as the human driver's maneuvering, train engine conditions, railway conditions (covered with rain, snow, or ice etc.), wind velocity etc. The interactions of these factors are highly random and nonlinear. So are many other states of the train.

6.2   Parametric Hybrid Automata

To address the problem raised in the modeling and verification of the CBTC system, we extended the original definition of HA and proposed the concept of *parametric hybrid automata* (PHA), where offline value-unknown context parameters are modeled as variables. Specifically, given a global set of real value *state parameter* variables $\mathcal{X}$, a global set of real value *context parameter* variables $\mathcal{P}$, where $\mathcal{P} \cap \mathcal{X} = \varnothing$, a global set of *event labels* $\mathcal{L}$, and a function $S : \mathcal{L} \mapsto 2^{\mathcal{X} \cup \mathcal{P}}$, where $S(l) \subseteq \mathcal{X} \cup \mathcal{P}$ ($\forall l \in \mathcal{L}$) specifies the set of state and context parameter variables *shared* (e.g. by data communications) by an event labeled l, we define the following.

Definition 10. A *parametric hybrid automaton* (PHA) is a tuple $H = (X, P, L, V, V^0, \Sigma, \alpha, \beta, \gamma)$, where

1. $X \subseteq \mathcal{X}$ and $P \subseteq \mathcal{P}$ are two finite set of variables respectively representing the *state parameters* and *context parameters* of H. Context parameters' dynamics are controlled by external entities (such as nature environment, or third party black box functions). Their values can be sampled online but are unknown offline. Given context parameters values, state parameters' dynamics are determined.

2. V is a finite set of *locations*; $V^0 \subseteq V$ is the set of *initial locations*.

3. E is a finite set of *events*, whose elements (i.e. events) are of the form $(v, \sigma, \phi, \psi, v')$, where

   (a) $v, v' \in V$ are respectively the *source* and *destination* locations for this event.

   (b) $\sigma \in \Sigma$ is the label for the event. If σ is used by this PHA alone, the event is called a *local* event. Otherwise, the event is a *shared* event.

   (c) ϕ is a finite set of *guards*. In case $\phi \neq \varnothing$, the ith ($i = 1, 2, \ldots$) element of ϕ is of the form $f_{\phi,i}(Y_{\phi,i}) \leqslant a_{\phi,i}$, where $Y_{\phi,i} \subseteq X \cup P$ is the set of state or context parameter variables involved in the guard, $a_{\phi,i} \in \mathbb{R}$ is a constant[2]. ϕ are conditions that must all sustain to trigger the event.

   (d) If the event is a shared event and $\phi = \varnothing$, i.e. the event cannot be triggered locally, then the event is called a *received* event. A received event must have $S(l) \cap (X \cup P) = \varnothing$. If the event is a shared event but not a received event, the it is called a *sent* event (when a sent event happens, $S(l) \cap (X \cup P)$ are the data sent to other PHAs in the system via matching received event(s)).

   (e) ψ is a finite set of *resets*. In case $\psi \neq \varnothing$, the ith ($i = 1, 2, \ldots$) element of ψ is of the form $x_{\psi,i} := f_{\psi,i}(Y_{\psi,i})$, where $x_{\psi,i} \in X \cup P$, and
   $$\begin{cases} Y_{\psi,i} \subseteq X \cup P \cup S(l) & \text{for a received event} \\ Y_{\psi,i} \subseteq X \cup P & \text{otherwise} \end{cases}.$$

4. $\Sigma \stackrel{\text{def}}{=} \{\delta | \exists (v, \delta, \phi, \psi, v') \in E\}$.

5. α is a labeling function, which maps each location $v \in V$ to a *location invariant*, which is a set of *parameter constraints*. In case $\alpha(v) \neq \varnothing$, the ith ($i = 1, 2, \ldots$) element of $\alpha(v)$ is of the form $f_{\alpha(v),i}(Y_{\alpha(v),i}) \leqslant a_{\alpha(v),i}$, where $Y_{\alpha(v),i} \subseteq X \cup P$, and $a_{\alpha(v),i} \in \mathbb{R}$.

6. β is a labeling function, which maps each location $v \in V$ to a set of *flow conditions*. In case $\beta(v) \neq \varnothing$, the ith ($i = 1, 2, \ldots$) element of $\beta(v)$ is of the form $\dot{x}_{\beta(v),i} = f_{\beta(v),i}(Y_{\beta(v),i})$, where $x_{\beta(v),i} \in X$, $Y_{\beta(v),i} \subseteq X \cup P$, and $f_{\beta(v),i}$ is a formula involving element(s) of $Y_{\beta(v),i}$. When $Y_{\beta(v),i} = \varnothing$, $f_{\beta(v),i}(Y_{\beta(v),i})$ can be either a constant in $\mathbb{R}$, or a range in $\mathbb{R}$. In the latter case (without loss of generality, suppose $f_{\beta(v),i}(\varnothing) = [a_{\beta(v),i}, b_{\beta(v),i}]$), we define $\dot{x}_{\beta(v),i} = [a_{\beta(v),i}, b_{\beta(v),i}]$ meaning $x_{\beta(v),i}$ is varying in a rate between $a_{\beta(v),i}$ and $b_{\beta(v),i}$. $\forall v \in V$, $\forall x \in X$, there is one and only one flow condition.

7. γ is a labeling function, which maps each location $v \in V^0$ to a set of *initial conditions*. In case $\gamma(v) \neq \varnothing$, the ith ($i = 1, 2, \ldots$) element of $\gamma(v)$ is of the

---

[2] Unless otherwise denoted, in this section, $a_{\bullet}$ and $b_{\bullet}$ represent real valued constants, and $c_{\bullet}$ represents real valued constant coefficients, where $\bullet$ is a subscript for identification purposes.

form $x_{\gamma(v),i} := a_{\gamma(v),i}$, where $x_{\gamma(v),i} \in X$, $a_{\gamma(v),i}$ is either a real constant or a context parameter in P. $\forall v \in V^0$, $\forall x \in X$, there is at the most one initial condition.   □

The definition of composed PHA can be extended from composed HA similarly. Thus, we omit the detail here, please refer to [10] if interested.

Definition 11 *(Concrete PHA, LHA)*. Given a PHA $H = (X, P, L, V, V^0, E, \alpha, \beta, \gamma)$, if $P = \varnothing$, we say H is a *concrete hybrid automaton* (HA), and simplify it as $H = (X, L, V, V^0, E, \alpha, \beta, \gamma)$. Furthermore, for the above HA H, if

1. all its guards, location invariants, and initial conditions are linear inequalities of X;
2. each reset is of the form $x := f_\psi(Y)$ (where $Y \subseteq \mathcal{X}$; $f_\psi(Y)$ is a linear expression of Y);
3. and each flow condition is of the form $\dot{x} = [a, b]$ (a, b are constants in $\mathbb{R}$ and $a \leqslant b$),

then H is a *linear hybrid automaton* (LHA) as shown in Definition 1.   □

6.3   Online Verification

As summarized in the last section, the offline verification of the parametric models of complex CPS system with high nondeterminism is very difficult. The main idea of model checking is traversing the complete state space of the system to find the bug. The free parameters and dynamic structure of CPS system make the state space undescribable and hence unverifiable.

To tackle this problem, we propose that the verification of such dynamic CPS system should be conducted online and focus on the system's runtime behavior in a time-bounded short-run future. The parametric model of the system can be concretized online using the runtime collected numeric values of these free parameters. The result will be a concretized model of the system's behavior in the time-bounded short-run future. As the model is concretized/built online, all the free parameters' running numeric values are fixed. Therefore, the high nondeterminism of the complete system behavior caused by the free parameters and dynamic structure are eliminated in the online concretized model. Furthermore, the nonlinear control functions can be substituted with the computation result of the functions under current input parameters. Therefore the nonlinear part can be eliminated from the online model too. As a result, the online model will be concrete and linear, which is much easier to handle.

Since the online concrete model only describes the behavior of the system in the time-bounded short-run future, whether the concrete model satisfies the given property means whether the system could encounter any errors in the time-bounded short-run future. The values of the parameters are updating frequently. Once the set of the values is updated means the current online model is outdated. Therefore, such an online modeling and verification procedure should be conducted respectively upon each update.

Now, let us present how our online modeling and verification framework can be integrated into the classical control loop. The general idea of classical control loop for complex CPS systems is shown in the left part of Fig. 9. Whenever a running system receives a new instruction/command/stimuli, it will compute/collect the numeric values of the control parameters, which will be deployed by the running system immediately. If we call the left part of Fig. 9 as "classical control system", our online modeling and verification framework, the right part of Fig. 9, can be used as a "runtime monitor" which works as a watchdog of the "classical control system" and strengthens the safety of system operation.

1. After the control functions are called by the running system and a new set of parameter values is generated, these values will be deployed on the running system immediately as in the classical control loop. In other words, the running system will not wait for the pass of the verification to deploy the control parameters. Otherwise the system has to work under the old set of parameter values during the verification period, which could be dangerous.
2. Meanwhile, once the new set of parameter values is generated, the online modeling module will be called to build the online model for the time-bounded behavior of the system by concretizing the free parameters in the model according to their running numeric values.
3. Then, the online verification module will verify the predefined verification tasks on the concretized models. If the verification is rejected, the online verification module will ask the system to stop the current parameters immediately and start a fall-back plan which is predefined by designers to increase the safety of system operation.

In such manner, the offline unverifiable parametric model can be verified online. The online modeling and verification module can be introduced as a runtime monitor into the classical control loop. Furthermore, such monitor will not interrupt the behavior of the system unless the verification is rejected.

6.4　Scenario-Oriented Online Verification

Furthermore, as discussed before, the designers pay special interest in checking whether any of the predefined safety-critical scenarios will happen in the systems' behavior, for example, the safety rule 1 presented in Sect. 6.1. Basically, each scenario can be presented as a sequence of control actions and control modes. Still taking safety rule 1 as an example, the scenario can be interpreted as follows. First, the train receives the new MA, enters location *Computing*. Then, after a series of adjustment, the train starts to operate in the new set of parameters, go through location *Adjusting* and enter location *cruising*. After the train has operated for 5 s without receiving any signal, the train changes the control mode to emergency braking, enters location *Ebraking*. Therefore, such scenario can be mapped into a path set in the concretized model naturally, for example, path $\left\langle \begin{smallmatrix} \text{WaitingMA} \\ \delta_{i,0} \end{smallmatrix} \right\rangle \xrightarrow{\text{UpdateMA}} \left\langle \begin{smallmatrix} \text{Computing} \\ \delta_{i,1} \end{smallmatrix} \right\rangle \xrightarrow{\text{UpdateSBP}_i} \left\langle \begin{smallmatrix} \text{Adjusting} \\ \delta_{i,2} \end{smallmatrix} \right\rangle \xrightarrow{\text{Adjusted}_i}$ $\left\langle \begin{smallmatrix} \text{Cruising} \\ \delta_{i,3} \end{smallmatrix} \right\rangle \xrightarrow{\text{EBrake}_i} \left\langle \begin{smallmatrix} \text{EBraking} \\ \delta_{i,4} \end{smallmatrix} \right\rangle$. for each train. As a result, whether the behavior of the system in time-bounded short-run future can satisfy the safety-critical scenario can be translated into the reachability of certain path (set) in the system. Therefore, the path-oriented efficient checking method introduced in last section can be deployed to solve the online verification problem quickly. Meanwhile, as the problem is LP-based, and the online model for different cycles are similar with each other, incremental LP solving as be used to boost the efficiency of solving furthermore. Please refer to [11] for detail.

By modeling the CBTC system by PHA, and conduct the scenario-based online LHA verification, we can verify the safety-critical scenarios in only 200 ms, which makes online prediction and safety assurance of dynamic CPS possible.

7 Systematically Modeling, Checking and Fixing of Real Time Home Automation IoT Systems

7.1 Background and Motivation

The Internet of Things (IoT) is a network of electronically embedded physical objects that are equipped with microcontrollers, transceivers for digital communication, and protocol stacks making them able to exchange information with each other and communicate with the users [4,28,32]. IoT systems are developing rapidly and penetrating various industry fields where safety is of vital importance, especially in fields such as smart homes and smart traffic management [19].

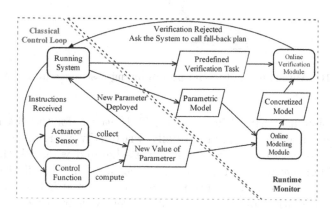

Fig. 9. Online modeling and verification framework

To handle and enhance the ability of programmable devices and to analog the environments in IoT, several IoT programming platforms are designed, such as If-This-Then-That (IFTTT.com), Apple HomeKit (ah 2016), and Google Brillo (gb 2016). These platforms all provide a trigger-action-programming (TAP) style functionality to help users to author their own customized command to link their devices. Without loss of generality, in the section, we focus on the IFTTT framework, which is a popular TAP home automation IoT (HA-IoT) framework for building event-driven applications.

An IFTTT-style TAP rule is in the from of if **A then do B**, where A is a triggering sensor event and B is a triggered device command. For example, there are two typical IFTTT-style rules to watch the CO concentration in a given space by sensors in a smart fan and make sure the CO concentration will not exceed 200 ppm by activating the smart fan.

$$
\begin{aligned}
&\text{IF Smart\_Fan.CO\_reading} == 195 \text{ THEN Alarm.TURN\_ON} \\
&\text{IF Alarm.TURN\_ON.Signal} == \text{TRUE THEN Smart\_Fan.ACTIVATE}
\end{aligned}
\tag{13}
$$

If a sensor in the smart fan detected the CO concentration is 195, then the alarm device executes the `Turn_on` action. If the alarm device sends a signal of `Turn_on`, then the smart fan device executes the `Activate` action.

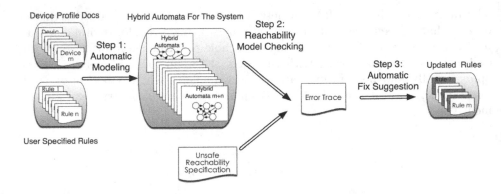

Fig. 10. Automated end-to-end programming assistance framework

Safety is obviously critical in the HA-IoT. However, for the HA-IoT in the home automation scene, rules are usually written by users who are mostly non-experts who have little background knowledge and who lack the comprehensive consideration regarding potential impact and chained effect of existing rules. Also, given the real-time continuous environments, it is hard to figure out whether the expectations of users can really be met by their written IFTTT rules and whether some unsafe consequences will occur under their written IFTTT rules. For example, in this CO example, if the smart fan is activated, it can decrease CO concentration according to dynamic law (ODE $dCO/dt = 2$). So, the 195 ppm threshold of the purifier seems is correct that CO level will not go over 200 ppm. However, due to the existence of time delay of rule reaction, the CO level could exceed the threshold before the smart fan is activated.

7.2   Solution

In this section, we introduce an end-to-end programming assistance system to model, check, and fix HA-IoT systems automatically, enhancing the confidence of users about their IFTTT-style rules and the safety of HA-IoT systems. The automated end-to-end programming assistance framework is shown in Fig. 10, where we input documents of devices' profiles and IFTTT-style rules specified by users and output model checking results together with updated rules.

Automatic System Modeling. In step 1, given devices' profiles and IFTTT rules, we generate the LHA models of the IoT system. We first design a specific device schema so that necessary information of devices can be presented in its schema by device manufacturers. The device schema consists of:

- Device *Type* and *SN* (serial number).
- Continuous System Variables, including environmental variables that can be affected by the device and internal data kept inside the device.
- Discrete Working Modes together with the dynamic information on how the system variables evolve in each mode by differential equations. A boolean signal is used to denote whether the execution of the transition is a observable triggering condition.
- Transitions describing the internal mode-changing logic of the device.
- APIs describing the actions of devices that can be triggered outside by users and other devices, having the same structure with transitions.

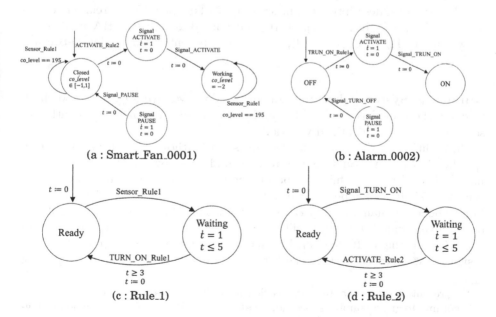

Fig. 11. Automated end-to-end programming assistance framework

Then, based on the schemas of all involved devices and the IFTTT rules, we show how to build the LHA model of the system in a formal way. To model the LHA model of each device by its schema:

- Generate name, variables X, locations V, transition relations E and flow conditions mapping function β directed by the schema.
- Generate shared labels by signal flags of transitions accordingly.
- Add transitions corresponding to APIs based on signals accordingly with share labels of 'API.Name_Caller.Name' or 'Signal_API.Name'.

To model the LHA model of each IFTTT rules:

- There are only two fixed locations in V: 'Ready' and 'Waiting', and E consists of the two fixed transitions between them. The transition from 'Waiting' to 'Ready' is related to triggering conditions and the triggered actions are executed in 'Ready'.
- The transition from 'Ready' to 'Waiting' is related to the triggering condition expression of observable variables or the occurrence of signals with label 'Sensor_Rule_i' or 'Signal_Transition.Name'.
- The transition from 'Waiting' to 'Ready' is related to the triggered commands, communicating with the device automaton the by shared label 'API.Name_Caller.Name'.
- We use invariants on the location 'Waiting' and guards condition on the transition from 'Waiting' to 'Ready' to model the time delay between the enabling of a triggering condition and the execution of its corresponding API.

More detailed description can be seen in [12]. For the example related devices and IFTTT rules given in Eq. 13, the automated generated LHA models are shown in Fig. 11. In Fig. 11(c)(d), we model a potential time delay between 3 and 5 s.

Automatic System Checking. In this section, we give approaches to check whether these models conform to specifications and systematically synthesize solutions to resolve identified violations.

In addition to the system model, users can author confidence/reachability specification which should be easy to read and write by the HA-IoT programming[3]. Therefore, we define the specification format as a conjunction of conditions that shall not happen. For example, if users want the room CO concentration to be lower than 200, they can write *SmartFan. CO $\geq$ 200*. The reachability of the given undesirable state will be checked after specifications are got from users. Conducting BMC checking by directly using off-the-shelf checkers will have a significant overhead because checkers always explore the entire state space of

---

[3] We present two ways of authoring specifications. First, users can author specifications according to given templates. Second, we also present a natural language processing-based method to translate specifications in the form of natural language sentence to LTL formulas. Please refer to [33] for detail.

devices and rules including meaningless interactions among devices. Therefore, we propose to only consider the subset of models that are related to reduce the state space.

Definition 12. *Given a composed LHA network $N = H_1 \| H_2 \| \cdots \| H_m$ and a reachability specification $\mathcal{R}(v, \varphi)$, if v is a location of H_i, φ consists of variables from $H_j (1 \leq i, j \leq m)$, we say H_i and H_j are $\mathcal{R}$ related.*

Definition 13. *If two LHA models have a shared label, these two models are related. Given three models H_1, H_2 and H_3, if H_1 is related to H_2, H_2 is related to H_3, then H_1 is related to H_3. Given a composed LHA network $N = H_1 \| H_2 \| \cdots \| H_m$, we call the sets of all the LHA models related to H_i the related closure $H_i (1 \leq i \leq m)$.*

Definition 14. *Given a composed LHA network $N = H_1 \| H_2 \| \cdots \| H_m$ and a reachability specification $\mathcal{R}(v, \varphi)$, if v is a location of H_i, φ consists of variables from $H_j (1 \leq i, j \leq m)$, we say H_i and H_j are $\mathcal{R}$ related. Then, the set of LHA models consisting of the related closure of H_i and the related closure of H_j is the $\mathcal{R}$ related closure.*

Given a reachability specification $\mathcal{R}(v, \varphi)$, we first compute the $\mathcal{R}$ related closure. Then we feed it to the BMC checker to check. Checking will have a smaller cost since the size of the system is reduced.

Automatic System Fixing. In this section, we give approaches to fix the system that can reach an undesirable state.

To resolve a specification violation, we need to identify the problematic automation rules. IoT users can realistically change only the automation rules rather than changing the installed IoT devices or specifications, which is different from debugging for general CPS software. It means that we can only adjust the triggering condition value of IFTTT rules. We propose parameterizing IFTTT rules and then solving for solutions to the parameterized system.

Instead of computing the potential range of each parameter directly, we propose a counterexample-guided approach. The algorithm is shown in Algorithm 2. Given a path in the model, whether it satisfies the specification is encoded to the feasibility of a formula Ψ. Then, we parameterize the threshold of the triggering conditions in the rules to free parameters $para_k$, and we modify Ψ to Ψ' accordingly (Lines 5–10). If we can find a valuation for these parameters to make Ψ' infeasible, the located counterexample is dismissed. We take the negation of all the subformulas in Ψ' and get new formula Ψ''. So we can find $para_k$ that make Ψ'' feasible to make Ψ' infeasible (Line 11). QE [25] can be used to transform this problem to an equivalent quantifier-free numerical formula about $para_k$ since all constraints in Ψ are linear. This formula gives the value range for each $para_k$ that can make Ψ' infeasible (Line 12–13). A value in the range can be chosen as a fix suggestion and the checker check the system again with this value.

Algorithm 2. Counterexample-Guided Fix Suggestion

Input: Counterexample Path ρ, Specification $\mathcal{R}(v,\varphi)$, Rule set RS
Output: value range for each free parameter
1: $\Psi \leftarrow$ Encoding the reachability of ρ according to $\mathcal{R}(v,\varphi)$
2: $\Theta \leftarrow$ The constraints related with all the rules in RS
3: $\Phi \leftarrow$ Other rules in Ψ
4: $\qquad\qquad\qquad\qquad\qquad$ $\triangleright$ $\Psi = (\bigwedge_{i=1}^{m} \phi_i) \wedge (\bigwedge_{i=1}^{m} \theta_i)$ where $\phi_i \in \Phi, \theta_i \in \Theta$
5: **for all** $\theta_i, (Device_i.variable_j == concrete\_value_k) \in \Theta$ **do**
6: $\qquad$ Parameterize $concrete\_value_k$ to a free parameter $para_k$
7: $\qquad$ New constraint $\theta_i' \leftarrow (Device_i.variable_j == para_k)$
8: **end for**
9: $\Theta' \leftarrow \bigwedge_{i=1}^{m} \theta_i'$
10: $\Psi' \leftarrow \bigwedge_{i=1}^{m} \phi_i$
11: $\Psi'' \leftarrow \bigvee_{\psi_i \in \Psi'} \neg\psi_i$ $\qquad\qquad$ $\triangleright$ Take the negation of all the subformulas
12: $Vari \leftarrow$ all the variables in Ψ
13: Use QE to check: Whether $\exists para_k$, such that $\forall x_i \in Vari, \Psi''$ is feasible. **return** the value range for each $para_k$

For example, the original rule in CO example is IF `Smart_Fan.CO_rea` `ding == 195 THEN Execute Alarm.TURN_ON`. This rule may cause a bad situation, the CO concentration can reach 200 before the smart fan is activated. We parameterized the rule to IF `Smart_Fan.CO_reading == A THEN Execute` `Alarm.TURN_ON`. Then we conduct the negation and QE procedure. The result tells us $0 \le A \le 190$, and solver selects a value from this range (e.g. 180). We use it as a potential fix and check the mole again. The system should pass the verification this time, and it subsequently presents the new value as a fix suggestion to the user.

7.3   System Implementation

We implemented a system, MenShen, which supports functionalities discussed in previous sections

1. automated LHA model generation from device schemas
2. template-based GUI for authoring IFTTT-style rules and specifications
3. automated system reachability checking,
4. violation fix suggestions.

MenShen is implemented in C# based on third-party libraries: BACH [7,8] for the LHA checker, Redlog [16] for the QE solver, Z3 [15] for the SMT solver, and Json.Net [1] for parsing the device schemas.

To evaluate the usefulness of MenShenâ we conducted a set of experiments with a benchmark which consists of 18 devices, including gas meters, HVAC, lights, air purifiers, GPS, water heater, etc., and 19 rules. MenShen finishes the checking by only 0.23 s and fixing by only 0.95 s.

Meanwhile, we also conduct user studies to see how normal users can handle such problem. We have two groups which both have 45 members: (1) researchers and interns from Microsoft Research Asia, and students in the software engineering discipline at Nanjing University; (2) non-computer science major college students, high school students, and also some housewives. We asked the participants to decide whether the connected IoT system can violate any of the three given specifications, and then we asked participants to attempt to fix these violations manually.

It is interesting to see that only 2 of 45 participants in each group can find the fix conflicts. All the other participants can not finish the problem after they spend 1 to 8 min. We can see that, for the majority of the participants, even for users with background in computer science, successfully realizing high-confidence HA-IoT systems is still a difficult task.

8 Tool Implementation and Conclusion

We have given a systematic review of our works from the bounded model checking of hybrid automata to the verification of industrial CPS and IoT. A path-oriented bounded reachability analysis method for a single linear hybrid automaton (LHA) was given first to control the complexity of verification. Then, the path-oriented method is extended to the bounded reachability analysis for LHA compositions as well as the unbounded reachability analysis of them. We then showed the possibility of applying the LHA model checking into the online verification for industrial cyber-physical systems and the automatic verification and fixing for IoT systems in the home automation scenario.

The above techniques are all implemented into a toolset: BACH, which stands for Bounded Reachability Checker of LHA. Now, the functionalities of BACH include graphical modeling, reachability verification, and online runtime verification of hybrid and CPS systems. Many editions of BACH are available, i.e., standalone C application, JAVA application, web application, and even Eclipse plugin.

The latest versions of BACH are publicly available online from http://seg.nju.edu.cn/BACH/. BACH joined the ARCH-COMP hybrid system model checker competition continuously. It outperforms many competitors on the well-recognized benchmarks[4]. Since its debut in 2008, BACH has attracted hundreds of registered users globally including researchers from top institutions, i.e., CMU, UC Berkeley, UBC and engineers from industry like AeroSpace, Railway, Telecom and etc.

Acknowledgement. We are grateful to Dingbao Xie, Yang Yang, Wen Xiong, Xinyue Ren, Shaopeng Xing all from Nanjing University, Qixin Wang from Hong Kong Polytechnic University, Mike Liang, Shi Han, Dongmei Zhang from Microsoft Research Asia, Stefano Tonetta, Alessandro Cimatti from Fondazione Bruno Kessler, Edmund Clarke from Carnegie Mellon University and all the other co-authors for their collaboration in

---

[4] As this paper is used as notes for the tutorial of SETSS 2019, and also due to the space limitation, we do not include experimental data in the paper. Please refer to the series works of BACH for detail.

previous works on verification of LHA, CPS, and IoT. This paper is supported in part by the National Natural Science Foundation of China (No. 61632015, No. 61572249, 61561146394).

References

1. Json.net (2009). https://www.newtonsoft.com/json
2. Alur, R., Henzinger, T.A., Ho, P.H.: Automatic symbolic verification of embedded systems. IEEE Trans. Softw. Eng. **22**(3), 181–201 (1996)
3. Asarin, E., Bournez, O., Dang, T., Maler, O.: Approximate reachability analysis of piecewise-linear dynamical systems. In: Lynch, N., Krogh, B.H. (eds.) HSCC 2000. LNCS, vol. 1790, pp. 20–31. Springer, Heidelberg (2000). https://doi.org/10.1007/3-540-46430-1_6
4. Atzori, L., Iera, A., Morabito, G.: The Internet of Things: a survey. Comput. Netw. **54**(15), 2787–2805 (2010)
5. Biere, A., Cimatti, A., Clarke, E.M., Strichman, O., Zhu, Y., et al.: Bounded model checking. Adv. Comput. **58**(11), 117–148 (2003)
6. Bu, L., Li, X.: Path-oriented bounded reachability analysis of composed linear hybrid systems. Int. J. Softw. Tools Technol. Transf. **13**(4), 307–317 (2011)
7. Bu, L., Li, Y., Wang, L., Chen, X., Li, X.: Bach 2: bounded reachability checker for compositional linear hybrid systems. In: 2010 Design, Automation & Test in Europe Conference & Exhibition (DATE 2010), pp. 1512–1517. IEEE (2010)
8. Bu, L., Li, Y., Wang, L., Li, X.: Bach: bounded reachability checker for linear hybrid automata. In: 2008 Formal Methods in Computer-Aided Design, pp. 1–4. IEEE (2008)
9. Bu, L., et al.: Toward online hybrid systems model checking of cyber-physical systems' time-bounded short-run behavior. ACM SIGBED Rev. **8**(2), 7–10 (2011)
10. Bu, L., Wang, Q., Ren, X., Xing, S., Li, X.: Scenario-based online reachability validation for CPS fault prediction. IEEE Trans. Comput.-Aided Des. Integr. Circuits Syst. (2019). https://doi.org/10.1109/TCAD.2019.2935062
11. Bu, L., Xing, S., Ren, X., Yang, Y., Wang, Q., Li, X.: Incremental online verification of dynamic cyber-physical systems. In: Teich, J., Fummi, F. (eds.) Design, Automation & Test in Europe Conference & Exhibition, DATE 2019, Florence, Italy, March 25–29, 2019, pp. 782–787. IEEE (2019)
12. Bu, L., et al.: Systematically ensuring the confidence of real-time home automation IoT systems. ACM Trans. Cyber-Phys. Syst. **2**(3), 1–23 (2018)
13. Chutinan, A., Krogh, B.H.: Verification of polyhedral-invariant hybrid automata using polygonal flow pipe approximations. In: Vaandrager, F.W., van Schuppen, J.H. (eds.) HSCC 1999. LNCS, vol. 1569, pp. 76–90. Springer, Heidelberg (1999). https://doi.org/10.1007/3-540-48983-5_10
14. Clarke Jr., E.M., Grumberg, O., Kroening, D., Peled, D., Veith, H.: Model Checking. MIT Press, Cambridge (2018)
15. de Moura, L., Bjørner, N.: Z3: an efficient SMT solver. In: Ramakrishnan, C.R., Rehof, J. (eds.) TACAS 2008. LNCS, vol. 4963, pp. 337–340. Springer, Heidelberg (2008). https://doi.org/10.1007/978-3-540-78800-3_24
16. Dolzmann, A.: Redlog (2006). http://redlog.eu
17. Frehse, G.: PHAVer: algorithmic verification of hybrid systems past HyTech. In: Morari, M., Thiele, L. (eds.) HSCC 2005. LNCS, vol. 3414, pp. 258–273. Springer, Heidelberg (2005). https://doi.org/10.1007/978-3-540-31954-2_17

18. Frehse, G., et al.: SpaceEx: scalable verification of hybrid systems. In: Gopalakrishnan, G., Qadeer, S. (eds.) CAV 2011. LNCS, vol. 6806, pp. 379–395. Springer, Heidelberg (2011). https://doi.org/10.1007/978-3-642-22110-1_30

19. Hassija, V., Chamola, V., Saxena, V., Jain, D., Goyal, P., Sikdar, B.: A survey on IoT security: application areas, security threats, and solution architectures. IEEE Access 7, 82721–82743 (2019)

20. Henzinger, T.A.: The theory of hybrid automata. In: Verification of Digital and Hybrid Systems, pp. 265–292. Springer (2000). https://doi.org/10.1007/978-3-642-59615-5_13

21. Henzinger, T.A., Ho, P.-H., Wong-Toi, H.: HyTech: a model checker for hybrid systems. In: Grumberg, O. (ed.) CAV 1997. LNCS, vol. 1254, pp. 460–463. Springer, Heidelberg (1997). https://doi.org/10.1007/3-540-63166-6_48

22. Henzinger, T.A., Kopke, P.W., Puri, A., Varaiya, P.: What's decidable about hybrid automata? In: Proceedings of the Twenty-seventh Annual ACM Symposium on Theory of Computing, pp. 373–382 (1995)

23. Lee, E.A.: Cyber-physical systems - are computing foundations adequate. In: Position Paper for NSF Workshop on Cyber-Physical Systems: Research Motivation, Techniques and Roadmap, vol. 2, pp. 1–9. CiteSeer (2006)

24. Li, X., Aanand, S.J., Bu, L.: Towards an efficient path-oriented tool for bounded reachability analysis of linear hybrid systems using linear programming. Electron. Notes Theor. Comput. Sci. 174(3), 57–70 (2007)

25. Monniaux, D.: A quantifier elimination algorithm for linear real arithmetic. In: Cervesato, I., Veith, H., Voronkov, A. (eds.) LPAR 2008. LNCS (LNAI), vol. 5330, pp. 243–257. Springer, Heidelberg (2008). https://doi.org/10.1007/978-3-540-89439-1_18

26. Pascoe, R.D., Eichorn, T.N.: What is communication-based train control? IEEE Veh. Technol. Mag. 4(4), 16–21 (2009)

27. Platzer, A., Quesel, J.-D.: European train control system: a case study in formal verification. In: Breitman, K., Cavalcanti, A. (eds.) ICFEM 2009. LNCS, vol. 5885, pp. 246–265. Springer, Heidelberg (2009). https://doi.org/10.1007/978-3-642-10373-5_13

28. Talal, M., et al.: Smart home-based IoT for real-time and secure remote health monitoring of triage and priority system using body sensors: multi-driven systematic review. J. Med. Syst. 43(3), 42 (2019)

29. Xie, D., Bu, L., Li, X.: Deriving unbounded proof of linear hybrid automata from bounded verification. In: 2014 IEEE Real-Time Systems Symposium, pp. 128–137. IEEE (2014)

30. Xie, D., Bu, L., Zhao, J., Li, X.: SAT-LP-IIS joint-directed path-oriented bounded reachability analysis of linear hybrid automata. Form. Methods Syst. Des. 45(1), 42–62 (2014)

31. Xie, D., Xiong, W., Bu, L., Li, X.: Deriving unbounded reachability proof of linear hybrid automata during bounded checking procedure. IEEE Trans. Comput. 66(3), 416–430 (2016)

32. Zanella, A., Bui, N., Castellani, A., Vangelista, L., Zorzi, M.: Internet of Things for smart cities. IEEE Internet Things J. 1(1), 22–32 (2014)

33. Zhang, S., Zhai, J., Bu, L., Wang, L., Li, X.: Natural language-based formal specification generation for trigger-action style smart home IoT system. In: Design, Automation & Test in Europe Conference & Exhibition, DATE 2020. IEEE (2020)

Weakest Preexpectation Semantics
for Bayesian Inference
Conditioning, Continuous Distributions and Divergence

Marcin Szymczak[(✉)][iD] and Joost-Pieter Katoen[iD]

Software Modelling and Verification Group, RWTH Aachen University,
52056 Aachen, Germany
`marcin.szymczak@cs.rwth-aachen.de`

Abstract. We present a semantics of a probabilistic while-language, with soft conditioning and continuous distributions, which handles programs diverging with positive probability. To this end, we extend the probabilistic guarded command language (pGCL), which draws from continuous distributions and a score operator. The main contribution is an extension of the standard weakest preexpectation semantics to support these constructs. As a sanity check of our semantics, we define an alternative trace-based semantics of the language and show that the two semantics are equivalent. Various examples illustrate the applicability of the semantics.

1 Introduction

Research on semantics of probabilistic languages for machine learning [5,6,15,28, 37] has so far focused almost exclusively on almost-surely terminating programs. These programs terminate on all possible inputs with probability one. This seems a reasonable assumption, because not only most probabilistic models used in practice terminate with probability one, but programs that may diverge with a positive probability also do not make much sense in the context of probabilistic inference.

However, one cannot simply assume that in the context of statistical probabilistic programming, divergence is a non-existant issue that can be ignored completely. For one thing, models that are not guaranteed to terminate actually exist and are not merely degenerate cases. Even if one cannot apply inference in this case, being able to reason about such programs is important, since it helps to define suitable approximations and check their correctness. Moreover, the line dividing almost-surely terminating and possibly diverging programs can sometimes be very thin and a small change to some parameter values may make a terminating program diverge.

To make a case for potentially diverging probabilistic programs, consider a variation of the tortoise and hare problem described by Icard [18] as a simple

This work is supported by the ERC Advanced Grant Project FRAPPANT (project number 787914).

J. P. Bowen et al. (Eds.): SETSS 2019, LNCS 12154, pp. 44–121, 2020.
https://doi.org/10.1007/978-3-030-55089-9_3

problem in intuitive physics: a tortoise is walking at some low constant speed and a hare, which was initially behind the tortoise and moves forward with random fast strides, is trying to catch it. Assuming that the tortoise is moving at a constant speed of $1 + $ e cm per second (where e is some small constant) and each second the hare moves with probability $\frac{1}{4}$ by a random Gaussian-distributed distance, being 4 cm on average, we would like to calculate the average time after which the hare will catch the tortoise. We can model this problem by the following probabilistic program:

```
t := 5.0;
h := 0.0;
time := 0.0;
while (h < t)
{
  t := t + 1 + e;
  if (flip(0.25))
     h := h + Gaussian(4,2);
  time := time + 1;
}
return time
```

where flip(p) returns true with probability p and false with probability $1 - p$ and Gaussian(μ, σ) draws a random value from the Gaussian distribution with mean μ and variance σ. It can be proven that if e $= 0$, the program terminates with probability one, but if e > 0, the program may diverge with positive probability, no matter how small e is. In other words, if the tortoise moves at a speed strictly greater than one, the hare may never catch it.

The above program is a simple forward simulation, which does not use conditioning at all. However, we may also invert the problem and ask what was the tortoise's head start given that the hare caught the tortoise in around one minute. This could be modelled by the following probabilistic program:

```
t := Gaussian(5,2);
h := 0.0;
time := 0.0;
while (h < t)
{
  t := t + 1 + e;
  if (flip(0.25))
     h := h + Gaussian(4,2);
  time := time + 1;
}
score(Gaussian_pdf(time, 10.0, 60.0));
return t
```

where score intuitively multiplies the probability of the current program run by its argument, and Gaussian_pdf$(\mu, \sigma, x) = \frac{1}{\sqrt{2\pi}\sigma}e^{-\frac{1}{2\sigma^2}(\mu - x)^2}$ is the value of the density function of the Gaussian distribution with mean μ and variance σ at point x. Now, although we assume that the hare caught the tortoise, the program may still diverge with a positive probability. In order to reason about programs like this, we need a framework which supports soft conditioning—as modelled by score in our setting—and is able to handle diverging programs.

As a more complicated example, let us consider the inverse intuitive physics example from [12][1]. In this model, using noisy approximate Newtonian dynamics, a ball is falling on the ground from a certain height, potentially hitting some fixed obstacles on the way. Given the observed final position of the ball, we want to find the distribution on initial locations of the ball. Similarly to the above example, this model is implemented as a simulation of the ball's movement from the random initial position (sampled from the prior), followed by soft conditioning on the ball's final position. Depending on the shapes and locations of the obstacles and the size of the floor on which the ball is supposed to land, the program may not terminate—the ball may get stuck in the air, blocked by obstacles, or may fail to land on the floor and keep falling indefinitely.

Issues with program divergence may also appear when implementing models which are not designed to be possibly diverging—be it because of mistakes in the implementation or intricacies and subtleties of the model itself. For instance, the implementation of the Pitman-Yor process [19] on forestdb.org, an online repository of probabilistic models in Church [10] and WebPPL [11], occasionally fails. According to a note on the website, a possible cause is that the program may not almost surely terminate.

Another issue related to program divergence is that some implementations of sampling-based algorithms do not handle detected divergence correctly—instead of throwing an appropriate error message, they simply ignore diverging runs after a given number of steps, which leads to misleading inference results. For instance, consider the following WebPPL program taken from [30]:

```
var three_calls = function () {
  if (flip(0.5)) {
    return 0;
  }
  else {
    return 1 + three_calls() + three_calls() + three_calls();
  }
}
var model = function () {three_calls()}
```

This program does not almost surely terminate and its expected outcome is infinite. However, applying WebPPL's enumeration (exact) inference algorithm with a bounded maximum number of executions to this program gives a distribution assigning a probability of over 0.8 to outcome 0 and minuscule probabilities to other outcomes. No warning about the maximum number of evaluation steps being reached is given.

---

[1] Available online under http://probmods.org/chapters/conditioning.html.

There has been research on the semantics of non-terminating probabilistic programs [13,26,27]. However, this research was mostly aimed at analysing randomised algorithms, rather than Bayesian inference. As a consequence, most languages used in this line of research have no features such as continuous distributions and soft conditioning, which are the cornerstone of Bayesian probabilistic programming. While some authors consider non-terminating programs in the context of Bayesian reasoning [20,21,29], they normally restrict their attention to discrete programs with hard conditioning by means of Boolean predicates. So far, to our knowledge, the only work which comprehensively treats non-termination in the context of semantics of Bayesian probabilistic programming with continuous distributions is [3]. This paper defines a semantics which calculates the probability of divergence and the probability of failing a hard constraint explicitly. Soft constraints are not considered for diverging programs, as the authors argue that the probability of divergence normalised by soft constraints may be undefined for some programs if unbounded scores are allowed. The authors do not attempt to restrict the language so that scores would make sense for diverging programs.

In this paper, we investigate how the addition of continuous distributions and soft conditioning, necessary for most machine learning applications, affects the semantics of potentially diverging procedural probabilistic programs. We discuss why dealing with divergence in programs with soft conditioning is very difficult (if at all possible) and why one cannot expect any sampling-based semantics to fully correspond to the intuitive meaning of a potentially diverging program. Nevertheless, we also aim to define the first semantics of a probabilistic language supporting both continuous distributions and hard and soft conditioning which is designed to handle diverging programs. We discuss the strengths and limitations of this semantics and state in what sense it can be considered correct.

We provide both a denotational weakest preexpectation semantics à la Kozen [24] and McIver and Morgan [26] together with an operational sampling-based semantics, and prove that the two semantics are equivalent. Hence, *this paper extends the standard weakest preexpectation framework to programs with continuous distributions and soft conditioning while being able to treat program divergence.*

2   A Bayesian Probabilistic While-Language

We start off by presenting the syntax of a simple probabilistic while-language, simply called *PL*, which will be used throughout this paper. Besides the usual ingredients such as skip and diverge statements, assignments, sequential composition, conditional statements and guarded loops, the language contains three additional constructs: (a) *random draws* from *continuous distributions*, (b) *observations* encoding hard conditioning, and (c) a *score* function used for soft conditioning. These forms of conditioning are central to Bayesian inference.

The syntax is presented in Fig. 1 where C, C_1, and C_2 are programs, x is a program variable, U denotes the continuous uniform distribution on the unit

$$\langle C \rangle ::= \texttt{skip} \qquad\qquad\qquad\qquad \text{no-operation}$$

```
⟨C⟩ ::= skip                          no-operation
      | diverge                         divergence
      | x := E                 variable assignment
      | x :≈ U          random variable assignment
      | observe(φ)              hard conditioning
      | score(E)                soft conditioning
      | C₁; C₂            sequential composition
      | if(φ){C}                      conditional
      | while(φ){C}                  guarded loop
```

Fig. 1. Syntax of PL

interval, ϕ is a predicate over the program variables, and E is an arithmetic expression over the program variables. We do not specify the syntax of expressions E and predicates ϕ—we assume these may be arbitrary, as long as the corresponding evaluation functions are measurable (as explained later).

A few remarks concerning the syntax are in order. In order to simplify the approximation of while loops (as used later), we use the if operator without an else clause. This does not change the expressiveness of the language. For the same reason, the explicit diverge statement is used as syntactic sugar for while(true){skip}. In random assignments, we only allow sampling from the uniform distribution U on the unit interval $[0,1]$. This does not limit the expressiveness of the language, as samples from an arbitrary continuous distribution can be obtained by sampling from the unit interval and applying the inverse cumulative distribution function (inverse cdf) of the given distribution to the generated sample. For instance, we can generate a sample from the Gaussian distribution with mean mu and variance sigma as follows

```
u := U;
x := Gaussian_inv_cdf(mu,sigma,u);
```

where $\texttt{Gaussian\_inv\_cdf}(\mu,\sigma,u)$ returns the value of the inverse cumulative distribution function of the Gaussian distribution with mean μ and variance σ at point u—in other words, $\texttt{Gaussian\_inv\_cdf}(\mu,\sigma,u)$ is a value $v \in \mathbb{R}$ such that $\int_{-\infty}^{v} \texttt{Gaussian\_pdf}(\mu,\sigma,x)\,dx = u^2$.

Random draws from discrete probability distributions can also be encoded by uniform draws from the unit interval, see e.g. [31]. For instance, the statement if(flip(0.25)){C} as used in the introduction is a shorthand for u :≈ U; if(u < 0.25){C}.

Let us briefly describe the semantics of the three new syntactic constructs at an intuitive level; the rest of this paper is devoted to make this precise. The execution of the random variable assignment $x :\approx U$ incorporates taking a

---

[2] Note that the value of $\texttt{Gaussian\_inv\_cdf}(\mu,\sigma,u)$ is technically only defined for $u \in (0,1)$, but we can safely extend it to $[0,1]$ by setting $\texttt{Gaussian\_inv\_cdf}(\mu,\sigma,0)$ and $\texttt{Gaussian\_inv\_cdf}(\mu,\sigma,1)$ to some arbitrary value (say, 0), as the probability of drawing 0 or 1 from the continuous uniform distribution on $[0,1]$ is zero, anyway.

sample from the uniform distribution U and assigning this sample to the program variable x. The observe(ϕ) statement is similar to the assert(ϕ) statement: it has no effect for program runs satisfying the predicate ϕ, but program runs violating ϕ are invalid. Such invalid runs are discontinued (aka: stopped). The crucial difference to the assert statement is that probabilities of valid program runs are normalised with respect to the total probability mass of all valid runs. For instance, the only valid runs of program

```
x := 0; y := 0;
if (flip(0.5))
    x := 1;
if (flip(0.5))
    y := 1;
observe(x+y=1)
```

are $x = 0, y = 1$ and $x = 1, y = 0$. Although in absence of the observe-statement the probability of each such run is $1/4$, their probability now becomes $1/2$ due to normalising $1/4$ with the probability of obtaining a valid run, i.e., $1/2$. (As discussed extensively in [29], the semantics becomes more tricky when program divergences are taken into account.) As runs are abandoned that violate the predicate ϕ, this is called *hard* conditioning.

In contrast, the statement score(E) models *soft* conditioning. As effect of executing this statement the probability of the current program run is scaled (i.e. multiplied) by the current value of the expression E. The higher the value of E, the more likely the combination of random variables sampled so far is considered to be.

To illustrate how soft conditioning works, suppose that we have a function softeq$(a, b) = e^{-(a-b)^2}$, whose value is 1 if both arguments are the same and moves closer to 0 as the arguments move further apart. Now, consider the following program:

```
u1 := U;
x  := Gaussian_inv_cdf(0,2,u1);
u2 := U;
y  := Gaussian_inv_cdf(1,2,u2);
score(softeq(x,y));
```

The use of score has the effect that program runs in which x and y are closer to each other are more likely.

3   Denotational Semantics

We will now define the semantics of *PL* in a weakest precondition style manner. This semantics builds upon the semantics of the probabilistic guarded command language pGCL [25] extended with hard conditioning as defined in [29]. The key object $\text{wp}[\![C]\!](f)(\sigma)$ defines the expected value of a function f with respect to the probability distribution of final states of program C, provided the program starts in the initial state σ. The key difference to [25,29] is that dealing with continuous distributions requires some sort of integration, and the integrated functions must be well-behaved.

Defining a denotational semantics of a language allowing unbounded computations requires the use of domain theory, which helps to ensure that all semantic functions used are well-defined. Some basic definitions from domain theory, which are needed to understand this paper, are included in Appendix B.

Probability theory with continuous random variables is usually formalised using measure theory and the semantics of *PL* follows this route. For the sake of completeness, the main relevant ingredients of measure theory are summarised in Appendix A. We start off by defining a measurable state space, and the domain of measurable expectations—the quantitative analogue of predicates. After shortly defining the (standard) semantics of expressions and predicates, we define a weakest preexpectation semantics of *PL* and subsequently generalise this towards a weakest liberal preexpectation semantics that takes program divergence explicitly into account.

3.1   Measurable Space of States

In the same vein as [25,29], the semantics $\mathbf{wp}[\![C]\!](f)(\sigma)$ will be defined as the expected value of the measurable function f mapping states to nonnegative reals (extended with ∞). In order to reason about measurable functions on states, we first define a measurable space of program states.

Let $\mathcal{N}$ be a countable set of variable names ranged over by x_i. A program state maps program variables to their current value. Formally, state σ is a set $\{(x_1, V_1), \ldots, (x_n, V_n)\}$ of pairs of unique variable names x_i and their corresponding values $V_i \in \mathbb{R}$. The set Ω_σ has the following form:

$$\Omega_\sigma = \biguplus_{n \in \mathbb{N}} (\{\{(x_1, V_1), \ldots, (x_n, V_n)\} \mid \forall i \in 1..n \; x_i \in \mathcal{N}, V_i \in \mathbb{R}. \forall j \neq i \; x_i \neq x_j\})$$

The state space Ω_σ is equipped with the functions: $\mathbf{dom}(\cdot) : \Omega_\sigma \to P(\mathcal{N})$, returning the domain of a state (i.e., the set of variables which are assigned values), and $\mathbf{elem}(\cdot, \cdot) : \Omega_\sigma \times \mathcal{N} \to \mathbb{R} \uplus \{\bot\}$ such that $\mathbf{elem}(\sigma, x)$ (for convenience, abbreviated $\sigma(x)$) returns the value assigned to variable x in σ or $\bot$ if $x \notin \mathbf{dom}(\sigma)$. The functions $\mathbf{dom}$ and $\mathbf{elem}$ are defined for $\sigma = \{(x_1, V_1), \ldots, (x_n, V_n)\}$ as:

$$\mathbf{dom}(\sigma) = \{x_1, \ldots, x_n\}$$

$$\mathbf{elem}(\sigma, y) = \sigma(y) = \begin{cases} V_i & \text{if } y = x_i \text{ for some } i \\ \bot & \text{otherwise.} \end{cases}$$

Let the metric d_σ on Ω_σ be defined as follows:

$$d_\sigma(\sigma_1, \sigma_2) = \begin{cases} \sum_{x \in \mathbf{dom}(\sigma_1)} |\sigma_1(x) - \sigma_2(x)| & \text{if } \mathbf{dom}(\sigma_1) = \mathbf{dom}(\sigma_2) \\ \infty & \text{otherwise} \end{cases}$$

It is easy to verify that d_σ is indeed a metric. Note that on the subset of states with a fixed domain $\{x_1, \ldots, x_n\}$, d_σ is essentially the Manhattan distance.

Lemma 1. *The metric space* $(\Omega_\sigma, d_\sigma)$ *is separable.*

Proof. Consider a subset $\Omega_\sigma^\mathbb{Q}$ of Ω_σ where all values are rational. Then the set $\Omega_\sigma^\mathbb{Q}$ is countable and it can be easily verified that it is a dense subset of Ω_σ. Hence, $(\Omega_\sigma, d_\sigma)$ is separable.   □

Finally, let Σ_σ be the Borel σ-algebra on Ω_σ induced by the metric d_σ. The pair $(\Omega_\sigma, \Sigma_\sigma)$ is our measurable space of states.

3.2   Domain of Measurable Expectations

As the weakest preexpectation semantics of *PL* is defined in terms of an operator transforming measurable functions, we need to show that measurable functions from Ω_σ to $\overline{\mathbb{R}}_+ = \mathbb{R}_+ \cup \{+\infty\}$ form a valid domain. More specifically, these functions must form a ω-*complete partial order* (whose definition is included in Appendix B). Similarly, we need to show that the domain of *bounded* measurable expectations, which will be used in the weakest liberal preexpectation semantics, is valid. Fortunately, these facts follow immediately from basic properties of measure theory.

Lemma 2. *The set of measurable functions* $f\colon \Omega_\sigma \to \overline{\mathbb{R}}_+$ *with point-wise ordering forms an* ω-*complete partial order* (ω-*cpo*). *Similarly, the set of bounded measurable functions* $f\colon \Omega_\sigma \to [0,1]$ *forms an* ω-*cpo.*

Proof. The bottom element of the set of measurable functions $f\colon \Omega_\sigma \to \overline{\mathbb{R}}_+$ is the function $\lambda\sigma.0$, mapping every state to 0. It is known that any increasing chain of functions with co-domain $\overline{\mathbb{R}}_+$ has a supremum, so this also holds for chains of measurable functions. The fact that point-wise supremum of measurable functions to $\overline{\mathbb{R}}_+$ is measurable is a standard result in measure theory. The argument for bounded measurable functions is the same.   □

3.3   Expression and Predicate Evaluation

The semantics makes use of two evaluation functions, $\sigma(E)$ and $\sigma(\phi)$, which evaluate the real-valued expression E and predicate ϕ, respectively, in state σ. We assume that for each E, the evaluation function on states $\lambda(\sigma, E).\sigma(E)$ is measurable and, similarly, for all ϕ, the function $\lambda(\sigma, \phi).\sigma(\phi)$ is measurable[3]. We also assume that the evaluation functions are total—this means that in case of evaluation errors, such as some variable in E not being in the domain of σ, some value (typically 0 or false) still needs to be returned. We convert truth values to reals by Iverson brackets $[\cdot]$: $[\text{true}] = 1$ and $[\text{false}] = 0$. We write E for $\lambda\sigma.\sigma(E)$ and ϕ for $\lambda\sigma.\sigma(\phi)$ if it is clear from the context that E or ϕ denotes a function.

---

[3] This assumption requires a σ-algebra on expressions and predicates. This can be defined as a Borel σ-algebra induced by a simple metric on syntactic terms, as in [5].

$$\mathtt{wp[\![skip]\!]}(f) = f$$

$$\mathtt{wp[\![diverge]\!]}(f) = 0$$

$$\mathtt{wp[\![}x := E\mathtt{]\!]}(f) = \lambda\sigma.f(\sigma[x \mapsto \sigma(E)])$$

$$\mathtt{wp[\![}x :\approx U\mathtt{]\!]}(f) = \lambda\sigma.\int_{[0,1]} f(\sigma[x \mapsto v])\,\lambda(dv)$$

$$\mathtt{wp[\![observe}(\phi)\mathtt{]\!]}(f) = \lambda\sigma.[\sigma(\phi)]\cdot f(\sigma)$$

$$\mathtt{wp[\![score}(E)\mathtt{]\!]}(f) = \lambda\sigma.[\sigma(E) \in (0,1]]\cdot\sigma(E)\cdot f(\sigma)$$

$$\mathtt{wp[\![}C_1; C_2\mathtt{]\!]}(f) = \mathtt{wp[\![}C_1\mathtt{]\!]}(\mathtt{wp[\![}C_2\mathtt{]\!]}(f))$$

$$\mathtt{wp[\![if}(\phi)\{C\}\mathtt{]\!]}(f) = [\phi]\cdot\mathtt{wp[\![}C\mathtt{]\!]}(f) + [\neg\phi]\cdot f$$

$$\mathtt{wp[\![while}(\phi)\{C\}\mathtt{]\!]}(f) = \mathtt{lfp}\ X.[\neg\phi]\cdot f + [\phi]\cdot\mathtt{wp[\![}C\mathtt{]\!]}(X)$$

Fig. 2. Weakest preexpectation semantics of *PL*

3.4 Weakest Preexpectation Semantics

We now have all ingredients in place to define the weakest preexpectation semantics of *PL*. This semantics is defined by the operator $\mathtt{wp[\![}C\mathtt{]\!]}(\cdot)$, which takes a measurable function f from Ω_σ to $\overline{\mathbb{R}}_+$—called the *postexpectation*—and returns a measurable function in the same domain—called the *preexpectation*)—which, for every initial state σ_0, computes the expected value of f after executing the program C starting in state σ_0. In other words, if $f\colon \Omega_\sigma \to \overline{\mathbb{R}}_+$ is a measurable function on states and $\sigma_0 \in \Omega_\sigma$ is the initial state, then $\mathtt{wp[\![}C\mathtt{]\!]}(f)(\sigma_0)$ yields the expected value of $f(\sigma)$, where σ is a final program state of C.

The wp-semantics of *PL* is defined by structural induction and is shown in Fig. 2. The semantics of most constructs matches the wp-semantics in [29], with the distinction that it is defined on the domain of nonnegative measurable functions on states, rather than arbitrary nonnegative functions. Let us briefly explain the individual cases one by one.

Skip. The skip statement leaves the expectation f unchanged.

Divergence. The expectation of any function f with respect to the diverge expression is 0, as no final state at which f can be evaluated is ever reached by the program.

Assignment. For assignment $x := E$, the semantics just evaluates E, updates x with the new value in the state and passes this updated state to the expectation.

Random draw. The expected value of a measurable function f on states with respect to the uniform random assignment $x :\approx U$, applied to the initial state σ, is the Lebesgue integral of $f(\sigma[x \mapsto v])$ (as a function of v) with respect to the Lebesgue measure μ_L on $[0,1]^4$. By the Fubini-Tonelli theorem, $\mathtt{wp}[\![x :\approx U]\!](f)$ is itself a measurable function.

Hard. The `observe` statement defines hard conditioning—it states that all runs of the program which do not satisfy ϕ should be discarded and should not affect the expectation of f.

Soft. Scoring multiplies the expectation by the argument to `score`, expected to evaluate to a number in $(0,1]$.

Sequencing. The semantics of a sequence $C_1; C_2$ of two commands is just the composition of the semantics of respective commands— the semantics of C_2 with respect to the given input function f is the input to the semantics of C_1.

Conditional. The semantics of an $\mathtt{if}(\phi)\{C\}$-expression is, for initial states satisfying the condition ϕ, the semantics of the body C. For other states, the semantics is equivalent to the `skip` statement, as the expression does not do anything.

Loops. The semantics of a `while`-loop is defined as the least fixpoint of a function which simply returns the input continuation f if ϕ is false (corresponding to exiting the loop) and applies the semantics of the body to the argument X otherwise (which corresponds to performing another iteration). As explained in the following paragraph (cf. Lemma 4), this has the desired effect that the semantics of a `while`-loop is equivalent to the semantics of the infinite unfolding of the loop.

Well-Definedness and Key Properties of **wp.** When defining the weakest preexpectation semantics of *PL*, we implicitly assumed that all mathematical objects used are well defined. Specifically, we assumed that the `wp` transformer preserves measurability and that the least fixpoint in the semantics of `while`-loops exists. These properties can be proven by structural induction on the program C. The key observations used in the proof (which would not be needed in the discrete case) are that $\lambda\sigma. \int_{[0,1]}(\sup_i f_i)(\sigma[x \mapsto v]) \, \mu_L(dv) = \lambda\sigma. \sup_i \int_{[0,1]} f_i(\sigma[x \mapsto v]) \, \mu_L(dv)$ by Beppo Levi's theorem and that $\lambda\sigma. \int_{[0,1]} f(\sigma[x \mapsto v]) \, \mu_L(dv)$ is measurable (as a function of σ) by the Fubini-Tonelli theorem. As both ω-continuity (as defined in Appendix B) and measurability are required for $\mathtt{wp}[\![C]\!]$ to be well defined, we need to prove both properties simultaneously, so that the induction hypothesis is strong enough.

Lemma 3. *For every program C:*

1. *the function $\mathtt{wp}[\![C]\!](\cdot)$ is ω-continuous, and*
2. *for every measurable $f \colon \Omega_\sigma \to \overline{\mathbb{R}}_+$, $\mathtt{wp}[\![C]\!](f)(\cdot)$ is measurable.*

Proof. By induction on the structure of C. $\qquad\square$

The continuity of $\mathtt{wp}[\![C]\!]$ also ensures that the expression $[\neg\phi]\cdot f + [\phi]\cdot\mathtt{wp}[\![C]\!](X)$ in the semantics of `while` loops is continuous as a function of X. Applying Kleene's Fixpoint Theorem immediately gives us the following result:

---

[4] The Lebesgue measure is usually denoted by λ in the literature. We write μ_L instead to avoid confusion with the use of $\lambda\sigma$ to define a function with formal parameter σ.

Lemma 4. *Let* $f\colon \Omega_\sigma \to \overline{\mathbb{R}}_+$ *be measurable,* C *be a PL program and* ϕ *be a predicate. Let* $_{\langle\phi,C\rangle}^{\text{wp}}\Phi_f(X) = [\neg\phi]\cdot f + [\phi]\cdot\text{wp}[\![C]\!](X)$. *Then* $\text{lfp } X._{\langle\phi,C\rangle}^{\text{wp}}\Phi_f(X)$ *exists and is equal to* $\sup_n {}_{\langle\phi,C\rangle}^{\text{wp}}\Phi_f^n(0)$. *Thus,* $\text{wp}[\![\text{while}(\phi)\{C\}]\!](f)$ *exists and*

$$\text{wp}[\![\text{while}(\phi)\{C\}]\!](f) = \sup_n {}_{\langle\phi,C\rangle}^{\text{wp}}\Phi_f^n(0)$$

3.5 Examples

Having defined the weakest preexpectation semantics, we explain it using a few examples. We first introduce two simple examples, which illustrate the key concepts, and then show how the semantics can be applied to the tortoise and hare program from the introduction.

Notation. To distinguish between program variables and metavariables, we write the former in fixed-width font (such as x1) and the latter in the usual italic form (such as x_1). In functions where only the original, non-updated input state appears in the body, we sometimes make the state implicit by removing "$\lambda\sigma.$" and replacing variable lookups of the form $\sigma(x)$ by just variables. For instance we write $\lambda\sigma.\sigma(\text{x}) + \sigma(\text{y})$ simply as $\text{x} + \text{y}$.

Example 1. Let us first consider a very simple instance of Bayesian linear regression. We want to fit a linear function approximately to two points $(0, 2)$ and $(1, 3)$, assuming that the coefficients of the function have Gaussian prior distributions. A *PL* implementation of such a regression, using the softeq distance squashing function mentioned at the end of Sect. 2, has the following form:

```
u1 := U;
a := Gaussian_inv_cdf(0,2,u1);
u2 := U;
b := Gaussian_inv_cdf(0,2,u2);
score(softeq(a*0 + b, 2));
score(softeq(a*1 + b, 3));
```

Let us now suppose that we want to calculate the expected value of the square of thea coefficient (recall that we can only compute expectations of nonnegative functions). We can do that by computing the weakest preexpectation of $\lambda\sigma.\sigma(\text{a})^2$ (written a^2 in short) with respect to the above program — that is, $\text{wp}[\![C]\!](\text{a}^2)$, where C is the given program. In the following derivation (as well as subsequent examples in this chapter), we adopt the notation used in [21], where the function directly below a statement C is a postexpectation, and the function directly above C is the corresponding preexpectation. That is, a block of the form:

$$// \ f_1$$
$$C$$
$$// \ f_2$$

states that $f_1 = \text{wp}[\![C]\!](f_2)$. We also use the letter G as an abbreviation for the Gaussian inverse cdf[5].

We can derive the expected value of a^2 as shown below. Note that the expressions between program lines are functions on program states, written using the implicit notation explained before.

$$// \int_{(0,1)} \int_{(0,1)} e^{-(G(0,2,v_2)-2)^2-(G(0,2,v_1)+G(0,2,v_2)-3)^2} \cdot G(0,2,v_1)^2 \, \mu_L(dv_2)\mu_L(dv_1)$$

u1 := U;

$$// \int_{(0,1)} e^{-(G(0,2,v_2)-2)^2-(G(0,2,u1)+G(0,2,v_2)-3)^2} \cdot G(0,2,u1)^2 \, \mu_L(dv_2)$$

a := Gaussian_inv_cdf(0, 2, u1);

$$// \int_{(0,1)} e^{-(G(0,2,v_2)-2)^2-(a+G(0,2,v_2)-3)^2} \cdot \text{a}^2 \, \mu_L(dv_2)$$

u2 := U;

$$// \; e^{-(G(0,2,u2)-2)^2-(a+G(0,2,u2)-3)^2} \cdot \text{a}^2$$

b := Gaussian_inv_cdf(0, 2, u2);

$$// \; e^{-(b-2)^2-(a+b-3)^2} \cdot \text{a}^2$$

score(softeq(a * 0 + b, 2));

$$// \; e^{-(a+b-3)^2} \cdot \text{a}^2$$

score(softeq(a * 1 + b, 3));

$$// \; \text{a}^2$$

We observe that the expected value of a^2 is independent on the initial state, which is not surprising as the program has no free variables. For any initial state σ, the expected value $\text{wp}[\![C]\!](\text{a}^2)(\sigma)$ of a is:

$$\int_{(0,1)} \int_{(0,1)} e^{-(G(0,2,v_2)-2)^2-(G(0,2,v_1)+G(0,2,v_2)-3)^2} \cdot G(0,2,v_1)^2 \, \mu_L(dv_2)\mu_L(dv_1).$$

We can also represent this expression as a double integral with respect to the Gaussian probability distribution $\mathcal{D}_G$ with mean 0 and variance 2, using the fact that a continuous probability distribution is a pushforward of the Lebesgue measure by the inverse cdf of the given distribution:

$$\text{wp}[\![C]\!](\text{a})(\sigma) = \int \int e^{-(x_2-2)^2-(x_1+x_2-3)^2} \cdot x_1^2 \, \mathcal{D}_G(dx_2)\mathcal{D}_G(dx_1).$$

This expression can also be represented as a double integral of Gaussian densities (denoted G_{pdf}) over $\mathbb{R}$:

$$\int \int e^{-(x_2-2)^2-(x_1+x_2-3)^2} G_{pdf}(0,2,x_1)G_{pdf}(0,2,x_2) \cdot x_1^2 \, \mu_L(dx_2)\mu_L(dx_1).$$

---

[5] We can integrate the Gaussian inverse over the interval $(0,1)$ instead of $[0,1]$, because the value of the Lebesgue integral at a single point does not contribute to the result.

Example 2. Let us now consider a very simple example of a potentially diverging program with continuous variables and soft conditioning. This example may be rather contrived and does not represent any machine learning model, but it illustrates well how the semantics works. Take the following program C:

```
b := 0;
k := 0;
while (b=0)
{
  u := U;
  k := k+1;
  if(u < 1/(k+1)^2)
  {
    b := 1;
    score(k/(k+1));
  }
}
```

Suppose we want to compute $\mathsf{wp}[\![C]\!](1)$, that is, the weakest preexpectation of the constant function $\lambda\sigma.1$ with respect to the program C. This may be interpreted as the probability that the program terminates, weighted by the scores.

As the program has a while-loop, we need to find the characteristic function $^{\mathsf{wp}}_{\langle b=0,C'\rangle}\Phi_1$ of this loop (whose body we denote by C'), with respect to the constant postexpectation 1. In this case, the characteristic function is

$$^{\mathsf{wp}}_{\langle b=0,C'\rangle}\Phi_1(X) = [\mathrm{b}\neq 0] + [\mathrm{b}=0]\cdot\mathsf{wp}[\![C']\!](X).$$

We first need to compute $\mathsf{wp}[\![C']\!](X)$:

$$// \quad \lambda\sigma.\frac{\sigma(\mathrm{k})+1}{(\sigma(\mathrm{k})+2)^3}\cdot X(\sigma[k\mapsto\sigma(k)+1][\mathrm{b}\mapsto 1]) + \frac{(\sigma(\mathrm{k})+2)^2 - 1}{(\sigma(\mathrm{k})+2)^2}\cdot X(\sigma[k\mapsto\sigma(k)+1])$$

$$=$$

$$// \quad \lambda\sigma.\int_{[0,1]}\left[v < \frac{1}{(\sigma(\mathrm{k})+2)^2}\right]\cdot\frac{\sigma(\mathrm{k})+1}{\sigma(\mathrm{k})+2}\cdot X(\sigma[k\mapsto\sigma(k)+1][\mathrm{b}\mapsto 1])$$

$$// \qquad + \left[v \geq \frac{1}{(\sigma(\mathrm{k})+2)^2}\right]\cdot X(\sigma[k\mapsto\sigma(k)+1])\,\mu_L(dv)$$

$$\mathrm{u} := \mathrm{U};$$

$$// \quad \lambda\sigma.\left[\sigma(\mathrm{u}) < \frac{1}{(\sigma(\mathrm{k})+2)^2}\right]\cdot\frac{\sigma(\mathrm{k})+1}{\sigma(\mathrm{k})+2}\cdot X(\sigma[k\mapsto\sigma(k)+1][\mathrm{b}\mapsto 1])$$

$$\qquad + \left[\sigma(\mathrm{u}) \geq \frac{1}{(\sigma(\mathrm{k})+2)^2}\right]\cdot X(\sigma[k\mapsto\sigma(k)+1])$$

```
k := k + 1;
```

$$// \ \lambda\sigma.\left[\sigma(u) < \frac{1}{(\sigma(k)+1)^2}\right]\cdot\frac{\sigma(k)}{\sigma(k)+1}\cdot X(\sigma[b \mapsto 1]) + \left[\sigma(u) \geq \frac{1}{(\sigma(k)+1)^2}\right]\cdot X(\sigma)$$

```
if(u < 1/(k + 1)²)
{
```

$$// \ \lambda\sigma.\frac{\sigma(k)}{\sigma(k)+1}\cdot X(\sigma[b \mapsto 1])$$

```
b := 1;
```

$$// \ \lambda\sigma.\frac{\sigma(k)}{\sigma(k)+1}\cdot X(\sigma)$$

```
score(k/(k + 1));
```

$$// \ X$$

```
}
```

$$// \ X$$

To simplify the presentation, we assumed in the last step that X does not depend directly on the variable u—we can show by a simple induction that this holds for $X = \overset{\text{wp}}{}_{\langle b=0,C'\rangle}\Phi_1^n(0)$ for any n, and we only need to apply $\text{wp}[\![C']\!](\cdot)$ to functions X of this form. By plugging

$$\text{wp}[\![C']\!](X) = \lambda\sigma.\frac{\sigma(k)+1}{(\sigma(k)+2)^3}\cdot X(\sigma[k \mapsto \sigma(k)+1][b \mapsto 1])$$

$$+ \ \frac{(\sigma(k)+2)^2 - 1}{(\sigma(k)+2)^2}\cdot X(\sigma[k \mapsto \sigma(k)+1])$$

into the equation for the characteristic function, we get

$$\overset{\text{wp}}{}_{\langle b=0,C'\rangle}\Phi_1(X) = \lambda\sigma.[\sigma(b) \neq 0] + [\sigma(b) = 0](\frac{\sigma(k)+1}{(\sigma(k)+2)^3}X(\sigma[k \mapsto \sigma(k)+1][b \mapsto 1])$$

$$+ \ \frac{(\sigma(k)+2)^2-1}{(\sigma(k)+2)^2}X(\sigma[k \mapsto \sigma(k)+1]))$$

We can now calculate subsequent terms of the sequence $\overset{\text{wp}}{}_{\langle b=0,C'\rangle}\Phi_1^n(0)$, whose supremum is the semantics of the while-loop:

$$\overset{\text{wp}}{}_{\langle b=0,C'\rangle}\Phi_1^0(0) = 0$$

$$\overset{\text{wp}}{}_{\langle b=0,C'\rangle}\Phi_1^1(0) = [b \neq 0]$$

$$\overset{\text{wp}}{}_{\langle b=0,C'\rangle}\Phi_1^2(0) = [b \neq 0] + [b = 0]\frac{k+1}{k+2}\cdot\frac{1}{(k+2)^2}$$

$$\overset{\text{wp}}{}_{\langle b=0,C'\rangle}\Phi_1^3(0) = [b \neq 0] + [b = 0]\frac{k+1}{k+2}\cdot\left(\frac{1}{(k+2)^2} + \frac{1}{(k+3)^2}\right)$$

$$\overset{\text{wp}}{}_{\langle b=0,C'\rangle}\Phi_1^4(0) = [b \neq 0] + [b = 0]\frac{k+1}{k+2}\cdot\left(\frac{1}{(k+2)^2} + \frac{1}{(k+3)^2} + \frac{1}{(k+4)^2}\right)$$

$$\cdots$$

It follows that $\overset{\text{wp}}{\langle b=0,C' \rangle}\Phi_1^n(0)$ can be represented in a closed form for any n:

$$\overset{\text{wp}}{\langle b=0,C' \rangle}\Phi_1^n(0) = [b \neq 0] + [b = 0]\cdot\frac{k+1}{k+2}\cdot\left(\sum_{i=2}^{n}\frac{1}{(k+i)^2}\right)$$

The correctness of this formula can be proven by a simple induction on n (which we omit here). This means that the semantics of the while-loop has the form:

$$\text{wp}[\![\texttt{while}(b=0)\{C'\}]\!](1) = \sup_n \overset{\text{wp}}{\langle b=0,C' \rangle}\Phi_1^n(0)$$

$$= [b \neq 0] + [b = 0]\frac{k+1}{k+2}\cdot\left(\sum_{i=2}^{\infty}\frac{1}{(k+i)^2}\right)$$

We can now use this result to compute the postexpectation of $\sigma.1$ with respect to the full program (where the while-loop is the program C', whose semantics has already been calculated):

```
//  π²/12 − 1/2
    =
//  1/2 · Σ∞_{i=2} 1/i²

    b := 0;

//  [b ≠ 0] + [b = 0] 1/2 · ( Σ∞_{i=2} 1/i² )

    k = 0;

//  [b ≠ 0] + [b = 0] (k+1)/(k+2) · ( Σ∞_{i=2} 1/(k+i)² )

    c′

    1
```

In the last step, we used the well-known fact that the series $\sum_{i=2}^{\infty}\frac{1}{i^2}$ converges to $\frac{\pi^2}{6} - 1$, to establish that $\text{wp}[\![C]\!](1) = \frac{\pi^2}{12} - \frac{1}{2}$.

Example 3. In order to illustrate the wp semantics on a more realistic program, let us recall the tortoise and hare example with soft conditioning from the introduction (with the time variable removed for simplicity and the Gaussian density in score replaced by softeq to ensure that scores are bounded). After expanding the syntactic sugar, this program has the following form:

```
u1 := U;
t  := Gaussian_inv_cdf(5,2,u1);
h  := 0.0;
while (h < t)
{
    t := t + 1 + e;
```

```
u2 := U;
if (u2 < 0.25)
{
    u3 := U;
    h := h + Gaussian_inv_cdf(4,2,u3);
}
}
score(softeq(t, 60.0));
```

Let us suppose we want to calculate the expected distance travelled by the tortoise before it gets caught. To this end, we need to calculate $\mathbf{wp}[\![C]\!](t)$ for the above program C and apply it to the empty initial state (or in fact any initial state, as the program contains no free variables).

Like in the previous example, we begin by calculating the characteristic function of the while-loop. We first need to compute $\mathbf{wp}[\![C']\!](X)$ for the loop body C'. We assume that X does not depend directly on variables u2 and u3—this is safe for X of the form $X = \substack{\mathbf{wp} \\ \langle h < t, C' \rangle} \Phi_f^n(0)$, as long as f does not depend directly on the aforementioned variables.

$$// \ \lambda\sigma. \, 0.25 \cdot \int_{(0,1)} X(\sigma[t \mapsto \sigma(t)+1+e][h \mapsto \sigma(h)$$
$$+ \, \mathsf{G}(4,2,v_3)]) \, \mu_L(dv_3) + 0.75 \cdot X(\sigma[t \mapsto \sigma(t)+1+e])$$

$\qquad$ t := t + 1 + e;

$$// \ \lambda\sigma. \, 0.25 \cdot \int_{(0,1)} X(\sigma[h \mapsto \sigma(h) + \mathsf{G}(4,2,v_3)]) \, \mu_L(dv_3) + 0.75 \cdot X(\sigma)$$

$$=$$

$$// \ \lambda\sigma. \int_{(0,1)} [v_2 < 0.25] \int_{(0,1)} X(\sigma[u2 \mapsto v_2][u3 \mapsto v_3][h \mapsto \sigma(h)$$
$$+ \, \mathsf{G}(4,2,v_3)]) \, \mu_L(dv_3) + [v_2 \geq 0.25] X(\sigma[u2 \mapsto v_2]) \, \mu_L(dv_2)$$

$\qquad$ u2 := U;

$$// \ \lambda\sigma. [\sigma(u2) < 0.25] \int_{(0,1)} X(\sigma[u3 \mapsto v_3][h \mapsto \sigma(h) + \mathsf{G}(4,2,v_3)] \, \mu_L(dv_3)$$
$$+ \, [\sigma(u2) \geq 0.25] \cdot X(\sigma)$$

$\qquad$ if(u2 < 0.25)

$\qquad$ {

$$// \ \lambda\sigma. \int_{(0,1)} X(\sigma[u3 \mapsto v_3][h \mapsto \sigma(h) + \mathsf{G}(4,2,v_3)] \, \mu_L(dv_3)$$

$\qquad\quad$ u3 := U;

$$// \ \lambda\sigma. X(\sigma[h \mapsto \sigma(h) + \mathsf{G}(4,2,\sigma(u3))])$$

$\qquad\quad$ h := h + Gaussian_inv_cdf(4, 2, u3);

$$// \ X$$

$\qquad$ }

$$// \ X$$

Thus, we have $\overset{\text{wp}}{_{\langle h<t,C'\rangle}}\Phi_f(X) = \lambda\sigma.\,[\sigma(\mathtt{h}) \geq \sigma(\mathtt{t})]\cdot f(\sigma) + [\sigma(\mathtt{h}) < \sigma(\mathtt{t})]\cdot(0.25\cdot$
$\int_{[0,1]} X(\sigma'_{\sigma,v_3})\,\mu_L(dv_3) + 0.75\cdot X(\sigma''_\sigma)))$, where $\sigma'_{\sigma,v_3} = \sigma[\mathtt{t}\mapsto \sigma(\mathtt{t})+1+e][\mathtt{h}\mapsto$
$\sigma(\mathtt{h})+\mathtt{G}(4,2,v_3)]$ is the state σ updated after a step where both the tortoise and
the hare moved (the latter by $\mathtt{G}(4,2,v_3)$) and $\sigma''_\sigma = \sigma[\mathtt{t}\mapsto\sigma(\mathtt{t})+1+e]$ is state
σ updated after a step where the hare stood still.

By the inductive definition of the wp operator, we have $\mathtt{wp}[\![\mathtt{while}(\mathtt{h}<\mathtt{t})\{C'\}]\!]$
$= \sup_n \overset{\text{wp}}{_{\langle h<t,C'\rangle}}\Phi_f^n(0)$. Then $\sup_n \overset{\text{wp}}{_{\langle h<t,C'\rangle}}\Phi_f^n(0)$ is guaranteed to exist, but unlike
in the previous example, it does not have a nice closed form. This is indeed the case
for most real-world programs.

We can now derive the formula for the expected final value of $\mathtt{t}$:

$$// \quad \lambda\sigma.\int_{(0,1)} \sup_n {}^{\text{wp}}_{\langle h<t,C'\rangle}\Phi_{e^{-(t-60.0)^2}t}^n(0)$$

$$// \qquad (\sigma[\mathtt{t}\mapsto \mathtt{G}(5,2,\sigma(v_1))][\mathtt{h}\mapsto 0])\,\mu_L(dv_1)$$

$$=$$

$$// \quad \lambda\sigma.\int_{(0,1)} \sup_n {}^{\text{wp}}_{\langle h<t,C'\rangle}\Phi_{e^{-(t-60.0)^2}t}^n(0)$$

$$(\sigma[\mathtt{u1}\mapsto v_1][\mathtt{t}\mapsto \mathtt{G}(5,2,\sigma(\mathtt{u1}))][\mathtt{h}\mapsto 0])\,\mu_L(dv_1)$$

$\mathtt{u1} := \mathtt{U};$

$$// \quad \lambda\sigma.\sup_n {}^{\text{wp}}_{\langle h<t,C'\rangle}\Phi_{e^{-(t-60.0)^2}t}^n(0)(\sigma[\mathtt{t}\mapsto \mathtt{G}(5,2,\sigma(\mathtt{u1}))][\mathtt{h}\mapsto 0])$$

$\mathtt{t} := \mathtt{Gaussian\_inv\_cdf}(5,2,\mathtt{u1});$

$$// \quad \lambda\sigma.\sup_n {}^{\text{wp}}_{\langle h<t,C'\rangle}\Phi_{e^{-(t-60.0)^2}t}^n(0)(\sigma[\mathtt{h}\mapsto 0])$$

$\mathtt{h} := 0.0;$

$$// \quad \sup_n {}^{\text{wp}}_{\langle h<t,C'\rangle}\Phi_{e^{-(t-60.0)^2}t}^n(0)$$

$\mathtt{while}(\mathtt{h}<\mathtt{t})\{...\}$

$$// \quad e^{-(t-60.0)^2}t$$

$\mathtt{score}(\mathtt{softeq}(\mathtt{t},60.0));$

$$// \quad \mathtt{t}$$

In the last step, we used the fact that $\overset{\text{wp}}{_{\langle h<t,C'\rangle}}\Phi_{\mathtt{softeq}(t,60.0)t}^n(0)$ does not
depend directly on $\mathtt{u1}$. We have now derived the expression for the weakest
preexpectation semantics of the program C:

$$\mathtt{wp}[\![C]\!](\mathtt{t}) = \lambda\sigma.\int_{(0,1)} \sup_n \Phi^n(0)(\sigma[\mathtt{t}\mapsto \mathtt{Gaussian\_inv\_cdf}(5,2,\sigma(v_1))][\mathtt{h}\mapsto 0])$$

where

$$\Phi(X) = \lambda\sigma.\,[\sigma(\mathtt{h}) \geq \sigma(\mathtt{t})]\cdot\mathtt{softeq}(\sigma(\mathtt{t}),60.0)\sigma(\mathtt{t})$$
$$+ [\sigma(\mathtt{h}) < \sigma(\mathtt{t})]\cdot(0.25\cdot\int_{(0,1)} X(\sigma'_{\sigma,v_3})\,\mu_L(dv_3)$$
$$+ 0.75\cdot X(\sigma''_\sigma)))$$

$$\sigma'_{\sigma,v_3} = \sigma[\mathtt{t} \mapsto \sigma(\mathtt{t}) + 1 + e][h \mapsto \sigma(\mathtt{h}) + \mathtt{Gaussian\_inv\_cdf}(4, 2, v_3)]$$
$$\sigma''_{\sigma} = \sigma[\mathtt{t} \mapsto \sigma(\mathtt{t}) + 1 + e].$$

3.6 Weakest Liberal Preexpectation Semantics

We now define a different variant of the above semantics, called the *weakest liberal preexpectation* semantics (wlp). In standard, discrete pGCL without scores [25, 29], the weakest liberal preexpectation defines the expected value of a function bounded by 1 (as per wp) plus the probability of divergence—in other words, in contrast to wp, the wlp operator considers the value of the input function to be 1, rather than 0, for diverging program runs. If the input function is a binary predicate ϕ, wlp defines the probability of this predicate being satisfied in the final state *or* the program never terminating.

$$
\begin{aligned}
\mathtt{wlp}[\![\mathtt{skip}]\!](f) &= f \\
\mathtt{wlp}[\![\mathtt{diverge}]\!](f) &= 1 \\
\mathtt{wlp}[\![x := E]\!](f) &= \lambda\sigma.f(\sigma[x \mapsto \sigma(E)]) \\
\mathtt{wlp}[\![x :\approx U]\!](f) &= \lambda\sigma. \int_{[0,1]} f(\sigma[x \mapsto v]) \, \mu_L(dv) \\
\mathtt{wlp}[\![\mathtt{observe}(\phi)]\!](f) &= \lambda\sigma.[\sigma(\phi)]{\cdot}f(\sigma) \\
\mathtt{wlp}[\![\mathtt{score}(E)]\!](f) &= \lambda\sigma.[\sigma(E) \in (0,1]]{\cdot}\sigma(E){\cdot}f(\sigma) \\
\mathtt{wlp}[\![C_1; C_2]\!](f) &= \mathtt{wlp}[\![C_1]\!](\mathtt{wlp}[\![C_2]\!](f)) \\
\mathtt{wlp}[\![\mathtt{if}(\phi)\{C\}]\!](f) &= [\phi]{\cdot}\mathtt{wlp}[\![C]\!](f) + [\neg\phi]{\cdot}f \\
\mathtt{wlp}[\![\mathtt{while}(\phi)\{C\}]\!](f) &= \mathtt{gfp}X.[\neg\phi]{\cdot}f + [\phi]{\cdot}\mathtt{wlp}[\![C]\!](X)
\end{aligned}
$$

Fig. 3. Weakest liberal preexpectation semantics of *PL*

In *PL*, the concept of weakest liberal preexpectation is similar, except that probabilities of all outcomes again have to be multiplied by scores encountered during the program's execution. Formally, $\mathtt{wp}[\![C]\!](\cdot)$, takes a measurable function f mapping Ω_σ to $[0,1]$ and returns another measurable function from Ω_σ to $[0,1]$. Note that, in contrast to wp, the domain of the input function is restricted to the unit interval.

The wlp operator is defined in Fig. 3, with changes from wp marked in blue.

The semantics of a while loop is now computed with the greatest fixpoint rather than the least fixpoint—this has the effect that the "default" outcome for diverging loops is 1 instead of 0. Similarly, diverge converts every function into a constant 1 function. The remaining changes are just that the recursive invocations to wp are replaced with calls to wlp.

Well-Definedness of `wlp`. To show that the liberal semantics is well-defined, we use a similar argument as for `wp`. First, note that if we restrict the set of measurable functions $f\colon \Omega_\sigma \to \overline{\mathbb{R}}_+$ to functions $f\colon \Omega_\sigma \to [0,1]$ with values in $[0,1]$, the constant function $\lambda\sigma.1$ (denoted 1 in short) is its top element. Hence, we can invert the complete partial order to get an ω-cpo with inverse pointwise ordering and a "bottom" element 1. The supremum of functions in this inverted cpo corresponds to the infimum in the original cpo, so continuity of `wlp` can again be proven by induction using the same domain-theoretic results. In the proof of measurability of $\texttt{wlp}[\![C]\!](f)$, we use the fact that the infimum of a sequence of measurable functions is measurable, just like with supremum. By Kleene's Fixpoint Theorem, we again know that $\texttt{gfp}\ X.[\neg\phi]\cdot f + [\phi]\cdot\texttt{wlp}[\![C]\!](X)$ exists and equals $\inf_n {}^{\texttt{wlp}}_{\langle\phi,C\rangle}\Phi_f^n(1)$, where ${}^{\texttt{wlp}}_{\langle\phi,C\rangle}\Phi_f(X) = [\neg\phi]\cdot f + [\phi]\cdot\texttt{wlp}[\![C]\!](X)$.

Note that the weakest liberal preexpectation is only defined for bounded postexpectations f, as we need some upper bound to set the preexpectation to in case of divergence. If we chose this bound to be $\lambda\sigma.\infty$, `wlp` would effectively always be set to ∞ for all non almost-surely terminating programs, rendering the semantics useless.

Example 4. To show how `wlp` differs from `wp`, let us consider Example 2 again. This time, we want to compute $\texttt{wlp}[\![C]\!](1)$, where C is again the full program. Like before, we begin by computing the semantics of the loop. As the body C' of the loop is itself loop (and `diverge`)-free, we have $\texttt{wlp}[\![C']\!](1) = \texttt{wp}[\![C']\!](1) = \lambda\sigma.\frac{\sigma(\mathrm{k})+1}{(\sigma(\mathrm{k})+2)^3}X(\sigma[\mathrm{k} \mapsto \sigma(\mathrm{k})+1][\mathrm{b} \mapsto 1]) + \frac{(\sigma(\mathrm{k})+2)^2-1}{(\sigma(\mathrm{k})+2)^2}X(\sigma[\mathrm{k} \mapsto \sigma(\mathrm{k})+1]))$, which implies ${}^{\texttt{wlp}}_{\langle\mathrm{b}=0,C'\rangle}\Phi_1(X) = {}^{\texttt{wp}}_{\langle\mathrm{b}=0,C'\rangle}\Phi_1(X) = \lambda\sigma.[\sigma(\mathrm{b}) \neq 0] + [\sigma(\mathrm{b}) = 0]\left(\frac{\sigma(\mathrm{k})+1}{(\sigma(\mathrm{k})+2)^3}X(\sigma[\mathrm{k} \mapsto \sigma(\mathrm{k})+1][\mathrm{b} \mapsto 1]) + \frac{(\sigma(\mathrm{k})+2)^2-1}{(\sigma(\mathrm{k})+2)^2}X(\sigma[\mathrm{k} \mapsto \sigma(\mathrm{k})+1])))$. The first terms of the sequence ${}^{\texttt{wlp}}_{\langle\mathrm{b}=0,C'\rangle}\Phi_1(1)$ are as follows:

$${}^{\texttt{wlp}}_{\langle\mathrm{b}=0,C'\rangle}\Phi_1^0(1) = [\mathrm{b} \neq 0]$$

$${}^{\texttt{wlp}}_{\langle\mathrm{b}=0,C'\rangle}\Phi_1^1(1) = [\mathrm{b} \neq 0]+[\mathrm{b} = 0]\left(\frac{\mathrm{k}+1}{\mathrm{k}+2}\frac{1}{(\mathrm{k}+2)^2} + \frac{(\mathrm{k}+2)^2-1}{(\mathrm{k}+2)^2}\right)$$

$${}^{\texttt{wlp}}_{\langle\mathrm{b}=0,C'\rangle}\Phi_1^2(1) = [\mathrm{b} \neq 0] + [\mathrm{b} = 0]\left(\frac{\mathrm{k}+1}{\mathrm{k}+2}\left(\frac{1}{(\mathrm{k}+2)^2} + \frac{1}{(\mathrm{k}+3)^2}\right)\right.$$
$$\left. + \frac{(\mathrm{k}+2)^2-1}{(\mathrm{k}+2)^2}\cdot\frac{(\mathrm{k}+3)^2-1}{(\mathrm{k}+3)^2}\right)$$

$${}^{\texttt{wlp}}_{\langle\mathrm{b}=0,C'\rangle}\Phi_1^3(1) = [\mathrm{b} \neq 0] + [\mathrm{b} = 0]\left(\frac{\mathrm{k}+1}{\mathrm{k}+2}\left(\frac{1}{(\mathrm{k}+2)^2} + \frac{1}{(\mathrm{k}+3)^2} + \frac{1}{(\mathrm{k}+4)^2}\right)\right.$$
$$\left. + \frac{(\mathrm{k}+2)^2-1}{(\mathrm{k}+2)^2}\cdot\frac{(\mathrm{k}+3)^2-1}{(\mathrm{k}+3)^2}\cdot\frac{(\mathrm{k}+4)^2-1}{(\mathrm{k}+4)^2}\right)$$

$$\cdots$$

We can now see what the pattern is:

$${}^{\texttt{wlp}}_{\langle b=0,C'\rangle}\Phi_1^n(0) = [b \neq 0] + [b = 0]\cdot\left(\frac{\mathrm{k}+1}{\mathrm{k}+2}\cdot\sum_{i=2}^{n+1}\frac{1}{(\mathrm{k}+i)^2} + \prod_{i=2}^{n+1}\frac{(\mathrm{k}+i)^2-1}{(\mathrm{k}+i)^2}\right)$$

Moreover, we can quickly check that $\prod_{i=2}^{n+1} \frac{(k+i)^2 - 1}{(k+i)^2} = \frac{k+1}{k+2} \cdot \frac{k+n+2}{k+n+1}$. We obtain $\mathtt{wlp}[\![C]\!]$ by computing the $\mathtt{wlp}$ of $\inf_n {}_{\langle b=0, C'\rangle}^{\mathtt{wlp}} \Phi_1^n(0)$ with respect to the two initial statements, $\mathtt{k} := 0$ and $\mathtt{b} := 0$. Thus,

$$\mathtt{wlp}[\![C]\!](1) = \frac{1}{2} \cdot \inf_n \sum_{i=2}^{n+1} \frac{1}{i^2} + \frac{1}{2} \frac{n+2}{n+1}$$

$$= \frac{1}{2} \cdot \lim_{n \to \infty} \sum_{i=2}^{n+1} \frac{1}{i^2} + \frac{1}{2} \frac{n+2}{n+1} = \frac{1}{2} \cdot \left(\frac{\pi^2}{6} - 1 \right) + \frac{1}{2} = \frac{\pi^2}{12}.$$

3.7 Redundancy of score

With respect to the weakest preexpectations semantics, the score operator admitting only arguments bounded by one is redundant, because scoring by a number in the unit interval can be simulated by rejection sampling without affecting the expected value of the given function. We show this result in this section.

To this end, we first need some additional concepts. Let $\mathtt{dom}(\sigma)$ be the set of variables which are assigned values in state σ. A function f is said to be *independent* of a variable x if $f(\sigma) = f(\sigma[x \mapsto V])$ for all $\sigma \in \Omega_\sigma$ and $V \in \mathbb{R}$. Let $\mathtt{fv}(E)$ be the set of free variables of an expression E, and $\mathtt{vars}(E)$ and $\mathtt{vars}(C)$ be the sets of all variables (free or bound) appearing in, respectively, the expression E and the program C.

Lemma 5. *For every expectation f, expression E and variable u such that $u \notin \mathtt{vars}(E)$ and f is independent of u, it holds:*

$$\mathtt{wp}[\![\mathtt{score}(E)]\!](f) = \mathtt{wp}[\![u :\approx U; \mathtt{observe}(E \in (0,1] \wedge u \le E)]\!](f)$$
$$\mathtt{wlp}[\![\mathtt{score}(E)]\!](f) = \mathtt{wlp}[\![u :\approx U; \mathtt{observe}(E \in (0,1] \wedge u \le E)]\!](f).$$

Proof. For $\mathtt{wp}$ we have:

$$\mathtt{wp}[\![u :\approx U]\!](\mathtt{wp}[\![\mathtt{observe}(E \in (0,1] \wedge u \le E)]\!](f))$$

$$= \lambda\sigma. \int_{[0,1]} \mathtt{wp}[\![\mathtt{observe}(E \in (0,1] \wedge u \le E)]\!](f)(\sigma[u \mapsto v]) \, \mu_L(dv)$$

$$= \lambda\sigma. \int_{[0,1]} [\sigma[u \mapsto v](E) \in (0,1]][v \le \sigma[u \mapsto v](E)] f(\sigma[u \mapsto v]) \, \mu_L(dv)$$

$$(*) = \lambda\sigma. \int_{[0,1]} [\sigma(E) \in (0,1]][v \le \sigma(E)] f(\sigma) \, \mu_L(dv)$$

$$= \lambda\sigma. f(\sigma) \int_{[0,1]} [\sigma(E) \in (0,1]][v \le \sigma(E)] \, \mu_L(dv)$$

$$(\text{Lebesgue}) = \lambda\sigma. f(\sigma) \cdot \sigma(E)$$

$$= \mathtt{wp}[\![\mathtt{score}(E)]\!](f).$$

Proof step ($*$) follows from the fact that $u \notin \mathtt{fv}(E)$ and that f is independent of u. The above result also proves the second item of the lemma, as $\mathtt{wp}$ and $\mathtt{wlp}$ coincide for programs without loops and $\mathtt{diverge}$ statements.   □

Let $\mathtt{noscore}(C)$ denote the program obtained from program C by replacing each expression of the form $\mathtt{score}(E)$ by $u :\approx U; \mathtt{observe}(u \leq E)$ for sufficiently fresh variable $u \notin \mathtt{vars}(E)$. By "sufficiently fresh" we mean that u does not appear in the program C and that no function f whose expected value we are interested in depends on u. (We do not formalise this notion for the sake of brevity.)

Lemma 6. *For every expectation f we have:*

$$\mathtt{wp}[\![\mathtt{noscore}(C)]\!](f) = \mathtt{wp}[\![C]\!](f) \quad and \quad \mathtt{wlp}[\![\mathtt{noscore}(C)]\!](f) = \mathtt{wlp}[\![C]\!](f).$$

Proof. By induction on the structure of C, with appeal to Lemma 5.   □

4   Operational Semantics

In addition to the denotational semantics, we also present an operational semantics of *PL*. Apart from serving as a sanity check for the wp-semantics, this semantics is of interest on its own: an operational semantics is typically closer to a sample-based semantics that provides the basis for simulation-based evaluation of probabilistic programs (such as MCMC and Metropolis Hasting), is closer to models that are amenable to automated verification techniques such as probabilistic model checking [23], and sometimes simplifies for the reasoning about probabilistic programs, such as proving some sort of program equivalence [39].

4.1   Entropy Space

A *small-step* operational semantics of a deterministic imperative language typically takes a program C and state σ and performs a single step of program evaluation, returning a new program C' and an updated state σ'. For probabilistic languages, this is not possible, as a probabilistic program has multiple updated states—in fact, infinitely and uncountably many of them for programs with continuous distributions—depending on the outcomes of random draws. A possible way around this is to define the operational semantics of probabilistic languages with respect to a fixed sequence of values sampled from subsequent distributions, called a *trace*. By fixing a trace, a probabilistic program can be evaluated deterministically.

Traces often have the form of finite [5] or infinite [31] lists of values. To obtain a compositional semantics, we will instead use an abstract, infinite structure called *entropy*, as defined by [8] and [39].

Definition 1 ([39]). *An* entropy space *is a measurable space* $(\mathbb{S}, \mathcal{S})$ *equipped with a measure $\mu_{\mathbb{S}}$ with $\mu_{\mathbb{S}}(\mathbb{S}) = 1$, and measurable functions $\pi_U \colon \mathbb{S} \to [0,1]$, $(::) \colon \mathbb{S} \times \mathbb{S} \to \mathbb{S}$, $\pi_L, \pi_R \colon \mathbb{S} \to \mathbb{S}$ such that:*

– *For all measurable functions* $f\colon [0,1] \to \overline{\mathbb{R}}_+$ *and Lebesgue measure* λ,

$$\int f(\pi_U(\theta))\,\mu_\mathbb{S}(d\theta) = \int_{[0,1]} f(x)\,\mu_L(dx)$$

– (::) *is a surjective pairing function defined by:* $\pi_L(\theta_L :: \theta_R) = \theta_L$ *and* $\pi_R(\theta_L :: \theta_R) = \theta_R$
– *For all measurable functions* $g\colon \mathbb{S} \times \mathbb{S} \to \overline{\mathbb{R}}_+$:

$$\int g(\pi_L(\theta), \pi_R(\theta))\,\mu_\mathbb{S}(d\theta) = \int \int g(\theta_L, \theta_R)\,\mu_\mathbb{S}(d\theta_L)\mu_\mathbb{S}(d\theta_R).$$

An element $\theta \in \mathbb{S}$ *of the entropy space is called an* entropy.

In the above definition, $\mathbb{S}$ is the set of all possible entropies and $\mathcal{S}$ a σ-algebra on it. The entropy space is abstract, so we do not specify what $\mathbb{S}$ and $\mathcal{S}$ are and what they look like, we only assume that they satisfy the above properties.

Example of an Entropy Space. A simple concrete realisation of the entropy space, for which the properties are satisfied, is the following:

– The set $\mathbb{S}$ is the set $[0,1]^\omega$ of infinite sequences of numbers in $[0,1]$ (the so-called Hilbert cube). Thus, each entropy $S \in \mathbb{S}$ is an infinite sequence $S = (s_1, s_2, s_3 \dots)$ such that $s_i \in [0,1]$ for all i.
– The σ-algebra $\mathcal{S}$ is, intuitively, the product of infinitely many copies of the Borel σ-algebra on $[0,1]$. More formally, $\mathcal{S}$ is the σ-algebra generated by cylinder sets of the form $A_1 \times A_2 \times \cdots \times A_k \times [0,1] \times [0,1] \times [0,1]\dots$, where $A_1, A_2, \dots, A_k$ are Borel subsets of $[0,1]$.
– The measure $\mu_\mathbb{S}$ on $(\mathbb{S}, \mathcal{S})$ is the extension of the Lebesgue measure to the infinite product space $(\mathbb{S}, \mathcal{S})$. Formally, it is the unique (by Kolmogorov's extension theorem) measure such that for all finite sequences of Borel subsets $A_1, A_2, \dots, A_k$ of $[0,1]$, we have $\mu_\mathbb{S}(A_1 \times A_2 \times \cdots \times A_k \times [0,1]^\omega) = \mu_L(A_1) \times \mu_L(A_2) \times \dots \times \mu_L(A_k) \times \mu_L([0,1]) \times \mu_L([0,1]) \cdots = \mu_L(A_1) \times \mu_L(A_2) \times \dots \times \mu_L(A_k)$
– The function π_U returns the first element of the given sequence—that is, $\pi_U((s_1, s_2, s_3, \dots)) = s_3$.
– The functions π_L and π_R return the subsequences consisting of odd and even elements of the input sequence, respectively. Thus, $\pi_L((s_1, s_2, s_3, s_4, \dots)) = (s_1, s_3, \dots)$ and $\pi_R((s_1, s_2, s_3, s_4, \dots)) = (s_2, s_4, \dots)$.
– The function :: interleaves the two input sequences, so that $(s_1, s_2, s_3, \dots) :: (t_1, t_2, t_3, \dots) = (s_1, t_1, s_2, t_2, s_3, t_3, \dots)$.

Observe that the functions π_L and π_R return two *disjoint* infinite subsequences of the input sequence. This means that if we want to perform two random computations, but only have a single entropy $s = (s_1, s_2, s_3, s_4 \dots)$, we can perform the first computation with the sequence $\pi_L((s_1, s_2, s_3, s_4 \dots)) = (s_1, s_3, \dots)$ and the second one with $\pi_R((s_1, s_2, s_3, s_4 \dots)) = (s_2, s_4, \dots)$ and no entropy component from the first computation will be reused in the second one.

In other words, for each new random sample we will have a "fresh" value in the entropy.

Results presented in this paper will, however, only depend on the abstract definition of entropy space.

4.2 Extended State Space

In order to define the operational semantics and the distributions induced by it, we need to extend the set of states Ω_σ with two exception states: $\frac{1}{2}$, denoting a *failed hard constraint or an evaluation error*, and $\uparrow$, denoting *divergence*. We denote this extended space by $\hat{\Omega}_\sigma$. A metric space on $\hat{\Omega}_\sigma$ is defined by extending the metric d_σ on Ω_σ to $\hat{\Omega}_\sigma$ as follows:

$$\hat{d}_\sigma(\sigma_1,\sigma_2) = \begin{cases} 0 & \text{if } \sigma_1 = \sigma_2 \in \{\frac{1}{2},\uparrow\} \\ d_\sigma(\sigma_1,\sigma_2) & \text{if } \sigma_1,\sigma_2 \in \Omega_\sigma \\ \infty & \text{otherwise.} \end{cases}$$

It is easy to check that the extended metric space $(\hat{\Omega}_\sigma, \hat{d}_\sigma)$ is separable. The σ-algebra $\hat{\Sigma}_\sigma$ on $\hat{\Omega}_\sigma$ is then induced by the metric $\hat{d}_\sigma$ and $(\hat{\Omega}_\sigma, \hat{\Sigma}_\sigma)$ is the measurable space of all program states.

In the remainder of this section, we will use two operators to extend real-valued functions on Ω_σ to the state space $\hat{\Omega}_\sigma$: for each function $f \colon \Omega_\sigma \to \overline{\mathbb{R}}_+$, the extended functions $\hat{f}, \check{f} \colon \hat{\Omega}_\sigma \to \overline{\mathbb{R}}_+$ are defined as follows:

$$\hat{f}(\tau) = \begin{cases} f(\tau) & \text{if } \tau \in \Omega_\sigma \\ 0 & \text{otherwise} \end{cases} \quad \text{and} \quad \check{f}(\tau) = \begin{cases} f(\tau) & \text{if } \tau \in \Omega_\sigma \\ 1 & \text{if } \tau = \uparrow \\ 0 & \text{otherwise.} \end{cases}$$

4.3 Reduction Relation

To ensure that the entropy is split correctly between partial computations, we use continuations, similarly to [39]. A continuation is represented by a list of expressions that are to be evaluated after completing the current evaluation. We keep track of two distinct entropies: one for the current computation and one to be used when evaluating the continuation.

The reduction relation is defined as a binary relation on *configurations*, i.e., tuples of the form

$$\langle \theta, C, K, \sigma, \theta_K, n, w \rangle$$

where C is the current program statement to be evaluated, σ is the current program state, K is the continuation, θ and θ_K are, respectively, the entropies to be used when evaluating C and the continuation K; finally, $n \in \mathbb{N}$ is the number of reduction rules applied so far and $w \in \mathbb{R} \cap [0,1]$ is the weight of the current program run so far. In order to access elements of a configuration κ, we use functions, e.g., for κ as given above $\mathsf{weight}(\kappa) = w$ and $\mathsf{state}(\kappa) = \sigma$. The *reduction relation* $\vdash$ is a binary relation on configurations where

$$\underbrace{\langle \theta, C, K, \sigma, \theta_K, n, w \rangle}_{\text{configuration } \kappa} \vdash \underbrace{\langle \theta', C', K', \sigma', \theta'_K, n', w' \rangle}_{\text{configuration } \kappa'}$$

means that the configuration κ reduces to configuration κ' in one step. Let $\vdash^*$ denote the reflexive and transitive closure of the reduction relation $\vdash$, i.e., $\kappa \vdash^* \kappa'$ means that κ reduces to κ' in zero or more reduction steps.

We present the reduction rules one-by-one for each syntactic construct of *PL*. The symbol $\downarrow$ means successful termination and $\frac{\iota}{}$ is a special state reached after a failed observation or an execution error.

Skip. As the `skip` statement cannot do anything, it has no reduction rule.

Divergence. The (diverge) rule states that the `diverge` statement reduces to itself indefinitely in any non-failure state σ:

$$\text{diverge} \frac{\sigma \neq \frac{\iota}{}}{\langle \theta, \texttt{diverge}, K, \sigma, \theta_K, n, w \rangle \vdash \langle \theta, \texttt{diverge}, K, \sigma, \theta_K, n{+}1, w \rangle}$$

Assignment. The rule (assign) evaluates the expression E in the current state σ and sets the value of x in the state to the outcome of this evaluation:

$$\text{assign} \frac{\sigma \neq \frac{\iota}{} \quad \sigma(E) = V}{\langle \theta, x := E, K, \sigma, \theta_K, n, w \rangle \vdash \langle \theta, \downarrow, K, \sigma[x \mapsto V], \theta_K, n{+}1, w \rangle}$$

Random draw. The rule (draw) evaluates a random draw from a uniform distribution:

$$\text{draw} \frac{\sigma \neq \frac{\iota}{}}{\langle \theta, x :\approx U, K, \sigma, \theta_K, n, w \rangle \vdash \langle \pi_R(\theta), \downarrow, K, \sigma[x \mapsto \pi_U(\pi_L(\theta))], \theta_K, n{+}1, w \rangle}$$

The outcome of this random draw is determined by the entropy θ and is set to $\pi_U(\pi_L(\theta))$, intuitively the first element of the "left" part of the entropy θ^6. The value of the sampled variable is assigned to variable x. The weight w is unchanged, as the density of the uniform distribution on $[0,1]$ is constant and equal to 1 for every point in the unit interval—as all outcomes are equally likely, there is no need to weigh the program runs.

---

[6] If we set this value to just $\pi_U(\theta)$, we would lose the property that an already used "element" of the entropy cannot appear in the entropy in the subsequent configuration, because we do not know what parts of θ the value of $\pi_U(\theta)$ depends on. In the Hilbert cube implementation discussed before, $\pi_U(\theta)$ is equivalent to $\pi_U(\pi_L(\theta))$ and "disjoint" from $\pi_R(\theta)$, but if we defined $\pi_U(\theta)$ to be, for instance, the second element of the sequence encoded by θ, this would not be the case. Obviously, this does not matter in practice, as after the (draw) rule, the expression to be evaluated with entropy $\pi_R(\theta)$ is empty, but it is still elegant to keep this property.

Hard. The rules (condition-true) and (condition-false) evaluate a hard condition in an observe statement. If the condition is satisfied, (condition-true) returns the current state and weight unchanged, otherwise the state is set to the error state $\frac{\iota}{\iota}$ by (condition-false):

$$\text{condition-true} \frac{\sigma \neq \frac{\iota}{\iota} \quad \sigma(\phi) = \texttt{true}}{\langle \theta, \texttt{observe}(\phi), K, \sigma, \theta_K, n, w \rangle \vdash \langle \theta, \downarrow, K, \sigma, \theta_K, n+1, w \rangle}$$

$$\text{condition-false} \frac{\sigma \neq \frac{\iota}{\iota} \quad \sigma(\phi) = \texttt{false}}{\langle \theta, \texttt{observe}(\phi), K, \sigma, \theta_K, n, w \rangle \vdash \langle \theta, \downarrow, [], \frac{\iota}{\iota}, \theta_K, n+1, w \rangle}$$

Soft. The rule (score) evaluates its argument, a real number in the unit interval, and multiplies it by the weight of the current run so far:

$$\text{score} \frac{\sigma \neq \frac{\iota}{\iota} \quad v = \sigma(E) \in (0, 1]}{\langle \theta, \texttt{score}(E), K, \sigma, \theta_K, n, w \rangle \vdash \langle \theta, \downarrow, K, \sigma, \theta_K, n+1, w \cdot v \rangle}$$

Sequencing. The rule (seq) is used to move statements from the current statement C to the continuation K:

$$\text{seq} \frac{\sigma \neq \frac{\iota}{\iota} \quad C_1 \neq C_1'; C_1''}{\langle \theta, C_1; C_2, K, \sigma, \theta_K, n, w \rangle \vdash \langle \pi_L(\theta), C_1, C_2 :: K, \sigma, \pi_R(\theta) :: \theta_K, n+1, w \rangle}$$

If the current statement is a sequence of statements, (seq) splits it into the first statement C_1 and the sequence of remaining statements C_2 in such a way that C_1 itself is a single concrete statement and not a sequence of statements—in other words, C_1 is as small as possible. The expression C_1 is then retained as the current expression to be evaluated, while C_2 is pushed onto the top of the expression stack in the continuation K. The expression C_1 is evaluated with only the "left" part of the entropy θ, and the right part is appended to the entropy of the continuation K; it is stored to be used later when C_2 is popped from the stack and evaluated. The reason that C_1 is required not to be a sequence is to ensure that there is a unique way to split the sequence of statements into C_1 and C_2. If the entropy could be split in different ways into sub-computations, this would make the semantics nondeterministic. Note that C_1 may be, e.g., an if-statement or a while loop which includes a sequence of statements as its sub-expression; we only require that it is not a sequence at the top level. The rule

$$\text{pop} \frac{\sigma \neq \frac{\iota}{\iota}}{\langle \theta, \downarrow, C :: K, \sigma, \theta_K, n, w \rangle \vdash \langle \pi_L(\theta_K), C, K, \sigma, \pi_R(\theta_K), n+1, w \rangle}$$

is the dual of (seq). After the current statement has been completely evaluated, (pop) fetches the top statement C from the continuation K and sets it as the next statement to be evaluated. The unused part θ of the entropy used in evaluating the last expression is discarded and replaced by the left part of the continuation entropy θ_K. If the evaluation started with an empty continuation, $\pi_L(\theta_K)$ will be the entropy "reserved" for evaluating C as it was pushed on the continuation by (seq). Obviously, the entropy reserved for C has to be removed from the entropy saved for evaluating the rest of the continuation, hence the latter is set to $\pi_R(\theta_K)$.

Conditional. The rules (if-true) and (if-false) are standard and self-explanatory.

$$\text{if-true}\frac{\sigma \neq \xi \qquad \sigma(\phi) = \texttt{true}}{\langle \theta, \texttt{if}(\phi)\{C\}, K, \sigma, \theta_K, n, w\rangle \vdash \langle \theta, C, K, \sigma, \theta_K, n{+}1, w\rangle}$$

$$\text{if-false}\frac{\sigma \neq \xi \qquad \sigma(\phi) = \texttt{false}}{\langle \theta, \texttt{if}(\phi)\{C\}, K, \sigma, \theta_K, n, w\rangle \vdash \langle \theta, \downarrow, K, \sigma, \theta_K, n{+}1, w\rangle}$$

Loops. The (while-true) and (while-false) rules are standard too. If the loop-guard ϕ is true, the loop body is to be executed possibly followed by the loop itself. Otherwise the loop terminates. The (while-true) rule reads

$$\frac{\sigma \neq \xi \qquad \sigma(\phi) = \texttt{true}}{\langle \theta, \texttt{while}(\phi)\{C\}, K, \sigma, \theta_K, n, w\rangle \vdash \langle \theta, C; \texttt{while}(\phi)\{C\}, K, \sigma, \theta_K, n{+}1, w\rangle}$$

$$\text{while-false}\frac{\sigma \neq \xi \qquad \sigma(\phi) = \texttt{false}}{\langle \theta, \texttt{while}(\phi)\{C\}, K, \sigma, \theta_K, n, w\rangle \vdash \langle \theta, \downarrow, K, \sigma, \theta_K, n{+}1, w\rangle}$$

The (final) rule is a dummy rule which applies to fully evaluated programs. It does nothing, except for increasing the step counter. Its purpose is to allow for reasoning about infinite evaluations, as explained later.

$$\text{final}\frac{\sigma \neq \xi}{\langle \theta, \downarrow, [], \sigma, \theta_K, n, w\rangle \vdash \langle \theta, \downarrow, [], \sigma, \theta_K, n{+}1, w\rangle}$$

The initial configuration for program C is of the form $\langle \theta, C, [], \sigma, \theta_K, 0, 1\rangle$ with the initial statement C, the empty continuation, initial state σ, a zero step count and initial weight one. Note that if the initial continuation is $[]$, the initial continuation entropy θ_K is irrelevant, as it can never be copied to the entropy of the current expression. A program is considered fully evaluated when the evaluation reaches a configuration where $C = \downarrow$ and $K = []$. In this case, only the dummy (final) rule can be applied. Thus, if

$$\langle \theta, C, [], \sigma, \theta_K, 0, 1\rangle \vdash^* \langle \theta', \downarrow, [], \sigma', \theta'_K, n, w\rangle$$

we say that the program C with initial state σ under entropy θ terminates in n steps in the state σ' with weight w.

Examples. We demonstrate how the semantics works by revisiting two of the examples in Sect. 3. For clarity, we now add line numbers to programs and write C_i for line i of the given program C and $C_{i,j}$ for the part of the program between lines i and j. We also write $\pi_{d_1,\ldots,d_n}(\theta)$ (where $d_1,\ldots,d_n \in \{L,R\}$) for $\pi_{d_1}(\pi_{d_2}\ldots(\pi_{d_n}(\theta)\ldots))$.

Example 5. We begin by revisiting the Bayesian linear regression example:

```
1        u1 := U;
2        a := Gaussian_inv_cdf(0,2,u1);
3        u2 := U;
4        b := Gaussian_inv_cdf(0,2,u2);
5        score(softeq(a*0 + b, 2));
6        score(softeq(a*1 + b, 3));
```

Let us suppose we want to evaluate this program with an empty initial state and with an entropy θ such that the two values sampled in the program (which are $\pi_U(\pi_{L,L}(\theta))$ and $\pi_U(\pi_{L,L,R,R}(\theta)))$), are, respectively, 0.5 and v, where $v \in (0,1)$ is a value such that Gaussian_inv_cdf$(0,2,v) = 2$. For the particular instantiation of the entropy space shown in Sect. 4.1, we have $\pi_U(\pi_{L,L}((s_1,s_2,s_3,\ldots))) = s_1$ and $\pi_U(\pi_{L,L,R,R}((s_1,s_2,s_3,\ldots))) = s_{13}$, so we can assume that θ is any infinite sequence $(s_1,s_2,s_3,\ldots)$ whose first element is 0.5 and thirteenth element is v. Note that Gaussian_inv_cdf$(0,2,0.5) = 0$, because the Gaussian distribution is symmetric, so exactly half of the total probability mass is below the mean.

The evaluation chain is shown below. We use colour to highlight states and scores which have changed from the previous configuration. Since the evaluation starts with a configuration with empty continuation, the initial continuation entropy θ_K is a "dummy" entropy whose values are irrelevant and do not affect the computation.

$$\langle\theta, \mathtt{u1} :\approx U; C_{2,6}, [], [], \theta_K, 0, 1\rangle \vdash$$

$(\text{seq})\ \langle\pi_L(\theta), \mathtt{u1} :\approx U, [C_{2,6}], [], \pi_R(\theta) :: \theta_K, 1, 1\rangle \vdash$

$(\text{draw})\ \langle\pi_{R,L}(\theta), \downarrow, [C_{2,6}], [\mathtt{u1} \mapsto 0.5], \pi_R(\theta) :: \theta_K, 2, 1\rangle \vdash$

$(\text{pop})\ \langle\pi_R(\theta), \mathtt{a} := \mathtt{G}(0,2,\mathtt{u1}); C_{3,6}, [], [\mathtt{u1} \mapsto 0.5], \theta_K, 3, 1\rangle \vdash$

$(\text{seq})\ \langle\pi_{L,R}(\theta), \mathtt{a} := \mathtt{G}(0,2,\mathtt{u1}), [C_{3,6}], [\mathtt{u1} \mapsto 0.5], \pi_{R,R}(\theta) :: \theta_K, 4, 1\rangle \vdash$

$(\text{assign})\ \langle\pi_{L,R}(\theta), \downarrow, [C_{3,6}], [\mathtt{u1}, \mathtt{a} \mapsto 0.5, 0], \pi_{R,R}(\theta) :: \theta_K, 5, 1\rangle \vdash$

$(\text{pop})\ \langle\pi_{R,R}(\theta), \mathtt{u2} :\approx U; C_{4,6}, [], [\mathtt{u1}, \mathtt{a} \mapsto 0.5, 0], \theta_K, 6, 1\rangle \vdash$

$(\text{seq})\ \langle\pi_{L,R,R}(\theta), \mathtt{u2} :\approx U, [C_{4,6}], [\mathtt{u1}, \mathtt{a} \mapsto 0.5, 0], \pi_{R,R,R}(\theta) :: \theta_K, 7, 1\rangle \vdash$

$(\text{draw})\ \langle\pi_{R,L,R,R}(\theta), \downarrow, [C_{4,6}], [\mathtt{u1}, \mathtt{a}, \mathtt{u2} \mapsto 0.5, 0, v], \pi_{R,R,R}(\theta) :: \theta_K, 8, 1\rangle \vdash$

$(\text{pop})\ \langle\pi_{R,R,R}(\theta), \mathtt{b} := \mathtt{G}(0,2,\mathtt{u2}); C_{5,6}, [], [\mathtt{u1}, \mathtt{a}, \mathtt{u2} \mapsto 0.5, 0, v], \theta_K, 9, 1\rangle \vdash$

$(\text{seq})\ \langle\pi_{L,R,R,R}(\theta), \mathtt{b} := \mathtt{G}(0,2,\mathtt{u2}), [C_{5,6}], [\mathtt{u1}, \mathtt{a}, \mathtt{u2} \mapsto 0.5, 0, v],$
$\qquad\qquad \pi_{R,R,R,R}(\theta) :: \theta_K, 10, 1\rangle \vdash$

$(\text{assign})\ \langle\pi_{L,R,R,R}(\theta), \downarrow, [C_{5,6}], [\mathtt{u1}, \mathtt{a}, \mathtt{u2}, \mathtt{b} \mapsto 0.5, 0, v, 2],$

$$\pi_{R,R,R,R}(\theta) :: \theta_K, 11, 1\rangle \vdash$$

(pop) $\langle \pi_{R,R,R,R}(\theta), C_{5,6}, [], [\text{u1}, \text{a}, \text{u2}, \text{b} \mapsto 0.5, 0, v, 2], \theta_K, 12, 1\rangle \vdash$

(seq) $\langle \pi_{L,R,R,R,R}(\theta), \texttt{score}(\texttt{softeq}(\text{a} * 0 + \text{b}, 2)), [C_6],$

$$[\text{u1}, \text{a}, \text{u2}, \text{b} \mapsto 0.5, 0, v, 2], \pi_{R,R,R,R}(\theta) :: \theta_K, 13, 1\rangle \vdash$$

(score) $\langle \pi_{L,R,R,R,R}(\theta), \downarrow, [C_6], [\text{u1}, \text{a}, \text{u2}, \text{b} \mapsto 0.5, 0, v, 2],$

$$\pi_{R,R,R,R}(\theta) :: \theta_K, 14, 1\rangle \vdash$$

(pop) $\langle \pi_{R,R,R,R,R}(\theta), \texttt{score}(\texttt{softeq}(\text{a} * 1 + \text{b}, 3)), [],$

$$[\text{u1}, \text{a}, \text{u2}, \text{b} \mapsto 0.5, 0, v, 2], \theta_K, 15, 1\rangle \vdash$$

(score) $\langle \pi_{R,R,R,R,R}(\theta), \downarrow, [], [\text{u1}, \text{a}, \text{u2}, \text{b} \mapsto 0.5, 0, v, 2], \theta_K, 16, e^{-1}\rangle.$

Hence, with the given entropy θ, the program evaluates with score e^{-1} to a state where $\text{a} = 0$ and $\text{b} = 0$.

Example 6. Let us now consider the program in Example 2:

```
1          b := 0;
2          k := 0;
3          while (b=0)
           {
4              u := U;
5              k := k+1;
6              if(u < 1/(k+1)^2)
               {
7                  b := 1;
8                  score(k/(k+1))
               }
           }
```

We want to compute the final state and weight for this program, assuming an empty initial state and an entropy θ such that the first value drawn (that is, $\pi_U(\pi_{L,L,R,R}(\theta))$) is 0.1, which also means the loop terminates after the first iteration. The evaluation proceeds as follows:

$$\langle \theta, \text{b} := 0; C_{2,8}, [], [], \theta_K, 0, 1\rangle \vdash$$

(seq) $\langle \pi_L(\theta), \text{b} := 0, [C_{2,8}], [], \pi_R(\theta) :: \theta_K, 1, 1\rangle \vdash$

(assign) $\langle \pi_L(\theta), \downarrow, [C_{2,8}], [\text{b} \mapsto 0], \pi_R(\theta) :: \theta_K, 2, 1\rangle \vdash$

(pop) $\langle \pi_R(\theta), C_{2,8}, [], [\text{b} \mapsto 0], \theta_K, 3, 1\rangle \vdash$

(seq) $\langle \pi_{L,R}(\theta), \text{k} := 0, [C_{3,8}], [\text{b} \mapsto 0], \pi_{R,R}(\theta) :: \theta_K, 4, 1\rangle \vdash$

(assign) $\langle \pi_{L,R}(\theta), \downarrow, [C_{3,8}], [\text{b}, \text{k} \mapsto 0, 0], \pi_{R,R}(\theta) :: \theta_K, 5, 1\rangle \vdash$

(pop) $\langle \pi_{R,R}(\theta), \texttt{while}(\text{b} = 0)\{C_{4,8}\}, [], [\text{b}, \text{k} \mapsto 0, 0], \theta_K, 6, 1\rangle \vdash$

(while-true) $\langle \pi_{R,R}(\theta), C_4; C_{5,8}; \texttt{while}(\text{b} = 0)\{C_{4,8}\}, [], [\text{b}, \text{k} \mapsto 0, 0], \theta_K, 7, 1\rangle \vdash$

(seq) $\langle \pi_{L,R,R}(\theta), \text{u} :\approx U, [C_{5,8}; \texttt{while}(\text{b} = 0)\{C_{4,8}\}], [\text{b}, \text{k} \mapsto 0, 0],$

$$\pi_{R,R,R}(\theta) :: \theta_K, 8, 1\rangle \vdash$$

(draw) $\langle \pi_{R,L,R,R}(\theta), \downarrow, [C_{5,8}; \texttt{while}(\text{b} = 0)\{C_{4,8}\}], [\text{b}, \text{k}, \text{u} \mapsto 0, 0, 0.1],$

$$\pi_{R,R,R}(\theta) :: \theta_K, 9, 1\rangle \vdash$$

(pop) $\langle \pi_{R,R,R}(\theta), \mathtt{k} := \mathtt{k} + 1; C_{6,8}; \mathtt{while}(\mathtt{b} = 0)\{C_{4,8}\}, [],$
$$[\mathtt{b}, \mathtt{k}, \mathtt{u} \mapsto 0, 0, 0.1], \theta_K, 10, 1\rangle \vdash$$

(seq) $\langle \pi_{L,R,R,R}(\theta), \mathtt{k} := \mathtt{k} + 1, [C_{6,8}; \mathtt{while}(\mathtt{b} = 0)\{C_{4,8}\}],$
$$[\mathtt{b}, \mathtt{k}, \mathtt{u} \mapsto 0, 0, 0.1], \pi_{R,R,R,R}(\theta) :: \theta_K, 11, 1\rangle \vdash$$

(assign) $\langle \pi_{L,R,R,R}(\theta), \downarrow, [C_{6,8}; \mathtt{while}(\mathtt{b} = 0)\{C_{4,8}\}], [\mathtt{b}, \mathtt{k}, \mathtt{u} \mapsto 0, 1, 0.1],$
$$\pi_{R,R,R,R}(\theta) :: \theta_K, 12, 1\rangle \vdash$$

(pop) $\langle \pi_{R,R,R,R}(\theta), C_{6,8}; \mathtt{while}(\mathtt{b} = 0)\{C_{4,8}\}, [], [\mathtt{b}, \mathtt{k}, \mathtt{u} \mapsto 0, 1, 0.1],$
$$\theta_K, 13, 1\rangle \vdash$$

(seq) $\langle \pi_{L,R,R,R,R}(\theta), \mathtt{if}(\mathtt{u} < 1/(\mathtt{k} + 1)^2)\{C_{7,8}\}, [\mathtt{while}(\mathtt{b} = 0)\{C_{4,8}\}],$
$$[\mathtt{b}, \mathtt{k}, \mathtt{u} \mapsto 0, 1, 0.1], \pi_{R,R,R,R,R}(\theta) :: \theta_K, 14, 1\rangle \vdash$$

(if-true) $\langle \pi_{L,R,R,R,R}(\theta), \mathtt{b} := 1; C_8, [\mathtt{while}(\mathtt{b} = 0)\{C_{4,8}\}],$
$$[\mathtt{b}, \mathtt{k}, \mathtt{u} \mapsto 0, 1, 0.1], \pi_{R,R,R,R,R}(\theta) :: \theta_K, 15, 1\rangle \vdash$$

(seq) $\langle \pi_{L,L,R,R,R,R}(\theta), \mathtt{b} := 1, [C_8, \mathtt{while}(\mathtt{b} = 0)\{C_{4,8}\}], [\mathtt{b}, \mathtt{k}, \mathtt{u} \mapsto 0, 1, 0.1],$
$$\pi_{R,L,R,R,R,R}(\theta) :: (\pi_{R,R,R,R,R}(\theta) :: \theta_K), 16, 1\rangle \vdash$$

(assign) $\langle \pi_{L,L,R,R,R,R}(\theta), \downarrow, [C_8, \mathtt{while}(\mathtt{b} = 0)\{C_{4,8}\}], [\mathtt{b}, \mathtt{k}, \mathtt{u} \mapsto 1, 1, 0.1],$
$$\pi_{R,L,R,R,R,R}(\theta) :: (\pi_{R,R,R,R,R}(\theta) :: \theta_K), 17, 1\rangle \vdash$$

(pop) $\langle \pi_{R,L,R,R,R,R}(\theta), \mathtt{score}(\mathtt{k}/(\mathtt{k} + 1)), [\mathtt{while}(\mathtt{b} = 0)\{C_{4,8}\}],$
$$[\mathtt{b}, \mathtt{k}, \mathtt{u} \mapsto 1, 1, 0.1], \pi_{R,R,R,R,R}(\theta) :: \theta_K, 18, 1\rangle \vdash$$

(score) $\langle \pi_{R,L,R,R,R,R}(\theta), \downarrow, [\mathtt{while}(\mathtt{b} = 0)\{C_{4,8}\}], [\mathtt{b}, \mathtt{k}, \mathtt{u} \mapsto 1, 1, 0.1],$
$$(\pi_{R,R,R,R,R}(\theta) :: \theta_K), 19, 1/2\rangle \vdash$$

(pop) $\langle \pi_{R,R,R,R,R}(\theta), \mathtt{while}(\mathtt{b} = 0)\{C_{4,8}\}, [], [\mathtt{b}, \mathtt{k}, \mathtt{u} \mapsto 1, 1, 0.1], \theta_K, 20, 1/2\rangle \vdash$$

(while-false) $\langle \pi_{R,R,R,R,R}(\theta), \downarrow, [], [\mathtt{b}, \mathtt{k}, \mathtt{u} \mapsto 1, 1, 0.1], \theta_K, 21, 1/2\rangle.$

Hence, the program evaluates to a state where $\mathtt{k} = 1$ with score $1/2$.

4.4   Measure on Final Program States

As mentioned before, the operational semantics so far only defines the final state and weight for a single program execution, for a fixed entropy. We now explain how a probability distribution on final states can be obtained by integrating the semantics over the entropy space.

Two Auxiliary Functions. In order to define a probability distribution over the final program states, two auxiliary functions are technically convenient. The function $\mathbf{O}_C^\sigma \colon \mathbb{S} \to \hat{\Omega}_\sigma$ determines the *final state* of program C with initial state σ for entropy $\theta \in \mathbb{S}$. It is defined by:

$$\mathbf{O}_C^\uparrow(\theta) = \uparrow$$

$$\mathbf{O}_C^\sigma(\theta) = \begin{cases} \tau & \text{if } \langle \theta, C, [], \sigma, \theta_K, 0, 1\rangle \vdash^* \langle \theta', \downarrow, [], \tau, \theta_K, n, w\rangle \text{ and } \tau \neq \lightning \\ \lightning & \text{if } \langle \theta, C, [], \sigma, \theta_K, 0, 1\rangle \vdash^* \langle \theta', C', K, \tau, \theta'_K, n, w\rangle \not\vdash \\ \uparrow & \text{otherwise.} \end{cases}$$

The final state of program C and proper initial state σ (i.e., $\sigma \neq \uparrow$ and $\sigma \neq \notz$) with entropy θ equals state τ provided its execution ends in configuration $\langle \cdot, [], \tau, \cdots \rangle$. For instance, for the program C and entropy θ from Example 6, we have $\mathbf{O}_C^{[]}(\theta) = [\mathbf{b} \mapsto 1, \mathbf{k} \mapsto 1, \mathbf{u} \mapsto 0.1]$. If the evaluation reaches a configuration which cannot be reduced any further (e.g., due to a failed hard constraint), the final state equals the error state $\notz$. Note that this is also applicable to the initial state $\sigma = \notz$. Finally, if the evaluation can neither be completed nor reach an irreducible configuration, this means that the evaluation of program C with state σ diverges with entropy θ. This results in the extended state $\uparrow$. For an example of a computation leading to such a state, consider Example 6 again. If we take an entropy θ' such that the value sampled in line 4 in each iteration is 0.5, the evaluation will never terminate and so we have $\mathbf{O}_C^{[]}(\theta') = \uparrow$. The final state of running C from initial state $\downarrow$ is the initial state. This way of handling exceptions ensures compositionality. We omit C and σ as sub- and superscript if they are clear from the context.

Besides the final state obtained from a program's run, we need also the *run's score*. The function $\mathbf{SC}_C^\sigma \colon \mathbb{S} \to \mathbb{R}_+$ yields the score of executing program C from initial state σ for a given entropy. This definition is a bit more complicated, due to the handling of diverging runs. A naive solution would be to define $\mathbf{SC}$ similarly to $\mathbf{O}$ and return 0 for diverging runs. This would, however, mean that the semantics would quietly ignore diverging runs, while a key motivation for this work is to handle divergence in the presence of soft conditioning in a meaningful way. Our proposal is to let the score for diverging runs be the *limit* of the weight w as the number of steps n goes to infinity. Formally, this is done as follows: Let us define an approximation function $\mathbf{SC}_C^\sigma \colon \mathbb{S} \times \mathbb{N} \to \mathbb{R}_+$, such that $\mathbf{SC}_C^\sigma(\theta, n)$ returns the score for program C with entropy θ and initial state σ after n evaluation steps:

$$\mathbf{SC}_C^\sigma(\theta, n) = \begin{cases} w & \text{if } \langle \theta, C, [], \sigma, \theta_K, 0, 1 \rangle \vdash^* \langle \theta', C', K, \tau, \theta'_K, n, w \rangle \text{ and } \tau \neq \notz \\ 0 & \text{otherwise.} \end{cases}$$

The function $\mathbf{SC}_C^\sigma \colon \mathbb{S} \to \mathbb{R}_+$ is now defined for proper state σ as the limit, or equivalently infimum, of its n-the approximation:

$$\mathbf{SC}_C^\sigma(\theta) = \lim_{n \to \infty} \mathbf{SC}_C^\sigma(\theta, n) = \inf_n \mathbf{SC}_C^\sigma(\theta, n).$$

For the special cases $\sigma = \notz$ and $\sigma = \uparrow$ we define:

$$\mathbf{SC}_C^\uparrow(\theta) = 1 \quad \text{and} \quad \mathbf{SC}_C^{\notz}(\theta) = 0.$$

Example 7. Let us revisit the program C from Example 6 to show how the $\mathbf{SC}$ function works. The program terminates with score $\frac{1}{2}$ after 16 steps with the original entropy θ used in the example. Thus, $\mathbf{SC}_C^{[]}(\theta, 16) = \frac{1}{2}$. The final configuration reduces to itself by (diverge) infinitely many times, so we have $\mathbf{SC}_C^{[]}(\theta, n) = \frac{1}{2}$ for all $n \geq 16$. Thus, $\mathbf{SC}_C^{[]}(\theta) = \frac{1}{2} = \lim_{n \to \infty} \mathbf{SC}_C^{[]}(\theta, n) = \frac{1}{2}$. This is the same result which would be returned by a naive definition of $\mathbf{SC}$, similar to $\mathbf{O}$. However, if we use the entropy θ' described above, where all values sampled are 0.5, this is no longer the case. In this case, we have $\mathbf{SC}_C^{[]}(\theta, n) = 1$ for all n, because the only score statement is never reached. Hence, $\mathbf{SC}_C^{[]}(\theta') = \lim_{n\to\infty} \mathbf{SC}_C^{[]}(\theta', n) = 1$, while the naive definition would return 0.

Example 8. For a more illustrative example, we consider the trivial program C':

```
i := 1;
while(true)
{
  i := i+1;
  score((i^2 - 1) / i^2)
}
```

Now, for any θ, we have $\mathbf{SC}_C^{[]}(\theta, n) = \frac{1}{2} \cdot \frac{i(n)+2}{i(n)+1}$, where $i(n)$ is the number of loop iterations completed after n steps. As the second factor converges to 1 as n (and so $i(n)$) goes to infinity, it follows that $\mathbf{SC}_C^{[]}(\theta) = \frac{1}{2}$, so the limit score is $\frac{1}{2}$ even though the program never terminates.

Note that by the monotone convergence theorem, the limit of approximations always exists. Thus, $\mathbf{SC}$ is well-defined. This can be seen as follows. As scores are bounded by 1, and no rule other than (score) affects the weight of a program run, a reduction step cannot increase the total score:

Lemma 7. $\kappa \vdash \kappa'$ *implies* $\mathsf{weight}(\kappa) \geq \mathsf{weight}(\kappa')$.

Thus, scores are antitone: $k \geq n$ implies $\mathbf{SC}_C^\sigma(\theta, k) \leq \mathbf{SC}_C^\sigma(\theta, n)$. The monotone convergence theorem now yields:

Lemma 8. *For each PL program C, state σ and entropy θ, $\lim_{n\to\infty} \mathbf{SC}_C^\sigma(\theta, n)$ exists and is finite.*

To define the probability distribution of states as a Lebesgue integral involving functions $\mathbf{O}$ and $\mathbf{SC}$, these functions need to be shown to be measurable. Although this is a property satisfied by almost all functions used in practice and it is known to be hard to construct non-measurable functions—to construct non-Lebesgue-measurable sets of reals, and hence non-measurable functions on reals, requires the Axiom of Choice [34]—measurability proofs tend to be lengthy and tedious. A detailed proof of measurability of functions similar to $\mathbf{O}_C$ and $\mathbf{SC}_C$, can be found in [5] when providing a semantics to a probabilistic functional programming language. More details are in Appendix F; we summarise here the main things:

Lemma 9. *For all C and $\sigma \in \hat{\Omega}_\sigma$:*

(1) $\mathbf{O}_C^\sigma(\cdot)$ *is $\mathcal{S}/\hat{\Omega}_\sigma$ measurable*   *and*   (2) $\mathbf{SC}_C^\sigma(\cdot)$ *is $\mathcal{S}/\mathcal{R}$ measurable.*

Proof. (1) Analogous to the proof of Lemma 92 in [5], more details in Appendix F. (2) Analogous to the proof of Lemma 93 in [5], it follows that $\mathbf{SC}_C^\sigma(\cdot, n)$ is $\mathcal{S}/\mathcal{R}$ measurable, for all n; more details in Appendix F. The result now follows by the fact that point-wise limits of measurable real-valued functions are measurable. $\square$

Distribution Over Final Program States. We are now in a position to define the distribution on final states in terms of the operational semantics. We first define the distribution on entropies $\langle C \rangle_\sigma \colon \mathcal{S} \to \mathbb{R}_+$, as an integral of score $\mathbf{SC}_C^\sigma$ with respect to the standard measure on entropy space:

$$\langle C \rangle_\sigma(B) = \int_B \mathbf{SC}_C^\sigma(\theta) \, \mu_{\mathbb{S}}(d\theta).$$

For each measurable subset $B \in \mathcal{S}$ of the entropy space, $\langle C \rangle_\sigma(B)$ is the probability that if we run program C with initial state σ, the random values sampled during execution will match some element of the set B of entropies.

The probability distribution $[\![C]\!]_\sigma \colon \hat{\Sigma}_\sigma \to \mathbb{R}_+$ on extended states can now be defined as the push-forward measure of $\langle C \rangle_\sigma$ with respect to $\mathbf{O}_C^\sigma(\theta)$:

$$[\![C]\!]_\sigma(A) = \langle C \rangle_\sigma(\{\theta \mid \mathbf{O}_C^\sigma(\theta) \in A\}) = \langle C \rangle_\sigma(\mathbf{O}_C^{\sigma-1}(A))$$
$$= \int [\mathbf{O}_C^\sigma(\theta)(A)] \cdot \mathbf{SC}_C^\sigma(\theta) \, \mu_{\mathbb{S}}(d\theta).$$

For program C with $\langle C \rangle_\sigma(\mathbb{S}) > 0$, this distribution can be normalised as follows:

$$[\![\hat{C}]\!]_\sigma(A) = \frac{[\![C]\!]_\sigma(A)}{\langle C \rangle_\sigma(\mathbb{S})}.$$

The measure $[\![C]\!]_\sigma(A)$ is a measure on $(\hat{\Omega}_\sigma, \hat{\Sigma}_\sigma)$. Let $[\![C]\!]_\sigma|_{\Omega_\sigma}$ be this measure restricted to $(\Omega_\sigma, \Sigma_\sigma)$, i.e., the space of proper states without ξ and $\uparrow$, such that $[\![C]\!]_\sigma|_{\Omega_\sigma}(A) = [\![C]\!]_\sigma(A)$ for $A \subseteq \Sigma_\sigma$.

Example 9. We go back once again to the Bayesian linear regression program from Example 5. We will first compute the measure $[\![C]\!]_\sigma$ on program outcomes.

If the value sampled in line 1 is v_1 and the value sampled in line 3 is v_2, it follows from the operational semantics that the final state is $[\mathtt{u1} \mapsto v_1, \mathtt{a} \mapsto \mathtt{G}(0,2,v_1), \mathtt{u2} \mapsto v_2, \mathtt{b} \mapsto \mathtt{G}(0,2,v_2)]$ and the final score is

$$e^{-(\mathtt{G}(0,2,v_2)-2)^2} e^{-(\mathtt{G}(0,2,v_1)+\mathtt{G}(0,2,v_2)-3)^2} = e^{-(\mathtt{G}(0,2,v_2)-2)^2 - (\mathtt{G}(0,2,v_1)+\mathtt{G}(0,2,v_2)-3)^2}.$$

Hence, for entropy θ with $\pi_u(\pi_{L,L}(\theta)) = v_1$ and $\pi_u(\pi_{L,L,R,R}(\theta)) = v_2$:

$$\mathbf{O}_C^{[]}(\theta) = [\mathtt{u1} \mapsto v_1, \mathtt{a} \mapsto \mathtt{G}(0,2,v_1), \mathtt{u2} \mapsto v_2, \mathtt{b} \mapsto \mathtt{G}(0,2,v_2)]$$
$$\mathbf{SC}_C^{[]}(\theta) = e^{-(\mathtt{G}(0,2,v_2)-2)^2 - (\mathtt{G}(0,2,v_1)+\mathtt{G}(0,2,v_2)-3)^2}.$$

This means that the integral $\int [\mathbf{O}_C^{[]}(\theta)(A)] \cdot \mathbf{SC}_C^{[]}(\theta) \, \mu_{\mathbb{S}}(d\theta)$ can be written as $\int f(\pi_u(\pi_{L,L}(\theta)), \pi_u(\pi_{L,L,R,R}(\theta))) \, \mu_{\mathbb{S}}(d\theta)$, where

$$f(v_1, v_2) = [[\mathtt{u1}, \mathtt{a}, \mathtt{u2}, \mathtt{b} \mapsto v_1, \mathtt{G}(0,2,v_1), v_2, \mathtt{G}(0,2,v_2)] \in A]$$
$$\cdot e^{-(\mathtt{G}(0,2,v_2)-2)^2 - (\mathtt{G}(0,2,v_1)+\mathtt{G}(0,2,v_2)-3)^2}.$$

By the definition of entropy, we have:

$$\int f(\pi_u(\pi_{L,L}(\theta)), \pi_u(\pi_{L,L,R,R}(\theta)))\, \mu_\mathbb{S}(d\theta)$$

$$= \int\int f(\pi_u(\pi_L(\theta_L)), \pi_u(\pi_{L,L,R}(\theta_R)))\, \mu_\mathbb{S}(d\theta_L)\mu_\mathbb{S}(d\theta_R)$$

$$= \int\int\int\int f(\pi_u(\theta_{L,L})), \pi_u(\pi_{L,L}(\theta_{R,R})))\, \mu_\mathbb{S}(d\theta_{L,L})\mu_\mathbb{S}(d\theta_{R,L})\, \mu_\mathbb{S}(d\theta_{L,R})\mu_\mathbb{S}(d\theta_{R,R})$$

$$= \int\int f(\pi_u(\theta_{L,L})), \pi_u(\pi_{L,L}(\theta_{R,R})))\, \mu_\mathbb{S}(d\theta_{L,L})\mu_\mathbb{S}(d\theta_{R,R}).$$

By repeatedly applying the definition of entropy like above, we get:

$$\int\int f(\pi_u(\theta_{L,L})), \pi_u(\pi_{L,L}(\theta_{R,R})))\, \mu_\mathbb{S}(d\theta_{L,L})\mu_\mathbb{S}(d\theta_{R,R})$$

$$\vdots$$

$$= \int\int f(\pi_u(\theta_{L,L})), \pi_u(\theta_{L,L,R,R}))\, \mu_\mathbb{S}(d\theta_{L,L})\mu_\mathbb{S}(d\theta_{L,L,R,R})$$

$$= \int_{[0,1]}\int_{[0,1]} f(v_1, v_2)\, \mu_L(dv_1)\mu_L(dv_2).$$

Thus,

$$[\![C]\!]_\sigma(A) = \int_{(0,1)}\int_{(0,1)} [[\mathtt{u1} \mapsto v_1, \mathtt{a} \mapsto \mathsf{G}(0,2,v_1), \mathtt{u2} \mapsto v_2, \mathtt{b} \mapsto \mathsf{G}(0,2,v_2)] \in A]$$

$$\cdot e^{-(\mathsf{G}(0,2,v_2)-2)^2 - (\mathsf{G}(0,2,v_1)+\mathsf{G}(0,2,v_2)-3)^2}\, \mu_L(dv_1)\mu_L(dv_2).$$

Now, suppose that A is a set of states such that $\mathtt{a} < 0$ and $\mathtt{b} < 0$. Then:

$$[\![C]\!]_\sigma(A) = \int_{(0,1)}\int_{(0,1)} [\mathsf{G}(0,2,v_1) < 0][\mathsf{G}(0,2,v_2)] < 0]$$

$$\cdot e^{-(\mathsf{G}(0,2,v_2)-2)^2 - (\mathsf{G}(0,2,v_1)+\mathsf{G}(0,2,v_2)-3)^2}\, \mu_L(dv_1)\mu_L(dv_2).$$

Like in Example 1, this expression can be rewritten as a double integral of Gaussian densities over the real line:

$$[\![C]\!]_\sigma(A) = \int\int [x_1 < 0][x_2 < 0]\cdot e^{-p(x)}\cdot \mathsf{G}_{pdf}(0,2,x_1)\cdot \mathsf{G}_{pdf}(0,2,x_2)\, \mu_L(dx_1)\mu_L(dx_2)$$

$$= \int_{(-\infty,0)}\int_{(-\infty,0)} \cdot e^{-p(x)}\cdot \mathsf{G}_{pdf}(0,2,x_1)\cdot \mathsf{G}_{pdf}(0,2,x_2)\, \mu_L(dx_1)\mu_L(dx_2)$$

where $e^{-p(x)} = e^{-(x_2-2)^2 - (x_1+x_2-3)^2}$. Let us now compute the normalising constant $\langle C \rangle_\sigma(\mathbb{S})$. By a similar reasoning as above, we get:

$$\langle C \rangle_\sigma(\mathbb{S}) = \int \mathbf{SC}_C^\sigma(\theta)\, \mu_\mathbb{S}(d\theta)$$

$$= \int_{(0,1)}\int_{(0,1)} e^{-(\mathsf{G}(0,2,v_2)-2)^2 - (\mathsf{G}(0,2,v_1)+\mathsf{G}(0,2,v_2)-3)^2}\, \mu_L(dv_1)\mu_L(dv_2)$$

$$= \int\int e^{-p(x)}\cdot \mathsf{G}_{pdf}(0,2,x_1)\cdot \mathsf{G}_{pdf}(0,2,x_2)\, \mu_L(dx_1)\mu_L(dx_2)$$

Hence, the normalised semantics $[\![\hat{C}]\!]_\sigma(A)$ applied to the above set A is:

$$[\![\hat{C}]\!]_\sigma(A) = \frac{\int_{(-\infty,0)} \int_{(-\infty,0)} e^{-p(x)} \cdot \mathsf{G}_{pdf}(0,2,x_1) \cdot \mathsf{G}_{pdf}(0,2,x_2)\, \mu_L(dx_1)\mu_L(dx_2)}{\int \int e^{-p(x)} \cdot \mathsf{G}_{pdf}(0,2,x_1) \cdot \mathsf{G}_{pdf}(0,2,x_2)\, \mu_L(dx_1)\mu_L(dx_2)}.$$

4.5 Expectations

The weakest preexpectation semantics determines the expected value of an arbitrary measurable function f on states with respect to a program. We can also obtain such expected value by integrating f with respect to the measure $[\![C]\!]_\sigma(A)$ defined just above. By change of variable, this integral can be easily transformed into an integral with respect to the default measure on entropies.

Lemma 10. *For all measurable f,*

$$\int f(\tau)[\![C]\!]_\sigma|_{\Omega_\sigma}(d\tau) = \int \hat{f}(\mathbf{O}_C^\sigma(\theta)) \cdot \mathbf{SC}_C^\sigma(\theta)\, \mu_\mathbb{S}(d\theta).$$

Proof.

$$\int f(\tau)[\![C]\!]_\sigma|_{\Omega_\sigma}(d\tau) = \int \hat{f}(\tau)[\![C]\!]_\sigma(d\tau)$$

$$\text{(by property of the pushforward)} = \int \hat{f}(\mathbf{O}_C^\sigma(\theta)) \langle C \rangle_\sigma(d\theta)$$

$$\text{(by Radon-Nikodým theorem)} = \int \hat{f}(\mathbf{O}_C^\sigma(\theta))\mathbf{SC}_C^\sigma(\theta)\, \mu_\mathbb{S}(d\theta).$$

$\square$

Example 10. Let us compute the expected value of the variable a in the Bayesian linear regression example. To this end, we take a function f such that $f(\sigma) = \sigma(\mathsf{a})$ if $\mathsf{a} \in \mathrm{dom}(\sigma)$ and $f(\sigma) = 0$ otherwise. By a similar reasoning as in Example 9, we get:

$$\int f(\tau)[\![C]\!]_{[]}|_{\Omega_\sigma}(d\tau)$$

$$= \int \hat{f}(\mathbf{O}_C^{[]}(\theta)) \cdot \mathbf{SC}_C^{[]}(\theta)\, \mu_\mathbb{S}(d\theta)$$

$$= \int_{(0,1)} \int_{(0,1)} \hat{f}([\mathsf{u1} \mapsto v_1, \mathsf{a} \mapsto \mathsf{G}(0,2,v_1), \mathsf{u2} \mapsto v_2, \mathsf{b} \mapsto \mathsf{G}(0,2,v_2)])$$

$$\cdot e^{-(\mathsf{G}(0,2,v_2)-2)^2 - (\mathsf{G}(0,2,v_1)+\mathsf{G}(0,2,v_2)-3)^2}\, \mu_L(dv_1)\mu_L(dv_2)$$

$$= \int_{(0,1)} \int_{(0,1)} \mathsf{G}(0,2,v_1) \cdot e^{-(\mathsf{G}(0,2,v_2)-2)^2 - (\mathsf{G}(0,2,v_1)+\mathsf{G}(0,2,v_2)-3)^2}\, \mu_L(dv_1)\mu_L(dv_2)$$

This is the same result as the one we obtain using wp in Example 1.

Example 11. Let us now revisit the program from Example 2 and calculate the expected value of the constant function $f(\sigma) = 1$ with respect to the program using the operational semantics. To this end, we need to calculate $\int \hat{f}(\mathbf{O}_C^{[]}(\theta)) \cdot \mathbf{SC}_C^{[]}(\theta)\,\mu_{\mathbb{S}}(d\theta)$ for the given program C. By evaluating the first two statements in the program, like in Example 5, we can check that $\mathbf{O}_C^{[]}(\theta) = \mathbf{O}_{C'}^{\sigma}(\pi_{R,R}(\theta))$ and $\mathbf{SC}_C^{[]}(\theta) = \mathbf{SC}_{C'}^{\sigma}(\pi_{R,R}(\theta))$, where $C' = \mathtt{while(b = 0)\{C''\}}$ (C'' being the loop body) and $\sigma = [\mathtt{b} \mapsto 0, \mathtt{k} \mapsto 0]$. It follows from the properties of entropy that $\int \hat{f}(\mathbf{O}_{C'}^{\sigma}(\pi_{R,R}(\theta))) \cdot \mathbf{SC}_{C'}^{\sigma}(\pi_{R,R}(\theta))\,\mu_{\mathbb{S}}(d\theta) = \int \hat{f}(\mathbf{O}_{C'}^{\sigma}(\theta)) \cdot \mathbf{SC}_{C'}^{\sigma}(\theta)\,\mu_{\mathbb{S}}(d\theta)$.

Now, let $C'_n = \mathtt{while}^n(\mathtt{b} = 0)\{C''\}$. We can show (using Proposition 3 from Appendix D and the Beppo Levi's theorem) that

$$\int \hat{f}(\mathbf{O}_{C'}^{\sigma}(\theta)) \cdot \mathbf{SC}_{C'}^{\sigma}(\theta)\,\mu_{\mathbb{S}}(d\theta) = \sup_n \int \hat{f}(\mathbf{O}_{C'_n}^{\sigma}(\theta)) \cdot \mathbf{SC}_{C'_n}^{\sigma}(\theta)\,\mu_{\mathbb{S}}(d\theta).$$

Since $\hat{f}$ has value 1 on all proper states and is 0 on state $\uparrow$, $\hat{f}(\mathbf{O}_{C'_n}^{\sigma}(\theta)) = 1$ if $\mathbf{O}_{C'}^{\sigma}(\theta)$ is a proper state (that is, if C' terminates with initial state σ and entropy θ) and $\hat{f}(\mathbf{O}_{C'_n}^{\sigma}(\theta)) = 0$ if C' does not terminate with θ. Thus, $\hat{f}(\mathbf{O}_{C'_n}^{\sigma}(\theta)) = [\theta \in S_1] + [\theta \in S_2] + \ldots + [\theta \in S_{n-1}]$, where S_i is the set of entropies resulting in termination after exactly i iterations[7].

The score is only multiplied by $\frac{k}{k+1}$ in the last iteration, after which the guard is satisfied. As long as the guard of the while-loop is false, the score stays at 1. Thus, we have $\mathbf{SC}_C^{[]}(\theta) = [\theta \in S_1] \cdot \frac{1}{2} + [\theta \in S_2] \cdot \frac{2}{3} + \ldots + [\theta \in S_n] \cdot \frac{n}{n+1} + [\theta \notin S_1 \cup \ldots \cup S_n]$[8].

Therefore, for each n,

$$\int \hat{f}(\mathbf{O}_{C'_n}^{\sigma}(\theta)) \cdot \mathbf{SC}_{C'_n}^{\sigma}(\theta)\,\mu_{\mathbb{S}}(d\theta) = \int \sum_{k=1}^{n-1} \frac{k}{k+1}[\theta \in S_k]\,\mu_{\mathbb{S}}(d\theta)$$

$$= \sum_{k=1}^{n-1} \frac{k}{k+1} \int [\theta \in S_k]\,\mu_{\mathbb{S}}(d\theta)$$

Now we need to calculate $\int [\theta \in S_k]\,\mu_{\mathbb{S}}(d\theta)$ for each k. Observe that whether $\theta \in S_k$, depends only on parts of θ which are sampled from (that is, on sub-entropies to which π_U is applied). The value of $[\theta \in S_k]$ depends only on the sub-entropies $\pi_{p_1}(\theta), \ldots, \pi_{p_k}(\theta)$, where $p_1, \ldots, p_k$ are the paths leading to values sampled in subsequent iterations. An entropy θ leads to termination in the k-th step if $\pi_U(\pi_{p_1}(\theta)) \geq \frac{1}{4}, \ldots, \pi_U(\pi_{p_{k-1}}(\theta)) \geq \frac{1}{k^2}$ and $\pi_U(\pi_{p_k}(\theta)) \leq \frac{1}{(k+1)^2}$. Thus, by the definition of entropy, we have

$$\int [\theta \in S_k]\,\mu_{\mathbb{S}}(d\theta) = \int \left[\pi_U(\pi_{p_1}(\theta)) \geq \frac{1}{4}\right] \cdot \ldots \cdot \left[\pi_U(\pi_{p_{k-1}}(\theta)) \geq \frac{1}{k^2}\right]$$

---

[7] The reason the last set is S_{n-1} and not S_n is that $\mathtt{while}^1(\phi)\{C''\} = C''; \mathtt{diverge}$ if ϕ is true, so $\mathtt{while}^n(\theta)\{C''\}$ only terminates if the loop body is executed at most $n-1$ times.

[8] This time, the last set is S_n, because the **score** statement will be executed even if the loop body is followed by **diverge**.

$$\cdot \left[\pi_U(\pi_{p_k}(\theta)) \le \frac{1}{(k+1)^2}\right] \mu_{\mathbb{S}}(\theta)$$

$$= \int \cdots \int \left[\pi_U(\pi_{p_1}(\theta)) \ge \frac{1}{4}\right] \cdot \cdots \cdot \left[\pi_U(\pi_{p_{k-1}}(\theta)) \ge \frac{1}{k^2}\right]$$

$$\cdot \left[\pi_U(\pi_{p_k}(\theta)) \le \frac{1}{(k+1)^2}\right] \mu_{\mathbb{S}}(\theta_{p_1}) \ldots \mu_{\mathbb{S}}(\theta_{p_k})$$

$$= \int \cdots \int \left[v_1 \ge \frac{1}{4}\right] \cdot \cdots \cdot \left[v_{k-1} \ge \frac{1}{k^2}\right]$$

$$\cdot \left[v_k \le \frac{1}{(k+1)^2}\right] \mu_L(dv_1) \ldots \mu_L(dv_k)$$

$$= \left(\prod_{i=1}^{k-1} \frac{(i+1)^2 - 1}{(i+1)^2}\right) \cdot \frac{1}{(k+1)^2}$$

$$= \frac{1}{2} \cdot \frac{1}{k \cdot (k+1)}.$$

Hence, $\sum_{k=1}^{n-1} \frac{k}{k+1} \int [\theta \in S_k] \mu_{\mathbb{S}}(d\theta) = \frac{1}{2} \cdot \sum_{k=1}^{n-1} \frac{1}{(k+1)^2}$, so we have

$$\int \hat{f}(\mathbf{O}_C^{\emptyset}(\theta)) \cdot \mathbf{SC}_C^{\emptyset}(\theta) \, \mu_{\mathbb{S}}(d\theta) = \int \hat{f}(\mathbf{O}_{C'}^{\sigma}(\theta)) \cdot \mathbf{SC}_{C'}^{\sigma}(\theta) \, \mu_{\mathbb{S}}(d\theta)$$

$$= \sup_n \int \hat{f}(\mathbf{O}_{C_n'}^{\sigma}(\theta)) \cdot \mathbf{SC}_{C_n'}^{\sigma}(\theta) \, \mu_{\mathbb{S}}(d\theta)$$

$$= \frac{1}{2} \sum_{k=1}^{\infty} \frac{1}{k \cdot (k+1)}$$

$$= \frac{\pi^2}{12} - \frac{1}{2}$$

This is exactly the result we obtained with the weakest preexpectation semantics in Example 2. The correspondence between the weakest preexpectation and operational semantics is the topic of the next section.

5   Equivalence of wp and Operational Semantics

The aim of this section is to show that the weakest preexpectation semantics of *PL* is equivalent to its operational semantics. This property is formalised by two theorems which relate the wp and wlp semantics to the operational semantics. The first result asserts that the expected value of an arbitrary function f defined by the weakest preexpectation operator equals the expected value of f computed as an integral of f with respect to the distribution induced by the operational semantics.

Theorem 1. *For all measurable functions* $f: \Omega_\sigma \to \overline{\mathbb{R}}_+$, *PL programs* C *and initial states* $\sigma \in \Omega_\sigma$:

$$\mathrm{wp}[\![C]\!](f)(\sigma) = \int f(\tau)[\![C]\!]_\sigma(d\tau).$$

Proof. By Lemma 10, it suffices to prove that for all f:

$$\int \hat{f}(\mathbf{O}_C^\sigma(\theta)) \cdot \mathbf{SC}_C^\sigma(\theta) \, \mu_{\mathbb{S}}(d\theta) \; = \mathtt{wp}[\![C]\!](f)(\sigma).$$

This can be proven by induction on the structure of C. The detailed proof can be found in Appendix E. The proof makes use of several compositionality properties of the operational semantics and properties of finite approximations of while-loops, which are also proven in the appendix. A key insight used in the proof is that Beppo Levi's theorem can be used to express the expectation of f with respect to a while-loop as the limit of expectations of f with respect to finite approximations of the loop. □

The second main theorem of this paper states that the weakest liberal preexpectation of a non-negative function f bounded by 1 is equivalent to the expected value of f with respect to the distribution defined by the operational semantics plus the probability of divergence weighted by scores.

Theorem 2. *For every measurable non-negative function $f \colon \Omega_\sigma \to \overline{\mathbb{R}}_+$ with $f(\sigma) \leq 1$ for all states σ, PL program C and initial state $\sigma \in \Omega_\sigma$:*

$$\mathtt{wlp}[\![C]\!](f)(\sigma) \; = \; \int f(\tau) \cdot [\![C]\!]_\sigma|_{\Omega_\sigma}(d\tau) + \underbrace{\int [\mathbf{O}_C^\sigma(\theta) = \uparrow] \cdot \mathbf{SC}_C^\sigma(\theta) \, \mu_{\mathbb{S}}(d\theta)}_{\substack{\text{probability of divergence} \\ \text{multiplied by the score}}}.$$

Proof. By induction on the structure of C. Details in Appendix E. □

Corollary 1. *For every PL program C and state σ:*

$$\mathtt{wlp}[\![C]\!](1)(\sigma) \; = \; \int \mathbf{SC}_C^\sigma(\theta) \, \mu_{\mathbb{S}}(d\theta).$$

6   Related Work

Semantics of Languages for bayesian Inference. Research on the semantics of probabilistic programs dates back to the pioneering work by Saheb-Djahromi [32] and Kozen [24], among others. However, this early work is mostly motivated by applications such as the analysis of randomised algorithms, so the languages involved mostly only supported discrete distributions and did not allow conditioning.

A recent explosion of popularity of machine learning, and the rise of probabilistic programming as a tool for Bayesian inference, have sparked a new line of work on semantics of languages with continuous random draws and conditioning. An early example of such work is the paper by Park et al. [31], who present an operational semantics for a higher-order language with conditioning, parametrised by an infinite trace of random values. Borgström et al. [6] define a denotational semantics of a first-order language with both discrete and continuous distributions, which also supports conditioning, including zero-probability observations. Nori et al. [28] define a denotational semantics of an imperative language with (hard) conditioning, similar to the weakest preexpectation semantics; they however do not consider possible program divergence. Toronto et al. [37] present a denotational semantics for a first-order functional language which interprets programs as deterministic functions on the source of randomness. Huang and Morrisett [16] define a semantics for a first-order language, restricted to computable operations. Heunen et at. [15] present a denotational semantics of a higher-order functional language with continuous random draws and conditioning. They manage to overcome the well-known problem with measurability of higher-order function application [2] by replacing standard Borel spaces with so-called quasi-Borel spaces. This idea, simplifying the authors' previous work [35], has since gained a lot of attraction in the community: Ścibior et al. [33] use quasi-Borel spaces to prove correctness of sampling-based inference algorithms, while Vákár et al. [38] define a domain theory for higher-order functional probabilistic programs, which extends the quasi-Borel space approach to programs with higher-order recursion and recursive types. A different approach is followed in a recent paper by Dahlqvist and Kozen [9], who define a semantics of a probabilistic language with conditioning in terms of Banach spaces.

The operational semantics presented in this chapter is strongly inspired by the semantics of Borgström et al. [5] and Wand et al. [39], both defined for functional programs. The former define a measure on program outcomes by integrating functions similar to our **O** and **SC**, defined in terms of an operational semantics, with respect to a stock measure on traces of random values. The latter use a similar approach, but define their operational semantics in terms of infinite entropies instead of finite traces, and use continuations to fix evaluation order and split entropies between continuations consistently.

Program Divergence. Another line of research on probabilistic programs, coming mostly from the algorithms and program verification community and inspired by earlier papers by Kozen [24] and McIver et al. [27], has focused on extending Dijkstra's weakest precondition calculus to probabilistic programs. In this line of work, correct handling of diverging programs has been a key issue from the start. Recent developments [7,13,22] focus on problems such as analysing runtimes, almost-sure termination (and variants thereof) and outcomes of algorithms. A weakest preexpectation semantics for recursive imperative probabilistic programs is given by Olmedo et al. [30]. Olmedo et al. [29] also extend the weakest preexpectation calculus to programs with hard conditioning and possible divergence, but their semantics only supports discrete distributions.

Combining Continuous Distributions, Conditioning and Divergence. The issue of program divergence has so far mostly been disregarded when defining semantics of Bayesian probabilistic programs, with most authors assuming that their semantics is only applicable to almost-surely terminating programs. Conversely, semantics designed to handle diverging programs usually did not support conditioning, and when they did, they were not applicable to programs with continuous distributions.

To our best knowledge, the only existing semantics supporting the combination of divergence, continuous random draws, and conditioning is the recent work by Bichsel et al. [3]. The authors define a semantics of an imperative probabilistic language with continuous and discrete distributions and hard conditioning, in which the probability of failing a hard constraint, the probability of an execution error and the probability of divergence are defined explicitly. The semantics calculates probability measures on final program states and the above exceptions are treated as special states, like $\frac{1}{2}$ and $\uparrow$ in our semantics.

Technically, the semantics in [3] is a superset of our semantics. A normalised expectation of the form $\frac{\mathtt{wp}[\![C]\!](f)(\sigma_0)}{\mathtt{wlp}[\![C]\!](1)(\sigma_0)}$ can be defined in their semantics as

$$\frac{\int_{\Omega_\sigma} f(\tau)[\![C]\!](\sigma_0)(d\tau)}{[\![C]\!](\sigma_0)(\Omega_\sigma) + [\![C]\!](\sigma_0)(\uparrow)}$$

where $[\![C]\!](\sigma_0)$ is the measure on final states of program C with initial state σ_0, as defined by the semantics, and Ω_σ is the set of proper states (excluding errors and divergence). However, we believe that extending the well-studied framework of weakest preexpectations to the continuous case is still a significant contribution, as it allows using established techniques, not applicable to the semantics in [3], to analyse programs with continuous distributions, conditioning, in the presence of possible program divergence.

7   Epilogue

In this paper, we have considered a probabilistic while-language that contains three important ingredients: (a) sampling from continuous probability distributions, (b) soft and hard conditioning, and (c) program divergence. We have provided a weakest (liberal) preexpectation semantics for our language and showed that soft conditioning can be encoded by hard conditioning. The wp-semantics is complemented by an operational semantics using the concept of entropies. The main results of this paper are the correspondence theorem between the wp-semantics (and wlp-semantics) and the operational semantics. The paper has been written in a tutorial-like manner with various illustrative examples.

Let us conclude with a short discussion. The interplay between divergence and conditioning is intricate. For the discrete probabilistic setting, this has been extensively treated in [29]. Intuitively speaking, the problem is how conditioning is taken into account by program runs that diverge and never reach the score statement. Consider the program:

```
t := 1;
x := U;
if (x > 0.5) {
    while(true) { t := t+1; }
```

```
}
score(softeq(t, 1));
return t;
```

This program terminates with probability $1/2$ with $t = 1$, and with the same probability diverges increasing t ad infinitum. One would perhaps expect the expected value of t to be 1, as the possibility of t going to infinity should be discarded by the `score` statement. However, for any function f, we have $\mathrm{wp}(\mathtt{while(true)}\{t = t{+}1\})(f) = 0$ and $\mathrm{wlp}(\mathtt{while(true)}\{t = t{+}1\})(f) = 1$. Hence, the expected value of t (for the empty initial state) will be:

$$\frac{\mathrm{wp}[\![C]\!](\lambda\sigma\ .t)([])}{\mathrm{wlp}[\![C]\!](\lambda\sigma\ .t)([])} \;=\; \frac{1/2}{1} \;=\; \frac{1}{2}.$$

A   Basics of Measure Theory

This section presents the basic definitions of measure theory used throughout this of the paper. For a more thorough introduction to measure theory, please consult one of the standard textbooks such as [4].

Measurable Spaces

Definition 2. *A σ-algebra Σ on a set Ω is a set consisting of subsets of Ω which satisfies the following properties:*

 - *$\emptyset \in \Sigma$*
 - *If $A \in \Sigma$, then $\Omega \setminus A \in \Sigma$ (closure under complements)*
 - *If $A_i \in \Sigma$ for all $i \in \mathbb{N}$, then $\bigcup_{i \in \mathbb{N}} A_i \in \Sigma$ (closure under countable unions)*

The tuple (Ω, Σ) of a set Ω and its σ-algebra Σ is called a measurable space. *A set $A \in \Sigma$ is called a* measurable set.

Definition 3. *A σ-algebra on a set Ω generated by a set S of subsets of Ω is the smallest σ-algebra containing S.*

Definition 4. *A countably generated σ-algebra on Ω is a σ-algebra generated by a countable set of subsets of Ω.*

Definition 5. *If (Ω_1, Σ_1) and (Ω_2, Σ_2) are measurable spaces, the* product *of the σ-algebras Σ_1 and Σ_2 is the σ-algebra $\Sigma_1 \otimes \Sigma_2$ on $\Omega_1 \times \Omega_2$ defined as $\Sigma_1 \otimes \Sigma_2 = \sigma(\{(A_1 \times A_2 \mid A_1 \in \Sigma_1, A_2 \in \Sigma_2\})$. This definition extends naturally to arbitrary finite products of measures.*

Definition 6. *A Borel σ-algebra $\mathcal{R}$ on $\mathbb{R}$ is the σ-algebra generated by the set of open intervals (a, ∞) for $a \in \mathbb{R}$. A Borel σ-algebra $\mathcal{R}_n$ on $\mathbb{R}^n$ is the n-fold product of $\mathcal{R}$.*

Measures

Definition 7. *A* measure *on the measurable space* (Ω, Σ) *is a function* $\mu : \Sigma \mapsto \overline{\mathbb{R}}_+$ *such that* $\mu(\emptyset) = 0$ *and for any collection of pairwise disjoint sets* $A_1, A_2, \ldots$, $\mu(\bigcup_{i \in \mathbb{N}} A_i) = \sum_{i \in \mathbb{N}} \mu(A_i)$ *(i.e.* μ *is countably additive).*

Definition 8. *A* product $\mu_1 \otimes \mu_2$ *of measures* μ_1 *and* μ_2 *on* (Ω_1, Σ_1) *and* (Ω_2, Σ_2), *respectively, is the unique measure on* $(\Omega_1 \times \Omega_2, \Sigma_1 \times \Sigma_2)$ *which satisfies* $(\mu_1 \otimes \mu_2)(A_1 \times A_2) = \mu_1(A_1)\mu_2(A_2)$ *for all* $A_1 \in \Sigma_1$, $A_2 \in \Sigma_2$. *This definition extends naturally to finite products of higher dimensions.*

Definition 9. *The* Lebesgue measure *on* $(\mathbb{R}, \mathcal{R})$ *is the unique measure* μ_L *which satisfies* $\mu_L([a, b]) = b - a$ *for all* $a, b \in \mathbb{R}$ *such that* $b \geq a$. *The Lebesgue measure on* $(\mathbb{R}^n, \mathcal{R}_n)$ *is the n-fold product of* μ_L.

Definition 10. *A* probability measure *on* (Ω, Σ) *is a measure* μ *such that* $\mu(\Omega) = 1$. *A* subprobability measure *on* (Ω, Σ) *is a measure* μ *with* $\mu(\Omega) \leq 1$.

Definition 11. *A measure* μ *on* (Ω, Σ) *is* σ-finite *if there exists a sequence of sets* $A_i \in \Sigma$ *such that* $A_i \subseteq A_{i+1}$ *for all* i *and* $\mu(A_i) < \infty$ *and* $\Omega = \bigcup_{i \in \mathbb{N}} A_i$.

Measurable Functions and Integrals

Definition 12. *A function* f *between measurable spaces* (Ω_1, Σ_1) *and* (Ω_2, Σ_2) *is* measurable Σ_1/Σ_2 *if for all* $B \in \Sigma_2$, $f^{-1}(B) \in \Sigma_1$. *If the* σ-algebras Σ_1 *and* Σ_2 *are clear from the context, we will simply call* f *measurable.*

Definition 13. *For a measurable space* (Ω, Σ), *a* simple function $g : \Omega \to \mathbb{R}_+$ *is a measurable* $\Sigma/\mathcal{R}$ *function with a finite image set, which can be expressed as* $g(x) = \sum_{i=1}^{n} \alpha_i [x \in A_i]$, *where* $A_i = f^{-1}(\alpha_1)$. *The* Lebesgue integral *of a simple function* $g(x) = \sum_{i=1}^{n} \alpha_i [x \in A_i]$ *with respect to a measure* μ *on* (Ω, Σ) *is defined as:*

$$\int g(x)\,\mu(dx) = \sum_{i=1}^{n} \alpha_i \mu(A_i)$$

The Lebesgue integral *of any measurable function* f *is then defined as the limit of integrals of simple functions pointwise smaller than* f:

$$\int f(x)\,\mu(dx) = \sup\left\{ \int g(x)\,\mu(dx) \mid g \text{ simple}, g \leq f \right\}$$

Theorem 3 (Beppo Levi). *Let* $f_i : X \to \overline{\mathbb{R}}_+$ *be a (pointwise) non-decreasing sequence of positive measurable functions and let* $f = \lim_{n \to \infty} \int f_i$ *be the pointwise limit of the sequence. Then* f *is measurable and*

$$\int f\,d\mu = \lim_{n \to \infty} \int f_n\,d\mu$$

The same holds for non-increasing sequences, provided that $\int f_0\,d\mu < \infty$.

Note that the limit and supremum of a non-decreasing sequence coincide. limit and infimum of a non-increasing sequence also coincide.

Metric and Topological Spaces

Definition 14. *A* metric *on a set Ω is a function $d\colon \Omega \times \Omega \to \overline{\mathbb{R}}_+$ such that $d(x,x) = 0$ and $d(x,y) + d(y,z) \geq d(x,z)$ for all $x,y,z \in \Omega$. The pair (Ω, d) is called a* metric space.

Definition 15. *If (Ω, d) is a metric space, $A \subseteq \Omega$ is* open *if every element $x \in A$ has a neighbourhood which is completely enclosed in A, i.e. there exists $\epsilon > 0$ such that $\{y \in \Omega \mid d(x,y) < \epsilon\} \subseteq A$.*

Definition 16. *If (Ω_1, d_1) and (Ω_2, d_2) are metric spaces, then a* product *of (Ω_1, d_1) and (Ω_2, d_2) is the metric space $(\Omega_1 \times \Omega_2, d_{12})$, where d_{12} is the Manhattan product of metrics d_1 and d_2, defined as*

$$d_{12}((x_1, y_1), (x_2, y_2)) = d_1(x_1, y_1) + d_2(x_2, y_2).$$

This definition naturally extends to finite products of higher dimensions.

A product of topological spaces can also be defined using the standard Euclidean product metric $d_{12}((x_1, y_1), (x_2, y_2)) = \sqrt{d_1(x_1, y_1)^2 + d_2(x_2, y_2)^2}$, both metrics induce the same topologies. We use Manhattan products as they are easier to work with.

Definition 17. *A* topology *on a set Ω is a set $\mathcal{O}$ of subsets of Ω such that*

- *$\emptyset \in \mathcal{O}$*
- *$\Omega \in \mathcal{O}$*
- *For all $O_1, \ldots, O_n \in \mathcal{O}$, $O_1 \cap O_2 \cap \cdots \cap O_n \in \mathcal{O}$*
- *If $O_i \in \mathcal{O}$ for all $i \in \mathbb{N}$, then $\bigcup_{n \in \mathbb{N}} O_i \in \mathcal{O}$.*

The pair $(\Omega, \mathcal{O})$ is called a topological space *and the elements of the topology $\mathcal{O}$ are called* open sets.

Definition 18. *If $(\Omega_1, \mathcal{O}_1)$ and $(\Omega_2, \mathcal{O}_2)$ are topological spaces, then a* product *of (Ω_1, d_1) and (Ω_2, d_2) is the metric space $(\Omega_1 \times \Omega_2, \mathcal{O}_1 \times \mathcal{O}_2)$, where the product of topologies $\mathcal{O}_1 \times \mathcal{O}_2$ is the smallest topology on $\Omega_1 \times \Omega_2$ which makes both left and right projections continuous. This definition naturally extends to final products of higher dimensions.*

Definition 19. *A function f between metric spaces (Ω_1, d_1) and (Ω_2, d_2) is* continuous *if for every $x \in \Omega_1$ and $\epsilon > 0$, there exists δ such that for all $y \in \Omega_1$, if $d_1(x,y) < \epsilon$, then $d_2(f(x), f(y)) < \delta$.*

Definition 20. *A function f between topological spaces $(\Omega_1, \mathcal{O}_1)$ and $(\Omega_2, \mathcal{O}_2)$ is* continuous *if for every open set $O \in \mathcal{O}_2$, $f^{-1}(O) \in \mathcal{O}_1$.*

From Metric to Measurable Spaces

Definition 21. *A topology on Ω induced by a metric d is the smallest topology which contains all open sets of the metric space (Ω, d).*

Definition 22. *The* Borel σ-algebra $\mathcal{B}(\Omega, \mathcal{O})$ *is the σ-algebra generated by a topology $\mathcal{O}$ on Ω.*

Definition 23. *We call the Borel σ-algebra on Ω generated by the topology induced by the metric d the σ-algebra induced by d. We denote such a σ algebra by $\mathcal{B}(\Omega, d)$.*

The following lemmas are well-established results:

Lemma 11. *If $\mathcal{O}_1$ and $\mathcal{O}_2$ are, respectively, topologies on Ω_1 and Ω_2 induced by metrics r_1 and r_2, and a function f between the metric spaces (Ω_1, d_1) and (Ω_2, d_2) is continuous, then f is also continuous as a function between topological spaces $(\Omega_1, \mathcal{O}_1)$ and $(\Omega_2, \mathcal{O}_2)$.*

Lemma 12. *If f is a continuous function between topological spaces $(\Omega_1, \mathcal{O}_1)$ and $(\Omega_2, \mathcal{O}_2)$ and Σ_1 and Σ_2 are the Borel σ-algebras on, respectively, Ω_1 and Ω_2 generated by topologies $\mathcal{O}_1$ and $\mathcal{O}_2$, then the function f is measurable.*

Corollary 2. *If (Ω_1, d_1) and (Ω_2, d_2) are metric spaces and f is a continuous function from Ω_1 to Ω_2, then f is measurable $\mathcal{B}(\Omega_1, d_1)/\mathcal{B}(\Omega_2, d_2)$.*

Lemma 13. *If (Ω_1, d_1) and (Ω_2, d_2) are separable metric spaces, then for the Manhattan product d_{12} of metrics d_1 and d_2*

$$\mathcal{B}(\Omega_1 \times \Omega_2, d_{12}) = \mathcal{B}(\Omega_1, d_1) \times \mathcal{B}(\Omega_2, d_2)$$

Corollary 3. *If (Ω_1, d_1), (Ω_2, d_2), (Ω_3, d_3) and (Ω_4, d_4) are separable metric spaces and f is a continuous function from $\Omega_1 \times \Omega_2$ to $\Omega_3 \times \Omega_4$ (with respect to corresponding product metrics) then f is measurable $\mathcal{B}(\Omega_1, d_1) \times \mathcal{B}(\Omega_2, d_2)/\mathcal{B}(\Omega_3, d_3) \times \mathcal{B}(\Omega_4, d_4)$.*

All the above results extend naturally to arbitrary finite products.

B   Basics of Domain Theory

This section includes some basic definitions from domain theory which are required to understand the paper. For readers wanting a more complete, tutorial-style introduction, there are many resources available, including [17] and [1].

Please note that we use the notions of ω-complete partial order and ω-continuity, defined in terms of countable sequences of increasing values (ω-chains), rather than the more general notions of complete partial order (requiring existence of suprema of directed sets) and continuity (requiring the given function to preserve suprema of all subsets of the domain). While ω-completeness and ω-continuity are technically weaker than completeness and continuity, respectively, they are sufficient for our purposes, as they allow applying the Kleene Fixpoint Theorem.

Definition 24 (Partially-ordered set). *A* partially-ordered set *is a pair* $(D, \sqsubseteq)$ *of set D and relation $\sqsubseteq$ such that:*

- *For each $a \in D$, $a \sqsubseteq a$ (reflexiveness)*
- *For each $a, b, c \in D$, if $a \sqsubseteq b$ and $b \sqsubseteq c$, then $a \sqsubseteq c$ (transitivity)*
- *For each $a, b \in D$, if $a \sqsubseteq b$ and $b \sqsubseteq a$, then $a = b$ (antisymmetry)*

Definition 25 (ω-chain and its supremum). *A ω-chain in a partially-ordered set $(D, \sqsubseteq)$ is an infinite sequence $d_0, d_1, d_2, \ldots$ such that for all i, $d_i \in D$ and $d_i \sqsubseteq d_{i+1}$. The supremum $\sup_i d_i$ of a chain $d_0, d_1, d_2, \ldots$ is the supremum of the set $\{d_0, d_1, d_2, \ldots\}$ of elements of the chain.*

Definition 26 (ω-complete partial order). *A ω-complete partial order (ω-cpo) is a partial order $(D, \sqsubseteq)$ such that for each ω-chain $d_0, d_1, d_2, \ldots$ in $(D, \sqsubseteq)$, the supremum $\sup_i d_i$ exists in D.*

Definition 27 (Monotone function). *A function $f \colon D \to D'$ between ω-cpos $(D, \sqsubseteq)$ and $(D', \sqsubseteq')$ is monotone if $f(d) \sqsubseteq' f(d')$ for each $d, d' \in D$ such that $d \sqsubseteq d'$.*

Definition 28 (ω-continuous function). *A function $f \colon D \to D'$ between ω-cpos $(D, \sqsubseteq)$ and $(D', \sqsubseteq')$ is ω-continuous if it is monotone and for each ω-chain $d_0, d_1, d_2, \ldots$ in $(D, \sqsubseteq)$, $f(\sup_i d_i) = \sup_i f(d_i)$.*

Note that in the definition above, the requirement that f is monotone ensures that $f(d_0)$, $f(d_1)$, $f(d_2)$, ... is a ω-chain.

Definition 29 (Least fixpoint). *Let $(D, \sqsubseteq)$ be a ω-cpo and $f \colon D \to D$ a function on $(D, \sqsubseteq)$. A fixpoint of f is an element $d \in D$ such that $f(d) = d$. A least fixpoint of f is a fixpoint d_0 of f such that for all other fixpoints d of f, $d_0 \sqsubseteq d$.*

Theorem 4 (Kleene Fixpoint Theorem). *Let $(D, \sqsubseteq)$ be a ω-cpo and $f \colon D \to D$ a ω-continuous function. Then f has a least fixpoint, which is the supremum of the chain $\bot$, $f(\bot)$, $f(f(\bot))$, $\ldots$, that is, $\sup_i f^i(\bot)$.*

C   Proofs for the wp and wlp Semantics

In order to prove that $\mathsf{wp}[\![C]\!](f)$ is measurable for all f, we first need to prove that the state update $\lambda(x, \sigma, E).\sigma[x \mapsto \sigma(E)]$ is measurable. Since states are a new structure, not discussed in the proofs of measurability in [36], we present the proof in more detail than other measurability proofs in this paper.

We define a metric $d_{\mathcal{N}}$ on variables as $d_{\mathcal{N}}(x, x) = 0$ and $d_{\mathcal{N}}(x, y) = \infty$ for $x \neq y$. The metric space $(\mathcal{N}, d_{\mathcal{N}})$ induces the usual discrete σ-algebra on $\mathcal{N}$.

Lemma 14. *The update function $h \colon \mathcal{N} \times \Omega_\sigma \times (\mathbb{R} \uplus \mathbb{Z}) \to \Omega_\sigma$ defined by $h(x, \sigma, v) = \sigma[x \mapsto v]$, is measurable.*

Proof. We prove that this function is continuous, which implies measurability. Take $x_1, x_2 \in \mathcal{N}$, $\sigma_1, \sigma_2 \in \Omega_\sigma$ and $V_1, V_2 \in \mathbb{R} \uplus \mathbb{Z}$. If $\mathbf{dom}(\sigma_1) \neq \mathbf{dom}(\sigma_2)$ then $d_\sigma(\sigma_1, \sigma_2) = \infty$, so trivially $d_\sigma(h(x_1, \sigma_1, V_1), h(x_2, \sigma_2, V_2)) \leq d_\mathcal{N}(x_1, x_2) + d_\sigma(\sigma_1, \sigma_2) + d_T(V_1, V_2) = \infty$. The same holds when $x_1 \neq x_2$ (which implies $d_\mathcal{N}(x_1, x_2) = \infty$). The inequality also immediately holds if $V_1 \in \mathbb{R}$ and $V_2 \in \mathbb{Z}$ (or vice versa), because then $d_T(V_1, V_2) = \infty$.

Now, suppose that $x_1 = x_2 = x$, $\mathbf{dom}(\sigma_1) = \mathbf{dom}(\sigma_2) = \{y_1, \ldots, y_n\}$ and either $V_1, V_2 \in \mathbb{R}$ or $V_1, V_2 \in \mathbb{Z}$. Now, if $x = y_k$ for some k, then

$$
\begin{aligned}
d_\sigma(h(x, \sigma_1, V_1), h(x, \sigma_2, V_2)) &= \sum_{i \in 1..n, i \neq k} d_T(\sigma_1(y_i), \sigma_2(y_i)) + d_T(V_1, V_2) \\
&\leq \sum_{i \in 1..n} d_T(\sigma_1(y_i), \sigma_2(y_i)) + d_T(V_1, V_2) \\
&= d_\sigma(\sigma_1, \sigma_2) + d_T(V_1, V_2) + d_\mathcal{N}(x, x)
\end{aligned}
$$

If $x \neq x_k$ for any k, we simply have:

$$
\begin{aligned}
d_\sigma(h(x, \sigma_1, V_1), h(x, \sigma_2, V_2)) &= \sum_{i \in 1..n} d_T(\sigma_1(y_i), \sigma_2(y_i)) + d_T(V_1, V_2) \\
&= d_\sigma(\sigma_1, \sigma_2) + d_T(V_1, V_2) + d_\mathcal{N}(x, x)
\end{aligned}
$$

Thus, h_x is continuous, and so measurable. $\qquad\square$

Restatement of Lemma 3. *For every program C, the function $\mathbf{wp}[\![C]\!](\cdot)$ is ω-continuous. Moreover, for every measurable $f \colon \Omega_\sigma \to \overline{\mathbb{R}}_+$, $\mathbf{wp}[\![C]\!](f)(\cdot)$ is measurable.*

Proof (of Lemma 3). By induction on the structure of C. The continuity part of the proof is largely similar to the proof of the analogous property in [13], with additional care needed because of the use of Lebesgue integration. We need to show that for any C and any ω-chain $f_1 \leq f_2 \leq f_3 \ldots$, $\mathbf{wp}[\![C]\!](\sup_i f_i) = \sup_i \mathbf{wp}[\![C]\!](f_i)$ and that $\mathbf{wp}[\![C]\!](f)$ is measurable for any measurable f.

– Case $C = x :\approx U$:
  • **Continuity:**

$$
\begin{aligned}
\mathbf{wp}[\![C]\!](\sup_i f_i) &= \lambda\sigma. \int_{[0,1]} (\sup_i f_i)(\sigma[x \mapsto v]) \, \mu_L(dv) \\
\text{(by Beppo Levi's theorem)} \quad &= \lambda\sigma. \sup_i \int_{[0,1]} f_i(\sigma[x \mapsto v]) \, \mu_L(dv) \\
\text{(sup taken wrt pointwise ordering)} \quad &= \sup_i \lambda\sigma. \int_{[0,1]} f_i(\sigma[x \mapsto v]) \, \mu_L(dv) \\
&= \sup_i \mathbf{wp}[\![C]\!](f_i)
\end{aligned}
$$

- **Measurability:**
  We have

  $$\mathrm{wp}[\![C]\!](f) = \lambda\sigma. \int_{[0,1]} g(x,\sigma,v)\,\mu_L(dv)$$

  where $g(x,\sigma,v) = f(\sigma[x \mapsto v])$. Now, take $h(x,\sigma,v) = \sigma[x \mapsto v]$. Then $g = f \circ h$. We know that substitutions are measurable (Lemmma 14), so h is measurable. This means that g is measurable, as it is a composition of measurable functions. Thus, by the Fubini-Tonelli theorem, $\lambda\sigma. \int_{[0,1]} g(x,\sigma,v)\,\mu_L(dv)$ is measurable, so $\mathrm{wp}[\![C]\!](f)$ is measurable.

- Case $C = \mathtt{score}(E)$:
  - **Continuity:**

  $$
  \begin{aligned}
  \mathrm{wp}[\![C]\!](\sup_i f_i) &= \lambda\sigma.\ [\sigma(E) \in (0,1]]\sigma(E) \cdot (\sup_i f_i)(\sigma) \\
  \text{\scriptsize(multiplying by a constant preserves sup)} &= \lambda\sigma.\sup_i([\sigma(E) \in (0,1]]\sigma(E) \cdot f_i(\sigma)) \\
  \text{\scriptsize(sup taken wrt pointwise ordering)} &= \sup_i \lambda\sigma.\ [\sigma(E) \in (0,1]]\sigma(E) \cdot f_i(\sigma) \\
  &= \sup_i \mathrm{wp}[\![C]\!](f_i)
  \end{aligned}
  $$

  - **Measurability:**
    We have $\mathrm{wp}[\![C]\!](f) = \lambda\sigma.\ [\sigma(E) \in (0,1]]\sigma(E) \cdot f(\sigma)$. The substitution $\sigma(E)$ is measurable by assumption (as a function of σ). Meanwhile, $[\sigma(E) \in (0,1]]$ is a composition of the measurable function $\sigma(E)$ and the indicator function of the measurable set $(0,1]$, which is obviously measurable. Finally, f is measurable by assumption, so the pointwise product of these three functions is measurable.

- Case $C = \mathtt{observe}(\phi)$:
  - **Continuity:**

  $$
  \begin{aligned}
  \mathrm{wp}[\![C]\!](\sup_i f_i) &= \lambda\sigma.[\sigma(\phi)](\sup_i f_i)(\sigma) \\
  \text{\scriptsize(multiplying by a constant preserves sup)} &= \lambda\sigma.\sup_i([\sigma(\phi)]f_i(\sigma)) \\
  \text{\scriptsize(sup taken wrt pointwise ordering)} &= \sup_i \lambda\sigma.\ [\sigma(\phi)]f_i(\sigma) \\
  &= \sup_i \mathrm{wp}[\![C]\!](f_i)
  \end{aligned}
  $$

  - **Measurability:**
    We have $\mathrm{wp}[\![C]\!](f) = \lambda\sigma.[\sigma(\phi)]f(\sigma)$. The function $\sigma.[\sigma(\phi)]$ is measurable by assumption (we only allow measurable predicates in the language), and f is measurable by assumption of the lemma, hence their pointwise product is measurable.

– Case $C = (x := E)$:
  • **Continuity:**

$$\text{wp}[\![C]\!](\sup_i f_i) = \lambda\sigma.(\sup_i f_i)(\sigma[x \mapsto \sigma(E)])$$

$$\text{(sup taken wrt pointwise ordering)} = \lambda\sigma.\sup_i f_i(\sigma[x \mapsto \sigma(E)])$$

$$\text{(sup taken wrt pointwise ordering)} = \sup_i \lambda\sigma.f_i(\sigma[x \mapsto \sigma(E)])$$

$$= \sup_i \text{wp}[\![C]\!](f_i)$$

  • **Measurability:**
  We have $\text{wp}[\![C]\!](f) = \lambda\sigma.f(\sigma[x \mapsto \sigma(E)])$. This can be represented as a composition of functions $\lambda\sigma.f \circ F_2 \circ F_1(\sigma)$, where $F_1(\sigma) = (\sigma, \sigma(E))$ and $F_2(\sigma, V) = \sigma[x \mapsto V]$. The function F_1 is measurable, because the identity function $\lambda\sigma.\sigma$ is trivially measurable, and $\lambda\sigma.\sigma(E)$ is measurable by assumption, so both components of F_1 are measurable. The function F_2 is measurable by Lemma 14. Hence, $\text{wp}[\![C]\!](f)$ is measurable as a composition of measurable functions.

– Case $C = \text{while}(\phi)\{C'\}$:
  • **Continuity:** We have:

$$\text{wp}[\![C]\!](\sup_i f_i) = \text{wp}[\![\text{while}(\phi)\{C'\}]\!](\sup_i f_i)$$

$$= \text{lfp } X.[\neg\phi](\sup_i f_i) + [\phi]\text{wp}[\![C']\!](X)$$

  Take $\Phi_f(X) = [\neg\phi]f + [\phi]\text{wp}[\![C']\!](X)$. By induction hypothesis, $\text{wp}[\![C']\!](\cdot)$ is continuous, so $\Phi_f(\cdot)$ is continuous for all $f: \Omega_\sigma \to \overline{\mathbb{R}}_+$. Moreover, it can be easily checked that for any X, $f \mapsto \Phi_f(X)$ is continuous as a function of f (which means that $f \mapsto \Phi_f$ is continuous). Thus,

$$\text{wp}[\![C]\!](\sup_i f_i) = \sup_n \Phi_{\sup_i f_i}^n(0) = \sup_n(\sup_i \Phi_{f_i})^n(0)$$

  By Theorem 2.1.19.2 from [1], the function $\Phi \mapsto \sup_n \Phi^n(0)$ is continuous. If $f_1, f_2, \dots$ is an increasing chain, then $\Phi_{f_1}, \Phi_{f_2}, \dots$ is also an increasing chain (because Φ_f is monotone in f). Thus, $\sup_n(\sup_i \Phi_{f_i})^n(0) = \sup_i(\sup_n \Phi_{f_i}^n(0)) = \sup_i \text{wp}[\![C]\!](f_i)$, as required.

  • **Measurability:**
  The function $\Phi_f(X) = [\neg\phi](f) + [\phi]\text{wp}[\![C']\!](X)$ is continuous for all measurable f by the induction hypothesis, so by the fixpoint theorem $\text{lfp } X.\Phi_f(X)$ exists in the domain of measurable functions.

– Case $C = C_1; C_2$:
  • **Continuity:**
  We have :

$$\text{wp}[\![C]\!](\sup_i f_i) = \text{wp}[\![C_1]\!](\text{wp}[\![C_2]\!](\sup_i f_i))$$

By induction hypothesis, $\text{wp}[\![C_2]\!](\sup_i f_i) = \sup_i \text{wp}[\![C_2]\!](f_i)$. The induction hypothesis also states that $\text{wp}[\![C_2]\!](f_i)$ is measurable for all measurable f_i, which also means that $\sup_i \text{wp}[\![C_2]\!](f_i)$ is measurable. Hence, $\text{wp}[\![C_1]\!](\sup_i \text{wp}[\![C_2]\!](f_i))$ is well-defined. By applying the induction hypothesis again, we get $\text{wp}[\![C_1]\!](\sup_i \text{wp}[\![C_2]\!](f_i)) = \sup_i \text{wp}[\![C_1]\!](\text{wp}[\![C_2]\!](f_i))$, as required.

- **Measurability:**

  By induction hypothesis, $\text{wp}[\![C_2]\!](f)$ is measurable, and so $\text{wp}[\![C_1]\!]$ $(\text{wp}[\![C_2]\!](f))$ is also measurable by induction hypothesis.

- The other cases are straightforward.

$\square$

D   Proofs for the Operational Semantics

D.1   Properties of the Operational Semantics

This section consists of proofs of properties of the operational semantics which are needed to prove Proposition 1.

Basic Properites. We begin by stating two basic properties: that reduction is deterministic and that the weight always stays positive.

Lemma 15 (Evaluation is deterministic). *For any configuration* κ, *if* $\kappa \vdash \kappa'$ *and* $\kappa \vdash \kappa''$, *then* $\kappa' = \kappa''$.

Lemma 16. *If* $\kappa \vdash \kappa'$ *and* $\text{weight}(\kappa) > 0$, *then* $\text{weight}(\kappa') > 0$.

Invariance of Reduction Relation. The functions $\mathbf{O}_C^\sigma$ and $\mathbf{SC}_C^\sigma$ are defined in terms of reduction chains which start at configurations with $K = []$, $n = 0$ and $w = 1$. However, in order to reason about evaluation of compositions of terms, we need to deal with reduction sequences starting at intermediate configurations, where this property does not hold. The following lemmas show that the reduction relation is preserved by modifying the initial and final step count, weight and continuation.

Proving invariance of the semantics under step count and weight change is straightforward:

Lemma 17. *If* $\langle \theta, C, K, \sigma, \theta_K, n, w \rangle \vdash^* \langle \theta', C', K', \sigma', \theta_K', n + n', w' \rangle$, *then for all* $w'' > 0$ *and integer* $n'' \geq -n$, $\langle \theta, C, K, \sigma, \theta_K, n + n'', w''w \rangle \vdash^* \langle \theta', C', K', \sigma', \theta_K', n + n'' + n', w''w' \rangle$.

Proof. Simple induction on n'. $\square$

The rest of this section shows that the semantics is also preserved by extending the initial continuation. In the following lemmas, we write $K @ K'$ for the concatenation of two continuations K and K' (recall that a continuation is a list of expressions).

Lemma 18. – *If* $\langle\theta, C, K', \sigma, \theta_K, n, w\rangle \vdash \langle\theta', C', K'', \sigma', \theta'_K, n+1, w'\rangle$ *and* $\sigma' \neq$ ξ *and* $(C, K') \neq (\downarrow, [])$, *then* $\langle\theta, C, K'@K, \sigma, \theta_K, n, w\rangle \vdash \langle\theta', C', K''@K, \sigma',$ $\theta'_K, n+1, w'\rangle$.

– *If* $\langle\theta, C, K', \sigma, \theta_K, n, w\rangle \vdash \langle\theta', C', K'', \xi, \theta'_K, n+1, w'\rangle$ *then* $\langle\theta, C, K'@K, \sigma, \theta_K,$ $n, w\rangle \vdash \langle\theta', C', [], \xi, \theta'_K, n+1, w'\rangle$.

Proof. By inspection of the reduction rules. □

Lemma 19. *If* $\langle\theta, C, K, \sigma, \theta_K, n, w\rangle \vdash^* \langle\theta', \downarrow, [], \sigma', \theta'_K, n+n', w'\rangle$, *then there exists a unique* $\hat{n} \leq n'$ *such that* $\langle\theta, C, K, \sigma, \theta_K, n, w\rangle \vdash^*_{\min} \langle\theta', \downarrow, [], \sigma', \theta'_K, n+\hat{n},$ $w'\rangle$

Proof. Obvious. □

Lemma 20. *If* $\langle\theta, C, K, \sigma, \theta_K, n, w\rangle \vdash^* \langle\theta', C', K', \sigma', \theta'_K, n+n', w'\rangle$ *and* $(C', K') \neq (\downarrow, [])$ *and* $\sigma' \neq \xi$, *then for all* K'', $\langle\theta, C, K@K'', \sigma, \theta_K, n, w\rangle \vdash^* \langle\theta',$ $C', K'@K'', \sigma', \theta'_K, n+n', w'\rangle$.

Proof. By induction on n':

– Base case: $n' = 0$: trivial

– Induction step: Let $n' > 0$. Then we have $\langle\theta, C, K, \sigma, \theta_K, n, w\rangle \vdash \langle\hat{\theta}, \hat{C}, \hat{K}, \hat{\sigma},$ $\hat{\theta_K}, n+1, \hat{w}\rangle \vdash^* \langle\theta', C', K', \sigma', \theta'_K, n+n', w'\rangle$. We now need to split on the derivation of $\langle\theta, C, K, \sigma, \theta_K, n, w\rangle \vdash \langle\hat{\theta}, \hat{C}, \hat{K}, \hat{\sigma}, \hat{\theta_K}, n+1, w\rangle$.

• If $\langle\theta, C, K, \sigma, \theta_K, n, w\rangle \vdash \langle\hat{\theta}, \hat{C}, \hat{K}, \hat{\sigma}, \hat{\theta_K}, n+1, \hat{w}\rangle$ was derived with (seq), then $C = C_1; C_2$, $\hat{K} = C_2 :: K$ and we have $\langle\theta, C_1; C_2, K, \sigma, \theta_K, n,$ $w\rangle \vdash \langle\pi_L(\theta), C_1, C_2 :: K, \sigma, \pi_L(\theta) :: \theta_K, n+1, w\rangle \vdash^* \langle\theta', C', K', \sigma', \theta'_K,$ $n+n', w'\rangle$.

By (seq), $\langle\theta, C_1; C_2, K@K'', \sigma, \theta_K, n, w\rangle \vdash \langle\pi_L(\theta), C_1, C_2 :: K@K'', \sigma,$ $\pi_L(\theta) :: \theta_K, n+1, w\rangle$, and by the induction hypothesis, $\langle\pi_L(\theta), C_1,$ $C_2 :: K@K'', \sigma, \pi_L(\theta) :: \theta_K, n+1, \hat{w}\rangle \vdash^* \langle\theta', C', K'@K'', \sigma', \theta'_K, n+n',$ $w'\rangle$.

• If $\langle\theta, C, K, \sigma, \theta_K, n, w\rangle \vdash \langle\hat{\theta}, \hat{C}, \hat{K}, \hat{\sigma}, \hat{\theta_K}, n+1, \hat{w}\rangle$ was derived with (pop), then $C = \downarrow$ and $K = C' :: K'''$ and we have $\langle\theta, \downarrow, C' :: K''', \sigma, \theta_K, n,$ $w\rangle \vdash \langle\pi_L(\theta_K), C', K''', \sigma, \pi_R(\theta_K), n+1, w\rangle \vdash^* \langle\theta', C', K', \sigma', \theta'_K, n+n',$ $w'\rangle$.

By (pop), $\langle\theta, \downarrow, C' :: K'''@K'', \sigma, \theta_K, n, w\rangle \vdash \langle\pi_L(\theta_K), C', K'''@K'', \sigma,$ $\pi_R(\theta_K), n+1, w\rangle$, and by induction hypothesis, $\langle\pi_L(\theta_K), C', K'''@K'',$ $\sigma, \pi_R(\theta_K), n+1, w\rangle \vdash^* \langle\theta', C', K'@K'', \sigma', \theta'_K, n+n', w'\rangle$.

• Otherwise, we have $\hat{K} = K$ and by inspection of the reduction rules, $\langle\theta, C,$ $K@K'', \sigma, \theta_K, n, w\rangle \vdash \langle\hat{\theta}, \hat{C}, K@K'', \hat{\sigma}, \hat{\theta_K}, n+1, \hat{w}\rangle$, so the result follows immediately by applying the induction hypothesis (note that $(C', K') \neq$ $(\downarrow, [])$ implies that $\langle\theta, C, K, \sigma, \theta_K, n, w\rangle \vdash \langle\hat{\theta}, \hat{C}, \hat{K}, \hat{\sigma}, \hat{\theta_K}, n+1, \hat{w}\rangle$ is not derived with (final)).

□

Corollary 4. *If $\langle\theta, C, K, \sigma, \theta_K, n, w\rangle \vdash^* \langle\theta', C', K', \sigma', \theta'_K, n+n', w'\rangle$ and $\sigma' \neq \xi$ and $(C', K') \neq (\downarrow, [])$, then for all $w'' > 0$, integer $n'' \geq -n$ and K'', $\langle\theta, C, K@K'', \sigma, \theta_K, n+n'', w''w\rangle \vdash^* \langle\theta', C', K'@K'', \sigma', \theta'_K, n+n''+n', w''w'\rangle$.*

The reason we added the condition $(C', K') \neq (\downarrow, [])$ to the premise of Lemma 20 is that in our semantics, a "final" configuration with statement $\downarrow$ and empty continuation reduces to itself (by the (final) rule) infinitely. If we replaced $[]$ with some non-empty continuation K, the rule (pop) would be applied instead of (final) and the reduction would be completely different. The statement $\langle\theta, C, K, \sigma, \theta_K, n, w\rangle \vdash^* \langle\theta', \downarrow, [], \sigma', \theta'_K, n+n', w'\rangle$ says nothing about how many times the rule (final) was applied at the end, so we do not know what the final configuration after n' steps would be if we appended some continuation K' to K.

Because of that, we need to treat the case $(C', K') = (\downarrow, [])$ separately. We first introduce some new notation: we write $\langle\theta, C, K, \sigma, \theta_K, n, w\rangle \vdash^*_{\min} \langle\theta', \downarrow, [], \sigma', \theta'_K, n+n', w'\rangle$ if $\langle\theta, C, K, \sigma, \theta_K, n, w\rangle \vdash^* \langle\theta', \downarrow, [], \sigma', \theta'_K, n+n', w'\rangle$ and there is no $n'' < n'$ such that $\langle\theta, C, K, \sigma, \theta_K, n, w\rangle \vdash^* \langle\theta'', \downarrow, [], \sigma'', \theta''_K, n+n'', w''\rangle$ (or, equivalently, $\langle\theta, C, K, \sigma, \theta_K, n, w\rangle \vdash^* \langle\theta', \downarrow, [], \sigma', \theta'_K, n+n', w'\rangle$ was derived without (final)).

Lemma 21 (Evaluation with continuation). *If $\langle\theta, C, [], \sigma, \theta_K, n, w\rangle \vdash^*_{\min} \langle\theta', \downarrow, [], \sigma', \theta'_K, n+n', w'\rangle$ and $\sigma' \neq \xi$, then $\langle\theta, C, K, \sigma, \theta_K, n, w\rangle \vdash^* \langle\theta', \downarrow, K, \sigma', \theta'_K, n+n', w'\rangle$.*

Proof. We will prove a more general statement:

If $\langle\theta, C, K', \sigma, \theta_K, n, w\rangle \vdash^*_{\min} \langle\theta', \downarrow, [], \sigma', \theta'_K, n+n', w'\rangle$, then $\langle\theta, C, K'@K, \sigma, \theta_K, n, w\rangle \vdash^* \langle\theta', \downarrow, K, \sigma', \theta'_K, n+n', w'\rangle$,

by induction on n':

- Base case: $n' = 0$: This implies that $C = \downarrow$ and $w' = w$ and $K' = []$ and $\theta'_K = \theta_K$, so the result follows trivially.
- Induction step: for $n' > 0$, we have $\langle\theta, C, K', \sigma, \theta_K, n, w\rangle \vdash \langle\hat{\theta}, \hat{C}, \hat{K}', \hat{\sigma}, \hat{\theta_K}, n+1, \hat{w}\rangle \vdash^*_{\min} \langle\theta', \downarrow, [], \sigma', \theta'_K, n+n', w'\rangle$, where $(C, K') \neq (\downarrow, [])$, as otherwise the configuration would reduce in 0 steps.
  By Lemma 18, $\langle\theta, C, K'@K, \sigma, \theta_K, n, w\rangle \vdash \langle\hat{\theta}, \hat{C}, \hat{K}'@K, \hat{\sigma}, \hat{\theta_K}, n+1, \hat{w}\rangle$ and by induction hypothesis, $\langle\hat{\theta}, \hat{C}, \hat{K}'@K, \hat{\sigma}, \hat{\theta_K}, n+1, \hat{w}\rangle \vdash^* \langle\theta', \downarrow, K, \sigma', \theta'_K, n+1+(n'-1), w'\rangle$, which ends the proof.

$\square$

Corollary 5. *If $\langle\theta, C, [], \sigma, \theta_K, n, w\rangle \vdash^*_{\min} \langle\theta', \downarrow, [], \sigma', \theta_K, n+n', w'\rangle$ and $\sigma' \neq \xi$, then $\langle\theta, C, K, \sigma, \theta_K, n, w\rangle \vdash^* \langle\theta', \downarrow, K, \sigma', \theta_K, n+n', w'\rangle$.*

We also need to show that reductions leading to a failed observation are also preserved when appending a continuation.

Lemma 22. *If $\langle\theta, C, K, \sigma, \theta_K, n, w\rangle \vdash^* \langle\theta', \downarrow, [], \xi, \theta'_K, n+n', w'\rangle$ then for all K'', $\langle\theta, C, K@K'', \sigma, \theta_K, n, w\rangle \vdash^* \langle\theta', C', [], \xi, \theta'_K, n+n', w'\rangle$.*

Proof. If $n' = 0$, the result follows trivially.

If $n' > 0$, then we have $\sigma \neq \frac{1}{2}$ (otherwise the initial configuration would not reduce), and so the last rule in the derivation of $\langle \theta, C, K, \sigma, \theta_K, n, w \rangle \vdash^* \langle \theta', C', K', \frac{1}{2}, \theta'_K, n + n', w' \rangle$ must have been (condition-false).

Hence, $\langle \theta, C, K, \sigma, \theta_K, n, w \rangle \vdash^* \langle \theta', \mathsf{observe}(\phi), \hat{K}, \sigma', \theta'_K, n + n' - 1, w' \rangle \vdash \langle \theta', \downarrow, [], \frac{1}{2}, \theta'_K, n + n', w' \rangle$, where $\sigma' \neq \frac{1}{2}$ and $\sigma'(\phi) = \mathtt{false}$. By Lemma 20, $\langle \theta, C, K@K'', \sigma, \theta_K, n, w \rangle \vdash^* \langle \theta', \mathsf{observe}(\phi), \hat{K}@K'', \sigma', \theta'_K, n + n' - 1, w' \rangle$. By applying (condition-false) again, we get $\langle \theta', \mathsf{observe}(\phi), \hat{K}@K'', \sigma', \theta'_K, n+n'-1, w' \rangle \vdash \langle \theta', \downarrow, [], \frac{1}{2}, \theta'_K, n + n', w' \rangle$, as required. $\qquad\square$

Lemma 23. *If $C_1 \neq C'_1; C''_1$ and $\langle \pi_L(\theta), C_1, [], \sigma, \pi_R(\theta) :: \theta_K, 0, 1 \rangle \vdash^* \langle \theta', \downarrow, [], \frac{1}{2}, \theta'_K, n, w \rangle$, then $\langle \theta, C_1; C_2, [], \sigma, \theta_K, 0, 1 \rangle \vdash^* \langle \theta', \downarrow, [], \frac{1}{2}, \theta'_K, n + 1, w \rangle$.*

Proof. By Lemma 22 $\langle \pi_L(\theta), C_1, [C_2], \sigma, \pi_R(\theta) :: \theta_K, 0, 1 \rangle \vdash^* \langle \theta', \downarrow, [], \frac{1}{2}, \theta'_K, n, w \rangle$. As $\langle \theta, C_1; C_2, [], \sigma, \theta_K, 0, 1 \rangle \vdash \langle \pi_L(\theta), C_1, [C_2], \sigma, \pi_R(\theta) :: \theta_K, 1, 1 \rangle$ by (seq), Lemma 17 yields $\langle \theta, C_1; C_2, [], \sigma, \theta_K, 0, 1 \rangle \vdash^* \langle \theta', \downarrow, [], \frac{1}{2}, \theta'_K, n + 1, w \rangle$. $\qquad\square$

Sequencing. We now use the above results to relate the final and intermediate configurations in the reduction of a statement C_1 to the intermediate configurations reached when reducing $C_1; C_2$.

Lemma 24 (Context evaluation for simple sequencing). *If $C_1 \neq C'_1; C''_1$ and $\langle \theta, C_1, [], \sigma, \theta_K, n, w \rangle \vdash^*_{\min} \langle \theta', \downarrow, [], \sigma', \theta_K, n + n', w' \rangle$ and $\sigma' \neq \frac{1}{2}$, then $\langle \theta::\pi_L(\theta_K), C_1; C_2, [], \sigma, \pi_R(\theta_K), n, w \rangle \vdash^* \langle \pi_L(\theta_K), C_2, [], \sigma', \pi_R(\theta_K), n + n' + 2, w' \rangle$.*

Proof. By (seq): $\langle \theta::\pi_L(\theta_K), C_1; C_2, [], \sigma, \pi_R(\theta_K), n, w \rangle \vdash \langle \theta, C_1, [C_2], \sigma, \theta_K, n+1, w \rangle$.

By Lemma 21 (and the fact that we can change n): $\langle \theta, C_1, [C_2], \sigma, \theta_K, n + 1, w \rangle \vdash^* \langle \theta', \downarrow, [C_2], \sigma', \theta_K, (n + 1) + n', w' \rangle$.

By (pop), $\langle \theta', \downarrow, [C_2], \sigma', \theta_K, (n + 1) + n', w' \rangle \vdash \langle \pi_L(\theta_K), C_2, [], \sigma', \pi_R(\theta_K), (n + 1) + n' + 1, w' \rangle$, as required. $\qquad\square$

Lemma 25. *If $C_1 \neq C'_1; C''_1$ and $\langle \theta, C_1, [], \sigma, \theta_K, n, w \rangle \vdash^* \langle \theta', C', K, \sigma', \theta'_K, n + n', w' \rangle$ and $\sigma' \neq \frac{1}{2}$ and $(C', K') \neq (\downarrow, [])$, then $\langle \theta::\pi_L(\theta_K), C_1; C_2, [], \sigma, \pi_R(\theta_K), n, w \rangle \vdash^* \langle \theta', C', K@[C_2], \sigma', \theta'_K, n + n' + 1, w' \rangle$.*

Proof. By (seq), we have $\langle \theta::\pi_L(\theta_K), C_1; C_2, [], \sigma, \pi_R(\theta_K), n, w \rangle \vdash \langle \theta, C_1, [C_2], \sigma, \theta_K, n+1, w \rangle$. Then, by Corollary 4, $\langle \theta, C_1, [C_2], \sigma, \theta_K, n+1, w \rangle \vdash^* \langle \theta', C', K@[C_2], \sigma', \theta'_K, n + n' + 1, w' \rangle$, as required. $\qquad\square$

Splitting a Sequence Evaluation. We now show that if a sequence $C_1; C_2$ of statements evaluates under entropy θ to a proper state, then C_1 in itself must evaluate under $\pi_L(\theta)$, and that if the evaluation of $C_1; C_2$ results in an error, then C_1 cannot diverge. These properties will be needed to show compositionality of the semantics.

To prove the first of the above properties, we first prove that if a configuration with an empty continuation reduces completely, then the continuation entropy θ_K in the final configuration will be identical to the original one (intermediate steps may extend θ_K, but all sub-entropies added to θ_K will subsequently be removed). In the following lemma, we write $|K|$ for the length of list K.

Lemma 26. *If $\langle \theta, C, K, \sigma, \hat{\theta_K}, n, w \rangle \vdash^* \langle \theta', \downarrow, [], \sigma', \theta'_K, n + n', w' \rangle$ and $\sigma' \neq \notdef$ and $\pi_R^{|K|}(\hat{\theta_K}) = \theta_K$, then $\theta'_K = \theta_K$.*

Proof. By induction on n':

- Base case: $n' = 0$: then obviously $|K| = 0$ and $\hat{\theta_K} = \theta_K$, so the result follows trivially.
- Induction step: if $n' > 0$, then $\langle \theta, C, K, \sigma, \hat{\theta_K}, n, w \rangle \vdash \langle \theta'', C'', K', \sigma'', \theta''_K, n + 1, w'' \rangle \vdash^* \langle \theta', \downarrow, [], \sigma', \theta'_K, n + n', w' \rangle$.
  Now we need to split on the first rule in this derivation chain.
  If the first transition was derived with (seq), then $|K'| = |K| + 1$ and $\theta''_K = \pi_R(\theta) :: \hat{\theta_K}$. We have $\pi_R^{|K'|}(\theta''_K) = \pi_R^{|K|+1}(\pi_R(\theta) :: \hat{\theta_K}) = \pi_R^{|K|}(\pi_R(\pi_R(\theta) :: \hat{\theta_K})) = \pi_R^{|K|}(\hat{\theta_K}) = \theta_K$, so by induction hypothesis, $\theta'_K = \theta_K$.
  If the first transition was derived with (pop), then $|K'| = |K| - 1$ and $\theta''_K = \pi_R(\hat{\theta_K})$. Thus, $\pi_R^{|K'|}(\theta''_K) = \pi_R^{|K|-1}(\pi_R(\hat{\theta_K})) = \pi_R^{|K|}(\hat{\theta_K}) = \theta_K$, so by induction hypothesis, $\theta'_K = \theta_K$.
  Otherwise, we have $K' = K$ (note that $\sigma' \neq \notdef$ implies $\sigma'' \neq \notdef$) and $\theta''_K = \hat{\theta_K}$, so $\pi_R^{|K'|}(\theta''_K) = \theta_K$. By induction hypothesis, $\theta'_K = \theta_K$.

$\qquad\square$

Corollary 6. *If $\langle \theta, C, [], \sigma, \theta_K, n, w \rangle \vdash^* \langle \theta', \downarrow, [], \sigma', \theta'_K, n + n', w' \rangle$ and $\sigma' \neq \notdef$, then $\theta'_K = \theta_K$.*

We now prove that if $C_1; C_2$ successfully evaluates with entropy θ, then C_1 also successfully evaluates with entropy $\pi_L(\theta)$.

Lemma 27 (Interpolation for Continuations). *If $\langle \theta, C, K_1@K_2, \sigma, \theta_K, n, w \rangle \vdash^* \langle \theta', \downarrow, [], \sigma', \theta'_K, n + n', w' \rangle$ and $\sigma' \neq \notdef$, then $\langle \theta, C, K_1, \sigma, \theta_K, n, w \rangle \vdash^* \langle \theta'', \downarrow, [], \sigma'', \theta''_K, n + n'', w'' \rangle$, where $\sigma'' \neq \notdef$.*

Proof. By induction on n'.

- Base case: $n' = 0$: in this case, $C = \downarrow$ and $K_1 = K_2 = []$, so the result follows trivially.
- Induction step: suppose $\langle \theta, C, K_1@K_2, \sigma, \theta_K, n, w \rangle \vdash \langle \hat{\theta}, \hat{C}, \hat{K}, \hat{\sigma}, \hat{\theta_K}, n + 1, \hat{w} \rangle \vdash^* \langle \theta', \downarrow, [], \sigma', \theta'_K, n + n', w' \rangle$.
  If $\langle \theta, C, K_1@K_2, \sigma, \theta_K, n, w \rangle \vdash \langle \hat{\theta}, \hat{C}, \hat{K}, \hat{\sigma}, \hat{\theta_K}, n+1, \hat{w} \rangle$ was derived with (seq), then $C = C_1; C_2$, $C_1 \neq C'_1; C''_1$, $\hat{K} = C_2 :: K_1@K_2$, $\hat{\theta} = \pi_L(\theta)$, $\hat{w} = w$ and $\hat{\theta_K} = \pi_R(\theta) :: \theta_K$. By (seq), we have $\langle \theta, C_1; C_2, K_1, \sigma, \theta_K, n, w \rangle \vdash \langle \pi_L(\theta), C_1, C_2 :: K_1, \sigma, \pi_R(\theta) :: \theta_K, n + 1, w \rangle$. By induction hypothesis, $\langle \pi_L(\theta), C_1, C_2 :: K_1, \sigma, \pi_R(\theta) :: \theta_K, n + 1, w \rangle \vdash^* \langle \theta'', \downarrow, [], \sigma'', \theta''_K, n + n'', w'' \rangle$ and $\sigma'' \neq \notdef$.

Hence, $\langle \theta, C_1; C_2, K_1, \sigma, \theta_K, n, w \rangle \vdash^* \langle \theta'', \downarrow, [], \sigma'', \theta_K'', n+n'', w'' \rangle$, as required. If $\langle \theta, C, K_1 @ K_2, \sigma, \theta_K, n, w \rangle \vdash \langle \hat{\theta}, \hat{C}, \hat{K}, \hat{\sigma}, \hat{\theta_K}, n+1, \hat{w} \rangle$ was derived with (pop), then $C = \downarrow$, $K_1 @ K_2 = \hat{C} :: \hat{K}$, $\hat{w} = w$, $\hat{\theta} = \pi_L(\theta_K)$ and $\hat{\theta_K} = \pi_R(\theta_K)$.

- If $K_1 \neq []$, then $K_1 = \hat{C} :: \hat{K_1}$ and $\hat{K} = \hat{K_1} @ K_2$ and we have $\langle \theta, \downarrow, \hat{C} :: \hat{K_1}, \sigma, \theta_K, n, w \rangle \vdash \langle \pi_L(\theta_K), \hat{C}, \hat{K_1}, \sigma, \pi_R(\theta_K), n+1, w \rangle$. By induction hypothesis, $\langle \pi_L(\theta_K), \hat{C}, \hat{K_1}, \sigma, \pi_R(\theta_K), n+1, w \rangle \vdash^* \langle \theta'', \downarrow, [], \sigma'', \theta_K'', n+n'', w'' \rangle$ and $\sigma'' \neq \text{\textreferencemark}$. Hence, we have $\langle \theta, \downarrow, \hat{C} :: \hat{K_1}, \sigma, \theta_K, n, w \rangle \vdash^* \langle \theta'', \downarrow, [], \sigma'', \theta_K'', n+n'', w'' \rangle$.

- If $K_1 = []$, then trivially $\langle \theta, \downarrow, [], \sigma, \theta_K, n, w \rangle \vdash^* \langle \theta, \downarrow, [], \sigma, \theta_K, n, w \rangle$ in zero steps.

Otherwise, $\hat{K} = K_1 @ K_2$ and $\hat{\theta_K} = \theta_K$ and by inspection of the reduction rules, $\langle \theta, C, K_1, \sigma, \theta_K, n, w \rangle \vdash \langle \hat{\theta}, \hat{C}, K_1, \hat{\sigma}, \theta_K, n+1, \hat{w} \rangle$. Hence, by induction hypothesis, $\langle \theta, C, K_1, \sigma, \theta_K, n, w \rangle \vdash \langle \hat{\theta}, \hat{C}, K_1, \hat{\sigma}, \theta_K, n+1, \hat{w} \rangle \vdash^* \langle \theta'', \downarrow, [], \sigma'', \theta_K'', n+n'', w'' \rangle$ and $\sigma'' \neq \text{\textreferencemark}$, as required. $\qquad\square$

Lemma 28 (Interpolation). *If $C_1 \neq C_1'; C_1''$ and $\langle \theta, C_1; C_2, [], \sigma, \theta_K, n, w \rangle \vdash^* \langle \theta', \downarrow, [], \sigma', \theta_K, n+n', w' \rangle$ and $\sigma' \neq \text{\textreferencemark}$, then $\langle \pi_L(\theta), C_1, [], \sigma, \pi_R(\theta) :: \theta_K, n, w \rangle \vdash^* \langle \theta'', \downarrow, [], \sigma'', \theta_K, n+n'', w'' \rangle$, where $\sigma'' \neq \text{\textreferencemark}$.*

Proof. The first rule applied in the derivation of $\langle \theta, C_1; C_2, [], \sigma, \theta_K, n, w \rangle \vdash^* \langle \theta', \downarrow, [], \sigma', \theta_K, n+n', w' \rangle$ is (seq), which gives $\langle \theta, C_1; C_2, [], \sigma, \theta_K, n, w \rangle \vdash \langle \pi_L(\theta), C_1, [C_2], \sigma, \pi_R(\theta) :: \theta_K, n+1, w \rangle$. Hence, $\langle \pi_L(\theta), C_1, [C_2], \sigma, \pi_R(\theta) :: \theta_K, n+1, w \rangle \vdash^* \langle \theta', \downarrow, [], \sigma', \theta_K, n+n', w' \rangle$. By applying Lemma 27 with $K_1 = []$ and Corollary 6, we get $\langle \pi_L(\theta), C_1, [], \sigma, \pi_R(\theta) :: \theta_K, n+1, w \rangle \vdash^* \langle \theta'', \downarrow, [], \sigma'', \pi_R(\theta) :: \theta_K, n+n'', w'' \rangle$, where $\sigma'' \neq \text{\textreferencemark}$, as required. $\qquad\square$

Finally, we show that if the evaluation of $C_1; C_2$ with entropy θ yields an error, then the evaluation of C_1 under $\pi_L(\theta)$ either terminates successfully or also results in an error (depending on where the error in the evaluation of $C_1; C_2$ occurred)—at any rate, C_1 does not diverge.

Lemma 29. *If $C_1 \neq C_1'; C_2'$ and $\langle \theta, C_1; C_2, [], \sigma, \theta_K, 0, 1 \rangle \vdash^* \langle \theta', C', K, \sigma', \theta_K', n, w \rangle \nvdash$, then either $\langle \pi_L(\theta), C_1, [], \sigma, \pi_R(\theta) :: \theta_K, 0, 1 \rangle \vdash^* \langle \theta'', \downarrow, [], \sigma'', \theta_K, n', w' \rangle$ or $\langle \pi_L(\theta), C_1, [], \sigma, \pi_R(\theta) :: \theta_K, 0, 1 \rangle \vdash^* \langle \theta'', C_1'', K'', \sigma'', \theta_K, n', w' \rangle \nvdash$.*

Proof. The statement in the lemma is equivalent to saying that it is *not* the case that for all k, $\langle \pi_L(\theta), C_1, [], \sigma, \pi_R(\theta) :: \theta_K, 0, 1 \rangle \vdash^* \langle \theta'', C_1'', K'', \sigma'', \pi_R(\theta) :: \theta_K, k, w' \rangle$ with $(C_1'', K'') \neq (\downarrow, [])$. Suppose for contradiction that the negation of this statement holds. By (seq), we have $\langle \theta, C_1; C_2, [], \sigma, \theta_K, 0, 1 \rangle \vdash \langle \pi_L(\theta), C_1, [C_2], \sigma, \pi_R(\theta) :: \theta_K, 1, 1 \rangle$, so $\langle \pi_L(\theta), C_1, [C_2], \sigma, \pi_R(\theta) :: \theta_K, 1, 1 \rangle \vdash^* \langle \theta', C', K, \sigma', \theta_K', n, w \rangle$.

Take $k = n - 1$. Then we have $\langle \pi_L(\theta), C_1, [], \sigma, \pi_R(\theta) :: \theta_K, 0, 1 \rangle \vdash^* \langle \theta'', C_1'', K'', \sigma'', \pi_R(\theta) :: \theta_K, n-1, w' \rangle \vdash \langle \hat{\theta}, \hat{C_1}, \hat{K}, \hat{\sigma}, \hat{\theta_K}, n, \hat{w} \rangle$, where $\sigma'' \neq \text{\textreferencemark}$ (otherwise the middle configuration would not reduce) and $(C_1'', K'') \neq (\downarrow, [])$. By Corollary 4, we have $\langle \pi_L(\theta), C_1, [C_2], \sigma, \pi_R(\theta) :: \theta_K, 1, 1 \rangle \vdash^* \langle \theta'', C_1'', K'' @ [C_2],$

$\sigma'', \pi_R(\theta) :: \theta_K, n, w'\rangle$. Hence, $\langle \theta, C_1; C_2, [], \sigma, \theta_K, 0, 1 \rangle \vdash^* \langle \theta'', C_1'', K''@[C_2], \sigma'',$
$\pi_R(\theta) :: \theta_K, n, w' \rangle$ and $\langle \theta'', C_1'', K''@[C_2], \sigma'', \pi_R(\theta) :: \theta_K, n, w' \rangle = \langle \theta', C', K, \sigma',$
$\theta_K', n, w \rangle$, since reduction is deterministic. By Lemma 18, this implies that $\langle \theta',$
$C', K, \sigma', \theta_K', n, w \rangle$ reduces, contradicting the assumption. □

Corollary 7. *If* $C_1 \neq C_1'; C_2'$ *and* $\langle \theta, C_1; C_2, [], \sigma, \theta_K, 0, 1 \rangle \vdash^* \langle \theta', C', K, \sigma', \theta_K',$
$n, w \rangle \not\vdash$, *then* $\mathbf{O}_{C_1}^\sigma(\pi_L(\theta)) \neq \uparrow$.

D.2 Properties of the Semantic Functions

Compositionality of Sequencing. A desirable and useful property of the
semantic functions is compositionality with respect to sequencing, i.e., the ability
to define $\mathbf{O}_{C_1;C_2}^\sigma$ in terms of $\mathbf{O}_{C_1}^{\sigma_1}$ and $\mathbf{O}_{C_2}^{\sigma_2}$ for some states σ_1 and σ_2. Similarly for
$\mathbf{SC}_{C_1;C_2}^\sigma$. We can easily express the semantics of $C_1; C_2$ in terms of the semantics
of C_1 and C_2 if C_1 is not a sequence of statements. (Recall the explanation of
the rule (seq).)

Proposition 1 (Simple sequencing for final states). *If* $C_1 \neq C_1'; C_2'$, *then:*

$$\mathbf{O}_{C_1;C_2}^\sigma(\theta) = \mathbf{O}_{C_2}^\tau(\pi_R(\theta)) \quad and \quad \mathbf{SC}_{C_1;C_2}^\sigma(\theta) = \mathbf{SC}_{C_1}^\sigma(\pi_L(\theta)) \cdot \mathbf{SC}_{C_2}^\tau(\pi_R(\theta))$$

where τ *stands for the state* $\mathbf{O}_{C_1}^\sigma(\pi_L(\theta))$.

Below, we prove Proposition 1. To simplify presentation, we split it into two
separate lemmas, one concerning final states and one concerning scores.

Lemma 30 (Simple sequencing for final states). *If* $C_1 \neq C_1'; C_2'$, *then*
$\mathbf{O}_{C_1;C_2}^\sigma(\theta) = \mathbf{O}_{C_2}^{\mathbf{O}_{C_1}^\sigma(\pi_L(\theta))}(\pi_R(\theta))$

Proof. If $\sigma = \uparrow$, then $LHS = RHS = \uparrow$ directly by definition.

If $\sigma = \frac{1}{2}$, the result also follows trivially, so let us suppose $\sigma \neq \frac{1}{2}$ and $\sigma \neq \uparrow$.
We need to consider several cases:

- If $\mathbf{O}_{C_1}^\sigma(\pi_L(\theta)) = \frac{1}{2}$, then $\langle \pi_L(\theta), C_1, [], \sigma, \pi_R(\theta) :: \theta_K, 0, 1 \rangle \vdash^* \langle \theta', C_1', K, \tau,$
  $\theta_K', n, w \rangle \not\vdash$. By (seq), we have $\langle \theta, C_1; C_2, [], \sigma, \theta_K, 0, 1 \rangle \vdash \langle \pi_L(\theta), C_1, [C_2], \sigma,$
  $\pi_R(\theta) :: \theta_K, 1, 1 \rangle$.
  If $\tau \neq \frac{1}{2}$, then by Lemmas 20 and 17, $\langle \pi_L(\theta), C_1, [C_2], \sigma, \pi_R(\theta) :: \theta_K, 1, 1 \rangle \vdash^*$
  $\langle \theta', C_1', K@[C_2], \tau, \theta_K', n + 1, w \rangle \not\vdash$. Moreover, $\langle \theta', C_1', K, \tau, \theta_K', n, w \rangle \not\vdash$ implies
  $C_1' \neq \downarrow$ (because otherwise the configuration would reduce by (final) or (pop)),
  so by inspection, $\langle \theta', C_1', K@[C_2], \tau, \theta_K', n + 1, w \rangle \not\vdash$. Thus, $\mathbf{O}_{C_1;C_2}^\sigma(\theta) = \frac{1}{2}$.
  If $\tau = \frac{1}{2}$, then $C_1' = \downarrow$, $K = []$ and by Lemmas 22 and 17 we have $\langle \pi_L(\theta), C_1,$
  $[C_2], \sigma, \pi_R(\theta) :: \theta_K, 1, 1 \rangle \vdash^* \langle \theta', \downarrow, [], \frac{1}{2}, \theta_K', n + 1, w \rangle \not\vdash$. Hence, $\mathbf{O}_{C_1;C_2}^\sigma(\theta) = \frac{1}{2}$.
- If $\mathbf{O}_{C_1}^\sigma(\pi_L(\theta)) = \uparrow$, then $RHS = \uparrow$. Moreover, we have neither $\langle \pi_L(\theta), C_1, [],$
  $\sigma, \pi_R(\theta) :: \theta_K, 0, 1 \rangle \vdash^* \langle \theta', \downarrow, [], \tau, \theta_K, n, w \rangle$ nor $\langle \pi_L(\theta), C_1, [], \sigma, \pi_R(\theta) :: \theta_K, 0,$
  $1 \rangle \vdash^* \langle \theta', C', K, \tau, \theta_K', n, w \rangle \not\vdash$.
  Now, suppose for contradiction that $LHS \neq \uparrow$. Then we have either $\langle \theta, C_1; C_2,$
  $[], \sigma, \theta_K, 0, 1 \rangle \vdash^* \langle \theta', \downarrow, [], \tau, \theta_K, n, w \rangle$ (with $\tau \neq \frac{1}{2}$) or $\langle \theta, C_1; C_2, [], \sigma, \theta_K, 0,$
  $1 \rangle \vdash^* \langle \theta', C', K, \tau, \theta_K', n, w \rangle \not\vdash$.

First, suppose that $\langle\theta, C_1; C_2, [], \sigma, \theta_K, 0, 1\rangle \vdash^* \langle\theta', \downarrow, [], \tau, \theta_K, n, w\rangle$, where $\tau \neq \not{\iota}$. By Lemma 28, this implies that $\langle\pi_L(\theta), C_1, [], \sigma, \pi_R(\theta) :: \theta_K, 0, 1\rangle \vdash^* \langle\theta'',$ $\downarrow, [], \tau', \pi_R(\theta) :: \theta_K, n', w'\rangle$ and so $\mathbf{O}^\sigma_{C_1}(\pi_L(\theta)) = \tau' \neq\uparrow$, contradicting the assumption.

If $\langle\theta, C_1; C_2, [], \sigma, \theta_K, 0, 1\rangle \vdash^* \langle\theta', C', K, \tau, \theta'_K, n, w\rangle \nvdash$, then by Corollary 7, we get a contradiction.

- If $\mathbf{O}^\sigma_{C_1}(\pi_L(\theta)) \notin \{\not{\iota}, \uparrow\}$, but $\mathbf{O}^{\mathbf{O}^\sigma_{C_1}(\pi_L(\theta))}_{C_2}(\pi_R(\theta)) = \not{\iota}$, we have $\langle\pi_L(\theta), C_1,$ $[], \sigma, \pi_R(\theta) :: \theta_K, 0, 1\rangle \vdash^*_{\min} \langle\theta', \downarrow, [], \tau', \pi_R(\theta) :: \theta_K, n, w\rangle$ for some $\tau' \neq \not{\iota}$, where $\mathbf{O}^\sigma_{C_1}(\pi_L(\theta)) = \tau'$, and $\langle\pi_R(\theta), C_2, [], \tau', \theta_K, 0, 1\rangle \vdash^* \langle\theta'', C'', K', \tau, \theta'_K,$ $n', w'\rangle \nvdash$. By Lemma 24, $\langle\theta, C_1; C_2, [], \sigma, \theta_K, 0, 1\rangle \vdash^* \langle\pi_R(\theta), C_2, [], \tau', \theta_K, n+2,$ $w\rangle$. By Lemma 17, $\langle\pi_R(\theta), C_2, [], \tau', \theta_K, n+2, w\rangle \vdash^* \langle\theta'', C'', K', \tau, \theta'_K, n+2+$ $n', ww'\rangle$, where the last configuration clearly does not reduce, as changing the last two components cannot make any rule apply. Hence, $\mathbf{O}^\sigma_{C_1; C_2}(\theta) = \not{\iota}$, as required.

- If $\mathbf{O}^\sigma_{C_1}(\pi_L(\theta)) \notin \{\not{\iota}, \uparrow\}$, but $\mathbf{O}^{\mathbf{O}^\sigma_{C_1}(\pi_L(\theta))}_{C_2}(\pi_R(\theta)) =\uparrow$, we have again $\langle\pi_L(\theta),$ $C_1, [], \sigma, \pi_R(\theta) :: \theta_K, 0, 1\rangle \vdash^*_{\min} \langle\theta', \downarrow, [], \tau', \pi_R(\theta) :: \theta_K, n, w\rangle$ for some $\tau' \neq \not{\iota}$. Again, by Lemma 24, we have $\langle\theta, C_1; C_2, [], \sigma, \theta_K, 0, 1\rangle \vdash^* \langle\pi_R(\theta), C_2, [], \tau',$ $\theta_K, n+2, w\rangle$, but we have neither $\langle\pi_R(\theta), C_2, [], \tau', \theta_K, 0, 1\rangle \vdash^* \langle\theta'', \downarrow, [], \tau'',$ $\theta_K, n', w'\rangle$ nor $\langle\pi_R(\theta), C_2, [], \tau', \theta_K, 0, 1\rangle \vdash^* \langle\theta'', C'', K', \tau, \theta'_K, n', w'\rangle \nvdash$.

  Suppose for contradiction that $LHS \neq\uparrow$. Then we have either $\langle\theta, C_1; C_2,$ $[], \sigma, \theta_K, 0, 1\rangle \vdash^* \langle\theta', \downarrow, [], \tau, \theta_K, \hat{n}, \hat{w}\rangle$ (with $\tau \neq \not{\iota}$) or $\langle\theta, C_1; C_2, [], \sigma, \theta_K, 0,$ $1\rangle \vdash^* \langle\theta', C', K, \tau, \theta'_K, \hat{n}, \hat{w}\rangle \nvdash$.

  In the former case, the determinicity of reduction implies $\langle\pi_R(\theta), C_2, [], \tau',$ $\theta_K, n+2, w\rangle \vdash^* \langle\theta', \downarrow, [], \tau, \theta_K, \hat{n}, \hat{w}\rangle$, so by Lemma 17, $\langle\pi_R(\theta), C_2, [], \tau', \theta_K, 0,$ $1\rangle \vdash^* \langle\theta', \downarrow, [], \tau, \theta_K, \hat{n}-n-2, \hat{w}/w\rangle$, which contradicts the assumption. Similarly, in the latter case, $\langle\pi_R(\theta), C_2, [], \tau', \theta_K, n+2, w\rangle \vdash^* \langle\theta', C', K, \tau, \theta'_K,$ $\hat{n}, \hat{w}\rangle \nvdash$, which violates the assumption.

  Hence, $\mathbf{O}^\sigma_{C_1; C_2}(\theta) =\uparrow$.

- Finally, suppose that $\mathbf{O}^\sigma_{C_1}(\pi_L(\theta)) \notin \{\not{\iota}, \uparrow\}$ and $\mathbf{O}^{\mathbf{O}^\sigma_{C_1}(\pi_L(\theta))}_{C_2}(\pi_R(\theta)) \notin \{\not{\iota}, \uparrow\}$. Then we have again $\langle\pi_L(\theta), C_1, [], \sigma, \pi_R(\theta) :: \theta_K, 0, 1\rangle \vdash^*_{\min} \langle\theta', \downarrow, [], \tau', \pi_R(\theta) ::$ $\theta_K, n', w'\rangle$ for some $\tau' \neq \not{\iota}$ and $\langle\theta, C_1; C_2, [], \sigma, \theta_K, 0, 1\rangle \vdash^* \langle\pi_R(\theta), C_2, [], \tau',$ $\theta_K, n', w'\rangle$ by Lemma 24. Since $\mathbf{O}^\sigma_{C_1}(\pi_L(\theta)) = \tau'$ and $\mathbf{O}^{\mathbf{O}^\sigma_{C_1}(\pi_L(\theta))}_{C_2}(\pi_R(\theta)) = \tau'' \neq \not{\iota}$, we have $\langle\pi_R(\theta), C_2, [], \tau', \theta_K, n', w'\rangle \vdash^* \langle\theta'', \downarrow, [], \tau'', \theta_K, n'', w''\rangle$. This also implies that
  $\langle\theta, C_1; C_2, [], \sigma, \theta_K, 0, 1\rangle \vdash^* \langle\theta'', \downarrow, [], \tau'', \theta_K, n'', w''\rangle$, and so $\mathbf{O}^\sigma_{C_1; C_2}(\theta) = \tau'' = \mathbf{O}^{\mathbf{O}^\sigma_{C_1}(\pi_L(\theta))}_{C_2}(\pi_R(\theta))$.

$\square$

Lemma 31 (Simple sequencing for scores).   *If $C_1 \neq C'_1; C'_2$ then*
$$\mathbf{SC}^\sigma_{C_1; C_2}(\theta) = \mathbf{SC}^\sigma_{C_1}(\pi_L(\theta)) \cdot \mathbf{SC}^{\mathbf{O}^\sigma_{C_1}(\pi_L(\theta))}_{C_2}(\pi_R(\theta))$$

Proof. If $\sigma = \not{\iota}$ or $\sigma =\uparrow$, the property holds trivially, so let us assume $\sigma \notin \{\not{\iota}, \uparrow\}$. We need to consider three cases:

– If $\mathbf{O}^{\sigma}_{C_1}(\pi_L(\theta)) = \sigma' \notin \{\not{z}, \uparrow\}$, then $\langle \pi_L(\theta), C_1, [], \sigma, \pi_R(\theta) :: \theta_K, 0, 1 \rangle \vdash^*_{\min} \langle \theta',$
$\downarrow, [], \sigma', \pi_R(\theta) :: \theta_K, n, w \rangle$ and $\mathbf{SC}^{\sigma}_{C_1}(\pi_L(\theta)) = w$.
By Lemma 24, $\langle \theta, C_1; C_2, [], \sigma, \theta_K, 0, 1 \rangle \vdash^* \langle \pi_R(\theta), C_2, [], \sigma', \theta_K, n + 2, w \rangle$.
Now, fix a $k \geq 0$.

- If $\langle \pi_R(\theta), C_2, [], \sigma', \theta_K, 0, 1 \rangle \quad \vdash^* \quad \langle \theta'', C_2', K, \sigma'', \theta_K', k, w' \rangle$, then
  $\mathbf{SC}^{\mathbf{O}^{\sigma}_{C_1}(\pi_L(\theta))}_{C_2}(\pi_R(\theta), k) = w'$. By Lemma 17, $\langle \pi_R(\theta), C_2, [], \sigma', \theta_K,$
  $n + 2, w \rangle \vdash^* \langle \theta'', C_2', K, \sigma'', \theta_K', n + 2 + k, ww' \rangle$, which implies $\langle \theta,$
  $C_1; C_2, [], \sigma, \theta_K, 0, 1 \rangle \vdash^* \langle \theta'', C_2', K, \sigma'', \theta_K', n + 2 + k, ww' \rangle$, and so
  $\mathbf{SC}^{\sigma}_{C_1; C_2}(\theta, n + 2 + k) = ww' = \mathbf{SC}^{\sigma}_{C_1}(\pi_L(\theta)) \mathbf{SC}^{\mathbf{O}^{\sigma}_{C_1}(\pi_L(\theta))}_{C_2}(\pi_R(\theta), k)$.
- If there is no configuration $\langle \theta'', C_2', K, \sigma'', \theta_K', k, w' \rangle$ such that $\langle \pi_R(\theta), C_2,$
  $[], \sigma', \theta_K, 0, 1 \rangle \vdash^* \langle \theta'', C_2', K, \sigma'', \theta_K', k, w' \rangle$, then $\mathbf{SC}^{\mathbf{O}^{\sigma}_{C_1}(\pi_L(\theta))}_{C_2}(\pi_R(\theta), k) =$
  0. If we had $\langle \theta, C_1; C_2, [], \sigma, \theta_K, 0, 1 \rangle \vdash^* \langle \theta'', C_2', K, \sigma'', \theta_K', n + 2 + k, ww' \rangle$,
  then, by determinacy of reduction, $\langle \pi_R(\theta), C_2, [], \sigma', \theta_K, n + 2, w \rangle \vdash^* \langle \theta'',$
  $C_2', K, \sigma'', \theta_K', n + 2 + k, ww' \rangle$. By Lemma 17 and Lemma 16 (which ensures
  $w > 0$), $\langle \pi_R(\theta), C_2, [], \sigma', \theta_K, 0, 1 \rangle \vdash^* \langle \theta'', C_2', K, \sigma'', \theta_K', k, w' \rangle$, which contradicts the assumption. Hence, there is no configuration $\langle \theta'', C_2', K, \sigma'',$
  $\theta_K', n + 2 + k, ww' \rangle$ such that $\langle \theta, C_1; C_2, [], \sigma, \theta_K, 0, 1 \rangle \vdash^* \langle \theta'', C_2', K, \sigma'',$
  $\theta_K', n + 2 + k, ww' \rangle$, and so $\mathbf{SC}^{\sigma}_{C_1; C_2}(\theta, n + 2 + k) = 0$.

In either case, $\mathbf{SC}^{\sigma}_{C_1; C_2}(\theta, n + 2 + k) = \mathbf{SC}^{\sigma}_{C_1}(\pi_L(\theta)) \cdot \mathbf{SC}^{\mathbf{O}^{\sigma}_{C_1}(\pi_L(\theta))}_{C_2}(\pi_R(\theta), k)$
for all $k \geq 0$. Thus, we have

$$\begin{aligned}
\mathbf{SC}^{\sigma}_{C_1; C_2}(\theta) &= \lim_{n \to \infty} \mathbf{SC}^{\sigma}_{C_1; C_2}(\theta, n) \\
&= \lim_{k \to \infty} \mathbf{SC}^{\sigma}_{C_1; C_2}(\theta, n + 2 + k) \\
&= \lim_{k \to \infty} \mathbf{SC}^{\sigma}_{C_1}(\pi_L(\theta)) \cdot \mathbf{SC}^{\mathbf{O}^{\sigma}_{C_1}(\pi_L(\theta))}_{C_2}(\pi_R(\theta), k) \\
&= \mathbf{SC}^{\sigma}_{C_1}(\pi_L(\theta)) \lim_{k \to \infty} \mathbf{SC}^{\mathbf{O}^{\sigma}_{C_1}(\pi_L(\theta))}_{C_2}(\pi_R(\theta), k) \\
&= \mathbf{SC}^{\sigma}_{C_1}(\pi_L(\theta)) \mathbf{SC}^{\mathbf{O}^{\sigma}_{C_1}(\pi_L(\theta))}_{C_2}(\pi_R(\theta))
\end{aligned}$$

– If $\mathbf{O}^{\sigma}_{C_1}(\pi_L(\theta)) = \not{z}$, then $\mathbf{SC}^{\mathbf{O}^{\sigma}_{C_1}(\pi_L(\theta))}_{C_2}(\pi_R(\theta)) = 0$, so $RHS = 0$. Moreover,
we have $\langle \pi_L(\theta), C_1, [], \sigma, \pi_R(\theta) :: \theta_K, 0, 1 \rangle \vdash^* \langle \theta', C', K, \tau, \theta_K', n, w \rangle \not\vdash$. If $\tau =$
$\not{z}$, then $C' = \not{z}$ and $K = []$ (as the last rule applied must have been (condition-
false)), so by Lemma 23, $\langle \theta, C_1; C_2, [], \sigma, \theta_K, 0, 1 \rangle \vdash^* \langle \theta', \downarrow, [], \not{z}, \theta_K', n + 1, w \rangle$.
Hence, $\mathbf{SC}^{\sigma}_{C_1; C_2}(\theta, n') = 0$ for all $n' > n + 1$, and so $\mathbf{SC}^{\sigma}_{C_1; C_2}(\theta) = 0$.
– If $\mathbf{O}^{\sigma}_{C_1}(\pi_L(\theta)) = \uparrow$, then $RHS = \mathbf{SC}^{\sigma}_{C_1}(\pi_L(\theta))$ and for all k, we have
$\langle \pi_L(\theta), C_1, [], \sigma, \pi_R(\theta) :: \theta_K, 0, 1 \rangle \vdash^* \langle \theta', C_1'', K, \sigma', \pi_R(\theta) :: \theta_K', k, w \rangle$, where
$(C_1'', K) \neq (\downarrow, K)$ and $\sigma' \neq \not{z}$. Fix $k \geq 0$. We have $\mathbf{SC}^{\sigma}_{C_1}(\pi_L(\theta), k) = w$ and by
Lemma 25, $\langle \theta, C_1; C_2, [], \sigma, \theta_K, 0, 1 \rangle \vdash^* \langle \theta', C_1'', K@[C_2], \sigma', \theta_K', k + 1, w \rangle$, which
implies $\mathbf{SC}^{\sigma}_{C_1; C_2}(\theta, k + 1) = w$. Hence, $\mathbf{SC}^{\sigma}_{C_1; C_2}(\theta, k + 1) = \mathbf{SC}^{\sigma}_{C_1}(\pi_L(\theta), k)$.

Thus,

$$\begin{aligned}
\mathbf{SC}^\sigma_{C_1;C_2}(\theta) &= \lim_{n \to \infty} \mathbf{SC}^\sigma_{C_1;C_2}(\theta, n) \\
&= \lim_{k \to \infty} \mathbf{SC}^\sigma_{C_1;C_2}(\theta, k+1) \\
&= \lim_{k \to \infty} \mathbf{SC}^\sigma_{C_1}(\pi_L(\theta), k) \\
&= \mathbf{SC}^\sigma_{C_1}(\pi_L(\theta))
\end{aligned}$$

as required.

□

Restatement of Proposition 1. *If* $C_1 \neq C'_1; C'_2$, *then* $\mathbf{O}^\sigma_{C_1;C_2}(\theta) = \mathbf{O}^{\mathbf{O}^\sigma_{C_1}(\pi_L(\theta))}_{C_2}(\pi_R(\theta))$ *and* $\mathbf{SC}^\sigma_{C_1;C_2}(\theta) = \mathbf{SC}^\sigma_{C_1}(\pi_L(\theta)) \cdot \mathbf{SC}^{\mathbf{O}^\sigma_{C_1}(\pi_L(\theta))}_{C_2}(\pi_R(\theta))$

Proof. This is a combination of Lemma 30 and Lemma 31.   □

Proposition 1 is not applicable when C_1 is not a sequence of statements, as we cannot know what part of the entropy θ will be used in the evaluation of which expression without knowing the length of the statement list in C_1. However, the above result can be generalised using *finite shuffling functions*, as defined by [39].

Definition 30 ([39]).

- *A* path *is a function* $[d_1, \ldots, d_n]: \mathbb{S} \to \mathbb{S}$ *parametrised by a list of directions* $d_1, \ldots, d_n \in \{L, R\}$, *such that* $[d_1, \ldots, d_n](\theta) = (\pi_{d_1} \circ \ldots \circ \pi_{d_n})(\theta)$.
- *A* finite shuffling function *(FSF) is a function* $\phi: \mathbb{S} \to \mathbb{S}$ *such that either* ϕ *is a path or* $\phi(\theta) = \phi_1(\theta) :: \phi_2(\theta)$, *where* ϕ_1 *and* ϕ_2 *are FSFs.*
- *A sequence of paths is* non-duplicating *if no path in the sequence is a suffix of another path.*
- *A FSF* ϕ *is* non-duplicating *if the sequence of all paths appearing in its definition is non-duplicating.*

The following key result shows that entropy rearrangements via FSFs have no effect under integration:

Lemma 32 ([39], **Th. 7.6**). *Any non-duplicating FSF* ϕ *is measure-preserving, i.e., for any measurable[9]* $g: \mathbb{S} \to \overline{\mathbb{R}}_+$:

$$\int g(\phi(\theta)) \, \mu(d\theta) \; = \; \int g(\theta) \, \mu(d\theta).$$

We now have everything in place to define a version of Proposition 1 for an arbitrary split of a sequencing statement:

---

[9] The result in [39] considers g with co-domain $[0, \infty)$ rather than $\overline{\mathbb{R}}_+$. It is however, not difficult to check that their result extends to the latter case.

Proposition 2 (Sequencing for final states). *If $C = C_1; C_2$, there exists a non-duplicating FSF ψ such that:*

$$\mathbf{O}_C^\sigma(\theta) = \mathbf{O}_{C_2}^\tau(\pi_R(\psi(\theta))) \quad and \quad \mathbf{SC}_C^\sigma(\theta) = \mathbf{SC}_{C_1}^\sigma(\pi_L(\psi(\theta))) \cdot \mathbf{SC}_{C_2}^\tau(\pi_R(\psi(\theta)))$$

with τ denoting $\mathbf{O}_{C_1}^\sigma(\pi_L(\psi(\theta)))$.

Proof. By induction on the structure of C.

- Base case: $C_1 \neq C_1'; C_1''$: the equality holds trivially for $\psi = Id$ by Lemma 30.
- Induction step: If C_1 is a sequence of statements, then $C_1 = C_1'; C_1''$ for some C_1' such that $C_1' \neq \hat{C}_1'\hat{C}_1''$.
  We have:

$$\mathbf{O}_{C_1';C_1'';C_2}^\sigma(\theta)_{\text{(by Lemma 30)}} = \mathbf{O}_{C_1'';C_2}^{\mathbf{O}_{C_1'}^\sigma(\pi_L(\theta))}(\pi_R(\theta))$$

$$_{\text{(by induction hypothesis)}} = \mathbf{O}_{C_2}^{\mathbf{O}_{C_1''}^{\mathbf{O}_{C_1'}^\sigma(\pi_L(\theta))}(\pi_L(\psi(\pi_R(\theta))))}(\pi_R(\psi(\pi_R(\theta))))$$

for some non-duplicating FSF ψ.
Thus, if $\theta = \theta_1 :: \theta_2$, then

$$\mathbf{O}_{C_1';C_1'';C_2}^\sigma(\theta_1 :: \theta_2) = \mathbf{O}_{C_2}^{\mathbf{O}_{C_1''}^{\mathbf{O}_{C_1'}^\sigma(\theta_1)}(\pi_L(\psi(\theta_2)))}(\pi_R(\psi(\theta_2)))$$

Now, take $\hat{\psi}$ such that $\hat{\psi}(\theta_1 :: \theta_2) = (\theta_1 :: \pi_L(\psi(\theta_2))) :: \pi_R(\psi(\theta_2))$.
Then

$$\mathbf{O}_{C_2}^{\mathbf{O}_{C_1';C_1''}^\sigma(\pi_L(\hat{\psi}(\theta_1::\theta_2)))}(\pi_R(\hat{\psi}(\theta_1 :: \theta_2))) = \mathbf{O}_{C_2}^{\mathbf{O}_{C_1';C_1''}^\sigma(\theta_1::\pi_L(\psi(\theta_2)))}(\pi_R(\psi(\theta_2)))$$

$$_{\text{(by Lemma 30)}} = \mathbf{O}_{C_2}^{\mathbf{O}_{C_1''}^{\mathbf{O}_{C_1'}^\sigma(\theta_1)}\pi_L(\psi(\theta_2))}(\pi_R(\psi(\theta_2)))$$

$$= \mathbf{O}_{C_1';C_1'';C_2}^\sigma(\theta_1 :: \theta_2)$$

as required.
For $\mathbf{SC}$, we have:

$$\mathbf{SC}_{C_1';C_1'';C_2}^\sigma(\theta)_{\text{(by Lemma 31)}} = \mathbf{SC}_{C_1'}(\pi_L(\theta))\mathbf{SC}_{C_1'';C_2}^{\mathbf{O}_{C_1'}^\sigma(\pi_L(\theta))}(\pi_R(\theta))$$

$$_{\text{(by induction hypothesis)}} = \mathbf{SC}_{C_1'}(\pi_L(\theta))\mathbf{SC}_{C_1''}^{\mathbf{O}_{C_1'}^\sigma(\pi_L(\theta))}(\pi_L(\psi(\pi_R(\theta))))$$

$$\mathbf{SC}_{C_2}^{\mathbf{O}_{C_1''}^{\mathbf{O}_{C_1'}^\sigma(\pi_L(\theta))}(\pi_L(\psi(\pi_R(\theta))))}(\pi_R(\psi(\pi_R(\theta))))$$

for the same ψ. Thus, for $\hat{\psi}$ defined above, we have:

$$\mathbf{SC}_{C_1';C_1''}(\pi_L(\hat{\psi}(\theta_1 :: \theta_2)))\mathbf{SC}_{C_2}^{\mathbf{O}_{C_1';C_1''}^{\sigma}(\pi_L(\hat{\psi}(\theta_1::\theta_2)))}(\pi_R(\hat{\psi}(\theta_1 :: \theta_2)))$$

$$= \mathbf{SC}_{C_1';C_1''}(\theta_1 :: \pi_L(\psi(\theta_2)))\mathbf{SC}_{C_2}^{\mathbf{O}_{C_1';C_1''}^{\sigma}(\theta_1::\pi_L(\psi(\theta_2)))}\pi_R(\psi(\theta_2))$$

$$(*) = \mathbf{SC}_{C_1'}(\theta_1)\mathbf{SC}_{C_1''}^{\mathbf{O}_{C_1'}^{\sigma}(\theta_1)}(\pi_L(\psi(\theta_2)))\mathbf{SC}_{C_2}^{\mathbf{O}_{C_1''}^{\sigma}(\pi_L(\psi(\theta_2)))}(\pi_R(\psi(\theta_2)))$$

$$= \mathbf{SC}_{C_1';C_1'';C_2}^{\sigma}(\theta_1 :: \theta_2)$$

as required, where the equality (*) follows from Lemmas 30 and 31.

Now we only need to show that $\hat{\psi}$ is a non-duplicating FSF.

First, let us show that $\hat{\psi}$ is indeed a FSF. To this end, we need to show that if ψ is a FSF, then $\psi'(\theta) = \psi(\pi_R(\theta))$ is also a FSF. We prove this by induction on the structure of ψ:

- Base case: if ψ is a path $[d_1, \ldots, d_n]$, then $\psi \circ \pi_R$ is the path $[d_1, \ldots, d_n, R]$, so it is a FSF.
- Induction step: Suppose that $\psi(\theta) = \psi_1(\theta) :: \psi_2(\theta)$ and that $\psi_1 \circ \pi_R$ and $\psi_2 \circ \pi_R$ are FSFs. Then we have $\psi(\pi_R(\theta)) = \psi_1(\pi_R(\theta)) :: \psi_2(\pi_R(\theta)) = (\psi_1 \circ \pi_R)(\theta) :: (\psi_2 \circ \pi_R)(\theta)$, so $\psi \circ \pi_R$ is a FSF by definition.

Now, we show that $\psi''(\theta) = \pi_L(\psi(\pi_R(\theta))) = \pi_L(\psi'(\theta))$ is a FSF: if ψ' is a path $[d_1, \ldots, d_n]$, then ψ'' is a path $[L, d_1, \ldots, d_n]$, and if $\psi' = \psi_1' :: \psi_2'$, then $\pi_L(\psi'(\theta)) = \pi_L(\psi_1'(\theta) :: \psi_2'(\theta)) = \psi_1'(\theta)$. Similarly, we can show that $\pi_R(\psi(\pi_R(\theta)))$ is a FSF. Hence, $\hat{\psi}$ is a FSF by definition.

Finally, we need to show that $\hat{\psi}$ is non-duplicating.

We can show by a simple induction that for any ψ, the set of paths $\mathcal{P}_{\psi \circ \pi_R}$ in $\psi \circ \pi_R$ is $\{pR \mid p \in \mathcal{P}_\psi\}$, where $\mathcal{P}_\psi$ is the set of paths in ψ and juxtaposition denotes concatenation.

If ψ is a path p, then $\pi_L \circ \psi \circ \pi_R$ and $\pi_R \circ \psi \circ \pi_R$ are paths LpR and RpR. Hence, the set of paths in $\hat{\psi}$ is $\{[L], LpR, RpR\}$. It is instantly clear that no path is a suffix of another, so $\hat{\psi}$ is non-duplicating.

If $\psi(\theta) = \psi_1(\theta) :: \psi_2(\theta)$, then $(\pi_L \circ \psi \circ \pi_R)(\theta) = \pi_L(\psi_1(\pi_R(\theta)) :: \psi_2(\pi_R(\theta))) = \psi_1(\pi_R(\theta))$, so the set of paths in $\pi_L \circ \psi \circ \pi_R$ is $\{pR \mid p \in \mathcal{P}_{\psi_1}\}$, where $\mathcal{P}_{\psi_1}$ is the set of paths in ψ_1. Similarly, the set of paths in $\pi_R \circ \psi \circ \pi_R$ is $\{pR \mid p \in \mathcal{P}_{\psi_2}\}$, where $\mathcal{P}_{\psi_2}$ is the set of paths in ψ_2. Since $\mathcal{P}_\psi = \mathcal{P}_{\psi_1} \cup \mathcal{P}_{\psi_2}$, the set of paths in the entire definition of $\hat{\psi}$ is $\{[L]\} \cup \{pR \mid p \in \mathcal{P}_\psi\}$. It is clear that $[L]$ is not a suffix of any path of the form pR (as all such paths end with R). Moreover, if there were paths $p_1, p_2 \in \mathcal{P}_\psi$ such that p_1R was a suffix of p_2R, then p_1 would be a suffix of p_2, which would contradict the assumption.

Hence, $\hat{\psi}$ is non-duplicating, which ends the proof.

□

D.3 Approximating While-Loops

To simplify reasoning about while-loops, it is useful—and common in program semantics—to consider finite approximations of loops in which the maximal number of iterations is bounded. To that end, we define the n-th unfolding of a guarded loop inductively as follows:

$$\texttt{while}^0(\phi)\{C\} = \texttt{diverge}$$
$$\texttt{while}^{n+1}(\phi)\{C\} = \texttt{if}(\phi)\{C; \texttt{while}^n(\phi)\{C\}\}.$$

In the limit, bounded $\texttt{while}$-loops behave as standard $\texttt{while}$-loops. We use this result to define the evaluation of measurable function f on successful termination states of a $\texttt{while}$-loop, scaled by its score as a limit of approximations. As we are interested in f on proper states, we use $\hat{f}$ rather than f.

Proposition 3. *Let loop* $C = \texttt{while}(\phi)\{C'\}$ *and* $C^n = \texttt{while}^n(\phi)\{C'\}$ *its n-th approximation. Then:*

$$\hat{f}(\mathbf{O}^\sigma_C(\theta)) \cdot \mathbf{SC}^\sigma_C(\theta) = \sup_n \hat{f}(\mathbf{O}^\sigma_{C^n}(\theta)) \cdot \mathbf{SC}^\sigma_{C^n}(\theta).$$

The following monotonicity property is relevant later when proving the relationship between the operational semantics of *PL* and its denotational semantics. As before let $C^n = \texttt{while}^n(\phi)\{C'\}$.

Proposition 4. *If* $n \geq k$ *and* $\hat{f}(\mathcal{\char"0024}) = \hat{f}(\uparrow) = 0$, *then* $\hat{f}(\mathbf{O}^\sigma_{C^n}(\theta)) \cdot \mathbf{SC}^\sigma_{C^n}(\theta) \geq \hat{f}(\mathbf{O}^\sigma_{C^k}(\theta)) \cdot \mathbf{SC}^\sigma_{C^k}(\theta).$

Similarly, we want to show that the sequence $\hat{f}(\mathbf{O}^\sigma_{C^n}(\theta)) \cdot \mathbf{SC}^\sigma_{C^n}(\theta)$ approximates $\hat{f}(\mathbf{O}^\sigma_C(\theta)) \cdot \mathbf{SC}^\sigma_C(\theta)$. This result allows us to express the anticipated value of the function $\hat{f}$ for a given fixed entropy as a limit of approximations, and by integrating both sides with respect to the measure on entropies we get that the expected value of $\hat{f}$ can also be expressed as a limit of approximations. We will use this result in the proof of Theorem 2. Recall that $\check{f}(\tau) = 1$ for $\tau = \uparrow$.

Proposition 5. *Let loop* $C = \texttt{while}(\phi)\{C'\}$ *and* $C^n = \texttt{while}(\phi)\{C'\}$ *its n-th approximation. Take a function* $f \leq 1$. *Then*

$$\check{f}(\mathbf{O}^\sigma_C(\theta)) \cdot \mathbf{SC}^\sigma_C(\theta) = \inf_n \check{f}(\mathbf{O}^\sigma_{C^n}(\theta)) \cdot \mathbf{SC}^\sigma_{C^n}(\theta).$$

Proposition 6. *If* $n \geq k$ *and* $f \leq 1$, *then*

$$\check{f}(\mathbf{O}^\sigma_{C^n}(\theta)) \cdot \mathbf{SC}^\sigma_{C^n}(\theta) \leq \check{f}(\mathbf{O}^\sigma_{C^k}(\theta)) \cdot \mathbf{SC}^\sigma_{C^k}(\theta).$$

The rest of this section is the proof of Propositions 3, 4, 5 and 6, which will be needed to prove the case of $\texttt{while}$-loops in Theorem 1 and Theorem 2. The first key fact that we want to show is that for non-diverging executions, a bounded $\texttt{while}$-loop of the form $\texttt{while}^n(\phi)\{C\}$ behaves just like $\texttt{while}(\phi)\{C\}$ for a sufficiently large n. We formalise and prove it using two auxiliary relations on configurations.

Replacing $\texttt{while}(\phi)\{C\}$ **with** $\texttt{while}^n(\phi)\{C\}$. We first prove that in all non-diverging configurations, if the expression is of the form $\texttt{while}(\phi)\{C\}$, we can replace it with $\texttt{while}^n(\phi)\{C\}$ for a large enough n, without changing the final configuration reached after reduction is completed. To this end, we first define an indexed relation $(\sim^n)$ on configurations. We begin with auxiliary relations $C \sim^n C'$ and $K \sim^n K'$, defined inductively as follows:

$$\overline{C \sim^0 C'}$$

For $n > 0$:

$$\overline{C \sim^n C}$$

$$\overline{\downarrow \sim^n \downarrow}$$

$$\frac{k \geq n}{\texttt{while}(\phi)\ \{C\} \sim^n \texttt{while}^k(\phi)\ \{C\}}$$

$$\frac{k \geq n}{\texttt{while}^k(\phi)\ \{C\} \sim^n \texttt{while}(\phi)\ \{C\}}$$

$$\frac{k \geq n \quad l \geq n}{\texttt{while}^k(\phi)\ \{C\} \sim^n \texttt{while}^l(\phi)\ \{C\}}$$

$$\frac{C_2 \sim^n C_2'}{C_1; C_2 \sim^n C_1; C_2'}$$

$$\frac{\forall i \in 1..n \quad C_i \sim^n C_i'}{[C_1, \ldots, C_n] \sim^n [C_1', \ldots, C_n']}$$

We then naturally extend the definition to configurations:

$$\overline{\langle \theta, C, K, \sigma, \theta_K, m, w \rangle \sim^0 \langle \theta', C', K', \sigma', \theta_K', m', w' \rangle}$$

For $n > 0$:
$$\frac{C \sim^n C' \quad K \sim^n K'}{\langle \theta, C, K, \sigma, \theta_K, m, w \rangle \sim^n \langle \theta, C', K', \sigma, \theta_K, m, w \rangle}$$

We can immediately check that if two configurations are related by $(\sim^n)$ for some $n > 0$, then if we perform one step of reductions on both of them, the resulting configurations are guaranteed to be related at least by $(\sim^{n-1})$.

Lemma 33. $\sim^n$ *is a stratified bisimulation—that is,* $\langle \theta, C, K, \sigma, \theta_K, m, w \rangle \sim^0$ $\langle \theta', C', K', \sigma', \theta_K', m', w' \rangle$ *and for* $n > 0$:

- *if* $\langle \theta, C, K, \sigma, \theta_K, m, w \rangle \sim^n \langle \theta, C', K', \sigma, \theta_K, m, w \rangle$ *and* $\langle \theta, C, K, \sigma, \theta_K, m, w \rangle \vdash \langle \theta'', C'', K'', \sigma'', \theta_K'', m+1, w'' \rangle$, *then* $\langle \theta, C', K', \sigma, \theta_K, m, w \rangle \vdash \langle \theta'', C''', K''', \sigma'', \theta_K'', m+1, w'' \rangle$ *and* $\langle \theta'', C'', K'', \sigma'', \theta_K'', m+1, w'' \rangle \sim^{n-1} \langle \theta'', C''', K''', \sigma'', \theta_K'', m+1, w'' \rangle$
- *if* $\langle \theta, C, K, \sigma, \theta_K, m, w \rangle \sim^n \langle \theta, C', K', \sigma, \theta_K, m, w \rangle$ *and* $\langle \theta, C', K', \sigma, \theta_K, m, w \rangle \vdash \langle \theta'', C''', K''', \sigma'', \theta_K'', m+1, w'' \rangle$, *then* $\langle \theta, C, K, \sigma, \theta_K, m, w \rangle \vdash \langle \theta'', C'', K'', \sigma'', \theta_K'', m+1, w'' \rangle$ *and* $\langle \theta'', C'', K'', \sigma'', \theta_K'', m+1, w'' \rangle \sim^{n-1} \langle \theta'', C''', K''', \sigma'', \theta_K'', m+1, w'' \rangle$

Proof. By inspection. □

This result naturally generalises to multi-step reduction.

Corollary 8. *If* $\langle \theta, C, K, \sigma, \theta_K, m, w \rangle \sim^n \langle \theta, C', K', \sigma, \theta_K, m, w \rangle$ *and* $\langle \theta, C, K,$ $\sigma, \theta_K, m, w \rangle \vdash^* \langle \theta'', C'', K'', \sigma'', \theta_K'', m + n', w'' \rangle$ *and* $n' < n$ *then* $\langle \theta, C', K', \sigma,$ $\theta_K, m, w \rangle \vdash^* \langle \theta'', C''', K''', \sigma'', \theta_K'', m + n', w'' \rangle$ *and* $\langle \theta'', C'', K'', \sigma'', \theta_K'', m + n',$ $w'' \rangle \sim^{n-n'} \langle \theta'', C''', K''', \sigma'', \theta_K'', m + n', w'' \rangle$ *(and vice versa).*

This leads us to the desired result for terminating runs.

Lemma 34. *If* $\langle \theta, \mathtt{while}(\phi)\{C\}, [], \sigma, \theta_K, n, w \rangle \vdash^* \langle \theta', \downarrow, [], \sigma', \theta_K, n + n', w' \rangle$, *then there exists* k *such that* $\langle \theta, \mathtt{while}^k(\phi)\{C\}, [], \sigma, \theta_K, n, w \rangle \vdash^* \langle \theta', \downarrow, [], \sigma', \theta_K,$ $n + n', w' \rangle$.

Proof. Take $k = n' + 1$. We clearly have $\mathtt{while}(\phi)\{C\} \sim^{n'+1} \mathtt{while}^{n'+1}(\phi)\{C\}$, and so $\langle \theta, \mathtt{while}(\phi)\{C\}, [], \sigma, \theta_K, n, w \rangle \sim^{n'+1} \langle \theta, \mathtt{while}^{n'+1}(\phi)\{C\}, [], \sigma, \theta_K, n,$ $w \rangle$. By Corollary 8, $\langle \theta, \mathtt{while}^{n'+1}(\phi)\{C\}, [], \sigma, \theta_K, n, w \rangle \vdash^* \langle \theta', C', K', \sigma, \theta_K,$ $n + n', w' \rangle$, where $\downarrow \sim^1 C'$ and $[] \sim^1 K'$, which implies $C' = \downarrow$ and $K' = []$. Thus, the statement always holds for $k = n' + 1$. □

This result leads to the following statement about the $\mathbf{O}_C^\sigma$ and $\mathbf{SC}_C^\sigma$ functions:

Lemma 35. *For each* ϕ, C, σ, θ, *such that* $\mathbf{O}_{\mathtt{while}(\phi)\{C\}}^\sigma(\theta) \in \Omega_\sigma$ *there is a* k *such that* $\mathbf{O}_{\mathtt{while}(\phi)\{C\}}^\sigma(\theta) = \mathbf{O}_{\mathtt{while}^k(\phi)\{C\}}^\sigma(\theta)$ *and* $\mathbf{SC}_{\mathtt{while}(\phi)\{C\}}^\sigma(\theta) = \mathbf{SC}_{\mathtt{while}^k(\phi)\{C\}}^\sigma(\theta)$

Proof. If $\mathbf{O}_{\mathtt{while}(\phi)\{C\}}^\sigma(\theta) \in \Omega_\sigma$, then by definition of $\mathbf{O}$, $\langle \theta, \mathtt{while}(\phi)\{C\}, [], \sigma,$ $\theta_K, 0, 1 \rangle \vdash^* \langle \theta', \downarrow, [], \sigma', \theta_K', n, w \rangle$, where $\sigma' \neq \frac{1}{2}$. This implies $\mathbf{O}_{\mathtt{while}(\phi)\{C\}}^\sigma(\theta) = \sigma'$ and $\mathbf{SC}_{\mathtt{while}(\phi)\{C\}}^\sigma(\theta) = w$. By Lemma 34, there is a k such that $\langle \theta,$ $\mathtt{while}^k(\phi)\{C\}, [], \sigma, \theta_K, 0, 1 \rangle \vdash^* \langle \theta', \downarrow, [], \sigma', \theta_K', n, w \rangle$. Thus, $\mathbf{O}_{\mathtt{while}^k(\phi)\{C\}}^\sigma(\theta) = \sigma'$ and $\mathbf{SC}_{\mathtt{while}^k(\phi)\{C\}}^\sigma(\theta) = w$. □

We can also show that if the evaluation of $\mathtt{while}(\phi)\{C\}$ gets stuck, so does the evaluation of $\mathtt{while}^k(\phi)\{C\}$ for large enough k.

Lemma 36. *If* $\langle \theta, \mathtt{while}(\phi)\{C\}, [], \sigma, \theta_K, n, w \rangle \vdash^* \langle \theta', C', K, \sigma', \theta_K', n + n',$ $w' \rangle \nvdash$, *then there exists* k *such that* $\langle \theta, \mathtt{while}^k(\phi)\{C\}, [], \sigma, \theta_K, n, w \rangle \vdash^* \langle \theta', C'',$ $K', \sigma', \theta_K', n + n', w' \rangle \nvdash$.

Proof. Again, take $k = n' + 1$. We have $\mathtt{while}(\phi)\{C\} \sim^{n'+1} \mathtt{while}^{n'+1}(\phi)\{C\}$, and so $\langle \theta, \mathtt{while}(\phi)\{C\}, [], \sigma, \theta_K, n, w \rangle \sim^{n'+1} \langle \theta, \mathtt{while}^{n'+1}(\phi)\{C\}, [], \sigma, \theta_K, n,$ $w \rangle$. By Corollary 8, $\langle \theta, \mathtt{while}^{n'+1}(\phi)\{C\}, [], \sigma, \theta_K, n, w \rangle \vdash^* \langle \theta', C'', K', \sigma', \theta_K,$ $n + n', w' \rangle$, where $C' \sim^1 C''$ and $K \sim^1 K'$. By case analysis on the derivation of $C' \sim^1 C''$, and using the fact that K and K' must have the same length, we conclude that $\langle \theta', C', K, \sigma', \theta_K', n + n', w' \rangle$ reduces if and only if $\langle \theta', C'', K', \sigma',$ $\theta_K', n + n', w' \rangle$ reduces. □

Replacing $\mathtt{while}^n(\phi)\{C\}$ with $\mathtt{while}(\phi)\{C\}$. We now prove the converse to the above result—that if $\mathtt{while}^n(\phi)\{C\}$ evaluates with some entropy θ, the unbounded loop $\mathtt{while}(\phi)\{C\}$ evaluates to the same configuration. We begin with another relation $\trianglelefteq$ on configurations, which effectively states that for two configurations κ_1 and κ_2, if $\kappa_1 \trianglelefteq \kappa_2$ and κ_1 evaluates, then κ_2 is guaranteed to evaluate to the same final configuration. This relation is defined inductively as follows:

$$C \trianglelefteq C$$

$$\downarrow \trianglelefteq \downarrow$$

$$\frac{\texttt{while}^k(\phi)\ \{C\} \trianglelefteq \texttt{while}(\phi)\ \{C'\} \qquad k \leq l}{\texttt{while}^k(\phi)\ \{C\} \trianglelefteq \texttt{while}^l(\phi)\ \{C'\}}$$

$$\texttt{diverge} \trianglelefteq C$$

$$\frac{C_2 \trianglelefteq C_2'}{C_1; C_2 \trianglelefteq C_1; C_2'}$$

$$\frac{\forall i \in 1..n \quad C_i \trianglelefteq C_i'}{[C_1, \ldots, C_n] \trianglelefteq [C_1, \ldots, C_n]}$$

$$\frac{C \trianglelefteq C' \quad K \trianglelefteq K'}{\langle \theta, C, K, \sigma, \theta_K, m, w \rangle \trianglelefteq \langle \theta, C', K', \sigma, \theta_K, m, w \rangle}$$

Lemma 37. $\trianglelefteq$ *is a simulation—that is, if* $\langle \theta, C, K, \sigma, \theta_K, m, w \rangle \trianglelefteq \langle \theta, C', K', \sigma,$ $\theta_K, m, w \rangle$ *and* $\langle \theta, C, K, \sigma, \theta_K, m, w \rangle \vdash \langle \theta'', C'', K'', \sigma'', \theta_K'', m+1, w'' \rangle$ *and* $C \neq$ $\texttt{diverge}$, *then* $\langle \theta, C', K', \sigma, \theta_K, m, w \rangle \vdash \langle \theta'', C''', K''', \sigma'', \theta_K'', m+1, w'' \rangle$ *and* $\langle \theta'',$ $C'', K'', \sigma'', \theta_K'', m+1, w'' \rangle \trianglelefteq \langle \theta'', C''', K''', \sigma'', \theta_K'', m+1, w'' \rangle$

Proof. By case analysis on the reduction rules. □

Corollary 9. *If* $\langle \theta, C, K, \sigma, \theta_K, m, w \rangle \trianglelefteq \langle \theta, C', K', \sigma, \theta_K, m, w \rangle$ *and* $\langle \theta, C, K, \sigma,$ $\theta_K, m, w \rangle \vdash^* \langle \theta'', C'', K'', \sigma'', \theta_K'', m+n', w'' \rangle$ *and* $C'' \neq \texttt{diverge}$, *then* $\langle \theta, C', K', \sigma, \theta_K, m, w \rangle \vdash^* \langle \theta'', C''', K''', \sigma'', \theta_K'', m+n', w'' \rangle$ *and* $\langle \theta'', C'', K'', \sigma'',$ $\theta_K'', m+n', w'' \rangle \trianglelefteq \langle \theta'', C''', K''', \sigma'', \theta_K'', m+n', w'' \rangle$

We can now show the desired result for terminating reductions.

Lemma 38. *If* $\langle \theta, \texttt{while}^k(\phi)\{C\}, [], \sigma, \theta_K, n, w \rangle \vdash^* \langle \theta', \downarrow, [], \sigma', \theta_K, n+n', w' \rangle$, *then* $\langle \theta, \texttt{while}(\phi)\{C\}, [], \sigma, \theta_K, n, w \rangle \vdash^* \langle \theta', \downarrow, [], \sigma', \theta_K, n+n', w' \rangle$.

Proof. We have $\langle \theta, \texttt{while}^k(\phi)\{C\}, [], \sigma, \theta_K, n, w \rangle \trianglelefteq \langle \theta, \texttt{while}(\phi)\{C\}, [], \sigma, \theta_K, n,$ $w \rangle$, so by Corollary 9, $\langle \theta, \texttt{while}(\phi)\{C\}, [], \sigma, \theta_K, n, w \rangle \vdash^* \langle \theta', C', K', \sigma', \theta_K, n+n',$ $w' \rangle$ where $\downarrow \trianglelefteq C'$ and $[] \trianglelefteq K'$, which implies $C' = \downarrow$ and $K' = []$. □

If the evaluation of $\texttt{while}^k(\phi)\{C\}$ gets stuck, so does the evaluation of $\texttt{while}(\phi)\{C\}$.

Lemma 39. *If* $\langle \theta, C, K, \sigma, \theta_K, n, w \rangle \vdash \langle \theta', C', K', \sigma', \theta_K', n', w' \rangle$ *and* $\hat{C} \trianglelefteq C$ *and* $\hat{K} \trianglelefteq K$, *then* $\langle \theta, \hat{C}, \hat{K}, \sigma, \theta_K, n, w \rangle \vdash \langle \theta'', C'', K'', \sigma'', \theta_K'', n'', w'' \rangle$.

Proof. By case analysis on the derivation of $\hat{C} \trianglelefteq C$. □

Lemma 40. *If* $\langle \theta, \text{while}^k(\phi)\{C\}, [], \sigma, \theta_K, n, w \rangle \vdash^* \langle \theta', C', K, \sigma', \theta'_K, n + n', w' \rangle \nvdash$, *then* $\langle \theta, \text{while}(\phi)\{C\}, [], \sigma, \theta_K, n, w \rangle \vdash^* \langle \theta', C'', K', \sigma', \theta'_K, n + n', w' \rangle \nvdash$.

Proof. If $C' \neq \text{diverge}$, then by Corollary 9, $\langle \theta, \text{while}(\phi)\{C\}, [], \sigma, \theta_K, n, w \rangle \vdash^* \langle \theta', C'', K', \sigma', \theta_K, n + n', w' \rangle$ where $C' \trianglelefteq C''$ and $K \trianglelefteq K'$. By Lemma 39, if $\langle \theta', C'', K', \sigma', \theta_K, n + n', w' \rangle$ reduces, then $\langle \theta', C', K, \sigma', \theta_K, n + n', w' \rangle$ also reduces, contradicting the assumption. Hence, $\langle \theta', C'', K', \sigma', \theta_K, n + n', w' \rangle \nvdash$, as required.

If $C' = \text{diverge}$, then $\sigma' = \xi$, as otherwise $\langle \theta', \text{diverge}, K, \sigma', \theta'_K, n + n', w' \rangle$ would reduce by (diverge). However, $\langle \theta', \text{diverge}, K, \xi, \theta'_K, n + n', w' \rangle$ is not derivable from any initial configuration other than itself. Hence, $n' = 0$ and $k = 0$ and $\sigma = \xi$. Since no configuration with state ξ reduces, we have $\langle \theta, \text{while}(\phi)\{C\}, [], \xi, \theta_K, n, w \rangle \nvdash$, as required. □

Corollary 10. $\mathbf{O}^\sigma_{\text{while}(\phi)\{C\}}(\theta) \geq \mathbf{O}^\sigma_{\text{while}^k(\phi)\{C\}}(\theta)$ *for all* k.

Replacing One Bounded Loop with Another. We now prove that a bounded loop $\text{while}^k(\phi)\{C\}$ can be safely replaced by another bounded loop with a higher bound.

Lemma 41. *If* $m \geq k$ *and* $\langle \theta, \text{while}^k(\phi)\{C\}, [], \sigma, \theta_K, n, w \rangle \vdash^* \langle \theta', \downarrow, [], \sigma', \theta_K, n + n', w' \rangle$, *then* $\langle \theta, \text{while}^m(\phi)\{C\}, [], \sigma, \theta_K, n, w \rangle \vdash^* \langle \theta', \downarrow, [], \sigma', \theta_K, n + n', w' \rangle$

Proof. We have $\langle \theta, \text{while}^k(\phi)\{C\}, [], \sigma, \theta_K, n, w \rangle \trianglelefteq \langle \theta, \text{while}^m(\phi)\{C\}, [], \sigma, \theta_K, n, w \rangle$, so by Corollary 9, $\langle \theta, \text{while}^m(\phi)\{C\}, [], \sigma, \theta_K, n, w \rangle \vdash^* \langle \theta', C', K', \sigma', \theta_K, n + n', w' \rangle$ where $\downarrow \trianglelefteq C'$ and $[] \trianglelefteq K'$, which implies $C' = \downarrow$ and $K' = []$. □

We show the same property for reductions which get stuck.

Lemma 42. *If* $m \geq k$ *and* $\langle \theta, \text{while}^k(\phi)\{C\}, [], \sigma, \theta_K, n, w \rangle \vdash^* \langle \theta', C', K, \sigma', \theta'_K, n + n', w' \rangle \nvdash$, *then* $\langle \theta, \text{while}^m(\phi)\{C\}, [], \sigma, \theta_K, n, w \rangle \vdash^* \langle \theta', C'', K', \sigma', \theta'_K, n + n', w' \rangle \nvdash$.

Proof. If $C' \neq \text{diverge}$, then by Corollary 9, $\langle \theta, \text{while}^m(\phi)\{C\}, [], \sigma, \theta_K, n, w \rangle \vdash^* \langle \theta', C'', K', \sigma', \theta_K, n + n', w' \rangle$ where $C' \trianglelefteq C''$ and $K \trianglelefteq K'$. By Lemma 39, if $\langle \theta', C'', K', \sigma', \theta_K, n + n', w' \rangle$ reduces, then $\langle \theta', C', K, \sigma', \theta_K, n + n', w' \rangle$ also reduces, contradicting the assumption. Hence, $\langle \theta', C'', K', \sigma', \theta_K, n + n', w' \rangle \nvdash$, as required.

If $C' = \text{diverge}$, then $\sigma' = \xi$, as otherwise $\langle \theta', \text{diverge}, K, \sigma', \theta'_K, n + n', w' \rangle$ would reduce by (diverge). However, $\langle \theta', \text{diverge}, K, \xi, \theta'_K, n + n', w' \rangle$ is not derivable from any initial configuration other than itself. Hence, $n' = 0$ and $k = 0$ and $\sigma = \xi$. Since no configuration with state ξ reduces, we have $\langle \theta, \text{while}^m(\phi)\{C\}, [], \xi, \theta_K, n, w \rangle \nvdash$, as required. □

The above results lead to the following properties of semantic functions:

Corollary 11. *If* $n \geq k$, *then* $\mathbf{O}^\sigma_{\text{while}^n(\phi)\{C\}}(\theta) \geq \mathbf{O}^\sigma_{\text{while}^k(\phi)\{C\}}(\theta)$ *(w.r.t. flat CPO with bottom* $\uparrow$*).*

Lemma 43. *If* $\mathbf{O}^{\sigma}_{\mathtt{while}^k(\phi)\{C\}}(\theta) \in \Omega_{\sigma}$ *and* $\mathbf{O}^{\sigma}_{\mathtt{while}^l(\phi)\{C\}}(\theta) \in \Omega_{\sigma}$, *then* $\mathbf{SC}^{\sigma}_{\mathtt{while}^k(\phi)\{C\}}(\theta) = \mathbf{SC}^{\sigma}_{\mathtt{while}^l(\phi)\{C\}}(\theta)$.

Proof. Assume w.l.o.g. that $l \geq k$. Then the result follows directly from Lemma 41. □

Proofs of Propositions 3 and 4. Having shown the above properties of while-loop approximations, we are now ready to prove Propositions 3 and 4.

Restatement of Proposition 4. *If* $n \geq k$, *then* $\hat{f}(\mathbf{O}^{\sigma}_{\mathtt{while}^n(\phi)\{C\}}(\theta))$ $\mathbf{SC}^{\sigma}_{\mathtt{while}^n(\phi)\{C\}}(\theta) \geq \hat{f}(\mathbf{O}^{\sigma}_{\mathtt{while}^k(\phi)\{C\}}(\theta))\mathbf{SC}^{\sigma}_{\mathtt{while}^k(\phi)\{C\}}(\theta)$.

Proof. (of Proposition 4). If $\mathbf{O}^{\sigma}_{\mathtt{while}^k(\phi)\{C\}}(\theta) = \frac{1}{2}$ or $\mathbf{O}^{\sigma}_{\mathtt{while}^k(\phi)\{C\}}(\theta) =\uparrow$, then $RHS = 0$, so the inequality holds trivially.

If $\mathbf{O}^{\sigma}_{\mathtt{while}^k(\phi)\{C\}}(\theta) \in \Omega_{\sigma}$, then by Corollary 11, $\mathbf{O}^{\sigma}_{\mathtt{while}^n(\phi)\{C\}}(\theta) = \mathbf{O}^{\sigma}_{\mathtt{while}^k(\phi)\{C\}}(\theta)$ and by Lemma 43, $\mathbf{SC}^{\sigma}_{\mathtt{while}^n(\phi)\{C\}}(\theta) = \mathbf{SC}^{\sigma}_{\mathtt{while}^k(\phi)\{C\}}(\theta)$. Hence, $f(\mathbf{O}^{\sigma}_{\mathtt{while}^n(\phi)\{C\}}(\theta))\mathbf{SC}^{\sigma}_{\mathtt{while}^n(\phi)\{C\}}(\theta) = f(\mathbf{O}^{\sigma}_{\mathtt{while}^k(\phi)\{C\}}(\theta))\mathbf{SC}^{\sigma}_{\mathtt{while}^k(\phi)\{C\}}(\theta)$. □

Restatement of Proposition 3. $\hat{f}(\mathbf{O}^{\sigma}_{\mathtt{while}(\phi)\{C\}}(\theta))\mathbf{SC}^{\sigma}_{\mathtt{while}(\phi)\{C\}}(\theta) = \sup_n \hat{f}(\mathbf{O}^{\sigma}_{\mathtt{while}^n(\phi)\{C\}}(\theta))\mathbf{SC}^{\sigma}_{\mathtt{while}^n(\phi)\{C\}}(\theta)$.

Proof (of Proposition 3). If $\mathbf{O}^{\sigma}_{\mathtt{while}(\phi)\{C\}}(\theta) \notin \Omega_{\sigma}$, then $LHS = 0$. If $\mathbf{O}^{\sigma}_{\mathtt{while}^n(\phi)\{C\}}(\theta) \in \Omega_{\sigma}$ for some n, then we get a contradiction by Lemma 38, so we have $\mathbf{O}^{\sigma}_{\mathtt{while}^n(\phi)\{C\}}(\theta) \notin \Omega_{\sigma}$, which implies $RHS = 0$.

Now, assume that $\mathbf{O}^{\sigma}_{\mathtt{while}(\phi)\{C\}}(\theta) \in \Omega_{\sigma}$. Then by Lemma 35, there exists k such that $\mathbf{O}^{\sigma}_{\mathtt{while}(\phi)\{C\}}(\theta) = \mathbf{O}^{\sigma}_{\mathtt{while}^k(\phi)\{C\}}(\theta)$ and $\mathbf{SC}^{\sigma}_{\mathtt{while}(\phi)\{C\}}(\theta) = \mathbf{SC}^{\sigma}_{\mathtt{while}^k(\phi)\{C\}}(\theta)$.

By Corollary 11 we know that $\mathbf{O}^{\sigma}_{\mathtt{while}^l(\phi)\{C\}}(\theta) = \mathbf{O}^{\sigma}_{\mathtt{while}^k(\phi)\{C\}}(\theta)$ for all $l \geq k$ and either $\mathbf{O}^{\sigma}_{\mathtt{while}^k(\phi)\{C\}}(\theta) = \mathbf{O}^{\sigma}_{\mathtt{while}^{l'}(\phi)\{C\}}(\theta)$ or $\mathbf{O}^{\sigma}_{\mathtt{while}^{l'}(\phi)\{C\}}(\theta) =\uparrow$ for all $l' \leq k$. Hence, for all l, either $\hat{f}(\mathbf{O}^{\sigma}_{\mathtt{while}^l(\phi)\{C\}}(\theta)) = \hat{f}(\mathbf{O}^{\sigma}_{\mathtt{while}^k(\phi)\{C\}}(\theta))$ or $\hat{f}(\mathbf{O}^{\sigma}_{\mathtt{while}^l(\phi)\{C\}}(\theta)) = 0$.

By Lemma 43, for all l, either $\mathbf{O}^{\sigma}_{\mathtt{while}^l(\phi)\{C\}}(\theta) \notin \Omega_{\sigma}$ or $\mathbf{SC}^{\sigma}_{\mathtt{while}^l(\phi)\{C\}}(\theta) = \mathbf{SC}^{\sigma}_{\mathtt{while}^k(\phi)\{C\}}(\theta)$. Hence, for all l, either $\hat{f}(\mathbf{O}^{\sigma}_{\mathtt{while}^l(\phi)\{C\}}(\theta))\mathbf{SC}^{\sigma}_{\mathtt{while}^l(\phi)\{C\}}(\theta) = \hat{f}(\mathbf{O}^{\sigma}_{\mathtt{while}^k(\phi)\{C\}}(\theta))\mathbf{SC}^{\sigma}_{\mathtt{while}^k(\phi)\{C\}}(\theta)$ or $\hat{f}(\mathbf{O}^{\sigma}_{\mathtt{while}^l(\phi)\{C\}}(\theta))\mathbf{SC}^{\sigma}_{\mathtt{while}^l(\phi)\{C\}}(\theta) = 0$.

Thus, $\sup_n \hat{f}(\mathbf{O}^{\sigma}_{\mathtt{while}^n(\phi)\{C\}}(\theta))\mathbf{SC}^{\sigma}_{\mathtt{while}^n(\phi)\{C\}}(\theta) = \hat{f}(\mathbf{O}^{\sigma}_{\mathtt{while}^k(\phi)\{C\}}(\theta))\mathbf{SC}^{\sigma}_{\mathtt{while}^k(\phi)\{C\}}(\theta)$, and so $\hat{f}(\mathbf{O}^{\sigma}_{\mathtt{while}(\phi)\{C\}}(\theta))\mathbf{SC}^{\sigma}_{\mathtt{while}(\phi)\{C\}}(\theta) = \sup_n \hat{f}(\mathbf{O}^{\sigma}_{\mathtt{while}^n(\phi)\{C\}}(\theta))\mathbf{SC}^{\sigma}_{\mathtt{while}^n(\phi)\{C\}}(\theta)$, as required. □

Proofs of Propositions 5 and 6. Finally, we prove Propositions 5 and 6, which are required by Theorem 2. One final additional result needed for these proofs is that $\mathbf{SC}^{\sigma}_{\mathtt{while}^n(\phi)\{C\}}(\theta)$ and $\mathbf{SC}^{\sigma}_{\mathtt{while}^n(\phi)\{C\}}(\theta, l)$ (for any l) are decreasing as functions of n.

Lemma 44. *If $n \geq k$, then $\mathbf{SC}^{\sigma}_{\mathtt{while}^n(\phi)\{C\}}(\theta) \leq \mathbf{SC}^{\sigma}_{\mathtt{while}^k(\phi)\{C\}}(\theta)$.*

Proof. If $\mathbf{O}^{\sigma}_{\mathtt{while}^k(\phi)\{C\}}(\theta) = \xi$, then $\mathbf{O}^{\sigma}_{\mathtt{while}^n(\phi)\{C\}}(\theta) = \xi$ by Corollary 11. Hence, $\mathbf{SC}^{\sigma}_{\mathtt{while}^k(\phi)\{C\}}(\theta) = \mathbf{SC}^{\sigma}_{\mathtt{while}^n(\phi)\{C\}}(\theta) = 0$.

Now, suppose that $\mathbf{O}^{\sigma}_{\mathtt{while}^k(\phi)\{C\}}(\theta) \neq \xi$. If there exists l such that $\langle \theta, \mathtt{while}^k(\phi)\{C\}, [], \sigma, \theta_K, 0, 1 \rangle \vdash^*_{\min} \langle \theta', \mathtt{diverge}, K, \tau, \theta'_K, l, w \rangle$, then by Lemma 45, $\langle \theta, \mathtt{while}^n(\phi)\{C\}, [], \sigma, \theta_K, 0, 1 \rangle \vdash^* \langle \theta', C, K', \tau, \theta'_K, l, w \rangle$ and $\langle \theta', \mathtt{diverge}, K, \tau, \theta'_K, l, w \rangle \trianglelefteq \langle \theta', C, K', \tau, \theta'_K, l, w \rangle$. Since $\langle \theta', \mathtt{diverge}, K, \tau, \theta'_K, m, w \rangle \vdash \langle \theta', \mathtt{diverge}, K, \tau, \theta'_K, m+1, w \rangle$, for all $l' \geq l$, we have $\mathbf{SC}^{\sigma}_{\mathtt{while}^{l'}(\phi)\{C\}}(\theta, l') = w$. For each $l' \geq l$, we either have $\langle \theta, \mathtt{while}^n(\phi)\{C\}, [], \sigma, \theta_K, 0, 1 \rangle \vdash^* \langle \theta', C, K', \tau, \theta'_K, l, w \rangle \vdash^* \langle \theta'', C', K'', \tau', \theta'_K, l', w' \rangle$, where $w' \leq w$ by Lemma 7, and so $\mathbf{SC}^{\sigma}_{\mathtt{while}^n(\phi)\{C\}}(\theta, l') = w'$ or $\mathtt{while}^n(\phi)\{C\}$ does not reduce in l' steps under θ, in which case $\mathbf{SC}^{\sigma}_{\mathtt{while}^n(\phi)\{C\}}(\theta, l') = 0$. In either case, $\mathbf{SC}^{\sigma}_{\mathtt{while}^n(\phi)\{C\}}(\theta, l') \leq \mathbf{SC}^{\sigma}_{\mathtt{while}^k(\phi)\{C\}}(\theta, l')$ for all $l' \geq l$, so the result holds by a property of the limit of a sequence.

If there exists no l such that $\langle \theta, \mathtt{while}^k(\phi)\{C\}, [], \sigma, \theta_K, 0, 1 \rangle \vdash^*_{\min} \langle \theta', \mathtt{diverge}, K, \tau, \theta'_K, l, w \rangle$, then for all l, we have $\langle \theta, \mathtt{while}^k(\phi)\{C\}, [], \sigma, \theta_K, 0, 1 \rangle \vdash^* \langle \theta', C, K, \tau, \theta'_K, l, w \rangle$, where $C \neq \mathtt{diverge}$. By Corollary 9, $\langle \theta, \mathtt{while}^n(\phi)\{C\}, [], \sigma, \theta_K, 0, 1 \rangle \vdash^* \langle \theta', C', K', \tau, \theta'_K, l, w \rangle$ for some C', K', and so $\mathbf{SC}^{\sigma}_{\mathtt{while}^k(\phi)\{C\}}(\theta, l) = \mathbf{SC}^{\sigma}_{\mathtt{while}^n(\phi)\{C\}}(\theta, l)$ for all l, which implies $\mathbf{SC}^{\sigma}_{\mathtt{while}^k(\phi)\{C\}}(\theta) = \mathbf{SC}^{\sigma}_{\mathtt{while}^n(\phi)\{C\}}(\theta)$. $\qquad\square$

Lemma 45. *If $\langle \theta, C, K, \sigma, \theta_K, m, w \rangle \trianglelefteq \langle \theta, C', K', \sigma, \theta_K, m, w \rangle$ and $\langle \theta, C, K, \sigma, \theta_K, m, w \rangle \vdash^*_{\min} \langle \theta'', \mathtt{diverge}, K'', \sigma'', \theta''_K, m+n', w'' \rangle$ then $\langle \theta, C', K', \sigma, \theta_K, m, w \rangle \vdash^* \langle \theta'', C''', K''', \sigma'', \theta''_K, m+n', w'' \rangle$ and $\langle \theta'', \mathtt{diverge}, K'', \sigma'', \theta''_K, m+n', w'' \rangle \trianglelefteq \langle \theta'', C''', K''', \sigma'', \theta''_K, m+n', w'' \rangle$*

Proof. Follows from Corollary 9 and Lemma 37. $\qquad\square$

Lemma 46. *If $n \geq k$, then for all l, $\mathbf{SC}^{\sigma}_{\mathtt{while}^n(\phi)\{C\}}(\theta, l) \leq \mathbf{SC}^{\sigma}_{\mathtt{while}^k(\phi)\{C\}}(\theta, l)$.*

Proof. If $\langle \theta, \mathtt{while}^k(\phi)\{C\}, [], \sigma, \theta_K, 0, 1 \rangle \vdash^* \langle \theta', C', K, \sigma', \theta'_K, l', w \rangle \nvdash$ for some $l' < l$, then $\langle \theta, \mathtt{while}^n(\phi)\{C\}, [], \sigma, \theta_K, 0, 1 \rangle \vdash^* \langle \theta', C'', K', \sigma', \theta'_K, l', w \rangle \nvdash$ by Lemma 42, and so $\mathbf{SC}^{\sigma}_{\mathtt{while}^n(\phi)\{C\}}(\theta, l) = \mathbf{SC}^{\sigma}_{\mathtt{while}^k(\phi)\{C\}}(\theta, l) = 0$.

If $\langle \theta, \mathtt{while}^k(\phi)\{C\}, [], \sigma, \theta_K, 0, 1 \rangle \vdash^* \langle \theta', \mathtt{diverge}, K, \sigma', \theta'_K, l, w \rangle$, then $\mathbf{SC}^{\sigma}_{\mathtt{while}^k(\phi)\{C\}}(\theta, l) = w$ and there must exist a $l' \leq l$ such that $\langle \theta, \mathtt{while}^k(\phi)\{C\}, [], \sigma, \theta_K, 0, 1 \rangle \vdash^*_{\min} \langle \theta', \mathtt{diverge}, K, \sigma', \theta'_K, l', w \rangle$. Moreover, by Lemma 45, $\langle \theta, \mathtt{while}^n(\phi)\{C\}, [], \sigma, \theta_K, 0, 1 \rangle \vdash^* \langle \theta', C'', K', \tau, \theta'_K, l', w \rangle$ and $\langle \theta', \mathtt{diverge}, K, \tau, \theta'_K, l', w \rangle \trianglelefteq \langle \theta', C'', K', \tau, \theta'_K, l', w \rangle$. If we have $\langle \theta', C'', K', \tau, \theta'_K, l', w \rangle \vdash^* \langle \theta', C''', K'', \tau, \theta''_K, l, w' \rangle$, then $\mathbf{SC}^{\sigma}_{\mathtt{while}^n(\phi)\{C\}}(\theta, l) = w' \leq w$ by Lemma 7. Otherwise, $\mathbf{SC}^{\sigma}_{\mathtt{while}^n(\phi)\{C\}}(\theta, l) = 0$. In either case, $\mathbf{SC}^{\sigma}_{\mathtt{while}^n(\phi)\{C\}}(\theta, l) \leq \mathbf{SC}^{\sigma}_{\mathtt{while}^k(\phi)\{C\}}(\theta, l) = 0$.

If $\langle \theta, \mathtt{while}^k(\phi)\{C\}, [], \sigma, \theta_K, 0, 1 \rangle \vdash^* \langle \theta', C', K, \sigma', \theta'_K, l, w \rangle$ and $C' \neq \mathtt{diverge}$, then by Corollary 9, $\langle \theta, \mathtt{while}^n(\phi)\{C\}, [], \sigma, \theta_K, 0, 1 \rangle \vdash \langle \theta', C'', K', \tau, \theta'_K, l, w \rangle$ and $\langle \theta', C', K, \tau, \theta'_K, l, w \rangle \trianglelefteq \langle \theta', C'', K', \tau, \theta'_K, l, w \rangle$. Thus, $\mathbf{SC}^{\sigma}_{\mathtt{while}^n(\phi)\{C\}}(\theta, l) \leq \mathbf{SC}^{\sigma}_{\mathtt{while}^k(\phi)\{C\}}(\theta, l) = w$. $\qquad\square$

Restatement of Proposition 5. *For all $f \leq 1$,*

$$\check{f}(\mathbf{O}^\sigma_{\texttt{while}(\phi)\{C\}}(\theta))\mathbf{SC}^\sigma_{\texttt{while}(\phi)\{C\}}(\theta) = \inf_n \check{f}(\mathbf{O}^\sigma_{\texttt{while}^n(\phi)\{C\}}(\theta))\mathbf{SC}^\sigma_{\texttt{while}^n(\phi)\{C\}}(\theta)$$

Proof (of Proposition 5). If $\mathbf{O}^\sigma_{\texttt{while}(\phi)\{C\}}(\theta) \in \Omega_\sigma$, then by Lemma 35, there exists k such that $\mathbf{O}^\sigma_{\texttt{while}(\phi)\{C\}}(\theta) = \mathbf{O}^\sigma_{\texttt{while}^k(\phi)\{C\}}(\theta)$ and $\mathbf{SC}^\sigma_{\texttt{while}(\phi)\{C\}}(\theta) = \mathbf{SC}^\sigma_{\texttt{while}^k(\phi)\{C\}}(\theta)$. By similar reasoning as in the proof of Proposition 3, for all l, either $\check{f}(\mathbf{O}^\sigma_{\texttt{while}^l(\phi)\{C\}}(\theta)) = \check{f}(\mathbf{O}^\sigma_{\texttt{while}^k(\phi)\{C\}}(\theta))$ or $\check{f}(\mathbf{O}^\sigma_{\texttt{while}^l(\phi)\{C\}}(\theta)) = 1$, so $\check{f}(\mathbf{O}^\sigma_{\texttt{while}^l(\phi)\{C\}}(\theta)) \geq \check{f}(\mathbf{O}^\sigma_{\texttt{while}^k(\phi)\{C\}}(\theta))$ for all l.

By Lemma 43, for all l, either $\mathbf{O}^\sigma_{\texttt{while}^l(\phi)\{C\}}(\theta) \notin \Omega_\sigma$ or $\mathbf{SC}^\sigma_{\texttt{while}^l(\phi)\{C\}}(\theta) = \mathbf{SC}^\sigma_{\texttt{while}^k(\phi)\{C\}}(\theta)$. If $\mathbf{O}^\sigma_{\texttt{while}^l(\phi)\{C\}}(\theta) \notin \Omega_\sigma$, then $l < k$ because of Corollary 11. Moreover, by Lemma 44, if $l < k$, then $\mathbf{SC}^\sigma_{\texttt{while}^k(\phi)\{C\}}(\theta) \leq \mathbf{SC}^\sigma_{\texttt{while}^l(\phi)\{C\}}(\theta)$. Hence, $\mathbf{SC}^\sigma_{\texttt{while}^k(\phi)\{C\}}(\theta) \leq \mathbf{SC}^\sigma_{\texttt{while}^l(\phi)\{C\}}(\theta)$ for all l. This implies $\inf_n \check{f}(\mathbf{O}^\sigma_{\texttt{while}^n(\phi)\{C\}}(\theta))\mathbf{SC}^\sigma_{\texttt{while}^n(\phi)\{C\}}(\theta) = \check{f}(\mathbf{O}^\sigma_{\texttt{while}^k(\phi)\{C\}}(\theta))\mathbf{SC}^\sigma_{\texttt{while}^k(\phi)\{C\}}(\theta) = \check{f}(\mathbf{O}^\sigma_{\texttt{while}(\phi)\{C\}}(\theta))\mathbf{SC}^\sigma_{\texttt{while}(\phi)\{C\}}(\theta)$.

If $\mathbf{O}^\sigma_{\texttt{while}(\phi)\{C\}}(\theta) = \frac{\ell}{2}$, then by Lemma 36, $\mathbf{O}^\sigma_{\texttt{while}^k(\phi)\{C\}}(\theta) = \frac{\ell}{2}$ for some k. Thus, $\inf_n \check{f}(\mathbf{O}^\sigma_{\texttt{while}^n(\phi)\{C\}}(\theta))\mathbf{SC}^\sigma_{\texttt{while}^n(\phi)\{C\}}(\theta) = 0 = \check{f}(\mathbf{O}^\sigma_{\texttt{while}(\phi)\{C\}}(\theta))\mathbf{SC}^\sigma_{\texttt{while}(\phi)\{C\}}(\theta)$.

If $\mathbf{O}^\sigma_{\texttt{while}(\phi)\{C\}}(\theta) = \uparrow$, then $\check{f}(\mathbf{O}^\sigma_{\texttt{while}(\phi)\{C\}}(\theta)) = 1$. By Lemma 10, $\mathbf{O}^\sigma_{\texttt{while}^k(\phi)\{C\}}(\theta) = \uparrow$ for all k. Since $\check{f}(\uparrow) = 1$, we only need to show that $\mathbf{SC}^\sigma_{\texttt{while}(\phi)\{C\}}(\theta) = \inf_n \mathbf{SC}^\sigma_{\texttt{while}^n(\phi)\{C\}}(\theta)$.

First, observe that from Corollary 8, it follows that for all l, for all $k \geq l$, $\mathbf{SC}^\sigma_{\texttt{while}(\phi)\{C\}}(\theta, l) = \mathbf{SC}^\sigma_{\texttt{while}^k(\phi)\{C\}}(\theta, l)$. Thus, for such fixed l, $\mathbf{SC}^\sigma_{\texttt{while}(\phi)\{C\}}(\theta, l) = \inf_n \mathbf{SC}^\sigma_{\texttt{while}^n(\phi)\{C\}}(\theta, l)$. Hence,

$$\mathbf{SC}^\sigma_{\texttt{while}(\phi)\{C\}}(\theta) = \inf_l \mathbf{SC}^\sigma_{\texttt{while}(\phi)\{C\}}(\theta, l)$$
$$= \inf_l \inf_n \mathbf{SC}^\sigma_{\texttt{while}^n(\phi)\{C\}}(\theta, l)$$
$$= \inf_n \inf_l \mathbf{SC}^\sigma_{\texttt{while}^n(\phi)\{C\}}(\theta, l)$$
$$= \inf_n \mathbf{SC}^\sigma_{\texttt{while}^n(\phi)\{C\}}(\theta)$$

In the equality $\inf_l \inf_n \mathbf{SC}^\sigma_{\texttt{while}^n(\phi)\{C\}}(\theta, l) = \inf_n \inf_l \mathbf{SC}^\sigma_{\texttt{while}^n(\phi)\{C\}}(\theta, l)$, we used the fact that $\inf_l \inf_n \mathbf{SC}^\sigma_{\texttt{while}^n(\phi)\{C\}}(\theta, l) = \lim_{l \to \infty} \lim_{n \to \infty} \mathbf{SC}^\sigma_{\texttt{while}^n(\phi)\{C\}}(\theta, l)$ and that $\mathbf{SC}^\sigma_{\texttt{while}^n(\phi)\{C\}}(\theta, l)$ is decreasing in both n and l, which means that by Theorem 4.2 from [14], $\lim_{l \to \infty} \lim_{n \to \infty} \mathbf{SC}^\sigma_{\texttt{while}^n(\phi)\{C\}}(\theta, l) = \lim_{n \to \infty} \lim_{l \to \infty} \mathbf{SC}^\sigma_{\texttt{while}^n(\phi)\{C\}}(\theta, l)$. □

Below, we write $\langle \theta, C, K, \sigma, \theta_K, n, w \rangle \vdash^*_{\min} \langle \theta', \texttt{diverge}, K', \sigma', \theta'_K, n + n', w' \rangle$ if $\langle \theta, C, K, \sigma, \theta_K, n, w \rangle \vdash^* \langle \theta', \texttt{diverge}, K', \sigma', \theta'_K, n + n', w' \rangle$ and there is no $n'' < n'$ such that $\langle \theta, C, K, \sigma, \theta_K, n, w \rangle \vdash^* \langle \theta'', \texttt{diverge}, K'', \sigma'', \theta''_K, n + n'', w'' \rangle$ (or, equivalently, $\langle \theta, C, K, \sigma, \theta_K, n, w \rangle \vdash^* \langle \theta', \texttt{diverge}, K', \sigma', \theta'_K, n + n', w' \rangle$ was derived without (diverge)).

Restatement of Proposition 6. *If $n \geq k$ and $f \leq 1$, then*

$$\check{f}(O^{\sigma}_{\mathtt{while}^n(\phi)\{C\}}(\theta))SC^{\sigma}_{\mathtt{while}^n(\phi)\{C\}}(\theta) \leq \check{f}(O^{\sigma}_{\mathtt{while}^k(\phi)\{C\}}(\theta))SC^{\sigma}_{\mathtt{while}^k(\phi)\{C\}}(\theta).$$

Proof (of Proposition 6). By Corollary 11, $O^{\sigma}_{\mathtt{while}^n(\phi)\{C\}}(\theta) \geq O^{\sigma}_{\mathtt{while}^k(\phi)\{C\}}(\theta)$. Since $\check{f}$ is antitone (we have $\check{f}(\tau) \leq \check{f}(\uparrow) = 1$ for all $\tau \geq \uparrow$), this implies $\check{f}(O^{\sigma}_{\mathtt{while}^n(\phi)\{C\}}(\theta)) \leq \check{f}(O^{\sigma}_{\mathtt{while}^k(\phi)\{C\}}(\theta))$. By Lemma 44, $SC^{\sigma}_{\mathtt{while}^n(\phi)\{C\}}(\theta) \leq SC^{\sigma}_{\mathtt{while}^k(\phi)\{C\}}(\theta)$, so $\check{f}(O^{\sigma}_{\mathtt{while}^n(\phi)\{C\}}(\theta))SC^{\sigma}_{\mathtt{while}^n(\phi)\{C\}}(\theta) \leq \check{f}(O^{\sigma}_{\mathtt{while}^k(\phi)\{C\}}(\theta))SC^{\sigma}_{\mathtt{while}^k(\phi)\{C\}}(\theta)$, as required. $\qquad\square$

E   Proofs of Theorems 1 and 2

Restatement of Theorem 1. *For all measurable functions $f \colon \Omega_\sigma \to \overline{\mathbb{R}}_+$, PL programs C and initial states $\sigma \in \Omega_\sigma$:*

$$\mathtt{wp}[\![C]\!](f)(\sigma) = \int f(\tau)[\![C]\!]_\sigma(d\tau).$$

Proof. By Lemma 10, it suffices to prove that for all f:

$$\int \hat{f}(O^{\sigma}_{C}(\theta)) \cdot SC^{\sigma}_{C}(\theta)\, \mu_{\mathbb{S}}(d\theta) = \mathtt{wp}[\![C]\!](f)(\sigma).$$

This can be proven by induction on the structure of C. We refrain from treating all cases but restrict ourselves to some interesting cases:

– Case $C = x :\approx U$.

$$\int \hat{f}(O^{\sigma}_{x:\approx U}(\theta)) \cdot SC^{\sigma}_{x:\approx U}(\theta)\, \mu_{\mathbb{S}}(d\theta)$$

$$= \int f(\sigma[x \mapsto \pi_U(\pi_L(\theta))])\, \mu_{\mathbb{S}}(d\theta)$$

$$\text{(property entropy)} = \int_{[0,1]} f(\sigma[x \mapsto v])\, \mu_L(dv)$$

$$\text{(definition wp)} = \mathtt{wp}[\![x :\approx U]\!](f)(\sigma).$$

– Case $C = C_1 ; C_2$ with $C_1 \neq C_1' ; C_2'$.

$$\int \hat{f}(O^{\sigma}_{C_1;C_2}(\theta)) \cdot SC^{\sigma}_{C_1;C_2}(\theta)\, \mu_{\mathbb{S}}(d\theta)$$

$$\text{(Proposition 1)} = \int \hat{f}(O^{\tau}_{C_2}(\pi_R(\theta))) \cdot SC^{\tau}_{C_2}(\pi_R(\theta)) \cdot SC^{\sigma}_{C_1}(\pi_L(\theta))\, \mu_{\mathbb{S}}(d\theta)$$

$$\text{(property entropy)} = \int \underbrace{\int \hat{f}(O^{\rho}_{C_2}(\theta_R)) \cdot SC^{\rho}_{C_2}(\theta_R)\, \mu_{\mathbb{S}}(d\theta_R)}_{=g(\rho)} \cdot SC^{\sigma}_{C_1}(\theta_L)\mu_{\mathbb{S}}(d\theta_L)$$

where $\tau = \mathbf{O}^\sigma_{C_1}(\pi_L(\theta))$ and $\rho = \mathbf{O}^\sigma_{C_1}(\theta_L)$. We have:

$$\int \hat{g}(\mathbf{O}^\sigma_{C_1}(\theta_L)) \cdot \mathbf{SC}^\sigma_{C_1}(\theta_L)\mu_\mathbb{S}(d\theta_L)$$

$$\text{(induction hypothesis)} \;=\; \mathtt{wp}[\![C_1]\!](g)(\sigma)$$

$$=\; \mathtt{wp}[\![C_1]\!](\lambda\tau. \int \hat{f}(\mathbf{O}^\tau_{C_2}(\theta_R)) \cdot \mathbf{SC}^\tau_{C_2}(\theta_R)\,\mu_\mathbb{S}(d\theta_R))(\sigma)$$

$$\text{(induction hypothesis)} \;=\; \mathtt{wp}[\![C_1]\!](\lambda\tau.\mathtt{wp}[\![C_2]\!](f)(\tau))(\sigma)$$

$$=\; \mathtt{wp}[\![C_1]\!](\mathtt{wp}[\![C_2]\!](f))(\sigma)$$

$$\text{(definition wp)} \;=\; \mathtt{wp}[\![C_1;C_2]\!](f)(\sigma)$$

– Case $C = \mathtt{score}(E)$. By inspecting the reduction rules, it follows:

$$\mathbf{O}^\sigma_{\mathtt{score}(E)}(\theta) \;=\; \begin{cases} \sigma & \text{if } \sigma(E) \in (0,1] \\ \lightning & \text{otherwise} \end{cases}$$

which implies $\hat{f}(\mathbf{O}^\sigma_{\mathtt{score}(E)}(\theta)) = [\sigma(E) \in (0,1]] \cdot \hat{f}(\sigma)$ and

$$\mathbf{SC}^\sigma_{\mathtt{score}(E)}(\theta) \;=\; \begin{cases} \sigma(E) & \text{if } \sigma(E) \in (0,1] \\ 0 & \text{otherwise} \end{cases} \;=\; [\sigma(E) \in (0,1]] \cdot \sigma(E).$$

Thus, we have:

$$\int \hat{f}(\mathbf{O}^\sigma_{\mathtt{score}(E)}(\theta)) \cdot \mathbf{SC}^\sigma_{\mathtt{score}(E)}(\theta)\,\mu_\mathbb{S}(d\theta)$$

$$=\; \int [\sigma(E) \in (0,1]] \cdot \hat{f}(\sigma) \cdot \sigma(E)\,\mu_\mathbb{S}(d\theta)$$

$$=\; [\sigma(E) \in (0,1]] \cdot \hat{f}(\sigma) \cdot \sigma(E)$$

$$(\sigma \in \Omega_\sigma \text{ by assumption}) \;=\; [\sigma(E) \in (0,1]] \cdot f(\sigma) \cdot \sigma(E)$$

$$=\; \mathtt{wp}[\![\mathtt{score}(E)]\!](f)(\sigma).$$

– Case $C = \mathtt{while}(\phi)\{C'\}$. Let $C^n = \mathtt{while}^n(\phi)\{C'\}$. We derive:

$$\int \hat{f}(\mathbf{O}^\sigma_C(\theta)) \cdot \mathbf{SC}^\sigma_C(\theta)\,\mu_\mathbb{S}(d\theta)$$

$$\text{(Proposition 3)} \;=\; \int \sup_n \hat{f}(\mathbf{O}^\sigma_{C^n}(\theta)) \cdot \mathbf{SC}^\sigma_{C^n}(\theta)\,\mu_\mathbb{S}(d\theta)$$

$$\text{(Beppo Levi's Theorem)} \;=\; \sup_n \int \hat{f}(\mathbf{O}^\sigma_{C^n}(\theta)) \cdot \mathbf{SC}^\sigma_{C^n}(\theta)\,\mu_\mathbb{S}(d\theta)$$

$$(*) \;=\; \sup_n {}^{\mathtt{wp}}_{\langle\phi,C'\rangle}\Phi^n_f(0)(\sigma)$$

$$\text{(Kleene's Fixpoint Theorem)} \;=\; \mathtt{wp}[\![\mathtt{while}(\phi)\{C'\}]\!](f)(\sigma).$$

When applying the Beppo Levi's Theorem, we used the fact that the sequence $\hat{f}(\mathbf{O}^\sigma_{C^n}(\theta)) \cdot \mathbf{SC}^\sigma_{C^n}(\theta)$ is monotonic in n (Proposition 4). In order to show that the proof step $(*)$ is correct, we need to show:

$$\int \hat{f}(\mathbf{O}^{\sigma}_{C^n}(\theta)) \cdot \mathbf{SC}^{\sigma}_{C^n}(\theta)\, \mu_{\mathbb{S}}(d\theta) \;=\; {}^{\mathrm{wp}}_{\langle\phi,C'\rangle} \varPhi^n_f(0)(\sigma) \text{ for all } n.$$

We prove this statement by induction on n, using Proposition 2:
- Base case: $n = 0$:

$$\int \underbrace{\hat{f}(\mathbf{O}^{\sigma}_{\mathrm{diverge}}(\theta))}_{=0} \cdot \underbrace{\mathbf{SC}^{\sigma}_{\mathrm{diverge}}(\theta)\, \mu_{\mathbb{S}}(d\theta)}_{=1} \;=\; 0 \;=\; {}^{\mathrm{wp}}_{\langle\phi,C'\rangle} \varPhi^0_f(0)(\sigma)$$

- Induction step: we distinguish $\sigma(\phi) = \texttt{true}$ and $\sigma(\phi) = \texttt{false}$. For the latter case we have:

$$\int \hat{f}(\sigma) \cdot 1\, \mu_{\mathbb{S}}(d\theta) \;=\; f(\sigma).$$

For the case $\sigma(\phi) = \texttt{true}$ we derive:

$$\int \hat{f}(\mathbf{O}^{\sigma}_{C^{n+1}}(\theta)) \cdot \mathbf{SC}^{\sigma}_{C^{n+1}}(\theta)\, \mu_{\mathbb{S}}(d\theta)$$

$$= \int \hat{f}(\mathbf{O}^{\sigma}_{C';C^n}(\theta)) \cdot \mathbf{SC}^{\sigma}_{C';C^n}(\theta)\, \mu_{\mathbb{S}}(d\theta)$$

$$\text{(Prop. 2)} \;=\; \int \hat{f}(\mathbf{O}^{\tau}_{C^n}(\pi_R(\psi(\theta)))) \cdot \mathbf{SC}^{\sigma}_{C'}(\pi_L(\psi(\theta))) \cdot \mathbf{SC}^{\tau}_{C^n}(\pi_R(\psi(\theta)))\, \mu_{\mathbb{S}}(d\theta)$$

$$\text{(Prop\ 32)} \;=\; \int \hat{f}(\mathbf{O}^{\rho}_{C^n}(\pi_R(\theta))) \cdot \mathbf{SC}^{\sigma}_{C'}(\pi_L(\theta)) \cdot \mathbf{SC}^{\rho}_{C^n}(\pi_R(\theta))\, \mu_{\mathbb{S}}(d\theta)$$

$$\text{(entropy)} \;=\; \int\int \hat{f}(\mathbf{O}^{\rho}_{C^n}(\theta_R)) \cdot \mathbf{SC}^{\rho}_{C^n}(\theta_R)\, \mu_{\mathbb{S}}(d\theta_R) \cdot \mathbf{SC}^{\sigma}_{C'}(\theta_L)\, \mu_{\mathbb{S}}(d\theta_L)$$

where $\tau = \mathbf{O}^{\sigma}_{C'}(\pi_L(\psi(\theta)))$ and $\rho = \mathbf{O}^{\sigma}_{C'}(\pi_L(\theta))$.
Now let $p(\tau) = \int \hat{f}(\mathbf{O}^{\tau}_{C^n}(\theta_R)) \cdot \mathbf{SC}^{\tau}_{C^n}(\theta_R)\, \mu_{\mathbb{S}}(d\theta_R)$ for $\tau \in \Omega_\sigma$. Then:

$$\int \hat{p}(\mathbf{O}^{\sigma}_C(\theta_L)) \cdot \mathbf{SC}^{\sigma}_C(\theta_L)\, \mu_{\mathbb{S}}(d\theta_L)$$

$$\text{(outer IH)} \;=\; \mathrm{wp}[\![C]\!](p)(\sigma)$$

$$= \mathrm{wp}[\![C]\!]\left(\lambda\tau.\int \hat{f}(\mathbf{O}^{\tau}_{C^n}(\theta_R)) \cdot \mathbf{SC}^{\tau}_{C^n}(\theta_R)\, \mu_{\mathbb{S}}(d\theta_R)\right)(\sigma)$$

$$\text{(inner IH)} \;=\; \mathrm{wp}[\![C]\!]\left(\lambda\tau.{}^{\mathrm{wp}}_{\langle\phi,C'\rangle}\varPhi^n_f(0)(\tau)\right)(\sigma)$$

$$= \mathrm{wp}[\![C]\!]\left({}^{\mathrm{wp}}_{\langle\phi,C'\rangle}\varPhi^n_f(0)\right)(\sigma)$$

$$\text{(definition } {}^{\mathrm{wp}}_{\langle\phi,C\rangle}\varPhi_f) \;=\; {}^{\mathrm{wp}}_{\langle\phi,C'\rangle}\varPhi^{n+1}_f(0)(\sigma).$$

Hence, the equality $(*)$ is correct, which finishes the proof. $\qquad\square$

The second main theorem of this paper states that the weakest liberal preexpectation of a non-negative function f bounded by 1 is equivalent to the expected value of f with respect to the distribution defined by the operational semantics plus the probability of divergence weighted by scores.

Restatement of Theorem 2. *For every measurable non-negative function* $f: \Omega_\sigma \to \overline{\mathbb{R}}_+$ *with* $f(\sigma) \leq 1$ *for all states* σ, *PL program* C *and initial state* $\sigma \in \Omega_\sigma$:

$$\texttt{wlp}\llbracket C \rrbracket(f)(\sigma) \;=\; \int f(\tau) \cdot \llbracket C \rrbracket_\sigma |_{\Omega_\sigma}(d\tau) + \underbrace{\int [\mathbf{O}_C^\sigma(\theta) = \uparrow] \cdot \mathbf{SC}_C^\sigma(\theta)\, \mu_\mathbb{S}(d\theta)}_{\text{probability of divergence multiplied by the score}} \quad .$$

Proof. By induction on the structure of C. The proof is essentially the same as the proof of Theorem 1, except that in the case of while-loops, we use Proposition 5 instead of Proposition 3 to show that the while-loop can be replaced by the limit of its finite approximations.

Similarly to Theorem 1, the equation we want to prove can be rewritten as:

$$\texttt{wlp}\llbracket C \rrbracket(f)(\sigma) \;=\; \int \check{f}(\mathbf{O}_C^\sigma(\theta)) \cdot \mathbf{SC}_C^\sigma(\theta)\, \mu_\mathbb{S}(d\theta)$$

The proof goes as follows. Let $C = \texttt{while}(\phi)\{C'\}$ and $C^n = \texttt{while}^n(\phi)\{C'\}$.

$$\int \check{f}(\mathbf{O}_C^\sigma(\theta)) \cdot \mathbf{SC}_C^\sigma(\theta)\, \mu_\mathbb{S}(d\theta)$$

$$\text{(Proposition 5)} \;=\; \int \inf_n \check{f}(\mathbf{O}_{C^n}^\sigma(\theta)) \cdot \mathbf{SC}_{C^n}^\sigma(\theta)\, \mu_\mathbb{S}(d\theta)$$

$$\text{(Beppo Levi's Theorem)} \;=\; \inf_n \int \check{f}(\mathbf{O}_{C^n}^\sigma(\theta)) \cdot \mathbf{SC}_{C^n}^\sigma(\theta)\, \mu_\mathbb{S}(d\theta)$$

$$(*) \;=\; \inf_n {}_{\langle\phi,C'\rangle}^{\texttt{wlp}} \Phi_f^n(1)(\sigma)$$

$$\text{(Kleene's Fixpoint Theorem)} \;=\; \texttt{wlp}\llbracket \texttt{while}(\phi)\{C'\} \rrbracket(f)(\sigma)$$

In order to show that step $(*)$ is correct, we need to show that $\int \check{f}(\mathbf{O}_{C^n}^\sigma(\theta)) \cdot \mathbf{SC}_{C^n}^\sigma(\theta)\, \mu_\mathbb{S}(d\theta) = \inf_n {}_{\langle\phi,C'\rangle}^{\texttt{wlp}} \Phi_f^n(1)(\sigma)$ for all n. This can be proven by induction on n; the proof is almost identical to the proof of $(*)$ from Theorem 1. When applying the Beppo Levi's Theorem, we used the fact that the sequence $\check{f}(\mathbf{O}_{C^n}^\sigma(\theta)) \cdot \mathbf{SC}_{C^n}^\sigma(\theta)$ is decreasing in n (Proposition 6) and that $\int \check{f}(\mathbf{O}_{C^0}^\sigma(\theta)) \cdot \mathbf{SC}_{C^0}^\sigma(\theta)\, \mu_\mathbb{S}(d\theta) < \infty$, which can be checked immediately.   □

F   Proving Measurability

The proofs of measurability are similar to [36], with the difference that we are working with an imperative language. In this section, we sketch the proofs of measurability of functions $\mathbf{O}_C^\sigma(\cdot)$ and $\mathbf{SC}_C^\sigma(\cdot, n)$, without going into the details, which are conceptually the same as in [36].

F.1   Measurability of Single-Step Reduction

Let us define:

$$g(\theta, C, K, \sigma, \theta_K, n, w) = \begin{cases} (\theta', C', K', \sigma', \theta'_K, n+1, w') \\ \quad \text{if } \langle \theta, C, K, \sigma, \theta_K, n, w \rangle \vdash \langle \theta', C', K', \sigma', \theta'_K, n+1, w' \rangle \\ (\theta, C, K, \xi, \theta_K, n+1, 0) \qquad \text{otherwise} \end{cases}$$

We need to show that g is measurable. The only interesting cases are (assign), which modifies state (we need to show g is still continuous in this case) and (draw), which modifies both state and trace, and (seq) and (pop), which modify both the main trace and the trace for continuation.

We can show that g is measurable by considering g as a disjoint union of sub-functions defined on measurable subsets of combinations corresponding to given reduction rules (e.g. $g_{if-true}$ and $g_{if-false}$ reducing conditional choices, $g_{while-true}$ and $g_{while-false}$ reducing while-loops, g_{sample} reducing sampling statements etc.) and showing that each sub-function is measurable. The reasoning is very similar to the one presented in Appendix E.1 of [36], so we omit the full proof and only show measurability of sub-functions modifying states and infinite traces, which were not present in [36].

From Continuity to Measurability. The easiest way of proving measurability of a function is often proving that this function is continuous as a function between the metric spaces which gave rise to the domain and codomain measurable spaces—by Corollary 2, continuity implies measurability. Moreover, Corollary 3 states that if a function f between products of separable metric spaces is continuous with respect to the Manhattan products of metrics, then it is measurable with respect to products of the given measurable spaces. We will make heavy use of these results in the proofs below.

Additional Borel σ-Algebras. In order to carry out the proofs, we need to define separable metric spaces on statements C, expressions E and continuations K, which will induce Borel σ-algebras. These metrics are straightforward metrics on syntactic terms, similar to the metrics on lambda-terms in [36]. We omit the details, but these metrics would be defined so that $d_C(C_1; C_2, C'_1; C'_2) = d_C(C_1; C'_1) + d_C(C_2; C'_2)$ and $d_K(C :: K, C' :: K') = d_C(C; C') + d_K(K, K')$ (where $d_K(K, K') = \infty$ if K and K' have different lengths).

It is easy to check that all the above metric spaces are separable—for each of them, a dense subset can be obtained by replacing reals with rationals. All subspaces of separable metric spaces can also be shown to be separable.

We also need to define σ-algebras on step sizes n and weights w—these will be the standard discrete σ-algebra on $\mathbb{Z}_+$ and the Borel σ-algebra on $[0, 1]$, respectively.

Measurability of (assign). We define:

$$g_{assign}(\theta, x := E, K, \sigma, \theta_K, n, w) = (\theta, \downarrow, K, \sigma[x \mapsto \sigma(E)], \theta_K, n + 1, w)$$
$$= (g_{assign1}(\theta, x := E, K, \sigma, \theta_K, n, w),$$
$$g_{assign2}(\theta, x := E, K, \sigma, \theta_K, n, w),$$
$$\dots,$$
$$g_{assign7}(\theta, x := E, K, \sigma, \theta_K, n, w))$$

where:

$$g_{assign1}(\theta, x := E, K, \sigma, \theta_K, n, w) = \theta$$
$$g_{assign2}(\theta, x := E, K, \sigma, \theta_K, n, w) = \downarrow$$
$$g_{assign3}(\theta, x := E, K, \sigma, \theta_K, n, w) = K$$
$$g_{assign4}(\theta, x := E, K, \sigma, \theta_K, n, w) = \sigma[x \mapsto \sigma(E)]$$
$$g_{assign5}(\theta, x := E, K, \sigma, \theta_K, n, w) = \theta_K$$
$$g_{assign6}(\theta, x := E, K, \sigma, \theta_K, n, w) = n + 1$$
$$g_{assign7}(\theta, x := E, K, \sigma, \theta_K, n, w) = w$$

Lemma 47. g_{assign} *is measurable.*

Proof. The functions $g_{assign1}$, $g_{assign3}$, $g_{assign5}$, $g_{assign7}$ are simple projections, so they are trivially measurable. The function $g_{assign2}$ is a constant function, so it is also measurable. Function $g_{assign4}$ is a composition of a function returning the tuple $(x, \sigma, \sigma(E))$ from the configuration, which can easily be shown measurable (projections are measurable, the function extracting E from $x := E$ can be shown continuous and substitution $\sigma(E)$ is measurable by assumption), and the state update function, which is measurable by Lemma 14. Function $g_{assign6}$ is a composition of a projection (returning the sixth component n from a tuple) and a function adding 1 to a number, which is continuous and measurable.

Hence, g_{assign} is measurable, as all its components are measurable. □

Measurability of (draw). Let us define:

$$g_{draw}((\theta, x :\approx U, K, \sigma, \theta_K, n, w)) = (\pi_R(\theta), \downarrow, K, \sigma[x \mapsto \pi_U(\pi_L(\theta))], \theta_K, n + 1, w)$$
$$= (g_{draw1}(\theta, x := E, K, \sigma, \theta_K, n, w),$$
$$g_{draw2}(\theta, x := E, K, \sigma, \theta_K, n, w),$$
$$\dots,$$
$$g_{draw7}(\theta, x := E, K, \sigma, \theta_K, n, w))$$

where:

$$g_{draw1}(\theta, x := E, K, \sigma, \theta_K, n, w) = \pi_R(\theta)$$
$$g_{draw2}(\theta, x := E, K, \sigma, \theta_K, n, w) = \downarrow$$
$$g_{draw3}(\theta, x := E, K, \sigma, \theta_K, n, w) = K$$
$$g_{draw4}(\theta, x := E, K, \sigma, \theta_K, n, w) = \sigma[x \mapsto \pi_U(\pi_L(\theta))]$$
$$g_{draw3}(\theta, x := E, K, \sigma, \theta_K, n, w) = \theta_K$$
$$g_{draw6}(\theta, x := E, K, \sigma, \theta_K, n, w) = n + 1$$
$$g_{draw7}(\theta, x := E, K, \sigma, \theta_K, n, w) = w$$

Lemma 48. *g_{assign} is measurable.*

Proof. We only need to show the measurability of g_{draw1} and g_{draw4}, as the other functions are identical to the ones used in the definition of g_{assign}.

The function g_{draw1} is a composition of the projection returning the first component θ of the configuration, and the function π_R, which is measurable by the axiomatisation of the entropy space, so it is measurable.

Function g_{draw4} is measurable by the same argument as $g_{assign4}$, except that the measurable evaluation $\sigma(E)$ is replaced by $\pi_U(\pi_L(\theta))$, which as a composition of two measurable (by assumption) functions and the measurable projection returning θ is also measurable. $\square$

Measurability of (seq) and (pop). Define:

$$g_{seq}((\theta, C_1; C_2, K, \sigma, \theta_K, n, w)) = (\pi_L(\theta), C_1, C_2 :: K, \sigma, \pi_R(\theta) :: \theta_K, n + 1, w)$$
$$= (g_{seq1}(\theta, x := E, K, \sigma, \theta_K, n, w),$$
$$g_{seq2}(\theta, x := E, K, \sigma, \theta_K, n, w),$$
$$\dots,$$
$$g_{seq7}(\theta, x := E, K, \sigma, \theta_K, n, w))$$

where:

$$g_{seq1}(\theta, C_1; C_2, K, \sigma, \theta_K, n, w) = \pi_L(\theta)$$
$$g_{seq2}(\theta, C_1; C_2, K, \sigma, \theta_K, n, w) = C_1$$
$$g_{seq3}(\theta, C_1; C_2, K, \sigma, \theta_K, n, w) = C_2 :: K$$
$$g_{seq4}(\theta, C_1; C_2, K, \sigma, \theta_K, n, w) = \sigma$$
$$g_{seq5}(\theta, C_1; C_2, K, \sigma, \theta_K, n, w) = \pi_R(\theta) :: \theta_K$$
$$g_{seq6}(\theta, C_1; C_2, K, \sigma, \theta_K, n, w) = n + 1$$
$$g_{seq7}(\theta, C_1; C_2, K, \sigma, \theta_K, n, w) = w$$

Lemma 49. *g_{seq} is measurable.*

Proof. The function g_{seq1} is measurable as a composition of projection and a function measurable by assumption. The metrics d_C and d_K on statements and continuations (whose formal definitions are omitted) satisfy $d_C(C_1; C_2, C_1'; C_2') = d_C(C_1; C_1') + d_C(C_2; C_2')$ and $d_K(C :: K, C' :: K') = d_C(C; C') + d_K(K, K')$, which makes it easy to show that g_{seq2} and g_{seq3} are measurable, as compositions of projections and continuous functions. Meanwhile, g_{seq5} is composed from measurable projections and the functions π_R and $(::)$, measurable by assumption, so it is measurable. $\square$

The proof of measurability of (pop) is analogous.

F.2 Measurability of $\mathbf{O}_C^\sigma(\cdot)$ and $\mathbf{SC}_C^\sigma(\cdot, n)$

Once we have proven the measurability of state updates, the proof of Lemma 9 (measurability of $\mathbf{O}_C^\sigma(\cdot)$) is analogous to the proof of Lemma 92 in [5].

The proof of measurability of $\mathbf{SC}_C^\sigma(\cdot, n)$ is even simpler—for each fixed n, we can represent $\mathbf{SC}_C^\sigma(\cdot, n)$ as an n-fold composition of g, followed by a projection returning the weight w from the configuration. The projection is obviously continuous, and so measurable. Since a composition of measurable functions is measurable, this shows that $\mathbf{SC}_C^\sigma(\cdot, n)$ is measurable.

References

1. Abramsky, S., Jung, A.: Domain theory. In: Abramsky, S., Gabbay, D.M., Maibaum, T.S.E. (eds.) Handbook of Logic in Computer Science, vol. 3, pp. 1–168. Oxford University Press, Inc. (1994). http://dl.acm.org/citation.cfm?id=218742. 218744
2. Aumann, R.J.: Borel structures for function spaces. Illinois J. Math. **5**(4), 614–630 (1961). http://projecteuclid.org/euclid.ijm/1255631584
3. Bichsel, B., Gehr, T., Vechev, M.: Fine-grained semantics for probabilistic programs. In: Ahmed, A. (ed.) ESOP 2018. LNCS, vol. 10801, pp. 145–185. Springer, Cham (2018). https://doi.org/10.1007/978-3-319-89884-1_6
4. Billingsley, P.: Probability and Measure, 3rd edn. Wiley, New York (1995)
5. Borgström, J., Dal Lago, U., Gordon, A.D., Szymczak, M.: A lambda-calculus foundation for universal probabilistic programming. In: Garrigue, J., Keller, G., Sumii, E. (eds.) Proceedings of the 21st ACM SIGPLAN International Conference on Functional Programming, ICFP 2016, Nara, Japan, 18–22 September 2016, pp. 33–46. ACM (2016). https://doi.org/10.1145/2951913.2951942
6. Borgström, J., Gordon, A.D., Greenberg, M., Margetson, J., Gael, J.V.: Measure transformer semantics for Bayesian machine learning. Log. Meth. Comput. Sci. **9**(3), 1–39 (2013). https://doi.org/10.2168/LMCS-9(3:11)201
7. Chatterjee, K., Novotný, P., Zikelic, D.: Stochastic invariants for probabilistic termination. In: Castagna, G., Gordon, A.D. (eds.) Proceedings of the 44th ACM SIGPLAN Symposium on Principles of Programming Languages, POPL 2017, Paris, France, January 18–20, 2017, pp. 145–160. ACM (2017). http://dl.acm.org/citation.cfm?id=3009873

8. Culpepper, R., Cobb, A.: Contextual equivalence for probabilistic programs with continuous random variables and scoring. In: Yang, H. (ed.) ESOP 2017. LNCS, vol. 10201, pp. 368–392. Springer, Heidelberg (2017). https://doi.org/10.1007/978-3-662-54434-1_14

9. Dahlqvist, F., Kozen, D.: Semantics of higher-order probabilistic programs with conditioning. Proc. ACM Program. Lang. 4(POPL), 57:1–57:29 (2020). https://doi.org/10.1145/3371125

10. Goodman, N.D., Mansinghka, V.K., Roy, D.M., Bonawitz, K., Tenenbaum, J.B.: Church: a language for generative models. In: McAllester, D.A., Myllymäki, P. (eds.) UAI 2008, Proceedings of the 24th Conference in Uncertainty in Artificial Intelligence, Helsinki, Finland, July 9–12, 2008, pp. 220–229. AUAI Press (2008), https://dslpitt.org/uai/displayArticleDetails.jsp?mmnu=1&smnu=2&article_id=1346&proceeding_id=24

11. Goodman, N.D., Stuhlmüller, A.: The design and implementation of probabilistic programming languages (2014). http://dippl.org

12. Goodman, N.D., Tenenbaum, J.B., Contributors, T.P.: Probabilistic Models of Cognition (2016). http://probmods.org/v2

13. Gretz, F., Katoen, J., McIver, A.: Operational versus weakest pre-expectation semantics for the probabilistic guarded command language. Perform. Eval. 73, 110–132 (2014). https://doi.org/10.1016/j.peva.2013.11.004

14. Habil, E.: Double sequences and double series. IUG J. Nat. Stud. 14(1), 1–32 (2006)

15. Heunen, C., Kammar, O., Staton, S., Yang, H.: A convenient category for higher-order probability theory. In: 32nd Annual ACM/IEEE Symposium on Logic in Computer Science, LICS 2017, Reykjavik, Iceland, June 20–23, 2017, pp. 1–12. IEEE Computer Society (2017). https://doi.org/10.1109/LICS.2017.8005137

16. Huang, D., Morrisett, G.: An application of computable distributions to the semantics of probabilistic programming languages. In: Thiemann, P. (ed.) ESOP 2016. LNCS, vol. 9632, pp. 337–363. Springer, Heidelberg (2016). https://doi.org/10.1007/978-3-662-49498-1_14

17. Hutton, G.: Introduction to Domain Theory (1994). lecture notes http://www.cs.nott.ac.uk/~pszgmh/domains.html

18. Icard, T.: Beyond almost-sure termination. In: Gunzelmann, G., Howes, A., Tenbrink, T., Davelaar, E.J. (eds.) Proceedings of the 39th Annual Meeting of the Cognitive Science Society, CogSci 2017, London, UK, 16–29 July 2017. cognitivesciencesociety.org (2017). https://mindmodeling.org/cogsci2017/papers/0430/index.html

19. Ishwaran, H., James, L.F.: Gibbs sampling methods for stick-breaking priors. J. Am. Stat. Assoc. 96(453), 161–173 (2001). http://www.jstor.org/stable/2670356

20. Jansen, N., Kaminski, B.L., Katoen, J., Olmedo, F., Gretz, F., McIver, A.: Conditioning in probabilistic programming. In: Ghica, D.R. (ed.) The 31st Conference on the Mathematical Foundations of Programming Semantics, MFPS 2015, Nijmegen, The Netherlands, 22–25 June 2015. Electronic Notes in Theoretical Computer Science, vol. 319, pp. 199–216. Elsevier (2015). https://doi.org/10.1016/j.entcs.2015.12.013

21. Kaminski, B.L.: Advanced Weakest Precondition Calculi for Probabilistic Programs. Ph.D. thesis, RWTH Aachen University, February 2019

22. Kaminski, B.L., Katoen, J., Matheja, C., Olmedo, F.: Weakest precondition reasoning for expected runtimes of randomized algorithms. J. ACM 65(5), 30:1–30:68 (2018). https://doi.org/10.1145/3208102

23. Katoen, J.: The probabilistic model checking landscape. In: Grohe, M., Koskinen, E., Shankar, N. (eds.) Proceedings of the 31st Annual ACM/IEEE Symposium on Logic in Computer Science, LICS 2016, New York, NY, USA, 5–8 July 2016, pp. 31–45. ACM (2016). https://doi.org/10.1145/2933575.2934574

24. Kozen, D.: Semantics of probabilistic programs. J. Comput. Syst. Sci. **22**(3), 328–350 (1981). https://doi.org/10.1016/0022-0000(81)90036-2

25. McIver, A., Morgan, C.: Abstraction, Refinement and Proof for Probabilistic Systems. Monographs in Computer Science. Springer, New York (2005). https://doi.org/10.1007/b138392

26. Morgan, C., McIver, A.: Unifying WP and WLP. Inf. Process. Lett. **59**(3), 159–163 (1996). https://doi.org/10.1016/0020-0190(96)00093-2

27. Morgan, C., McIver, A., Seidel, K.: Probabilistic predicate transformers. ACM Trans. Program. Lang. Syst. **18**(3), 325–353 (1996). https://doi.org/10.1145/229542.229547

28. Nori, A.V., Hur, C., Rajamani, S.K., Samuel, S.: R2: an efficient MCMC sampler for probabilistic programs. In: Brodley, C.E., Stone, P. (eds.) Proceedings of the Twenty-Eighth AAAI Conference on Artificial Intelligence, Québec City, Québec, Canada, 27–31 July 2014, pp. 2476–2482. AAAI Press (2014). http://www.aaai.org/ocs/index.php/AAAI/AAAI14/paper/view/8192

29. Olmedo, F., Gretz, F., Jansen, N., Kaminski, B.L., Katoen, J., McIver, A.: Conditioning in probabilistic programming. ACM Trans. Program. Lang. Syst. **40**(1), 41–450 (2018). https://doi.org/10.1145/3156018

30. Olmedo, F., Kaminski, B.L., Katoen, J., Matheja, C.: Reasoning about recursive probabilistic programs. In: Grohe, M., Koskinen, E., Shankar, N. (eds.) Proceedings of the 31st Annual ACM/IEEE Symposium on Logic in Computer Science, LICS 2016, New York, NY, USA, 5–8 July 2016, pp. 672–681. ACM (2016). https://doi.org/10.1145/2933575.2935317

31. Park, S., Pfenning, F., Thrun, S.: A probabilistic language based on sampling functions. ACM Trans. Program. Lang. Syst. **31**(1) (2008). https://doi.org/10.1145/1452044.1452048

32. Saheb-Djahromi, N.: Probabilistic LCF. In: Winkowski, J. (ed.) MFCS 1978. LNCS, vol. 64, pp. 442–451. Springer, Heidelberg (1978). https://doi.org/10.1007/3-540-08921-7_92

33. Ścibior, A., Kammar, O., Ghahramani, Z.: Functional programming for modular Bayesian inference. Proc. ACM Program. Lang. **2**(ICFP), 83:1–83:29 (2018). https://doi.org/10.1145/3236778

34. Solovay, R.M.: A model of set-theory in which every set of reals is Lebesgue measurable. Ann. Math. **92**(1), 1–56 (1970). http://www.jstor.org/stable/1970696

35. Staton, S., Yang, H., Wood, F., Heunen, C., Kammar, O.: Semantics for probabilistic programming: higher-order functions, continuous distributions, and soft constraints. In: Proceedings of the 31st Annual ACM/IEEE Symposium on Logic in Computer Science, LICS 2016, pp. 525–534. ACM, New York (2016). https://doi.org/10.1145/2933575.2935313

36. Szymczak, M.: Programming Language Semantics as a Foundation for Bayesian Inference. Ph.D. thesis, University of Edinburgh (2018). https://www.era.lib.ed.ac.uk/handle/1842/28993

37. Toronto, N., McCarthy, J., Van Horn, D.: Running probabilistic programs backwards. In: Vitek, J. (ed.) ESOP 2015. LNCS, vol. 9032, pp. 53–79. Springer, Heidelberg (2015). https://doi.org/10.1007/978-3-662-46669-8_3

38. Vákár, M., Kammar, O., Staton, S.: A domain theory for statistical probabilistic programming. Proc. ACM Program. Lang. **3**(POPL), 36:1–36:29 (2019). https://doi.org/10.1145/3290349

39. Wand, M., Culpepper, R., Giannakopoulos, T., Cobb, A.: Contextual equivalence for a probabilistic language with continuous random variables and recursion. Proc. ACM Program. Lang. **2**(ICFP), 87:1–87:30 (2018). https://doi.org/10.1145/3236782

𝕂—A Semantic Framework for Programming Languages and Formal Analysis

Xiaohong Chen[(✉)] and Grigore Roşu

University of Illinois at Urbana-Champaign, Champaign, USA
{xc3,grosu}@illinois.edu

Abstract. We give an overview on the applications and foundations of the 𝕂 language framework, a semantic framework for programming languages and formal analysis tools. 𝕂 represents a 20-year effort in pursuing the ideal language framework vision, where programming languages must have formal definitions, and tools for a given language, such as parsers, interpreters, compilers, semantic-based debuggers, state-space explorers, model checkers, deductive program verifiers, etc., can be derived from just one reference formal definition of the language, which is executable, and no other semantics for the same language should be needed. The correctness of the language tools is guaranteed on a case-by-case basis by proof objects, which encode rigorous mathematical proofs as certificates for every individual task that the tools do and can be mechanically checked by third-party proof checkers.

Keywords: 𝕂 framework · Matching logic · Formal semantics

1 What Is 𝕂?

𝕂 is a language semantic framework and a suite of tools that allow and encourage the language designers to formally define their languages once and for all, using an intuitive and attractive notation, and then obtain language implementations as well as analysis tools for free. This represents a long-standing ideal vision held by the programming languages community. 𝕂 is aimed at developing the foundations, techniques, and tools to realize this vision.

1.1 The State-of-the-Art of Programming Languages Design

The state-of-the-art of programming language design is still far from the above ideal vision. The programming languages and formal methods communities still develop language analysis tools for each individual programming language. For

This paper follows the lecture notes presented by the second author at the School on Engineering Trustworthy Software Systems (SETSS) in 2019.

J. P. Bowen et al. (Eds.): SETSS 2019, LNCS 12154, pp. 122–158, 2020.
https://doi.org/10.1007/978-3-030-55089-9_4

example, the C programming language has well-known compilers such as gcc [2] and clang [1], but there are also C interpreters such as TrustInSoft [3] that target detecting undefined behaviors of C programs, model checkers for C such as CBMC [24] that aim at exploring exhaustively the state space of C programs up to a bounded depth, and symbolic execution and deductive verification tools for C such as VCC [14] that formally verify functional properties of C programs. However, the development of these language tools not only for C but also for other languages suffer from the following problems:

- They are built in an ad-hoc fashion, in the sense that language or program analysis experts must rely on their informal understanding of the language to develop the language tools. This informal understanding may not be consistent with the formal definitions of the language, not to mention that most languages do not even have an official formal semantic definition.
- They are time-consuming to develop and may not be thoroughly tested and validated with respect to the formal definition, due to a lack of a mechanized connection between the formal definition and the actual implementation; again, the formal definition might not even exist in the first place;
- Many tools are developed from scratch, sharing very little code or functionality with each other; as a result, not only are there waste of resource and duplicates of work in "re-inventing the wheels", but also we can hardly claim that these tools are implemented for the *same* language;
- They need be updated when the language evolves (e.g., from C11 to C18); in other words, they are inclined to become deprecated;

In conclusion, these language tools that we use to ensure the correctness, reliability, and security of other programs and software systems may themselves be unreliable.

The above story unfolded for various languages over and over again, for more than 50 years, and it is still going on. This is at best uneconomical. Figure 1 shows the state-of-the-art of programming languages design. Suppose we have L programming languages and T tools. Then we need to develop and maintain at least $L \times T$ systems, which share little code or functionality. The cost is waste of talent and resources in doing essentially the same thing, the same tools, but for different languages.

Challenges Reinforced by Blockchains. The above situation of programming language design is facing more challenges when it comes to the recent burgeoning blockchain industry. Blockchain technology has led to a variety of new programming languages and virtual machines designed specifically for the blockchains, including high-level languages such as Solidity [17] and Vyper [18] to low-level virtual machine bytecode languages such as EVM [22] and IELE [23].

Smart contracts are computer programs running on blockchains that implement communication protocols, often of a kind of digital assets called *cryptocurrencies* that handle economic or financial transactions, withholding a total market capitalization of more than 80 billion US dollars at the time of writing. Therefore, there is enormous demand for formally designing and verifying

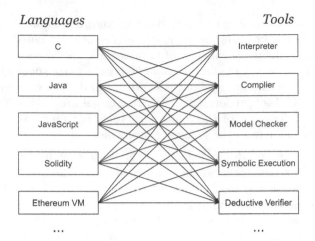

Fig. 1. The state-of-the-art of programming language design

these highly valuable smart contracts. On the other hand, blockchains and their virtual machine languages have a rapid development cycle with new versions being released on a weekly basis. The state-of-the-art approaches fail to have a canonical reference formal definition of the languages from which language tools are derived. Instead, language designers and tool developers need to implement the language tools and update them whenever a newer version of the languages is released. This has caused a lot of challenges in applying the state-of-the-art approaches to blockchain languages and smart contract formal analysis and verification. As we will see in Sect. 1.2, these challenges would not exist if one had an ideal language semantic framework.

1.2 The Ideal Language Semantic Framework

Our main motivation is to make programming language design a more organized and scientifically principled process, to reduce duplicated work and waste of resource in programming languages implementation, to increase the reusability and reliability of formal analysis tools, and to increase the reliability and security of the execution, verification, and testing environment of programs and software systems.

We look for an ideal language semantic framework, where all programming languages must be rigorously designed using formal methods and implementations of language tools must be provably correct. We depict this vision of an ideal language framework in Fig. 2, where the central yellow bubble denotes the canonical reference formal definition of a given (but arbitrary) programming language, and the surrounding blue bubbles denote language tools for that language, such as interpreters, compilers, state-space explorers, model checkers, deductive program verifiers, etc., which are all derived from the reference formal definition

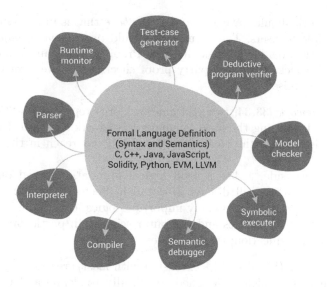

Fig. 2. The vision of an ideal language framework, pursued by 𝕂

of that language by the framework. We identify the following characteristics of an ideal language framework:

- The framework should be *language-independent*, in the sense that it uses the same generic method to generate language tools from the formal definitions for all programming languages.
- The framework should be *expressive*, to define the formal syntax and semantics of any programming language, with an intuitive and user-friendly *frontend interface*, so the formal definitions can be understood not only by experts but also by non-semanticists. In particular, the framework should provide easy-to-use facilities that help the language designers handle sophisticated features, such as non-deterministic computations, interaction, concurrency, and more, which are not uncommon in the real-world programming languages (see Sect. 2).
- The framework should support *modular development*, where formal definitions of large languages can be divided into smaller and more primitive modules. Language features should be loosely coupled, and language designers can easily add new features without revisiting existing definitions.
- The framework should support *testing-driven development*, where basic language tools such as the parser and the interpreter and/or compiler are automatically generated from language definitions for language designers to execute and test the semantics while they are defining it, by running lots of test programs and see if they get the intended results.
- The framework should have a mathematically solid logical foundation, in the sense that every semantic definition yields a *logical theory* of a foundational logic (see Sect. 4) and all language tools are best-effort implementations of logical reasoning of the foundational logic within the given logical theory.

- The framework should have a *minimal trustbase* that is fully comprehensible and accessible to users. The framework should provide *proof objects* as correctness certificates for all tasks it does. Proof objects can be mechanically and quickly checked by third-party proof checkers, so their correctness can not be compromised.

The $\mathbb{K}$ *framework* [33,34] (www.kframework.org) represents a 20-year effort in pursuing and realizing the ideal language framework shown in Fig. 2. There is enough evidence that the ideal vision is within our reach in the short term with $\mathbb{K}$.

On the theory side, $\mathbb{K}$ has a solid logical foundation based on matching logic [11,30], which we will discuss in detail in Sect. 4. Matching logic is an expressive logic that subsumes many important logics, calculi, and models that are used in both mathematics and computer science, in particular in program specification and verification; these include:

- First-order logic (FOL) and its extension with least/greatest fixpoints;
- Separation logic, which is designed specifically to define and reason about mutable data structures on heaps;
- Modal logic and modal μ-logic, as well as the various temporal logic and dynamic logic variants;
- Reachability logic, which supports $\mathbb{K}$'s program verification tools in a language-independent fashion; reachability logic captures the classic Hoare logic as a special instance.

Therefore, matching logic allows us to use $\mathbb{K}$ to specify and reason about properties written in all the above logics in a systematic and uniform way.

On the practical side, the current $\mathbb{K}$ implementations take the respective operational semantics of programming languages such as C [21], Java [8], and JavaScript [27] as well as emerging blockchain languages such as EVM [22] as parameters, and automatically generates language tools such as parsers, program interpreters, and program verifiers, for these languages. The auto-generated interpreters have competitive performance against hand-crafted interpreters and the automatic verifiers are capable of verifying challenging heap-manipulating programs at performance comparable to that of state-of-the-art verifiers specifically crafted for those languages. A precursor verifier specialized to the C programming language, MatchC [31] (http://matching-logic.org), has a user-friendly online interface for one to verify dozens of predefined or new programs.

The rest of the paper is organized as follows. In Sect. 2, we discuss some real-world languages whose formal semantics have been completely defined in $\mathbb{K}$, in order to demonstrate that $\mathbb{K}$ scales to complex, real languages. In Sect. 3, we present the complete $\mathbb{K}$ definitions of two example languages, in order to illustrate the basic $\mathbb{K}$ features and functionalities, including its parsing and program execution tools. In Sect. 4, we introduce matching logic, which is the logical foundation of $\mathbb{K}$. In Sect. 5, we discuss the language-independent program verification tools of $\mathbb{K}$. We conclude the paper in Sect. 6.

This paper is *not* peer reviewed and, indeed, aims at making no novel contributions. It is meant to simply give the students attending the SETSS'19 summer school an overview of the 𝕂 framework and its applications. Specifically, this paper extends the lecture notes of the Marktoberdorf'16 summer school [29], sometimes ad litteram, with material presented in the following papers: [10–12, 30].

2   𝕂 Scales

Many real programming languages have a formal semantics defined in 𝕂, with their language tools being automatically generated in a correct-by-construction manner. Here we list some representative milestone examples.

C [21]. A complete formal semantics of C11 has been defined, aiming at capturing all the *undefined behaviors* of C. This semantics powers the commercial RV-Match tool, developed and maintained by Runtime Verification Inc. (RV) founded by the second author, aiming at mathematically rigorous dynamic checking of C programs in compliance with the ISO C11 Standard.

Java [8]. A complete formal semantics of Java 1.4 has been defined, which captures all language features and has been extensively tested using a test suite developed in parallel with the semantics, in a test-driven development methodology. The test suite itself was itself an important outcome of the semantics, because at that time Java did not appear to have any publicly available conformance testsuite.

JavaScript [27]. A complete formal semantics of JavaScript has been defined and thoroughly tested against the ECMAScript 5.1 conformance test suite, passing all 2,782 core language tests. The semantics also yields a simple coverage metric for the existing test suites, which is the set of 𝕂 *semantic rules* they exercise; see Sect. 3. It turned out that the ECMAScript 5.1 conformance test suite was incomplete and failed to cover several semantic rules. The authors of [27] wrote additional tests to exercise those rules and found bugs in commercial JavaScript engines.

Python [20]. Defining the complete formal semantics of Python is one of the first efforts that demonstrated the ability of 𝕂 to formalize complex programming languages. The semantics of Python 3.3 provided an interpreter and several analysis tools for exploring program state space and performing static reasoning and formal verification. The semantics was thoroughly tested against a number of unit tests and was shown to perform as efficiently as CPython, the reference implementation of Python, on those tests.

x86-64 [15] Not being a high-level programming language, ×86-64 can also be given a formal semantics in 𝕂 similar to the other high-level languages. The formal semantics of ×86-64 faithfully formalizes all the non-deprecated, sequential user-level instructions of the ×86-64 Haswell instruction set architecture, including 3,155 instruction variants that correspond to 774 mnemonics. The semantics is fully executable and has been tested against over 7,000 instruction-level test cases and the GCC torture test suite. This extensive testing paid off, revealing bugs in both the ×86-64 reference manual and other existing semantics. The formal semantics can be used for formal analyses such as processor verification.

EVM [22]. Ethereum virtual machine (EVM) is a bytecode stack-based language that all smart contracts on the Ethereum blockchain are compiled to and then executed by EVM interpreters. A complete formal semantics of EVM, called KEVM, has been defined in $\mathbb{K}$. The correctness and performance of KEVM have been experimentally evaluated using the official Ethereum test suite, consisting of over 40,000 EVM programs. As a pleasant surprise, the EVM interpreter that is automatically generated by $\mathbb{K}$ from KEVM is as efficient as the reference JavaScript implementation, suggesting that virtual machines for blockchains (and not only) can realistically be automatically generated from their formal semantics and performance is no longer a main obstacle issue.

IELE [23]. Like EVM, IELE [23] is another virtual machine bytecode language. Unlike EVM, IELE was designed in the spirit of *easy formal verification*, making it significantly different from EVM in various aspects. For example, IELE is a register-based machine instead of a stack-based one; IELE supports unbounded integers, whose reasoning is often easier than bounded integers. IELE was designed in a semantic-driven methodology using $\mathbb{K}$, and a virtual machine was automatically generated from the formal semantics, making it the first virtual machine whose development and implementation were completely powered by formal methods.

3   Example Language Definitions in $\mathbb{K}$

In this section, we illustrate the basic features and functionalities of $\mathbb{K}$ in terms of two example programming languages: one is functional and the other imperative. For more example languages defined in $\mathbb{K}$, we refer to the online $\mathbb{K}$ tutorial (www. kframework.org).

3.1   LAMBDA: A Functional Language

Here we show the complete $\mathbb{K}$ definition of a simple functional language definition called LAMBDA. LAMBDA is named after λ-calculus [13], one of the earliest mathematical models of computation, proposed by Alonzo Church in the 1930s, even earlier than when Alan Turing proposed Turing machines. The simplest form of the λ-calculus is untyped λ-calculus, which consists of only untyped variables, function application, and function abstraction. Function abstraction is also called λ-abstraction, written $\lambda x . e$, which defines a function object as a process from argument x to return value e, which is a λ-calculus expression that mostly likely contains x. There are many extensions of λ-calculus with *types*. In there, functions can only be applied to arguments of matched types. Typical examples of typed extensions of λ-calculus include the simply-typed and poly-morphic typed λ-calculus, as well as type systems, which form the foundations of proof assistants such as Coq [7], Agda [26], and Idris [9].

In the following, we assume readers are familiar with the basic concepts of λ-calculus, such as λ-binder and its binding behavior, α-renaming and α-equivalence, capture-avoiding substitution, and β-reduction. Background knowledge about λ-calculus can be found in [5].

The functional language LAMBDA is a direct incarnation of the untyped λ-calculus in K.

Importing Substitution Module. We need the predefined substitution module[1] to define β-reduction in λ-calculus (discussed later). We *require* the substitution definition with the command below and then *import* the SUBSTITUTION module in our LAMBDA module below.

```
require "substitution.k"

module LAMBDA
  imports SUBSTITUTION
```

Basic Syntax: Call-by-value. We define the conventional call-by-value syntax of λ-calculus, making sure that the λ-abstraction construct `lambda` is declared to be a *binder*, the function application to be *strict*, and the parentheses used for grouping as a *bracket* (explained shortly after).

```
syntax Val ::= Id
             | "lambda" Id "." Exp   [binder]
syntax Exp ::= Val
             | Exp Exp               [left, strict]
             | "(" Exp ")"           [bracket]
syntax KVariable ::= Id
syntax KResult ::= Val
```

Syntax is defined using the keyword `syntax` and may contain one or more pro-duction rules, separated with the vertical bar |. Every production rule is defined using the conventional BNF notation, with terminals enclosed in quotes and nonterminals starting with capital letters. Nonterminals are sometimes called *sorts* or *syntactic categories*.

In the above, `Val` is the syntactic category of the *values* in λ-calculus, which are irreducible λ-calculus expressions. `Exp` is the syntactic category of all λ-calculus expressions. Parentheses are used only for grouping. The [bracket] tells K to not construct internal nodes for parentheses when it generates the parse trees of λ-calculus expressions, so we do not need to bother giving explicit idle semantics for parentheses. `Id`, `KVariable`, and `KResult` are three builtin nonterminals that are predefined in K. `Id` contains all identifiers (in a syntax

---

[1] Substitution can be defined fully generically in K (not shown here) and then used to give semantics to various constructs in various languages.

that is similar to the identifiers in C), which are used to represent λ-calculus variables. KVariable is used to define the binding behavior of lambda. KResult is used to specify the evaluation strategies of $\mathbb{K}$, which are explained below.

Attributes. $\mathbb{K}$ associates the BNF syntax definitions with *attributes*. Attributes are put in square braces [...]. Some attributes contain only syntactic meanings and only affect parsing. The other attributes may contain semantic information and can affect program execution. The bracket attribute is used for grouping and has been discussed before. The left attribute specifies that function application $e_1\,e_2$ is associative to the left, so $\mathbb{K}$ parses $e_1\,e_2\,e_3$ as $(e_1\,e_2)\,e_3$. The strict attribute defines *evaluation context* that determines $\mathbb{K}$'s strategy to evaluate expressions and execute programs. Language constructs with a strict attribute can evaluate their arguments in any (fully nondeterministic) order. Therefore, $\mathbb{K}$ evaluates the expression $e_1\,e_2$ by first evaluating e_1 to value v_1 and e_2 to value v_2, fully nondeterministically, and finally evaluates $v_1\,v_2$.

KResult is a builtin nonterminal predefined in $\mathbb{K}$. It contains all syntactic categories and domain values that should be regarded as *results of computation*. $\mathbb{K}$ uses this information to decide when to continue and stop evaluation. Note that $\mathbb{K}$ does not infer results of computation automatically. The language designer should explicitly specify the results of computation by defining KResult properly.

KVariable includes all identifiers in Id and it tells $\mathbb{K}$ to "hook" λ-calculus variables to $\mathbb{K}$'s internal identifiers. This triggers the capture-avoiding substitution in $\mathbb{K}$, which we will discuss in the next paragraph.

Substitution and β-reduction. Here we define β-reduction in λ-calculus using $\mathbb{K}$'s rewrite rules. Recall that β-reduction refers to the following axiom schema:

$$(\lambda x\,.\,e)\,e' = e[e'/x] \qquad \text{for variable } x \text{ and expressions } e, e'$$

where $e[e'/x]$ denotes capture-avoiding substitution, where bound variables are implicitly renamed (called α-*renaming*) to avoid unintended variable capture during the substitution. For example, consider this instance of the β-reduction schema: $(\lambda x.\lambda y.xy)\,y = (\lambda y.xy)[y/x]$. If we simply replace all occurrences of x for y in $\lambda y.xy$, we would get $\lambda y.yy$, which is *not* the right result of capture-avoiding substitution because the former y is accidentally captured by λy after substitution. To avoid that, capture-avoiding substitution first renames the bound variable y in $\lambda y.xy$ to a fresh variable, say z, and gets $\lambda z.xz$. Then, the substitution $(\lambda z.xz)[y/x]$ will not cause variable capture, and we can get the correct result $\lambda z.yz$.

The above axiom is often called the β-reduction *rule* when it is oriented and applied from left to right. In $\mathbb{K}$, we use *rewrite rules* to implement β-reduction. $\mathbb{K}$ uses the keyword rule to define a rewrite rule, or simply a rule. In addition, $\mathbb{K}$ has builtin support for capture-avoiding substitution, which is predefined in the module SUBSTITUTION that we imported in the beginning. To use $\mathbb{K}$'s builtin capture-avoiding substitution, we must explicitly tell $\mathbb{K}$ what syntactic category is the one for variables, so $\mathbb{K}$ knows how to generate fresh variables during substitution. This is done by defining the KVariable and let it include Id, which is used to represent all λ-calculus variables.

The following is the 𝕂 rule that implements β-reduction.

```
rule (lambda X:Id . E:Exp) V:Val => E[V / X]
```

Here, `X:Id` is a 𝕂 variable, decorated with its syntactic category `Id`, or called *sort* of `X`. Note that we use `V:Val` with sort `Val` instead of `Exp`, because function application is `strict`, so 𝕂 will always first evaluate both its arguments to values. In other words, if `V` is not yet a value (i.e., `KResult`), 𝕂 does not apply the β-reduction rule. Instead, 𝕂 will evaluate `V` further, until it becomes a value.

Nontermination. The `strict` attribute drives 𝕂's evaluation strategy. Together with `KResult`, the `strict` attributes offer hints to 𝕂 to help it execute programs (i.e., to apply rewrite rules) more efficiently. The `strict` attributes do *not* mean to guarantee the termination of program execution. For example, the following expression `(lambda x . (x x)) (lambda x . (x x))` does not terminate. In fact, it represents the famous λ-calculus Ω combinator, which is the simplest λ-expression whose β-reduction process does not terminate.

Integer and Boolean Builtins. We can define arithmetic and Boolean expression constructs, which are simply rewritten to their builtin counterparts once their arguments are evaluated.

```
syntax Val ::= Int | Bool
syntax Exp ::= Exp "*" Exp          [strict, left]
             | Exp "/" Exp          [strict]
             > Exp "+" Exp          [strict, left]
             > Exp "<=" Exp         [strict]
rule I1 * I2 => I1 *Int I2
rule I1 / I2 => I1 /Int I2   requires I2 =/=Int 0
rule I1 + I2 => I1 +Int I2
rule I1 <= I2 => I1 <=Int I2
```

The operations with sort suffixes (such as `*Int` and `/Int`) are 𝕂's builtin arithmetic operations and come with the corresponding builtin sort. Note that the variables appearing in these rules have `Int` sort. That means that these rules will only be applied after the arguments of the arithmetic constructs are fully evaluated to 𝕂 results. This happens thanks to their strictness attributes declared as annotations to their syntax declarations.

The keyword `requires` specifies the condition when a rewrite rule can be matched and applied. Therefore, `I1 / I2` is only defined when `I2` is not zero. When `I2` is zero, `I1 / I2` can not be matched by any rewrite rules and thus the execution gets stuck.

Conditional Expressions. We can define conditional expressions as follows. Note that the `if` construct is strict only in its first argument. Therefore, 𝕂 will only evaluate its first argument (the condition) to a result and will not touch its second and third argument.

```
syntax Exp ::= "if" Exp "then" Exp "else" Exp     [strict(1)]
rule if true  then E else _ => E
rule if false then _ else E => E
```

Let Binder. The let binder is a derived construct, because it can be defined using the λ-binder. The `macro` attribute means that the rule that desugars `let` is applied statically during compilation on all expressions that it is matched, and statically *before* evaluating the given λ-expressions.

```
syntax Exp ::= "let" Id "=" Exp "in" Exp
rule let X = E in E':Exp => (lambda X . E') E          [macro]
```

Letrec Binder. Similarly, `letrec` can also be defined in K. Here, we prefer a definition based on the μ-binder that constructs the fixpoints in λ-calculus.

```
syntax Exp ::= "letrec" Id Id "=" Exp "in" Exp
             | "mu" Id "." Exp                         [binder]
rule letrec F:Id X:Id = E in E' => let F = mu F . lambda X . E in E' [macro]
rule mu X . E => E[(mu X . E) / X]
endmodule
```

Finally, we finish the definition of module LAMBDA with the keyword `endmodule`.

Compiling K *definitions and executing programs.* The K definition of LAMBDA is now complete. We can compile it using the command

```
$ kompile lambda.k
```

Then we can execute programs, i.e., evaluating λ-expressions using the `krun` command. For example, if the file `factorial.lambda` contains the LAMBDA program

```
letrec f x = if x <= 1 then 1 else (x * (f (x + -1)))
in (f 10)
```

then the command

```
$ krun factorial.k
```

yields the expected result 3628800.

3.2   IMP: An Imperative Language

In this section, we discuss the K definition of the prototypical IMP language. IMP is a simple imperative language. It is considered as a folklore language, without an official inventor, and has been used in many textbooks and papers, often with slight syntactic variations and often without being called IMP. It includes the most basic imperative language constructs, namely basic constructs for arithmetic and Boolean expressions, and variable assignment, conditional, while loop and sequential composition constructs for statements.

The K definition of IMP has two modules: IMP-SYNTAX that defines the syntax of IMP and IMP that imports IMP-SYNTAX and defines the formal semantics in terms of K's rewrite rules.

Syntax of IMP

`module IMP-SYNTAX`

This module defines the syntax of IMP as shown below.

```
syntax AExp  ::= Int | Id
               | AExp "/" AExp        [left, strict]
               > AExp "+" AExp        [left, strict]
               | "(" AExp ")"         [bracket]
syntax BExp  ::= Bool
               | AExp "<=" AExp  [seqstrict, latex({#1}\leq{#2})]
               | "!" BExp             [strict]
               > BExp "&&" BExp        [left, strict(1)]
               | "(" BExp ")"         [bracket]
syntax Block ::= "{" "}"
               | "{" Stmt "}"
syntax Stmt  ::= Block
               | Id "=" AExp ";"      [strict(2)]
               | "if" "(" BExp ")"
                 Block "else" Block   [strict(1)]
               | "while" "(" BExp ")" Block
               > Stmt Stmt            [left]
syntax Pgm ::= "int" Ids ";" Stmt
syntax Ids ::= List{Id,","}
endmodule
```

As in LAMBDA, the syntax of the language is defined using the conventional BNF grammar. Syntax productions are separated by "|" and ">", where "|" means the two productions have the same precedence while ">" means the previous production has higher precedence (binds tighter) than the one that follows. In our example, all language constructs bind tighter than the sequential operator in IMP. Int and Id are two built-in categories of integers and identifiers (program variables), respectively. Exp is the category of expressions, which subsumes Int and Id, and contains two other productions for plus and minus. Pgm is the category of IMP programs.

A wellformed IMP program declares a list of program variables in the beginning and then executes a statement in the state obtained after initializing all those variables to 0. Ids is the category for lists of program variables, and it is defined using 𝕂's built-in template List. The first argument is the base category Id, and second argument is the separating character ",".

The seqstrict attribute specifies that <= is sequentially strict, so its arguments will be evaluated *in order* from left to right. <= also has a LaTeX attribute making it display as ≤, and that && is strict only in its first argument, because we want to give it a short-circuit semantics.

We are done with the definition of IMP's syntax.

Semantics of IMP

```
module IMP
  imports IMP-SYNTAX
```

The module IMP defines the semantics of IMP as a set of $\mathbb{K}$ rewrite rules.

Values and Results. IMP only has two types of results of computations: integers and Booleans, as defined below:

```
syntax KResult ::= Int | Bool
```

Configurations. Unlike LAMBDA, the execution of IMP programs requires an execution environment. Specifically, we need to define *program states* that map variables to their values.

In general, $\mathbb{K}$ uses *configurations* to organize the execution environment. A configuration represents a program execution state, holding all information that is needed for program execution. Configurations are organized into *cells*, which are labeled and can be nested. Simple languages such as IMP have only a few cells, while complex real languages such as C have a lot more. Configurations are defined in XML format as below:

```
configuration <T color="yellow">
                <k color="green"> $PGM:Pgm </k>
                <state color="red"> .Map </state>
              </T>
```

An IMP configuration has two cells: a <k/> cell and a <state/> cell. For clarity, we gather both cells and put them in a top-level cell <T/> cell. For better readability, we color the <k/> in green, color the <state/> in red, and color the <T/> cell in yellow. The <k/> cell holds the rest computation (i.e., program fragments) that needs to execute and the <state/> cell holds a map from program variables to their values in the memory. Initially, the <state/> cell holds the empty map, denoted as .Map. In $\mathbb{K}$, we write "." for "nothing", and .Map means the type of the "nothing" is Map.

The special configuration variable $PGM tells the $\mathbb{K}$ tool where to place the program. More precisely, the command "krun file.imp" parses the IMP program in file file.imp and places the resulting $\mathbb{K}$ abstract syntax tree in the <k/> cell before invoking the semantic rules described in the sequel.

Arithmetic and Boolean Expressions. The $\mathbb{K}$ semantics of each arithmetic construct is defined below.

Variable Lookup. A program variable X is looked up in the state by matching a binding of the form $X \mapsto I$ in the state cell. If such a binding does not exist, then the rewriting process gets stuck. In other words, we disallow uses of uninitialized variables in IMP. Note that variable lookup is the first task performed while evaluating the statement in the <k/> cell (the cell is closed to the left and open to the right, as marked by the "..." on the right), while the binding can be anywhere in the <state/> cell (the cell is open at both sides, as marked by the "..." on both sides). Specifically, "..." means something "that exists but does not change in the rewrite". The rule, therefore, says that if a program variable X:Id is the current computation fragment in the <k/> cell, and X binds to the integer I somewhere in the <state/> cell, then X:Id is rewritten to I and nothing else should change.

```
rule <k> X:Id => I ...</k> <state>... X |-> I ...</state>
```

In the above, we color the two cells in blue and red, respectively, for readability. The above shows an important characteristic of 𝕂's rewrite rules: 𝕂 supports *local rewrites*, which are rewrite rules whose rewrite symbols "=>" occur not necessarily at the top but locally at where the rewrites happen. Without local rewrites, the above variables looking up rule has to be written as below:

```
rule <k> X:Id ...</k> <state>... X |-> I ...</state>
  => <k> I    ...</k> <state>... X |-> I ...</state>
```

As we can see, local rewrites avoid writing duplicate expressions on both the LHS and RHS of the rewrites.

Arithmetic Operators. We can define the semantics of arithmetic operators in the usual way.

```
rule I1 / I2 => I1 /Int I2  requires I2 =/=Int 0
rule I1 + I2 => I1 +Int I2
```

Note that 𝕂's *configuration abstraction* mechanism is at work here. In other words, rewrite rules do not need to explicitly mention all configuration cells but only those related. 𝕂 will infer the implicit cells, compete the configuration automatically, and apply the rewrite rule. Without configuration abstraction, the above rule for arithmetic operators has to be written as:

```
rule <k> I1 + I2 => I1 +Int I2 ... </k> <state> ... </state>
```

Not only is the rule using configuration abstraction more succinct, but it is also more modular. Suppose we need to modify the semantics and add a new configuration cell, we do not need to modify the rules with configuration abstraction because the new added cells can be automatically inferred and completed by 𝕂. Configuration abstraction is one of the most important features that makes 𝕂 definitions extensible and easy to adapt to language changes.

Boolean Expressions. The following rules for Boolean expressions are straightforward.

```
rule I1 <= I2 => I1 <=Int I2
rule ! T => notBool T
rule true && B => B
rule false && _ => false
```

Program Statements

Blocks. The empty block {} is simply dissolved. The dot symbol "." represents the unit of the computation list structure, i.e., the empty task. Similarly, the nonempty blocks are dissolved and replaced by their statement contents, thus effectively giving them a bracket semantics; we can afford to do this only because we have no block-local variable declarations yet in IMP. Since we tagged the rules below with attribute **structural**, 𝕂 structurally erases the block constructs from the computation structure, without considering their erasure as computational steps in the resulting transition systems. In other words, these rules are not regarded as computational steps.

```
rule {} => .   [structural]
rule {S} => S  [structural]
```

Assignments. The variable X is assigned a new integer value I and then the program state is updated accordingly.

```
rule <k> X = I:Int; => . ...</k> <state>... X |-> (_ => I) ...</state>
```

Sequential Composition. Sequential composition is simply structurally translated to 𝕂's builtin task sequentialization operation "~>". In other words, the effect of executing the sequential composition statement S1 S2 is equivalent to the effect of first executing S1 and then executing S2.

```
rule S1:Stmt S2:Stmt => S1 ~> S2   [structural]
```

Conditional Statements. The conditional statement has two semantic cases. We have seen them in defining LAMBDA.

```
rule if (true)  S else _ => S
rule if (false) _ else S => S
```

While Loops. The semantics of a **while** loop is defined simply by unfolding the loop once.

```
rule while (B) S => if (B) {S while (B) S} else {}  [structural]
```

Note that the above rule works because conditional statement (on the right-hand side) has the attribute **strict(1)**, so the inner **while** loop in the then-branch of the **it**-statement will not be unfolded.

Programs. An IMP program is a list of program variables declarations followed by a statement. The semantics is that the statement is executed in the initial state where all declared variables have value 0. 𝕂's syntactic lists are internally interpreted as cons-lists (i.e., lists constructed with a head element followed by a tail list), we have two cases. One is when the list has at least one element. The other is when the list is empty. In the first case, we initialize the variable to 0 in the state, but only when it is not already declared (we use juxtaposition to denote list concatenation in the following 𝕂 rules). In the second case, we dissolve the residual empty **int;** declaration as a structural cleanup.

```
rule <k> int (X,Xs => Xs);_ </k>
     <state> Rho:Map (.Map => X|->0) </state>
requires notBool (X in keys(Rho))
rule int .Ids; S => S  [structural]
endmodule
```

We have finished the definition of module IMP.

Compiling the Definition and Executing IMP Programs. After compilation with the command kompile imp.k, we can execute programs. Suppose sum.imp contains the following program:

```
int n, sum;
n = 100;
sum = 0;
while (!(n <= 0)) {
  sum = sum + n;
  n = n + -1;
}
```

then **krun** sum.imp yields the following final configuration

```
<T>
  <k> . </k>
  <state>
    n |-> 0
    sum |-> 5050
  </state>
</T>
```

Notice that in the final configuration, the <k/> cell is empty, meaning that the program was completely executed, or consumed. In the end of the execution, the program variable n has value 0 and s has value 5050, which is the total of numbers up to 100, as expected.

K is able to automatically generate a parser and an interpreter of any language from its formal definition, as we have seen in LAMBDA and IMP. This capability of K is crucial for testing language semantics and thus for increasing confidence in its adequacy. The above also illustrates another useful K tool: the K *unparser*, which is used by almost any other tool. Indeed, the above configuration result uses concrete language syntax (i.e. the syntax of IMP) to display the cells and their contents, although internally these are all represented as abstract data types.

We point out that the interpreters automatically generated by K can be *reasonably efficient*. For example, the formal definition of the Ethereum virtual machine (EVM) bytecode language, one of the most popular virtual machine languages for the blockchain, yields an EVM interpreter that is as efficient as the hand-written reference JavaScript implementation of EVM [22].

4   Matching Logic: The Logical Foundations of 𝕂

In this section, we introduce matching logic [10,11,30], the foundational logic underlying 𝕂. In Sect. 4.1, we discuss the motivation behind the design of matching logic. In Sect. 4.2, we formally define the syntax and semantics of matching logic. In Sect. 4.4, we introduce the Hilbert-style proof system of matching logic, using which we can carry out all logical reasoning in the logics and calculi mentioned in Sect. 1.2, all of which have been defined as theories and/or notations in matching logic, as shown in Sect. 4.3.

4.1   Matching Logic: Motivations

One main motivation for the design of matching logic is to give language semantic frameworks, such as 𝕂, a mathematically sound and rigorous logical foundation. Specifically, we want a foundational logic that is able to:

1. specify and reason about static program structures and configurations;
2. specify and reason about dynamic program behaviors and properties;
3. specify and reason about (least/greatest) fixpoints, which occur in both static structures (such as inductive/co-inductive data types) and dynamic properties (such as temporal and reachability properties).

We discuss the three motivations respectively in the following.

Motivation 1: Specifying and Reasoning About Static Program Structures and Configurations. Traditionally, static structures are specified using first-order logic (FOL) *terms*, which are built from variables, constants, and function symbols and can be used to define data constructors and language constructs. On the other hand, the properties about static structures are specified using FOL *formulas* as logical constraints, which are built from the primitive predicate symbols and composed using logical connectives.

However, such a clear distinction between terms (that represent data) and formulas (that represent the properties of data) can be inconvenient when it comes to specifying and reasoning about *program configurations*.

Consider as an example the program shown in Fig. 3, which reads n elements and outputs them in reversed order. The reader need not to understand all details; we will explain what are necessary below. The formal specifications of the program are given in gray. Note that in the specifications, we need to match an *abstract* sequence of n elements in the input buffer, and then to match its reverse at the end of the output buffer when the function terminates. Furthermore, in order to state the invariants of the two loops, we need to identify a singly linked list pattern in the heap, which is a finitely-supported partial map. Many such sequence or map patterns, as well as functions and operations on them, can be defined using conventional algebraic data types (ADTs) and/or FOL terms.

However, there are limitations. A major limitation is that function symbols must be interpreted as functions in models, which sometimes is insufficient.

```
struct listNode { int val; struct listNode *next; };

void list_read_write(int n) {
  rule ⟨$Pgm ⇒ return;  ···⟩code ⟨A ⇒ ·  ···⟩in ⟨··· · ⇒ rev(A)⟩out ∧ n = len(A)
    int i=0;
    struct listNode *x=0;
  inv  ⟨β ∧ len(β) = n − i ∧ i ≤ n ···⟩in ⟨list(x, α) ···⟩heap ∧ A = rev(α)@β
    while (i < n) {
      struct listNode *y = x;
      x = (struct listNode*) malloc(sizeof(struct listNode));
      scanf("%d", &(x->val));
      x->next = y;
      i += 1; }
  inv  ⟨··· α⟩out ⟨list(x, β) ···⟩heap ∧ rev(A) = α@β
    while (x) {
      struct listNode *y;
      y = x->next;
      printf("%d␣",x->val);
      free(x);
      x = y; }
}
```

Fig. 3. Reading, storing, and reverse writing a sequence of integers

For example, a two-element linked list in the heap starting with location 7 and holding values 9 and 5, written as $list(7, 9@5)$, can allow infinitely many heap values, one for each location where the value 5 may be stored. So we cannot define $list$ as an operation symbol $Int \times Seq \rightarrow Map$. The FOL alternative is to define $list$ as a predicate $Int \times Seq \times Map$, taking an additional heap argument. But mentioning the map all the time as an argument makes specifications verbose and hard to read, use and reason about. An alternative, proposed by separation logic [28], is to fix and move the map domain from explicit in models to implicit in the logic, so that $list(7, 9@5)$ is interpreted as a predicate but the non-deterministic map choices are implicit in the logic. The drawback of that, is that we may need customized separation logics for different languages that require different variations of map models or different configurations making use of different kinds of resources. This may also require specialized separation logic tools and provers, or otherwise encodings that need to be proved correct. Finally, since the map domain is not available as data, one cannot use FOL variables to range over maps and thus proof rules like "heap framing" need to be added to the logic explicitly.

Matching logic avoids the limitations of the approaches above, by interpreting its terms/formulae uniformly as *sets* of values. Matching logic's formulas, called *patterns*, are built using variables, symbols from a signature, and FOL connectives and quantifiers, and their semantics are the sets of values that *match* them; see Sect. 4.2.

Motivation 2: Specifying and Reasoning About Dynamic Program Behaviors and Properties. Traditionally, dynamic behaviors and properties can be specified in modal logic and/or modal μ-logic, as well as their temporal logics and dynamic logics fragments. Modal logic uses *modal operators* to specify various dynamic properties of transition systems. For example, the "next" operator $\circ\varphi$ holds on a state if the next state satisfies φ; $\Box\varphi$ holds if φ always holds; the "eventually" operator $\Diamond\varphi$ holds if φ eventually holds; etc.

A major limitation of modal logic is that it has no direct support for specifying the static structures of states. Indeed, in modal logic models, which are transition systems, states are structureless "points". Therefore, it is insufficient to specify and reason about program configurations, especially $\mathbb{K}$ configurations, which are nested structures built from basic mathematical domain values, data constructors, language constructs, and configuration cells.

Matching logic overcomes this limitation by defining modal logic operators uniformly using *symbols*. Recall that symbols and matching logic patterns are interpreted as the sets of elements that match them, so matching logic symbols are naturally interpreted as relations and can thus be used to capture the transition relations in transition systems. In addition, matching logic can use symbols and its FOL connectives and quantifiers to re-construct FOL formulas and structures, which are ideal in defining program configurations.

Motivation 3: Specifying and Reasoning About Least/Greatest Fixpoints. Fixpoints, especially least and greatest fixpoints, play an important role in programming languages semantics. Many real-world programming languages support inductive data types, which are mathematical domains that are defined as the smallest sets closed under user-defined constructors. Some programming languages, such as Haskell, support co-inductive data types (also called infinite data types). Both inductive and co-inductive data types are special instances of least/greatest fixpoints about static structures.

Fixpoints also play an important role in defining dynamic program behaviors and properties. For example, modal operators $\Box\varphi$ (always φ), $\Diamond\varphi$ (eventually φ), $\varphi_1 \,U\, \varphi_2$ (φ_1 until φ_2, meaning that φ_1 holds from now until the first time φ_2 holds), can all be defined using least/greatest fixpoints from the basic transition relations, i.e., the "next" operator $\circ\varphi$. For program verification, we define *reachability properties* $\varphi_1 \Rightarrow \varphi_2$, read "$\varphi_1$ reaches φ_2", to mean that φ_1 can reach φ_2 on some finite execution paths, which corresponds to the partial correctness semantics in the traditional Hoare-style verification; see Sect. 5.3.

Matching logic provides built-in support for fixpoint reasoning that occurs in both static structures and configurations and dynamic behaviors and properties, and in particular program verification.

4.2   Matching Logic: Syntax and Semantics

Matching logic formulas, called *patterns*, are built using variables, symbols, propositional connectives, FOL quantifiers, and fixpoints. Matching logic has a *powerset semantics*, where patterns are interpreted as the sets of elements that match them.

We assume readers are familiar with the basic notions and concepts about FOL and modal μ-logic.

Definition 1. *A* matching logic signature *or simply a* signature *is a triple* (S, V, Σ), *where*

- *S is a nonempty set of* sorts *written* $s_1, s_2, \ldots$;
- $V = EV \cup SV$ *with* $EV \cap SV = \emptyset$ *is a disjoint union of two sets of variables, where* $EV = \{EV_s\}_{s \in S}$ *contains* sorted element variables *written* $x:s, y:s, \ldots$ *and* $SV = \{SV_s\}_{s \in S}$ *contains* sorted set variables *written* $X:s, Y:s, \ldots$;
- $\Sigma = \{\Sigma_{s_1 \ldots s_n, s}\}_{s_1, \ldots, s_n, s \in S}$ *is a set of many-sorted symbols written* $\sigma \in \Sigma_{s_1 \ldots s_n, s}$, *where* $s_1, \ldots, s_n$ *are called the argument sorts and s is called the return sort.*

Given a signature (S, V, Σ), *matching logic patterns are inductively defined as follows for all* $s, s' \in S$:

$$\varphi_s ::= x:s \mid X:s \mid \sigma(\varphi_{s_1}, \ldots, \varphi_{s_n}) \quad \text{where } \sigma \in \Sigma_{s_1 \ldots s_n, s}$$
$$\mid \varphi_s \wedge \varphi'_s \mid \neg\varphi_s \mid \exists x:s'.\varphi_s \mid \mu X:s.\varphi_s$$

where $\mu X:s.\varphi_s$ *requires all free occurrences of* $X:s$ *are under an even number of negations in* φ_s. *The logical connectives* $\vee, \rightarrow, \leftrightarrow, \forall$ *are defined in the usual way.*

ML patterns are interpreted on an underlying carrier set of elements, and each pattern is then interpreted as a *set of elements*, which are those that *match* the pattern. This is called the *pattern matching semantics* of ML, and is what inspired the name "matching logic". For example, pattern *zero* is matched by the natural number 0; pattern *succ(zero)* is matched by the number 1; the (disjunctive) pattern *zero* $\vee$ *succ(zero)* is matched by 0 and 1; to put it another way, an element a matches *zero* $\vee$ *succ(zero)*, if a matches *zero* or a matches *succ(zero)*. Intuitively, $\varphi_s \wedge \varphi'_s$ is matched by those matching both φ_s and φ'_s. Pattern $\neg\varphi_s$ is matched by the elements (of sort s) that do not match φ_s. Element variable $x:s$ is a pattern that is matched by exactly one element to which $x:s$ evaluates (evaluation of variables is defined later). Set variable $X:s$ is a pattern that is matched by exactly the elements in the set to which $X:s$ evaluates to.

The meaning of $\sigma(\varphi_{s_1}, \ldots, \varphi_{s_n})$, called a symbol application, depends on how we interpret σ. For example, if σ is interpreted as a *constructor*, then $\sigma(\varphi_{s_1}, \ldots, \varphi_{s_n})$ is matched by the *structures* built by σ on elements matching $\varphi_{s_1}, \ldots, \varphi_{s_n}$, respectively. If σ is interpreted as a *function*, then $\sigma(\varphi_{s_1}, \ldots, \varphi_{s_n})$ is matched by the *return values* obtained by applying σ on elements matching $\varphi_{s_1}, \ldots, \varphi_{s_n}$. If σ is interpreted as a *relation* (such as the modal operators in modal logic). Then $\sigma(\varphi_{s_1}, \ldots, \varphi_{s_n})$ is matched by the elements that have the relation σ with elements matching $\varphi_{s_1}, \ldots, \varphi_{s_n}$, respectively. In conclusion, matching logic symbols can be used to uniformly represent constructors, functions, and relations (predicates).

There are two *binders* in matching logic. The $\exists$-binder binds element variables and builds *abstraction* $\exists x\!:\!s'.\varphi_s$, which is matched by the elements that match φ_s for *some valuations* of $x\!:\!s'$. In other words, it "abstracts away" the irrelevant part (i.e., $x\!:\!s'$) from the matched part (i.e., φ_s). Note that the sort of the binding variable $x\!:\!s'$ needs not to be the same as the sort of the pattern φ_s.

The μ-binder builds *least fixpoints*. Intuitively, φ_s with free occurrences of $X\!:\!s$ defines a function $\mathcal{F}_{\varphi_s,X\!:\!s}$ that maps (the set of elements matching) $X\!:\!s$ to (the set of elements matching) φ_s. Since $X\!:\!s$ occurs positively in φ_s, we can verify that $\mathcal{F}_{\varphi_s,X\!:\!s}$ is a monotone function, so it has a unique least fixpoint denoted as $\mu\mathcal{F}_{\varphi_s,X\!:\!s}$, guaranteed by the Knaster-Tarski fixpoint theorem (Theorem 1). The least fixpoint pattern $\mu X\!:\!s.\varphi_s$ is then matched by the elements in set $\mu\mathcal{F}_{\varphi_s,X\!:\!s}$.

We define the notions of free variables, capture-avoiding substitution, α-renaming, etc. in the usual way. We use $\varphi[\psi/x\!:\!s]$ (resp. $\varphi[\psi/X\!:\!s]$) to denote the result of substituting ψ for $x\!:\!s$ (resp. $X\!:\!s$) in φ, where α-renaming happens implicitly to prevent variable captures.

We review the Knaster-Tarski fixpoint theorem [35].

Theorem 1 (Knaster-Tarski). *Let M be a nonempty set and $\mathcal{P}(M)$ be the powerset of M. Let $\mathcal{F}\colon \mathcal{P}(M) \to \mathcal{P}(M)$ be a monotone function, i.e., $\mathcal{F}(A) \subseteq \mathcal{F}(B)$ for all subsets $A \subseteq B$ of M. Then $\mathcal{F}$ has a unique least fixpoint, written $\mu\mathcal{F}$, and a unique greatest fixpoint, written $\nu\mathcal{F}$, given as:*

$$\mu\mathcal{F} = \bigcap\{A \in \mathcal{P}(M) \mid \mathcal{F}(A) \subseteq A\},$$
$$\nu\mathcal{F} = \bigcup\{A \in \mathcal{P}(M) \mid A \subseteq \mathcal{F}(A)\}.$$

We call A a pre-fixpoint of $\mathcal{F}$ whenever $\mathcal{F}(A) \subseteq A$, and a post-fixpoint of $\mathcal{F}$ whenever $A \subseteq \mathcal{F}(A)$.

We now define matching logic models and interpretations of patterns.

Definition 2. *An (S, V, Σ)-model is a pair $M = (\{M_s\}_{s\in S}, \{\sigma_M\}_{\sigma\in\Sigma})$, consisting of a nonempty carrier set M_s for every $s \in S$ and an interpretation $\sigma_M\colon M_{s_1} \times \cdots \times M_{s_n} \to \mathcal{P}(M_s)$ for every $\sigma \in \Sigma_{s_1\ldots s_n,s}$. We extend σ_M to its pointwise extension, $\sigma_M\colon \mathcal{P}(M_{s_1}) \times \cdots \times \mathcal{P}(M_{s_n}) \to \mathcal{P}(M_s)$, defined as*

$$\sigma_M(A_1,\ldots,A_n) = \bigcup_{a_i \in A_i, 1\le i\le n} \sigma_M(a_1,\ldots,a_n)$$

for $A_i \subseteq M_{s_i}$, $1 \le i \le n$. An M-valuation $\rho\colon V \to M \cup \mathcal{P}(M)$ is one such that $\rho(x\!:\!s) \in M_s$ and $\rho(X\!:\!s) \subseteq M_s$ for all $x\!:\!s, X\!:\!s \in V$. Its extension $\bar{\rho}$ interprets (S, V, Σ)-patterns to sets as follows:

- $\bar{\rho}(x\!:\!s) = \{\rho(x\!:\!s)\}$;
- $\bar{\rho}(\sigma(\varphi_{s_1},\ldots,\varphi_{s_n})) = \sigma_M(\bar{\rho}(\varphi_{s_1}),\ldots,\bar{\rho}(\varphi_{s_n}))$ *for all $\sigma \in \Sigma_{s_1\ldots s_n,s}$*

- $\bar{\rho}(X\!:\!s) = \rho(X\!:\!s)$
- $\bar{\rho}(\varphi_s \wedge \varphi'_s) = \bar{\rho}(\varphi_s) \cap \bar{\rho}(\varphi'_s)$
- $\bar{\rho}(\exists x\!:\!s'.\varphi_s) = \bigcup_{a \in M_{s'}} \rho[a/x\!:\!s'](\varphi_s)$
- $\bar{\rho}(\neg\varphi_s) = M \setminus \bar{\rho}(\varphi_s)$
- $\bar{\rho}(\mu X\!:\!s.\varphi_s) = \mu \mathcal{F}^{\rho}_{\varphi, X\,:\,s}$ with $\mathcal{F}^{\rho}_{\varphi, X\,:\,s}(A) = \overline{\rho[A/X\!:\!s]}(\varphi_s)$ for $A \subseteq M_s$

We say φ_s holds in M, written $M \vDash \varphi_s$, iff $\bar{\rho}(\varphi_s) = M_s$ for all ρ. A theory is a set Γ of patterns. We write $M \vDash \Gamma$, iff $M \vDash \varphi$ for all $\varphi \in \Gamma$. We write $\Gamma \vDash \varphi_s$, iff $M \vDash \varphi_s$ for all models with $M \vDash \Gamma$.

Predicate Patterns. A difference between FOL formulas and ML patterns is that FOL formulas can only be interpreted as either true or false, while ML patterns can be interpreted as any subsets of the carrier set. To represent the (logical) true and false using patterns, we identify two special sets M and $\emptyset$, and use M to represent the logical truth and $\emptyset$ to represent the logical false. Obviously, not all patterns are interpreted as M or $\emptyset$. Given a model M, we call φ an *M-predicate*, if $\bar{\rho}(\varphi) \in \{\emptyset, M\}$ for all ρ. We call φ a *predicate* (or *predicate pattern*), if it is an M-predicate in all M. Predicate patterns can be built from $\bot$, $\top$, and ML logical constructs. More interesting patterns can be built from symbols and application. We will see more predicate patterns in Sect. 4.3 and throughout the paper. Roughly speaking, predicate patterns are the ML counterparts of FOL formulas. They make "statements", and can take only two possible values: M if the statements are facts, and $\emptyset$ if the statements are not facts.

4.3 Matching Logic Expressiveness

In this section, we discuss the expressiveness of matching logic by showing that FOL, inductive data types, transition systems, temporal logics, and reachability logic (for language-independent program verification) can be defined as theories and/or notations.

Important Mathematical Instruments. Several mathematical instruments of practical importance, such as definedness, totality, equality, membership, set containment, functions and partial functions, and constructors, can all be defined/axiomatized in matching logic.

Definition 3. *For any (not necessarily distinct) sorts s, s', let us consider a unary symbol $\lceil \_ \rceil_s^{s'} \in \Sigma_{s,s'}$, called the* definedness *symbol, and the pattern/axiom $\lceil x\!:\!s \rceil_s^{s'}$, called (DEFINEDNESS). We define totality "$\lfloor \_ \rfloor_s^{s'}$", equality "$=_s^{s'}$", membership "$\in_s^{s'}$", and set containment "$\subseteq_s^{s'}$" as derived constructs:*

$$\lfloor \varphi \rfloor_s^{s'} \equiv \neg\lceil \neg\varphi \rceil_s^{s'} \qquad\qquad \varphi_1 =_s^{s'} \varphi_2 \equiv \lfloor \varphi_1 \leftrightarrow \varphi_2 \rfloor_s^{s'}$$

$$x \in_s^{s'} \varphi \equiv \lceil x \wedge \varphi \rceil_s^{s'} \qquad\qquad \varphi_1 \subseteq_s^{s'} \varphi_2 \equiv \lfloor \varphi_1 \rightarrow \varphi_2 \rfloor_s^{s'}$$

and feel free to drop the (not necessarily distinct) sorts s, s'.

Intuitively, the axiom (DEFINEDNESS) states that every individual element x is defined. This is true, because x is matched by *exactly one element* to which it evaluates. Therefore, in any model that validates (DEFINEDNESS), $\lceil x \rceil$ is interpreted as the total set, according to ML validity (Definition 2). Now, consider any pattern φ that is defined, and that φ is matched by one element, say x. By *pointwise extension* (Definition 2), the interpretation of $\lceil \varphi \rceil$ must include the interpretation of $\lceil x \rceil$, which we know is the total set. Therefore, $\lceil \varphi \rceil$ is also interpreted as the total set, which is intended. On the other hand, if φ is *undefined*, its interpretation is the empty set, and by pointwise extension, $\lceil \varphi \rceil$ is also interpreted as the empty set. The above intuition is made formal below.

Proposition 1. *Let M be a matching logic model satisfying* (DEFINEDNESS). *Let ρ be any valuation. Then the following hold:*

- $\bar{\rho}(\lceil \varphi_s \rceil) = M_s$ *if* $\bar{\rho}(\varphi_s) \neq \emptyset$, *i.e.,* φ_s *is defined;*
- $\bar{\rho}(\lceil \varphi_s \rceil) = \emptyset$ *if* $\bar{\rho}(\varphi_s) = \emptyset$, *i.e.,* φ_s *is not defined;*
- $\bar{\rho}(\lfloor \varphi_s \rfloor) = M_s$ *if* $\bar{\rho}(\varphi_s) = M_s$, *i.e.,* φ_s *is total;*
- $\bar{\rho}(\lfloor \varphi_s \rfloor) = \emptyset$ *if* $\bar{\rho}(\varphi_s) \neq M_s$, *i.e.,* φ_s *is not total;*
- $\bar{\rho}(\varphi_s =_s^{s'} \varphi'_s) = M_{s'}$ *if* $\bar{\rho}(\varphi_s) = \bar{\rho}(\varphi'_s)$;
- $\bar{\rho}(\varphi_s =_s^{s'} \varphi'_s) = \emptyset$ *if* $\bar{\rho}(\varphi_s) \neq \bar{\rho}(\varphi'_s)$;
- $\bar{\rho}(x\!:\!s \in_s^{s'} \varphi_s) = M_{s'}$ *if* $\rho(x\!:\!s) \in \bar{\rho}(\varphi_s)$;
- $\bar{\rho}(x\!:\!s \in_s^{s'} \varphi_s) = \emptyset$ *if* $\rho(x\!:\!s) \notin \bar{\rho}(\varphi_s)$;
- $\bar{\rho}(\varphi_s \subseteq_s^{s'} \varphi'_s) = M_{s'}$ *if* $\bar{\rho}(\varphi_s) \subseteq \bar{\rho}(\varphi'_s)$;
- $\bar{\rho}(\varphi_s \subseteq_s^{s'} \varphi'_s) = \emptyset$ *if* $\bar{\rho}(\varphi_s) \not\subseteq \bar{\rho}(\varphi'_s)$.

As seen in Definition 2, symbols in matching logic are interpreted as relations. Specifically speaking, consider a symbol $\sigma \in \Sigma_{s_1 \ldots s_n, s}$ and its interpretation $\sigma_M \colon M_{s_1} \times \cdots \times M_{s_n} \to \mathcal{P}(M_s)$. Obviously, functions and partial functions are special instances of matching logic symbols. Functions are when $|\sigma_M(a_1, \ldots, a_n)| = 1$ for all $a_1 \in M_{s_1}, \ldots, a_n \in M_{s_n}$. Partial functions are when $|\sigma_M(a_1, \ldots, a_n)| \leq 1$ for all $a_1 \in M_{s_1}, \ldots, a_n \in M_{s_n}$. In the following, we show that functions and partial functions can be defined by axioms:

(FUNCTION)	$\exists y \,.\, \sigma(x_1, \ldots, x_n) = y$
PARTIAL FUNCTION	$\exists y \,.\, \sigma(x_1, \ldots, x_n) \subseteq y$

Intuitively, (FUNCTION) requires $\sigma(x_1, \ldots, x_n)$ to contain exactly one element and (PARTIAL FUNCTION) requires it to contain at most one element (recall that variable y evaluates to a singleton set). For brevity, we use the function notation $\sigma \colon s_1 \times \cdots \times s_n \to s$ to mean we automatically assume the (FUNCTION) axiom of σ. Similarly, partial functions are written as $\sigma \colon s_1 \times \cdots \times s_n \rightharpoonup s$.

First-Order Logic. We can use the above definitions of functions to capture first-order logic (FOL) in matching logic. Specifically, given a FOL signature (S, Σ, Π) with *function symbols* Σ and *predicate symbols* Π, the *syntax* of FOL is given by:

$$t_s ::= x \in \text{VAR}_s \mid f(t_{s_1}, \ldots, t_{s_n}) \text{ with } f \in \Sigma_{s_1 \ldots s_n, s}$$
$$\varphi ::= \pi(t_{s_1}, \ldots, t_{s_n}) \text{ with } \pi \in \Pi_{s_1 \ldots s_n} \mid \varphi \rightarrow \varphi \mid \neg \varphi \mid \forall x . \varphi$$

To capture FOL, we define a matching logic signature $\Sigma^{\text{FOL}} = (S^{\text{FOL}}, \Sigma^{\text{FOL}})$ where $S^{\text{FOL}} = S \cup \{Pred\}$ contains all FOL sorts plus a distinguished sort $Pred$ for FOL formulas and $\Sigma^{\text{FOL}} = \{f : s_1 \times \cdots \times s_n \rightarrow s \mid f \in \Sigma_{s_1 \ldots s_n, s}\} \cup \{\pi \in \Sigma^{\text{FOL}}_{s_1 \ldots s_n, Pred} \mid \pi \in \Pi_{s_1 \ldots s_n}\}$ contains FOL function symbols as matching logic functions and FOL predicate symbols as matching logic symbols that return $Pred$. Let Γ^{FOL} be the resulting ML theory of signature Σ^{FOL}.

Proposition 2. *All FOL formulas φ are Σ^{FOL} -patterns of sort Pred, and we have $\models_{FOL} \varphi$ iff $\Gamma^{\text{FOL}} \models \varphi$ (see [30]), where $\models_{FOL} \varphi$ means that φ is valid in FOL.*

Inductive Data Structures. Here we show how configurations and inductive data structures can be *precisely axiomatized* in matching logic.

Definition 4. *Let $\Sigma = (\{Term\}, \Sigma)$ be a signature with one sort Term and at least one constant. Σ -terms are defined as:*

$$t ::= c \in \Sigma_{\lambda, Term} \mid c(t_1, \ldots, t_n) \text{ for } c \in \Sigma_{Term \ldots Term, Term}$$

The Σ -term algebra $T^{\Sigma} = (\{T^{\Sigma}_{Term}\}, \{c_{T^{\Sigma}}\}_{c \in \Sigma})$ consists of:

- *a carrier set T^{Σ}_{Term} of all Σ -terms;*
- *a function $c_{T^{\Sigma}} : T^{\Sigma}_{Term} \times \cdots \times T^{\Sigma}_{Term} \rightarrow T^{\Sigma}_{Term}$ for all $c \in \Sigma_{Term \ldots Term, Term}$ defined as $c_{T^{\Sigma}}(t_1, \ldots, t_n) = c(t_1, \ldots, t_n)$.*

Proposition 3. *Let $\Sigma = (\{Term\}, \Sigma)$ be a signature with one sort Term and at least one constant. Define a Σ -theory $\Gamma^{\text{term}}_{\Sigma}$ with (FUNCTION) axioms for all constructors, plus the following axioms:*

NO CONFUSION I *for all $i \neq j$ and $s_i = s_j$:*
$$\neg(c_i(x_i^1, \ldots, x_i^{m_i}) \wedge c_j(x_j^1, \ldots, x_j^{m_j}))$$
NO CONFUSION II *for all $1 \leq i \leq n$:*
$$(c_i(x_i^1, \ldots, x_i^{m_i}) \wedge c_i(y_i^1, \ldots, y_i^{m_i})) \rightarrow c_i(x_i^1 \wedge y_i^1, \ldots, x_i^{m_i} \wedge y_i^{m_i})$$
INDUCTIVE DOMAIN
$$\mu D . \bigvee_{c \in \Sigma} c(D, \ldots, D)$$

Then for all Σ-models $M \models \Gamma^{\text{term}}_{\Sigma}$, M is isomorphic to T^{Σ}..

Intuitively, (INDUCTIVE DOMAIN) forces that for all models M, the carrier set M_{Term} must be the *the smallest set* that is closed under all symbols in Σ, while (FUNCTION) and (NO CONFUSION) force all symbols in Σ to be interpreted as injective functions, and different symbols construct different terms.

Transition Systems. At a high level, every $\mathbb{K}$ definition defines a transition system over program configurations. Here we show how to specify and reason about transition systems in matching logic. We first recall the definition of transition systems.

Definition 5. *A transition system $\mathbb{S} = (S, R)$ consists of a nonempty set S of states/configurations and a binary relation $R \subseteq S \times S$ called transition relation. For $s, t \in S$ such that $s\,R\,t$, we say that s is an R-predecessor of t and t is an R-successor of s.*

To capture transition systems in matching logic, we define a signature $\Sigma^{\mathsf{TS}} = (\{State\}, \{\bullet \in \Sigma^{\mathsf{TS}}_{State, State}\})$ where $State$ is the sort of states and $\bullet \in \Sigma^{\mathsf{TS}}_{State, State}$ is a symbol called *one-path next*.

An important observation is that matching logic models of the signature Σ^{TS} are *exactly* the transition systems, where $\bullet \in \Sigma^{\mathsf{TS}}_{State, State}$ is interpreted as the transition relation R. Specifically, for any transition system $\mathbb{S} = (S, R)$, we can regard $\mathbb{S}$ as a model where S is the carrier set of $State$ and $\bullet_{\mathsf{S}}(t) = \{s \in S \mid s\,R\,t\}$ contains all R-predecessors of t. The intuition is illustrated as follows:

$$\cdots \quad s \xrightarrow{R} s' \xrightarrow{R} s'' \cdots \quad // \text{ states}$$
$$\bullet\bullet\varphi \quad \bullet\varphi \quad \varphi \quad // \text{ patterns}$$

In other words, $\bullet\varphi$ is matched by states that have a next state matching φ.

Other dynamic properties about transition systems can be defined as patterns. As an example, let us define *all-path next* $\circ\varphi \equiv \neg\bullet\neg\varphi$. It is straightforward to show that $\circ\varphi$ is matched by states if all their R-successors matching φ. In particular, if s has no R-successor, i.e. it is terminating, then s matches $\circ\varphi$ for any φ. In other words, the pattern $\circ\bot$ is matched by exactly states that are terminating.

We define more dynamic properties as patterns. In the following, $\varphi, \varphi_1, \varphi_2$, and X have sort $State$.

$$\text{"all-path next"} \quad \circ\varphi \equiv \neg\bullet\neg\varphi$$
$$\text{"eventually"} \quad \diamond\varphi \equiv \mu X . \varphi \vee \bullet X$$
$$\text{"always"} \quad \Box\varphi \equiv \nu X . \varphi \wedge \circ X$$
$$\text{"(strong) until"} \quad \varphi_1 \mathsf{U} \varphi_2 \equiv \mu X . \varphi_2 \vee (\varphi_1 \wedge \bullet X)$$
$$\text{"well-founded"} \quad \mathsf{WF} \equiv \mu X . \circ X \quad // \text{ no infinite paths}$$

The following proposition justifies the above definitions.

Proposition 4. *Let $\mathbb{S} = (S, R)$ be a transition system regarded as a Σ^{TS}-model, and let ρ be any valuation and $s \in S$. Then:*

- *$s \in \bar{\rho}(\bullet\varphi)$ if there exists $t \in S$ such that $s\,R\,t$, $t \in \bar{\rho}(\varphi)$; in particular, $s \in \bar{\rho}(\bullet\top)$ if s has an R-successor;*
- *$s \in \bar{\rho}(\circ\varphi)$ if for all $t \in S$ such that $s\,R\,t$, $t \in \bar{\rho}(\varphi)$; in particular, $s \in \bar{\rho}(\circ\bot)$ if s has no R-successor;*

- $s \in \bar{\rho}(\Diamond\varphi)$ *if there exists* $t \in S$ *such that* $s R^* t$, $t \in \bar{\rho}(\varphi)$;
- $s \in \bar{\rho}(\Box\varphi)$ *if for all* $t \in S$ *such that* $s R^* t$, $t \in \bar{\rho}(\varphi)$;
- $s \in \bar{\rho}(\varphi_1 U\varphi_2)$ *if there exists* $n \geq 0$ *and* $t_1, \ldots, t_n \in S$ *such that* $s R t_1 R \ldots R t_n$, $t_n \in \bar{\rho}(\varphi_2)$, *and* $s, t_1, \ldots, t_{n-1} \in \bar{\rho}(\varphi_1)$;
- $s \in \bar{\rho}(\mathsf{WF})$ *if* s *is* R-*well-founded, meaning that there is no infinite sequence* $t_1, t_2, \cdots \in S$ *with* $s R t_1 R t_2 R \ldots$;

where $R^* = \bigcup_{i \geq 0} R^i$ *is the reflexive transitive closure of* R.

Modal μ-Logic and Temporal Logics. We have seen that transition systems can be captured in matching logic by the one-path next symbol $\bullet \in \Sigma_{State,State}$. Here, we show that we can define modal μ-logic and various temporal logics such as linear temporal logic (LTL) and computation tree logic (CTL) as matching logic theories, whose axioms constrain the underlying transition relations. The resulting theories are simple, intuitive, and faithfully capture both the syntax (provability) and the semantics of these temporal logics.

We assume readers are familiar with the basic syntax of modal μ-logic and the various temporal logic. The following table summarizes the assumptions that these logics make on the traces of the underlying transition systems, and the corresponding matching logic axioms that capture the assumptions.

Target logic	Assumption on traces	Matching logic axioms
Modal μ-logic	Any traces, no assumptions	No axioms
Infinite-trace LTL	Infinite and linear traces	(INF) + (LIN)
Finite-trace LTL	Finite and linear traces	(FIN) + (LIN)
CTL	Infinite traces	(INF)

where (INF) is the pattern/axiom $\bullet\top$ stating that all states are non-terminal states, (FIN) is the pattern/axiom $\mathsf{WF} \equiv \mu X . \circ X$ stating that all states are well-founded, and (LIN) is the pattern/axiom $\bullet X \to \circ X$ enforcing the linear paths: X holds on one next state implies X holds on all next states.

In conclusion, modal μ-logic is the empty theory over one-path next $\bullet \in \Sigma_{State,State}$ that contains no axioms. Adding (INF) yields precisely CTL. Adding (INF) yields precisely infinite-trace LTL and replacing (INF) with (FIN) yields finite-trace LTL. Therefore, matching logic over the one-path next symbol $\bullet$ gives a playground for defining variants of temporal logics.

It also shows that matching logic can serve as a convenient and uniform framework to define and study temporal logics. For example, finite-trace CTL (which is not shown in the above) can be trivially obtained as the theory containing only the axiom (FIN); LTL with both finite and infinite traces is the theory containing only the axiom (LIN), etc.

Reachability Logic (Program Verification in K). We can define reachability properties as patterns using one-path next $\bullet \in \Sigma_{State,State}$. We will discuss it and K's program verification tools in Sect. 5.

(Propositional Tautology)	φ if φ is a propositional tautology over patterns of the same sort
(Modus Ponens)	$\dfrac{\varphi_1 \quad \varphi_1 \to \varphi_2}{\varphi_2}$
(∃-Quantifier)	$\varphi[y/x] \to \exists x . \varphi$
(∃-Generalization)	$\dfrac{\varphi_1 \to \varphi_2}{(\exists x . \varphi_1) \to \varphi_2}$ if $x \notin \mathrm{FV}(\varphi_2)$
(Propagation$_\bot$)	$C_\sigma[\bot] \to \bot$
(Propagation$_\lor$)	$C_\sigma[\varphi_1 \lor \varphi_2] \to C_\sigma[\varphi_1] \lor C_\sigma[\varphi_2]$
(Propagation$_\exists$)	$C_\sigma[\exists x . \varphi] \to \exists x . C_\sigma[\varphi]$ if $x \notin \mathrm{FV}(C_\sigma[\exists x . \varphi])$
(Framing)	$\dfrac{\varphi_1 \to \varphi_2}{C_\sigma[\varphi_1] \to C_\sigma[\varphi_2]}$
(Existence)	$\exists x . x$
(Singleton Variables)	$\neg(C_1[x \land \varphi] \land C_2[x \land \neg\varphi])$ where C_1 and C_2 are nested symbol contexts.
(Set Variable Substitution)	$\dfrac{\varphi}{\varphi[\psi/X]}$
(Pre-Fixpoint)	$\varphi[\mu X . \varphi / X] \to \mu X . \varphi$
(Knaster-Tarski)	$\dfrac{\varphi[\psi/X] \to \psi}{\mu X . \varphi \to \psi}$

Fig. 4. Matching logic proof system

4.4   Matching Logic Proof System

We have discussed the syntax and semantics of matching logic and have seen many important mathematical instruments as well as other important logics and models can be defined as theories/notations using patterns. In this section, we discuss the proof system of matching logic; that is, how to carry out formal reasoning in matching logic.

We first need the following definition of contexts.

Definition 6. *A* context *C is a pattern with a distinguished placeholder variable $\square$. We write $C[\varphi]$ to mean the result of* replacing *$\square$ with φ without any α-renaming, so free variables in φ may become bound in $C[\varphi]$, different from capture-avoiding substitution. A* single symbol context *has the form*

$$C_\sigma \equiv \sigma(\varphi_1, \ldots, \varphi_{i-1}, \square, \varphi_{i+1}, \ldots, \varphi_n)$$

where $\sigma \in \Sigma_{s_1 \ldots s_n, s}$ and $\varphi_1, \ldots, \varphi_{i-1}, \varphi_{i+1}, \ldots, \varphi_n$ are patterns of appropriate sorts. A nested symbol context *is inductively defined as follows:*

- *$\square$ is a nested symbol context, called the* identity context;
- *if C_σ is a single symbol context, and C is a nested symbol context, then $C_\sigma[C[\square]]$ is a nested symbol context.*

Intuitively, a context C is a nested symbol context iff the path to $\Box$ in C contains only symbols and no logic connectives.

Figure 4 shows the Hilbert-style proof system of matching logic. It has four categories of proof rules. The first category (containing the first four rules) consists of all FOL proof rules. This makes the normal FOL reasoning available in matching logic. The second category (containing the next four rules) that supports *framing reasoning*, which allows one to lift the local reasoning in a context (in particular a symbol) to the top level. Separation logic, for example, has a specific framing rule for heap reasoning that allows one to lift the reasoning over a heap fragment to the entire heap. Matching logic, on the other hand, supports generic frame reasoning for all symbols and structures, where heap reasoning is just an special instance. The third category contains two technical proof rules (EXISTENCE) and (SINGLETON VARIABLES) that are needed for certain completeness result (see [11]). The last category contains three proof rules borrowed from modal μ-logic that support fixpoint reasoning. The (KNASTER-TARSKI) proof rule is a logical incarnation of the Knaster-Tarski fixpoint theorem (Theorem 1) that is the key proof rule for carrying out inductive and co-inductive reasoning; it is known as (PARK INDUCTION) in some literature.

Definition 7. *Let Γ be a theory and φ be a pattern. We write $\Gamma \vdash \varphi$ if φ can be proved by the proof system shown in Fig. 4 with patterns in Γ regarded as additional axioms.*

As we have seen earlier, matching logic can capture precisely inductive data structures. As a consequence, matching logic can capture precisely natural numbers (which are inductive data structures built from two constructors *zero* and *succ*) and define the addition and multiplication of natural numbers using pattern axioms in the usual way. Therefore, the proof system of matching logic cannot be both sound and complete for all theories. Some completeness results have been shown for some theories or fragments of matching logic in [11]. In the following, we only state the soundness theorem of the matching logic proof system.

Theorem 2 (Soundness). *$\Gamma \vdash \varphi$ implies $\Gamma \vDash \varphi$.*

Since the proof system of matching logic contains the normal proof rules for FOL reasoning, framing reasoning, and fixpoint reasoning as in modal μ-logic, all these reasonings are sound and available in matching logic, too.

5   Program Verification in K

Here we discuss the logical foundations and the K tools for program verification. We first review the classic approaches to program verification in Sect. 5.1 and then show the K tools for program verification in Sect. 5.2. Finally, we discuss the logical foundations of K's verification tools, reachability logic, and show that is can be defined in matching logic in Sect. 5.3.

5.1   Classic Approaches to Program Verification

Program verification is a decision problem that asks if a given program satisfies a given specification. If so, a collection of proof objects is expected to be generated as evidence. If not, counterexamples are given often in the form of concrete program execution traces that violate the specification.

Hoare-Style Program Verification. Hoare-style program verification refers to the program verification approaches where the formal semantics of a programming language is given as a *program logic*, which has several proof rules that are specific to the constructs of that language. The program logic, which is often called an axiomatic semantics or the Hoare logic of the language, derives sentences called *Hoare triples* that have the form $\{\varphi\}P\{\varphi'\}$ where P is the program, φ is a logic formula called the *pre-condition* of the triple, and φ' is a formula called the *post-condition*. The semantics of the Hoare triple is that if P is executed on a state satisfying the pre-condition φ, and if P terminates on a final state, then the final state satisfies the post-condition φ'. The requirement that P terminates implies that the Hoare triple unconditionally holds if P does not terminate. This is known as *partial correctness* in literature.

Hoare logic remains one of the most popular program logics since the day it was born. Obviously, Hoare logic is a *language-specific* logic because different languages must have their own variants of Hoare logic. This makes the development of verification tools based on Hoare logic difficult to adapt to language changes. Such inconvenience is being made worse when it comes to blockchain languages that have a rapid development cycle with new versions of the languages being released on a weekly basis.

Another notable characteristic of Hoare logic is that it is not directly executable. This makes it difficult to test Hoare logic semantics. In practice, language semanticists may need to define a separate trusted operational semantics that is executable, and carry out complex proofs of equivalence between the two semantics, which can take years to complete.

All the above makes language design with Hoare logic a highly expensive task, and *changing* the language rather inconvenient and demotivating, as it requires a thorough change of the Hoare logic proof system for that language and thus of all the related verification tools. If a trusted operational semantics is given, it needs to change, too, and a new proof of equivalence between the new Hoare logic and the new operational semantics should be carried out. This high cost brings us poor *reusability* of verification tools. Considering the fact that these tools often need several man-years to develop, the lack of reusability leads to a remarkable waste of resources and talent, as well as to duplicate work.

In $\mathbb{K}$, such drawbacks are overcome by using only one *language-independent* proof system to verify any programs written in any programming languages, given that the formal language definitions are given in $\mathbb{K}$. We will explain it in detail in Sect. 5.2.

Intermediate Verification Languages. A common alternative practice to Hoare-style verification is to design *intermediate verification languages* (IVL) such as Boogie [6] and Why [19], to develop verification tools for these IVL languages, and to translate the target languages to IVL. This brings some reusability, as verification tools are designed and implemented for IVL, in isolation from the target languages. However, correct program translation can be hard to develop. The proof of its correctness (called *soundness proof*) often involves the usage of higher-order theorem provers such as Coq [25] and Isabelle [36], not to mention that many real languages such as Java do not even have an official formal specification of the semantics. Thus, research about language-specific program logics and IVL tools sometimes have to compromise and claim "no intention of formally proving the soundness result" [4].

5.2 Program Verification by Reachability Logic

Ҝ's program verification tools are based on *reachability logic* [32], which has been shown to be a fragment of matching logic in [11]. One appealing aspect of reachability logic is that it is *language independent*, that is, it uses one fixed proof system to reason about any programs written in any programming languages, given that their formal semantics have been defined in Ҝ. Some selected proof rules of reachability logic are shown in Fig. 5. The proof system derives judgments of the form $A \vdash_C \varphi_1 \Rightarrow \varphi_2$, where $\varphi_1 \Rightarrow \varphi_2$ is a *reachability rule* that specifies that any configurations matching φ_1 will eventually reach a configuration matching φ_2, on termination. (Readers who are more familiar with the traditional Hoare-style verification can intuitively regard φ_1 as the *pre-condition* and φ_2 as the *post-condition*). A and C are two sets of reachability rules, where rules in A are considered as *axioms* and can be directly used to discharge the proof obligations, rules in C are called *circularities* and cannot be directly used. The distinguished proof rule (CIRCULARITY) adds the current proof obligation to the circularity set, which is then flushed to the axiom set by (TRANSITIVITY). In other words, circularities become axioms after making any progress on program execution.

$$(\text{AXIOM}) \quad \frac{\varphi_1 \Rightarrow \varphi_2 \in A}{A \vdash_C \varphi_1 \Rightarrow \varphi_2}$$

$$(\text{TRANSITIVITY}) \quad \frac{A \vdash_C \varphi_1 \Rightarrow \varphi_2 \quad A \cup C \vdash \varphi_2 \Rightarrow \varphi_3}{A \vdash_C \varphi_1 \Rightarrow \varphi_3}$$

$$(\text{CONSEQUENCE}) \quad \frac{M^{\text{cfg}} \vDash \varphi_1 \rightarrow \varphi_1' \quad A \vdash_C \varphi_1' \Rightarrow \varphi_2' \quad M^{\text{cfg}} \vDash \varphi_2' \rightarrow \varphi_2}{A \vdash_C \varphi_1 \Rightarrow \varphi_2}$$

$$(\text{CIRCULARITY}) \quad \frac{A \vdash_{C \cup \{\varphi_1 \Rightarrow \varphi_2\}} \varphi_1 \Rightarrow \varphi_2}{A \vdash_C \varphi_1 \Rightarrow \varphi_2}$$

Fig. 5. Some selected proof rules in the proof system of reachability logic

We use the following sum program as an example to illustrate program verification in K by reachability logic.

```
int n, sum;
n = N;
sum = 0;
while (!(n <= 0)) {
  sum = sum + n;
  n = n + -1;
}
```

We will use K's generic program verification tool to prove that the above sum program correctly computes the total of 1 to N, where N is a symbolic value denoting any natural number.

The first step to verify sum using reachability logic and K is to formally define the specifications as K's rewrite rules.

```
module SUM_SPEC
  imports IMP

  rule    // invariant spec
      <k> while(n){ s = s + n; n = n - 1; } => .K ... </k>
      <state>
        n |-> (N:Int => 0)
        s |-> (S:Int => S +Int ((N +Int 1) *Int N /Int 2)
      </state>
  requires N >=Int 0

  rule    // main spec
      <k> int n, s; n = N:Int; while(n){ s = s + n; n = n - 1; }
          => .K
      </k>
      <state> .Map =>
        n |-> 0
        s |-> ((N +Int 1) *Int N /Int 2)
      </state>
  requires N >=Int 0
endmodule
```

The above specification contains two sub-specifications as reachability claims. The first is the invariant reachability claim that specifies the behavior of the while-loop. It is provided as a *lemma* to prove the main claim. The second claim is the main verification claim. It specifies that if the sum program (where n is now initialized to a symbolic value n, written as a K variable N:Int) terminates, then the final value of s equals $n(n + 1)/2$. The condition after the keyword requires has the similar meaning of a pre-condition in Hoare logic. It asks K to prove the mentioned reachability claim given that $n \geq 0$.

Then, K proves the claims via *circular proofs*, based on reachability logic proof system (see Fig. 5). We take the proof of the invariant claim as an example.

We put the formal proof in Fig. 6 and explain it in the following. 𝕂 starts with a configuration with a while-loop in the <k/> cell and a state that maps n to n and s mapping to s, as required by the left-hand side of the claim. Then, 𝕂 rewrites the configuration *symbolically* using exactly the same rewrite rules used to execute IMP programs. After the rewrites, the while-loop is de-sugared to an if-statement and the two assignments are resolved accordingly. After that, 𝕂 reaches a configuration with the same while-loop in <k/> cell, but in the <state/> cell, n maps to $n - 1$ and s maps to $s + n$. For clarity, let us denote *that* configuration as γ and let $n' = n - 1$ and $s' = s + n$. At this point, the (CIRCULARITY) proof rule of the reachability logic proof system (see, Fig. 5) is applied, and the invariant claim itself becomes a regular *axiom* which can be used in further proofs. Therefore, we can *instantiate* the variables n and s in the invariant claim by n' and s', yielding exactly the configuration γ, and the invariant claim immediately tells us that γ will terminate at a state where n maps to 0 and s maps to $s' + n'(n' + 1)/s$. And this tells us that the initial configuration, with n mapping to n and s mapping to s, can reach γ and then terminate at the same state. Finally, 𝕂 calls SMT solvers (such as Z3 [16]) to prove that $s' + n'(n' + 1)/2 = s + n(n + 1)/2$, and concludes the proof successfully.

5.3 Reachability Logic Is a Fragment of Matching Logic

We have seen a program verification example using reachability logic. In this section, we show that we can faithfully capture reachability logic in matching logic, and all reachbaility logic reasoning, including the key proof rule (CIRCULARITY), can be derived by the matching logic proof system. In other words, reachability logic is the fragment of matching logic for program verification.

where WHILE ≡ while(n){s=s+n; n=n-1;} and IF ≡ IF(n){s=s+n; n=n-1; WHILE}{}. We use A to denote the axiom set that contains all semantic rules of IMP and let $C = \{\langle\text{WHILE}\rangle_k \langle N \mapsto N, S \mapsto S\rangle_{\text{state}} \Rightarrow \langle .K\rangle_k \langle N \mapsto 0, S \mapsto S + (N + 1)N/2\rangle_{\text{state}}\}$ contain the original invariant proof goal, which is added to C by (CIRCULARITY) in the first proof step and moved to A by (TRANSITIVITY) in the second proof step. This circularity pattern is then used in the second to last proof step, where we instantiate N by $N - 1$ and S by $S + N$. The last proof step is done by calling external SMT solvers such as Z3 [16].

$$\frac{(S + N) + ((N - 1) + 1)(N - 1)/2 = S + (N + 1)N/2}{\frac{A \cup C \vdash_\emptyset \langle\text{WHILE}\rangle_k \langle N \mapsto N - 1, S \mapsto S + N\rangle_{\text{state}} \Rightarrow \langle .K\rangle_k \langle N \mapsto 0, S \mapsto S + (N + 1)N/2\rangle_{\text{state}}}{\frac{A \cup C \vdash_\emptyset \langle\text{n=n-1;WHILE}\rangle_k \langle N \mapsto N, S \mapsto S + N\rangle_{\text{state}} \Rightarrow \langle .K\rangle_k \langle N \mapsto 0, S \mapsto S + (N + 1)N/2\rangle_{\text{state}}}{\frac{A \cup C \vdash_\emptyset \langle\text{s=s+n;n=n-1;WHILE}\rangle_k \langle N \mapsto N, S \mapsto S\rangle_{\text{state}} \Rightarrow \langle .K\rangle_k \langle N \mapsto 0, S \mapsto S + (N + 1)N/2\rangle_{\text{state}}}{\frac{A \cup C \vdash_\emptyset \langle\text{IF}\rangle_k \langle N \mapsto N, S \mapsto S\rangle_{\text{state}} \Rightarrow \langle .K\rangle_k \langle N \mapsto 0, S \mapsto S + (N + 1)N/2\rangle_{\text{state}}}{\frac{A \vdash_C \langle\text{WHILE}\rangle_k \langle N \mapsto N, S \mapsto S\rangle_{\text{state}} \Rightarrow \langle .K\rangle_k \langle N \mapsto 0, S \mapsto S + (N + 1)N/2\rangle_{\text{state}}}{A \vdash_\emptyset \langle\text{WHILE}\rangle_k \langle N \mapsto N, S \mapsto S\rangle_{\text{state}} \Rightarrow \langle .K\rangle_k \langle N \mapsto 0, S \mapsto S + (N + 1)N/2\rangle_{\text{state}}}}}}}$$

Fig. 6. Reachability logic proof of the inyariant of sum program.

Reachability Logic Preliminaries. Reachability logic is a "top-most" logic that builts on top of matching logic (without μ). Reachability logic is parametric in a model of configurtaions. Specifically, fix a signature (of static program configurations) Σ^{cfg} which may have various sorts and symbols, among which there is a distinguished sort *Cfg*. A model of signature Σ^{cfg}, denoted M^{cfg}, is called the configuration model where M^{cfg}_{Cfg} is the set of all configurations. Reachability logic formulas are called *reachability rules* of the form $\varphi_1 \Rightarrow \varphi_2$ where φ_1, φ_2 are matching logic patterns matched by the (static) program configurations. A *reachability system* S is a finite set of rules, which yields a transition system $\mathbb{S} = (M^{\mathsf{cfg}}_{Cfg}, R)$ where $s\, R\, t$ iff there exist a rule $\varphi_1 \Rightarrow \varphi_2 \in S$ and an M^{cfg}-valuation ρ such that $s \in \bar\rho(\varphi_1)$ and $t \in \bar\rho(\varphi_2)$. A rule $\psi_1 \Rightarrow \psi_2$ is *S-valid*, denoted $S \vDash_{\mathsf{RL}} \psi_1 \Rightarrow \psi_2$, iff for all M^{cfg}_{Cfg}-valuations ρ and configurations $s \in \bar\rho(\psi_1)$, either there is an infinite trace $s\, R\, t_1\, R\, t_2\, R \ldots$ in $\mathbb{S}$ or there is a configuration t such that $s\, R^*\, r$ and $t \in \bar\rho(\psi_2)$. Therefore, validity in RL is defined in the spirit of *partial correctness*.

The reachability logic proof system (Fig. 5) derives *reachability logic sequents* of the form $A \vdash_C \varphi_1 \Rightarrow \varphi_2$ where A (called *axioms*) and C (called *circularities*) are finite sets of rules. Initially, we start with $A = S$ and $C = \emptyset$. As the proof proceeds, more rules can be added to C via (CIRCULARITY) and then moved to A via (TRANSITIVITY), which can then be used via (AXIOM). We write $S \vdash_{\mathsf{RL}} \psi_1 \Rightarrow \psi_2$ to mean that $S \vdash_\emptyset \psi_1 \Rightarrow \psi_2$. Notice (CONSEQUENCE) consults the configuration model M^{cfg} for validity, so the completeness result is *relative to* M^{cfg}. We recall the following result [32] that shows that program verification with reachability logic is relative complete to the reason about the static program configurations.

Theorem 3. *For all reachability systems S satisfying some reasonable technical assumptions (see [32]) and all rules $\psi_1 \Rightarrow \psi_2$, we have $S \vDash_{\mathsf{RL}} \psi_1 \Rightarrow \psi_2$ iff $S \vdash_{\mathsf{RL}} \psi_1 \Rightarrow \psi_2$.*

Defining Reachability Logic in Matching Logic. As how we define modal μ-logic and the various temporal logics, we can faithfully define reachability logic in matching logic using the one-path next $\bullet \in \Sigma_{Cfg,Cfg}$ that captures the underlying transition relation defined by the rewrite rules. Specifically, we define the following reachability properties as patterns:

$$\text{"weak eventually"} \quad \diamond_w \varphi \equiv \nu X.\, \varphi \vee \bullet X \quad // \text{equal to } \neg\mathsf{WF} \vee \diamond\varphi$$

$$\text{"reaching star"} \quad \varphi_1 \Rightarrow^* \varphi_2 \equiv \varphi_1 \rightarrow \diamond_w \varphi_2$$

$$\text{"reaching plus"} \quad \varphi_1 \Rightarrow^+ \varphi_2 \equiv \varphi_1 \rightarrow \bullet \diamond_w \varphi_2$$

Notice that the "weak eventually" $\diamond_w \varphi$ is defined similarly to the "eventually" $\diamond\varphi \equiv \mu X.\, \varphi \vee \bullet X$, but instead of using least fixpoint μ-binder, we define it as a greatest fixpoint. One can prove that $\diamond_w \varphi = \neg\mathsf{WF} \vee \diamond\varphi$, that is, a configuration γ satisfies $\diamond_w \varphi$ if either it satisfies $\diamond\varphi$, or it is not well-founded, meaning that there exists an infinite execution path from γ. Also notice that "reaching plus"

$\varphi_1 \Rightarrow^+ \varphi_2$ is a stronger version of "reaching star", requiring that $\diamond_w \varphi_2$ should hold *after at least one step*. This *progressive condition* is crucial to the soundness of RL reasoning: as shown in (TRANSITIVITY), circularities are flushed into the axiom set only *after one reachability step is established*. This leads us to the following translation from RL sequents to MmL patterns.

Definition 8. *Given a rule $\varphi_1 \Rightarrow \varphi_2$, define the MmL pattern $\Box(\varphi_1 \Rightarrow \varphi_2) \equiv \Box(\varphi_1 \Rightarrow^+ \varphi_2)$ and extend it to a rule set A as follows: $\Box A \equiv \bigwedge_{\varphi_1 \Rightarrow \varphi_2 \in A} \Box(\varphi_1 \Rightarrow \varphi_2)$. Define the translation RL2ML from RL sequents to MmL patterns as follows:*

$$RL2ML(A \vdash_C \varphi_1 \Rightarrow \varphi_2) = (\forall \Box A) \wedge (\forall \circ \Box C) \rightarrow (\varphi_1 \Rightarrow^\star \varphi_2)$$

where $\star = *$ if C is empty and $\star = +$ if C is nonempty. We use $\forall \varphi$ as a shorthand for $\forall x . \varphi$ where $x = \mathrm{FV}(\varphi)$. Recall that the "$\circ$" in $\forall \circ \Box C$ is "all-path next".

Hence, the translation of $A \vdash_C \varphi_1 \Rightarrow \varphi_2$ depends on whether C is empty or not. When C is nonempty, the RL sequent is *stronger* in that it requires *at least one step* being made in $\varphi_1 \Rightarrow \varphi_2$. Axioms (those in A) are also *stronger* than circularities (those in C) in that axioms *always* hold, while circularities only hold *after at least one step* because of the leading all-path next "$\circ$"; and since the "next" is an "all-path" one, it does not matter which step is actually made, as circularities hold on *all* next states.

Theorem 4. *Let Γ^{RL} be the set of all matching logic patterns of sort Cfg that hold in the configuration model M^{cfg}. For all reachability systems S and rules $\varphi_1 \Rightarrow \varphi_2$ satisfying the same technical assumptions in [32], the following are equivalent: (1) $S \vdash_{RL} \varphi_1 \Rightarrow \varphi_2$; (2) $S \vDash_{RL} \varphi_1 \Rightarrow \varphi_2$; (3) $\Gamma^{RL} \vdash RL2ML(S \vdash_\emptyset \varphi_1 \Rightarrow \varphi_2)$; (4) $\Gamma^{RL} \vDash RL2ML(S \vdash_\emptyset \varphi_1 \Rightarrow \varphi_2)$.*

Therefore, given an oracle for validity of matching logic patterns in the configuration model M^{cfg}, the matching logic proof system is capable of deriving any reachability property that can be derived with the reachability logic proof system. This result makes matching logic an even more fundamental logic foundation for the 𝕂 framework and thus for programming language specification and verification than reachability logic, because it can express significantly more properties than partial correctness reachability.

6 Conclusion

We have discussed the ideal language framework vision pursued by 𝕂, where programming languages must have formal definitions and language tools are automatically generated by the framework from the definitions at no additional costs. Then, we presented two example languages, LAMBDA and IMP, to illustrate the basic features and functionality of the 𝕂 tools, such as parsers, interpreters, etc. Next, we presented in detail the foundational logic of the 𝕂 framework, matching logic, and showed that many important mathematical instruments as well as other common logics and/or models can be faithfully captured in matching logic. Finally, we discussed the language-independent program verification tools of $\mathbb{K}$ and showed that its logical foundation, reachability logic, can also be faithfully captured by matching logic.

References

1. Clang: A C language family frontend for LLVM. https://clang.llvm.org/
2. GCC, the GNU compiler collection. https://gcc.gnu.org/
3. TrustInSoft–cybersecurity and safety provider. https://trust-in-soft.com/
4. Ahrendt, W., Beckert, B., Bubel, R., Hahnle, R., Schmitt, P.H., Ulbrich, M.: Deductive Software Verification-The KeY Book. Springer, Heidelberg (2016). https://doi.org/10.1007/978-3-319-49812-6
5. Barendregt, H.: The lambda calculus: its syntax and semantics. Studies in Logic and the Foundations of Mathematics, Elsevier Science Publishers (1984)
6. Barnett, M., Chang, B.-Y.E., DeLine, R., Jacobs, B., Leino, K.R.M.: Boogie: a modular reusable verifier for object-oriented programs. In: de Boer, F.S., Bonsangue, M.M., Graf, S., de Roever, W.-P. (eds.) FMCO 2005. LNCS, vol. 4111, pp. 364–387. Springer, Heidelberg (2006). https://doi.org/10.1007/11804192_17
7. Bertot, Y., Castran, P.: Interactive Theorem Proving and Program Development. Coq'Art the Calculus of Inductive Constructions. Springer, Heidelberg (2010). https://doi.org/10.1007/978-3-662-07964-5
8. Bogdănaş, D., Roşu, G.: K-Java: a complete semantics of Java. In: Proceedings of the 42nd Symposium on Principles of Programming Languages (POPL 2015), pp. 445–456. ACM, January 2015. https://doi.org/10.1145/2676726.2676982
9. Brady, E.: IDRIS – systems programming meets full dependent types. In: Proceedings of the 5th ACM Workshop on Programming Languages Meets Program Verification (PLPV 2011), pp. 43–54. ACM (2011). https://doi.org/10.1145/1929529.1929536
10. Chen, X., Roşu, G.: Applicative matching logic. Technical Report, University of Illinois at Urbana-Champaign, July 2019. http://hdl.handle.net/2142/104616
11. Chen, X., Roşu, G.: Matching μ-logic. In: Proceedings of the 34th Annual ACM/IEEE Symposium on Logic in Computer Science (LICS 2019) (2019)
12. Chen, X., Roşu, G.: A language-independent program verification framework. In: Proceedings of the 8th International Symposium on Leveraging Applications of Formal Methods (ISoLA 2018), vol.11245, pp. 92–102. Springer (2018). https://doi.org/10.1007/978-3-030-03421-4
13. Church, A.: The Calculi of Lambda-Conversion. Princeton University Press, New Jersey (1941)
14. Cohen, E., et al.: VCC: a practical system for verifying concurrent C. In: Berghofer, S., Nipkow, T., Urban, C., Wenzel, M. (eds.) TPHOLs 2009. LNCS, vol. 5674, pp. 23–42. Springer, Heidelberg (2009). https://doi.org/10.1007/978-3-642-03359-9_2
15. Dasgupta, S., Park, D., Kasampalis, T., Adve, V.S., Roşu, G.: A complete formal semantics of x 86–64 user-level instruction set architecture. In: Proceedings of the 40th ACM SIGPLAN Conference on Programming Language Design and Implementation (PLDI 2019), pp. 1133–1148. ACM, June 2019. https://doi.org/10.1145/3314221.3314601

16. De Moura, L., Bjørner, N.: Z3: an efficient SMT solver. In: Proceedings of the 14th International Conference on Tools and Algorithms for the Construction and Analysis of Systems (TACAS 2008). pp. 337–340. Springer, Cham (2008). https://doi.org/10.1007/978-3-540-78800-3_24
17. Ethereum: Solidity documentation (2019). http://solidity.readthedocs.io
18. Ethereum: Vyper documentation (2019). https://vyper.readthedocs.io
19. Filliâtre, J.-C., Marché, C.: The Why/Krakatoa/caduceus platform for deductive program verification. In: Damm, W., Hermanns, H. (eds.) CAV 2007. LNCS, vol. 4590, pp. 173–177. Springer, Heidelberg (2007). https://doi.org/10.1007/978-3-540-73368-3_21
20. Guth, D.: A formal semantics of Python 3.3. Master's thesis, University of Illinois at Urbana-Champaign (2013). http://hdl.handle.net/2142/45275
21. Hathhorn, C., Ellison, C., Roşu, G.: Defining the undefinedness of C. In: Proceedings of the 36th ACM SIGPLAN Conference on Programming Language Design and Implementation (PLDI 2015). pp. 336–345. ACM, June 2015. https://doi.org/10.1145/2813885.2737979
22. Hildenbrandt, E., et al.: KEVM: a complete semantics of the Ethereum virtual machine. In: Proceedings of the 2018 IEEE Computer Security Foundations Symposium (CSF 2018). IEEE (2018). http://jellopaper.org
23. Kasampalis, T., et al.: IELE: a rigorously designed language and tool ecosystem for the blockchain. In: Proceeding of the 23rd International Symposium on Formal Methods (FM 2019) (2019)
24. Kroening, D., Tautschnig, M.: CBMC – C bounded model checker. In: Ábrahám, E., Havelund, K. (eds.) TACAS 2014. LNCS, vol. 8413, pp. 389–391. Springer, Heidelberg (2014). https://doi.org/10.1007/978-3-642-54862-8_26
25. The Coq development team: The Coq proof assistant reference manual. LogiCal Project (2004). http://coq.inria.fr
26. Norell, U.: Dependently typed programming in agda. In: Koopman, P., Plasmeijer, R., Swierstra, D. (eds.) AFP 2008. LNCS, vol. 5832, pp. 230–266. Springer, Heidelberg (2009). https://doi.org/10.1007/978-3-642-04652-0_5
27. Park, D., Ştefănescu, A., Roşu, G.: KJS: a complete formal semantics of JavaScript. In: Proceedings of the 36th ACM SIGPLAN Conference on Programming Language Design and Implementation (PLDI 2015), pp. 346–356. ACM, June 2015. https://doi.org/10.1145/2737924.2737991
28. Reynolds, J.C.: Separation logic: a logic for shared mutable data structures. In: Proceedings of the 17th Annual IEEE Symposium on Logic in Computer Science (LICS 2002), pp. 55–74. IEEE (2002). https://doi.org/10.1109/lics.2002.1029817
29. Roşu, G.: K–a semantic framework for programming languages and formal analysis tools. In: Dependable Software Systems Engineering. IOS Press (2017)
30. Roşu, G.: Matching logic. Logic. Methods Comput. Sci. **13**(4), 1–61 (2017). https://doi.org/10.23638/lmcs-13(4:28)2017
31. Roşu, G., Ştefănescu, A.: Checking reachability using matching logic. In: Proceedings of the 27th Conference on Object-Oriented Programming, Systems, Languages, and Applications (OOPSLA 2012), pp. 555–574. ACM, October 2012. http://dl.acm.org/citation.cfm?doid=2384616.2384656
32. Roşu, G., Ştefănescu, A., Ciobâcă, Ş., Moore, B.M.: One-path reachability logic. In: Proceedings of the 28th Symposium on Logic in Computer Science (LICS 2013), pp. 358–367. IEEE (2013). https://doi.org/10.1109/lics.2013.42
33. Roşu, G., Serbanuta, T.F.: K overview and simple case study. In: Proceedings of International K Workshop (K 2011). ENTCS, vol. 304, pp. 3–56. Elsevier, June 2014. https://doi.org/10.1016/j.entcs.2014.05.002

34. Roşu, G., Şerbănuţă, T.F.: An overview of the K semantic framework. J. Logic Algebraic Program. **79**(6), 397–434 (2010). https://doi.org/10.1016/j.jlap.2010.03.012
35. Tarski, A.: A lattice-theoretical fixpoint theorem and its applications. Pacific J. Math. **5**(2), 285–309 (1955). https://doi.org/10.2140/pjm.1955.5.285
36. The Isabelle development team: Isabelle (2018). https://isabelle.in.tum.de/

Software Abstractions
and Human-Cyber-Physical Systems
Architecture Modelling

Zhiming Liu[1], Jonathan P. Bowen[1,2]([✉]), Bo Liu[1],
Shmuel Tyszberowicz[1,3], and Tingting Zhang[1]

[1] RISE – Centre for Research and Innovation in Software Engineering,
Southwest University, Chongqing, China
{zhimingliu88,liubocq}@swu.edu.cn
[2] School of Engineering,
London South Bank University, London, UK
jonathan.bowen@lsbu.ac.uk
[3] Afeka Academic College of Engineering, Tel Aviv, Israel
tyshbe@tau.ac.il

Abstract. It is over fifty years since the subject discipline of *software engineering* and more than forty years from when the area of *formal methods* have been established. During this period, the academic community has accomplished extensive research in foundations and methods of software engineering, as well as developing and teaching a large body of software engineering knowledge and techniques. At the same time, the IT industry has produced larger, more complex, and better (in many aspects) software systems. Yet, these large projects are largely developed using a trial and error approach, without systematic use of the developed software engineering methods and tools. The cost of these projects is high, the percentage of project delay and cancellation is significant, and the dependability of the systems is low in many requirements. The most serious problem of this ad hoc development approach is that the development process is not repeatable and the systems developed are not well evolvable. This problem is particularly crucial for the design and implementation of modern networked distributed software systems, known as *Human-Cyber-Physical Systems* (HCPS).

In this tutorial paper, we reflect the development of software engineering through software abstractions and show that these abstractions are integral in the notion of software system architectures. We discuss the importance of architecture modelling and argue for a seamless combination of informal and formal activities in the modelling and design of the architecture. A point that we make is that it is important to engineer systems using formal methods in relation to the definition and management of development processes, and how a model of the software architecture, with rich semantics and refinement relations, plays an important role in this process. We consider development of two typical types of software components and use examples to discuss the traditional processes for their *domain modelling* and *software requirements modelling*. We then

© Springer Nature Switzerland AG 2020
J. P. Bowen et al. (Eds.): SETSS 2019, LNCS 12154, pp. 159–219, 2020.
https://doi.org/10.1007/978-3-030-55089-9_5

propose to combine these modelling approaches and this naturally leads to a *unified modelling process* for HCPS architecture modelling, design, and evolution. Based on the unified processes, we outline a framework in engineering formal methods for HCPS modelling, including the mapping of the system architecture to the technology architecture and organization of the development team with the expertise required, and decide the appropriate formal methods and tools to be used.

Keywords: Formal methods · Human-Computer-Physical System · Abstraction · Architecture modelling · Conceptual integrity · System evolution

1   Introduction

Although the term was used earlier, the notion of "Software Engineering" with its *intention* and *extension*, was first proposed at the world's first conference on software engineering that was held in 1968, sponsored and facilitated by NATO [77]. The challenges which it intended to address were characterized by "*software crisis*". Symptoms of the crisis had been that large software projects resulted in a high percentage of cancellations, late deliveries, over-spending of the budget, and systems that often failed to meet critical requirements. The cause of the crisis was regarded to be due to the growing power of computing machines [30], and as a consequence increase in software demand, complexity, and challenges, yet without changing the methods and tools being used.

From the viewpoint with respect to software construction, however, the fundamental problem of the software crisis was that it lacked systematic engineering methods for the production of computer programs. Unlike well-established branches of engineering, where the construction of a complex product was undertaken using well defined *engineering processes* employing proper *methods* and *tools*, software production was carried in an ad hoc manner, without the systematic use of standard methods and tools. Here, by methods and tools, we mean approaches that have been developed based on scientific and sound mathematical theories for modelling, validation, and verification. An improvised development process with best-effort methods is more likely to fail and is not repeatable. Neither the process nor the artefacts can be validated and the final product is not maintainable. This is why in the days of the software crisis, "various large software projects were almost all one-off projects, developed for specific customers, and all too many of the largest projects were characterized by underestimates and overexpectations" as Randell recalls [90].

The participants of NATO's Conference set the intent of software engineering to provide the construction of software systems with a sound mathematical foundation and based on this foundation to develop *systematic methods*, *tools*, and *standards* for software *design*, *analysis*, *implementation*, *verification*, and *validation*—like the traditional branches of engineering disciplines [77].

The report on the NATO conference demonstrates that it was very stimulating and history also proves it created great impact. Brian Randell pointed out in his keynote presentation at the 2018 International Conference on Software Engineering (ICSE) [90], among other software engineering subject areas, some people who attended NATO's conference were motivated by the problem of how to create programs that were mathematically-proven to be free from errors, becoming pioneers of *formal methods* (e.g., Edsger Dijkstra [29]), and some started the area of *fault-tolerant programming*, concerning how to design programs that could be usefully relied upon even if it was admitted that they still contained yet-to-be found bugs (e.g., Randell himself [88]). The first author of the present paper has worked on formal techniques in fault-tolerant programming [62,67].

In the half-century since the NATO conference, as well as these aspects of software engineering, intensive research has been conducted on "all aspects of software production from the early stages of system specification through to maintaining the system after it has gone into use" [99]. A rich body of knowledge, principles, and methods, including development processes, architecture styles, design patterns, programming paradigms, as well as techniques and tools for verification, validation, program construction, synthesis, etc., have been proposed and developed [45]. Research on formal methods [10] has also advanced with the development of comprehensive theories of formal semantics of languages, specification and verification techniques, and related tools [104].

At the same time, the software industry is still producing increasingly complex as well as larger software systems. However, it appears that there is a common concern about the degree of systematic adoption of the concepts, principles, and methods developed by the research community. Software practitioners do not necessarily see that research software engineering methods solve their problems. Common complains are that methods developed by the research community, and in particular formal methods, are difficult to understand and hard to scale up, and therefore they cannot meet their market requirements.

Hence, large systems which are constructed in an ad hoc way are costly, likely to fail or are not delivered on time. The construction process is not repeatable and have poor system reliability. Our understanding is that the main reasons for the gap between systematic software engineering methods and industry practice include, among some other issues, that theories, techniques, and tools developed in software engineering fundamental research:

(a) generally lack a seamless and coherent combination of theories, techniques, and tools for the various dimensions of the multi-scale design space, such as behaviour, quality of service (QoS), space and time, and thus
(b) usually consider only local solutions of methodology, tools, and models that ease part of the development, rather than the definition, management, and execution of the entire process, and especially
(c) they do not effectively address project management problems.

These problems are especially true for existing formal methods. Each formal method is based on an abstract model, which only considers one or at least very few aspects of the system, thus not addressing problems concerning all aspects of the design. In addition, there no systematic, sound, and coherent combination of different formal methods to solve combined issues in the design. This is also true to some extend for informal software engineering methods (or *empirical methods*), and informal methods themselves are less systematic because they are prone to ambiguity and different interpretations.

For two decades, we have believed that model-driven development [63] is the key to closing the gap, as it naturally provide the linkage between the concepts and methods in empirical methods and those in formal methods. In principle, model-driven development can be used to define the development process, the technology architecture that consists of methods, techniques and tools needed in the process, and the (models of) the system architecture of the system under development. This means that use model-driven method as meta-method to *engineering formal methods* in defining a development process and technology architecture for a system construction (or for solving a software system problem in its life cycle).

In this chapter, we recall the history of principles of abstraction, in programming languages in particular, which have driven the increase of software productivity and at the same, together with increasing power of computers, have led to the development of ever-larger software systems. We argue that these abstractions are integrated and reflected in software system architecture. The increasing size and complexity of software systems requires the use of engineering disciplines, processes, and modelling. Effectively modelling a complex system always needs certain degree of formality.

Software modelling involves both informal and formal activities and they need to be managed carefully for a seamless combination. Therefore, we propose the idea of engineering formal methods where systematic and effective use is possible. We consider the main concepts, the theoretical challenges, and technical challenges, involved in establishing the framework of engineering formal methods together. The process and techniques for system architecture modelling are the core of the framework. We study the traditional separation of application domain modelling and the software requirements modelling and show how to combine them into a unified modelling of *Human-Computer-Physical System* (HCPS) architecture modelling. From that point, the approach is intended to allow a smooth transition into discussions of problems in HCPS modelling and to provide an outline framework for engineering formal methods for HCPS development.

The remainder of this tutorial paper is organized as follows. Section 2 provides a discussion on the nature of software and software system development, as well as the difference between programming and software. Section 3 summarizes some major ideas of abstraction, which mark milestones in the history of software engineering development. With this discussion, we demonstrate the importance of abstraction in a systematic approach. This provides the background for the discussion in Sect. 4 about the development processes, the architecture of software systems, and technology architectures for their development. The point we wish to emphasize is that the architecture of the software systems as produced through the development process from the requirements for the system. The architecture plays a determining role in the definition and management of the development process.

In Sect. 5, we provides a review of formal methods, mainly to show that there are a large number of formal methods. There is no single one formal method can solve all the problems in a system's development, and there can be more than one formal method used for a particular design problem in the development. Therefore, there is need for the architecture model and development process to consider the use of formal methods and tools. We propose an approach with a combination of application domain modelling and requirements modelling for software systems. Further, in Sect. 6, we present a component-based, multi-view and multi-level approach to domain modelling, including a definition of the notion of *domain architecture*. Then we continue with a discussion in Sect. 7 concerning how to produce a model for the requirements of a software system, based on a model of the application domain architecture. The combination of requirements model and domain model naturally forms a general model of an HCPS. Based on this conceptual approach, in Sect. 8 we discuss the evolution of the concept of HCPS during the last 15 years, the new challenges in modelling and design based on the *unified domain and software requirements modelling* in Sect. 6 and Sect. 7, identifying the shortcomings in the theories, techniques, and tools of existing formal methods. A conceptual architecture model is proposed in this section, and based on it, we propose a framework for engineering formal methods for the development and evolution of HCPS. Section 9 summarizes this tutorial paper.

This tutorial paper is based on a number of lectures and talks on concepts, abstractions, principles, and challenges, in software engineering, in relation to HCPS.

2   Software Development Is Different from Programming

We often wonder about the definition of software and what is the difference between programs and software. In fact, the notion of software evolved from that of a program. Here we quote some software engineering pioneers.

> A program is something that I write and I use. Software is something that I write and you use. This requires more work. It has to be generalized, it has be tested, it has to be documented, and usually it has to be maintained.

> Fred Brooks
> ICSE 2018 Keynote [14].

Note that the key words in Brooks talk are *generalization, testing, documentation,* and *maintenance,* and these are about the term *program* and *software (product)* in the early 1950s. Brooks went on to introduce the software entity *software systems.*

> The next kind of entity ... is a software system—a system of many separate programs working together. And this requires more work because you have to define the interfaces, and many many system debugging troubles are because my understanding of the at least the connotations of the

interface and your understanding of the unit connotations of the interface are different, and they don't work, so now we have to do set of system integration and test ...

Fred Brooks
ICSE 2018 Keynote [14].

These are Brooks' notes about software in the late 1950s. The form of software was software systems, in which many systems were integrated through their interfaces. However, the interfaces then were not defined with rigorous semantics, which was the cause of integration problems. Margret Hamlton, who is regarded to be the first to coin term "software engineering", went even further when she talked about the insight gained in her Apollo experiences [35] to understand software [38]:

With multi-programming, shared responsibilities and more interfaces within and between every mission phase (8 tasks based on timing, 7 jobs based on priority); man-in-the-loop multi-processing within the overall system of systems.

Margaret Hamilton
ICSE 2018 Keynote [14].

What Hamilton emphasized, in addition to the integration of many programs, was the relation between software and hardware and human interaction, with the aim of better system reliability, more parallelism, and improved reuse and evolution.

Brian Randell, a participant and editor of the report of the 1968 and 1969 NATO Software Engineering Conferences [77,91] drew "a harsh distinction" between "bespoke" and "off-the-peg software" [89,90]:

Since [the NATO conferences] not just one, but rather many, types of software industry have come into existence, in particular those that design or tailor "bespoke" software for particular clients and environments, and those that produce "off-the-peg" software packages that are sold to thousands or even millions of customers. The first type is a recognisable successor to the software activities of the '60s. In the second, very different, type of software industry economies of scale, and Darwinian-style evolution, have a large impact on what sorts of software get implemented, and how such implementation is undertaken, e.g. involving getting hundreds or thousands of users involved, willingly or unwillingly, to help with software validation and refinement ...

Any reasonable account of how far we've come since the late '60s (and where we have got to) has to treat these two types of software and software industry very differently. The first type of software industry has gone on to attempt ever larger and more complex tasks. But it is still subject to many of the same challenges concerning implementation cost, project schedule, performance and (especially) dependability that so exercised the NATO conference participants. The second now provides a wonderful marketplace of usable and useful software systems, utilities and applications that has utterly transformed society's utilisation and perception of computers. But technical monoculturalism, allied to the growth of computer networking, has led to this industry and its customers also suffering from all sorts of malicious, indeed criminal, activities that were not in any way foreseen in the discussions at the NATO conferences.

Brian Randell
Keynote at COMPSAC 2008
and reiterated in a Keynote at ICSE 2018 [90].

With our understanding of the above quotes by the software engineering pioneers, we confirm the definition of software system which we gave in the lectures at SETSS 2014 [63]:

We thus define a *software system* to consist of set of architected programs and data that tell a set interrelated computers what to do and how to it. Computers include all devices with programmable processing capacity, all kinds of "smart devices" as well as "computers", that now affects all aspects of daily life.

Zhiming Liu
Lecture at SETSS 2014 [63].

In this section, we had a detailed discussion on some different views concerning software and software systems, before we summarized our views in the above definition. This definition gives an explicit emphasize on *the architectural aspects of system of systems and the significance of data.* In most cases, a software system is still an engineering product or artefact. Therefore, it must be delivered with enough documentation and subsequent maintenance is required after it has become operational. Later in Sect. 4, we will see the open architecture that we propose used to combine continuous system evolution with system construction, operation, and maintenance, with data used as a resource for system evolution.

3 A History of Abstractions in Software Engineering

We now consider the historical development of software engineering based on notes given by some software engineering pioneers, literature, and Internet sources. We emphasis on the abstractions proposed historically, which had led to significant advances in software technology. In any other engineering discipline, the construction (or development) of a complex system or product is done in a well defined *process* by employing proper methods and tools. These methods and tools are developed with applications of mathematical and scientific theories and/or experiments, and preferably standardized. The requirement for a defined process and the use of proper (and standard) methods and tools is for overall trustworthiness of the product, including the demand that the process is repeatable and certifiable, and that the product can be verified and validated according to the requirements of the product.

3.1   The Motivation and Aims of Software Engineering

The notion of software engineering, as well as issues discussed at and the aims of the 1968 NATO conference on software engineering [77], implies that construction of complex software systems should be done systematically, in a repeatable and certifiable process using sound methods and tools, like other traditional engineering branches. The consequence of increasing engineering in software production is improved quality, dependability and productivity, and deduced cost and development time. This understanding is consistent with the following definition given in Ian Sommerville's widely-used software engineering textbook [99]:

> Software engineering is an engineering discipline that is concerned with all aspects of software production from the early stages of system specification through to maintaining the system after it has gone into use.

In general, the theoretical foundations for the development of methods and tools that are used for general and systematic construction of engineering products are often based on ideas of *abstractions*. This seems even more true for the construction of a software product, since it is purely made of logical mathematical objects, unlike engineering products such as a building houses or bridges, where the functionality is mostly determined by their structure and the materials used. A software product does not exhibit physical characteristics and its functional behaviour is more complex to understand [8,12,13]. Note that a software system behaves very differently when its environment changes, which often happens. Indeed, the development of software engineering theories and methods has been driven by the idea of abstraction. We give a brief account of this below.

Abstraction in Computer Architecture. In the early 1940s, when the first digital electronic computers were designed, the commands to operate the computers were wired with the hardware [58]. It was soon realized that this design made programming these machines inflexible, and the idea of *stored program architecture* was developed, evolving to *von Neumann architecture* [103]. This was an important idea of abstraction to separate "software" from "hardware", to deal with the complexity of computing, enabling common principles to be used flexibly to program different machines.

3.2   Abstraction in Programming and Programming Languages

Along with the abstraction in the design of computer architecture, abstractions also developed in programming data structures and languages for programming the computers in the 1950s. The computers then were bare machines, and programs in the early 1940s were written, using binary (or octal) machine codes for instructions and explicit reference to absolute address represented in binary code too. The programs written on paper had to be transferred to punched paper tapes [14]. This way of programming was very slow and error-prone. It was hard to find and correct errors in programs, as when the result was wrong there was little feedback about when and how the program execution went wrong.

In the late 1940s, low-level *assembly language* was introduced to eliminate much of the error-prone, tedious, and time-consuming programming in machine instructions. Then a program called an *assembler* was responsible for translating assembly language to machine language. The introduction of this *layer of indirection* was very important in freeing programmers from tedium such as remembering binary or octal codes and calculating addresses. Early hand-written programs were used by those who wrote them. Assembly language enabled much faster program writing and programs could be distributed to be used by others as well as the original programmers. A software product was possible, to be used by customers or clients other than the program authors. Thus, the notion of *software product* emerged (in the early 1950s) and a program could be delivered to many customers for their use. For this, documentation, testing, and ongoing maintenance are required. These became possible with programs in assembly language.

With the support of assembly language, functionalities that needed to repeatedly execute in a program or commonly needed in several programs were defined and implemented as *subroutines* [72, 106, 107]. From the middle of the 1950s, *high-level programming languages* became avaiable. The first widely used high-level programming languages were Fortran (1956 by John Backus), Cobol (1959), and Algol (1958–1960). These languages (or their descendant) are still in use today to a greater or lesser extent, partly due to legacy code produced over the years. The main idea of high-level programming language appeared much earlier due to Konrad Zuse in 1943–1945 [33]. A high-level programming language uses natural language word elements (such "**if** ... **then** ..." and " **while** ... **do** ...") together with mathematical expressions. It provides programmers with *strong abstraction from the details of the computer.*

Compared to low-level assembly language, high-level programming languages provided another *layer of indirection.* This layer was realized through an *interpreter* or a *compiler,* or a combination of both. The interpreter of a high-level programming language is a program that follows the program flow, reads each program statement, and then executes it by interpreting it directly as a series of machine code instruction. A compiler translates the syntax of a program into an *executable form* ("object code") before running it, and the executable form can be either machine code or an intermediate representation.

With high-level languages, more programs structures were defined and implemented as programming language facilities (or mechanisms), e.g., *functions, procedures, data types,* etc. This allowed programmers to identify and design significant algorithms, a major challenge in programming at that time. It also provided better standardization, generalization, and thus reuse in many aspects of programming thinking, program design, program implementation, program operation, and its maintenance.

Apart from algorithm design, another major concern of programming in the 1960s was data structures. Data types were introduced in high-level languages like Fortran and Algol. A data type defines a set of permissible data and the permissible operations on these data. Thus, data types liberated programmers from error-prone ad hoc design and use of data in programs.

While the level of abstraction in programming languages was increasing, software systems such as input and output converters, symbolic assemblers, and compilers, became available, together with new hardware devices. The notion of a *software system*, a system of many programs working together, evolved. However, new problems were raised with this new layer of abstraction such as interface definition, system integration, system testing, and system debugging. This was due to the lack of a means for rigorous definition and understanding the semantics of program interfaces. Different people's understanding of the connotations of the interfaces can easily vary if formal definitions are lacking. In fact, the notion of software system was first practiced in building the first known operating system, GM-NAA I/O [95]. This was an integration of a number of component programs, including an input translator, an output converter, a SHARE Assembly program, and a compute monitor program. Operating systems in general were yet another layer of abstraction, realized as a software system to manage the computer hardware and software resources, providing common functionalities for computer programs.

Advances in programming languages and tools can therefore be characterized as having been gradually increasing the abstraction level, by introducing high-level language constructs that represent common concepts and design patterns of software designers.

3.3   Abstractions in Software Development

Compared to low-level languages, high-level programming languages greatly improved productivity for software systems in the 1960s. Increasingly large and complex systems were produced. Meanwhile, computers were becoming more powerful, especially those with hardware designed for operating systems, e.g., *multiprogramming and time sharing operating systems* [23], which ended the era of bare machines with no operating system. Therefore, requirements for large and complex software systems were rapidly increasing. Software system development worldwide started to encounter issues. The growth in complexity due to combinatorial possibiities for interaction was nonlinear and this caused major concerns in project management. With this background, computer scientists and software development practitioners started to consider the notion of writing programs as an engineering discipline and the 1968 NATO conference [77] recognized the problem of the software crisis, discussed it, and called for establishing *engineering foundations, principles and methods* for the production of software systems. Many of the fundamental theories and principles and methods were then developed with important ideas concerning abstraction, including those outlined below.

Objects, Classes, and Inheritance. The concepts of *objects*, *classes*, and *inheritance* were introduced in the Simula programming language by Kristen Nygaard and Ole-Johan Dahl in 1967 [79]; Simula is regarded as the first object-oriented programming language. The important concept of class, and thus the essential notion of object-orientation, was to separate the implementation from the interface, representing the data layer and the control layer.

Information Hiding, Modularity and Encapsulation. The ideas of sub-routines, procedures, functions, and data types, were further developed to cover the notion of *modules for information hiding* [80]. This was also introduced into programming language design and resulted in languages with *modularity* [59] to provide protection for related procedures and data structures, through separation of the use of functionality and data from the implementation. The concept of modularity was then further used to reflect the general engineering principles of *divide and conquer*, *separation of concern*, and *reuse*, such that the overall design problem of a large software system should be decomposed into the design of a set of modules of logically discrete functions for subproblems.

The *interfaces* of modules aught to be well-defined with respect to legitimate inputs, expected outputs, and the associated valid operations. How the functionality was to be done (i.e., the implementation) inside the module should not be visible from the outside of the module. Therefore, the overall design problem of a large software system could be divided into subproblems. These formed the basis for a *structured analysis and design technique* approach or *structured software development paradigm*. In this paradigm, *software architecture* was defined as a set of modules interacting with interfaces between them.

Theoretical study of the separation of the specification from the implementation of modules led to the establishment of the theory of *abstract data types* (ADT) [60]. In ADTs, the notion of algebraic specification of data types was defined as axiomatic (using a many-sorted algebra) and as a composition of data types. ADTs were then generalized from data type specifications to program algebraic specifications [16]. ADTs allowed software engineers to consider the requirements for data structures and specify them in early stages of the software development before the programming stage.

Information hiding and modularity were also introduced in object-oriented programming languages as *encapsulation* with *private fields* of *classes* (and *private classes*). In the object-orientated approach, the access to the functionality or the data from outside the object can only be done through the object interface, i.e., its public methods. Language facilities were provided for different levels of information hiding (or encapsulation). The notion of encapsulation was also used to raise the design level of classes and packages above the level of the programming language to *object-oriented requirements analysis and design* [8].

4 Software Development Processes and Software Architecture

In all traditional engineering disciplines, complex systems are produced in well-defined processes to improve the design, product management, and project management, in order to ensure the quality of the engineering product. Also, any serious engineering system construction is undertaken with the system architecture in mind. When software systems become more complex, the implementation requires a development process and an architecture.

4.1 Software Development Process

With software systems increasing in size, it was natural to consider the problems of planning, budgeting, and management of their development. This has to consider the development activities with their corresponding requirements, proposed techniques, and available expertise. Therefore, the notion of *software development process* emerged, dividing the development into distinct phases, identifying when and what to do at each phase, who (i.e., people) are needed to do it, and what methods, techniques, and tools should be used [61]. Notice that this definition emphasizes the relationships between development jobs, people, and expertise. This includes the definition of software artefacts to be produced at each phase. We believe that these relations form the basis for principles and techniques to improve the design, product management, and project management in large software system development [11].

The earliest ideas for the principles associated with the development process were the *top-down incremental build* [74] and stepwise refinement of Niklaus Wirth [108]. The earliest widely cited process model is the Waterfall Model [94]. Further well-known extended models include the Spiral Model [7] and the V-Model [32]. These models refine and extend the Waterfall approach with an emphasis on risks analysis for the former and verification and validation for the latter. They both emphasize the iterative and incremental nature of the development of large software systems. With the popularity of the Unified Modeling Language (UML), the *(Rational) Unified Process* (RUP) [52] emerged in the early 2000s as a combination of the Spiral process and the V-model, with more activities and the production of executable models using tools.

Software development process models are defined in terms of activities in workflows of software development. However, they are described with principles, techniques, and conditions for quality and risk control/management. This is because the development of software system activities in any nontrivial case must be done using design, construction, and verification and validation techniques/tools, as for any engineering system development. The body of principles and techniques required and availability is extremely large, as is the design space. Considering, for example, the issue of selecting a programming language (taking into account the expertise of the programmers in the development team), there are no less than 8,945 different programming languages [26,90]. Thus, it is extremely difficult to define a concrete development process for a particular project before the project starts and to decide the activities with mappings to artefacts and techniques. We believe that this is the main reason that software development models often attract criticisms for being unrealistic or impractical. However, we take a more positive view on the importance of the notion of a software development process and accept the essential characteristics of software system development due to its inherent multi-dimensional complexity described and reiterated in the literature [8,11–14,99]. We quote Brooks:

> There is no single development in technology or management which alone promises a 10× gain in 10 years – is again true 30 years later.

Fred Brooks
ICSE 2018 Keynote [14].

We also the quote Randall from Ian Sommerville's book [99]:

> There are no universal software engineering methods and techniques that are suitable for all systems and all companies. Rather, a diverse set of software engineering methods and tools has evolved over the past 50 years.

Brian Randall
ICSE 2018 Keynote [90].

In this tutorial paper we propose, or more precisely we promote, a unified and evolutionary development processe that should accommodate *agile methodologies* [2], to allow flexible changes during system development and evolution.

4.2 Software Architecture

Routines, modules, data types, classes, and packages in high-level programming languages made software systems development increasingly systematic and disciplined, thus enabling collaborative development processes by teams of developers. However, they were still very much at the programming level for the implementation and reuse of algorithms and data structures. The interactions among the modules were mainly local invocations of functionalities.

With advances of computer systems from a single processor running a program one at a time, through *multiprogramming systems* and *multitasking systems*, to *multi-processors computers and networks of computers*, with increasingly programmable input, output, and communication devices, the size of software systems for the evermore powerful and complex computers were increasing rapidly and the interactions of their components were becoming more complicated. Designers of software systems with this level of complexity started to realize and consider design problems related to the system's overall structural organization at a level of abstraction above the algorithms and data structures. This was then the notion of software architecture design, developed from intuitions of hardware and network architecture, as well as the classical computer architecture [82,83].

Roughly speaking, software architecture is the fundamental structure of a software system, comprising *software components*, *connections* among the components, and *properties* or *constraints* concerning the components and connections. Software architecture design reflects the engineering principles of decomposition and separation of concern of the overall system requirements, beyond the level of algorithms and data structures. Its concerns cover the following issues. The software architecture should:

- reflect the architecture of the computer system on which the software is to run;
- reflect the structure of the domain business organization, business processes, and their interactions;
- represent the decomposition of the functional requirements, including its behaviour or functionality, data flows, interaction protocols, synchronization, etc., through the system [46];
- relate to the software system quality of service (QoS) attributes such as fault-tolerance, extensibility, reliability, maintainability, availability, security, usability, and other *architecturally significant requirements*, sometimes called the "ilities" [18].

Therefore, software architecture can and should serve the following purposes:

- It is the vehicle to carry the defined requirements of the software system.
- It is used as the map for identification of principles, techniques, languages, models, and tools to be employed in the further design and implementation of the software system. This means there is *a correspondence relation* between the software architecture of the system and the technology architecture for its development.
- It serves as the basis for defining and managing the project development process:
  - organizing the development teams and assigning jobs to team members according to their expertise;
  - guiding the communication and collaboration between members of the development team in their development activities, as well as their management and coordination;
  - planning the development job and estimating the costs;
  - helping in risk identification and management.
- Its design and documentation facilitates and guides communication between stakeholders, captures early decisions about the high-level design, and allows reuse of design components between projects.

Though the importance of software architecture is commonly recognized in the software engineering community, research on software architecture has been largely dispersed and there is no established theory of software architecture. Effort in software architecture research has been mostly devoted to *architectural styles*. A software architecture style or an *architectural pattern* is a general, reusable solution to a commonly occurring problem in software architecture within a given context or a kind of software system.

There are a significant number of architectural styles, described in different levels of formality, from descriptive terms used informally to describe systems, through those with precisely define components and connectors, to some that are more carefully documented as industry and scientific standards. Early and well-known architecture styles include *Blackboard, Repository, Pipes and filters, Client-Server, Layered*, etc., and model architecture styles including *Object-Oriented Architecture, Component-Based Architecture, Service-Oriented Architecture*, and *Microservice Architecture*.

A conclusion of our discussion in the previous and the current sections is that systematic engineering design of software systems has been developed through a regular increase of abstraction level in programming language design and software architecture. The establishment of software architecture and software development processes gives software design better engineering characteristics. However, our observation shows that software development has not harvested enough from software architecture and development processes, in the application of formal methods in particular. In subsequent sections, we will re-emphasize the importance of software architecture and development processes, especially their relationship, in the development and evolution of software systems for emerging networked systems, including cloud-based services systems, *Internet of Things* (IoT), and *Human-Cyber-Physical Systems* (HCPS).

5   A Review of Formal Methods

While software systems were becoming larger and more complex, their verification and validation for correctness and quality of service were becoming extremely challenging. Techniques and tools for testing and code inspection based on the semantics of programming languages could not be systematic enough or comprehensive. Without a sound mathematical model of program languages, fully systematic and comprehensive program correctness verification was not be possible. No matter what could be done, some bugs would always remain in any realistically-sized system. Here we quote:

> The major cause of the software crisis is that the machines have become several orders of magnitude more powerful. To put it quite bluntly: as long as there were no machines, programming was no problem at all; when we had a few weak computers, programming became a mild problem, and now we have gigantic computers, programming has become an equally gigantic problem.

> Edsger Dijkstra
> "The Humble Programmer", *CACM* [30].

In this section, we present a review of the development of formal methods [10]. Unlike earlier more comprehensive surveys with a focus on the state of the art (e.g. [104,109]), we instead discuss the development of the important ideas, the common theoretical roots, and relationship with technology developments. Our main purpose is to consider the selection and integratation of different techniques into a development process.

5.1   Formal Semantics of Programming Languages

The idea that we can prove the correctness of programs was widely established in the late 1960s, with Floyd's paper on *Assigning Meanings to Programs* [31] and Sir Tony Hoare's paper on *An Axiomatic Basis for Computer Programs* (known as *Hoare Logic*) [42]. Both showed how proof of program (functional) correctness based on an *abstract* and *formal* semantics defined for the programming language. We say that semantics is "abstract" because it defines an abstraction model of the execution of each program in the programming language, instead of execution of the machine code of the program generated by the language compiler. It is formal as the model is defined precisely using mathematics from the formally defined syntax of the language, and this rules out any ambiguity. The ideas and importance of program formal verification and formal semantics of programming languages were proposed earlier, e.g., Turing's idea of "checking a large routine" [102] and McCarthy's talk on "mathematical science of computation" [73]. Thus, formal semantics of programming languages established a precise abstraction of their execution. Both Floyd and Hoare used formal first-order logic to define the semantics and the associated proofs. Later, the expressiveness, soundness, and completeness to the completeness of Hoare Logic were proved [4].

The notion of formal semantics of programming languages therefore provides a level of abstraction of program execution beyond the semantics defined by a compiler in terms of direct machine code execution. Later, formal semantics at different levels of abstraction were defined, which are mainly represented by Scott-Strachey *denotational semantics* [98,101] and Plotkin's *structural operational semantics* (SOS) [85]. Formal semantics theories are usually classified into four kinds and they are *operational semantics* as such Plotkin's structural operational semantics, *denotational semantics* such as Scott-Strachey semantics, *algebraic semantics* such as abstract data types (ADT), and *axiomatic semantics* such as Hoare Logic, in increasing levels of abstraction (but algebraic semantics and axiomatic semantics are at about the same level). These different kinds of semantics are defined for various programming languages of different programming paradigms, including structured programming languages, concurrent programming languages with shared variables, concurrent and communicating programs, object-oriented and service-oriented programming languages. A theory of unification of these different semantic theories is best studied in *Unifying Theories of Programming* (UTP) of Hoare in He [44].

Since the 1968 NATO software conference [77], theories of formal semantics became the foundation for the development of formal methods, including formal *specification, verification,* and *refinement,* forming a subfield of software engineering. As surveyed in [104], over a dozen Turing Award laureates have made pioneering contributions to the development of formal methods, as shown in Table 1.

Table 1. Turing Award Laureates in formal methods

Year of award	Name of Laureate	Area of contribution
1971	John McCarthy	Computational theory, semantics of LISP
1972	Edsger W. Dijkstra	Calculus of predicate transformers
1976	Dana Scott	Denotational semantics and modal logic
1978	Robert Floyd	Axiomatic semantics and verification
1980	Tony Hoare	Axiomatic semantics and CSP
1984	Niklaus Wirth	Programming language formal specification
1991	Robin Milner	CCS, bisimulation, LCF, ML
1996	Amir Pnueli	Temporal logic and verification
2007	Edmund Clarke E. Allen Emerson Joseph Sifakis	Model checking
2008	Barbara Liskov	Abstract data types, Larch
2013	Leslie Lamport	Temporal logic of actions

5.2 Formal Specification and Models

The rigorous study and analysis of program correctness based on formal semantics necessitates the requirements of the program to be specified formally, describing *what* the program should do rather than *how* the program does it. This implies that the language used for requirements specification is at a level of abstraction above the programming languages to be specified. Since the 1970s, a large number of specification languages have been developed.

There are mainly two kinds of specification languages. The first kind of languages are for specification of whole system behaviour, including data functionality, control flow, and data flow. A specification language of this kind has a well-defined semantics and a specification in the language defines a model of the software system under design. The specifications can be at different levels of abstraction and similarly for their models, formally related by partial orders (*refinement*) between specifications and *refinement* between models. We will discuss this further in the next subsection. Table 2 gives a list of major specification languages of this kind.[1]

All the specification languages in Table 2 have denotational or axiomatic semantics (or algebraic semantics), and allow specifications of different levels of abstraction. They also have the notion and rules (though in different degrees of formality) of specification refinement and thus support the top-down derivation of a program from a specification and bottom-up software systems integration.

---

[1] The years and features of the methods in the table are not guaranteed to be accurate or comprehensive.

Table 2. A list of software system formal specification languages

Year	Name of language	Features	Key Originators
1972	VDM [50]	Denotational semantics derivative design	D. Bjørner C. B. Jones
1974	Z [9,100]	Axiomatic semantics refinement	J.-R. Abrial
1975	Guarded commands [28] Action Systems	Logic based refinement [3]	E. W. Dijkstra R.-J. Back
1987	OBJ [34]	Algebraic semantics	J. A. Goguen
1988	B-Method [1]	Abstract machine semantics refinement	J.-R. Abrial
1988	UNITY [17]	Axiomatic semantics	K. M. Chandy, J. Misra
1990	TLA [53]	Temporal logic	L. Lamport
1992	Larch [36]	Algebraic semantics	J. Guttag, S. Garland, J. Wing, *et al.*
1999	JML [56]	Contract-based design	G. T. Leavens
2001	Stream Calculus [15]	Algebraic semantics	M. Broy
2004	rCOS [40,41,64]	Contract-based design component-based development (CBD), OO, refinement	Z. Liu, J. He, X. Li, *et al.*

Therefore, formal methods based on these languages provide formalization of notions of a software system development process and principles. There is the yet to be developed capability of supporting the definition and management of the entire processes and not to consider only point solutions of methodology, tools, and models that ease part of the design.

The other kind of specification languages and theories focuses on the abstraction of specific aspects or design problems of software execution, including *control flow, data, concurrency*, and *synchronization*. These theories mainly concern *concurrent software systems* (although the theories in Table 2 can deal with concurrency too). In Table 3, we list some well-known theories of this kind. There are further similar theories or extended versions of them. Compared to the theories in Table 2, these theories mainly deal with interaction, communication, and synchronization, with or without real-time aspects.

CSP and CCS both provide theories for algebraic reasoning of equivalence and refinement or simulation of software systems (although they can model and reason about hardware behaviour). The automata or state transition system-based models (i.e., I/O automata, Statecharts, and Uppaal) support algorithm-based verification, i.e., *model checking*. The synchronous languages Lustre and Esterel are for real-time control and monitoring systems. They have tool support for code generation and they are the basis for the implementation of the industry tool SCADE.

Table 3. A list of feature specific formal specification languages

Year	Name of theory	Features	Key originators
1962	Petri nets [84]	True concurrency event based interaction	C. A. Petri
1977	Temporal logics [86]	Property oriented	A. Pnueli
1978	CSP [43]	Channel and event based synchronous communication algebraic reasoning denotational semantics	C. A. R. Hoare
1980	CCS [75]	Event based synchronous communication operational semantics algebraic reasoning	R. Milner
1987	I/O automata [69]	Asynchronous communication distributed system model	N. A. Lynch
1987	Statecharts [39]	State machine & diagram hierarchy communication	D. Harel
1991	Lustre [37]	Data flow synchronous language signal communication	N. Halbwachs, P. Gaspi, *et al.*
1992	Esterel [5]	Synchronous language signal communication	G. Berry
1995	Uppaal [55]	Real-time model checking	K. G. Larsen, W. Yi
2001	Interface automata [27]	Component-based model	L. de Alfaro, T. A. Henzinger

5.3 Formal Techniques in Software Development

We take the definition that a method is a set of techniques and tools for solving a class of problems which are developed based on a sound theoretical foundation. In software systems, a technique means *a way of carrying out a particular task in a software development process, especially the execution or performance of phases, such as requirements specification, design, or verification.* The term *formal software development* actually means a development that involve intensive use of mathematically-based techniques, such as formal specification and verification. We do not consider separate fully formalized development or *formal engineering methods.* However, we rather propose seamlessly to integrate formal methods, more precisely formal techniques and tools, into overall software development processes, that is to engineer formal methods in software development.

The Trinity of Formal Methods – Specification Languages, Models, and Software Correctness. The specifications languages in Table 2 and CSP, CCS, Lustre and Esterel in Table 3 have a formally (mathematically) defined syntax and semantics. They can specify both the static structural view and dynamic behaviours of software systems (we only consider functionality at the moment) and thus are *system specification languages.*

With a temporal logic-based formal method, abstract execution modes of software systems are defined, such as state machines and labelled state transition systems or automata. These provide the *semantics (interpretations)* of the underlying logic. The formal language of the logic is used for the specification of properties as logical formulas that the system being studied, or under construction, is required to satisfy. The formulas form the *formal specification* of *requirements.*

The *correctness* of the system with respect to the specification is defined as the satisfaction of the relevant formula by the model of the system.

This is denoted as $M \models Spec$ where M is the model of the software system and $Spec$ is the specification of a formula. The theories of input-output automata are mainly about models for behavioural or execution of concurrent and communication systems. They are used with one or more temporal logic statements when dealing with software system verification. Therefore, the fundamental relation among specification languages, models, logic, and software correctness, is a direct inheritance of the trinity of logic, that is language, interpretation, and proofs.

Refinement and Code Generate. A system specification language usually is expressive enough to specify models of a software system at different levels of abstraction. These languages can specify *non-deterministic behaviour*. A specification $Spec_2$ is said to be a *refinement* of a specification $Spec_1$, denoted by $Spec_1 \sqsubseteq Spec_2$, if $Spec_2$ is not more non-deterministic than $Spec_1$. More formally, if the semantics of a specification $Spec$ is defined as the set of non-deterministic behaviours $[\![Spec]\!]$, $Spec_2$ is a *refinement* of a specification $Spec_1$ means the behaviour set of $Spec_2$ is a subset of that of $Spec_1$, i.e., $[\![Spec_2]\!] \subseteq [\![Spec_1]\!]$.

If the semantics $[\![Spec]\!]$ of a specification $Spec$ is defined as, or it itself is, a logical formula, such as a TLA (temporal logic of actions) specification, $Spec_2$ is a *refinement* of a specification $Spec_1$ if $Spec_2$ implies $Spec_1$, i.e., $Spec_2 \Rightarrow Spec_1$. This is why we say in general *specification and program refinement means behaviours inclusion and logical implication*. Therefore, the refinement relation between specification is a partial order, and two specifications are *equivalent* if they are a refinement of each other.

The behaviours of a specification are defined in different forms for different languages, and a language can have different but related semantics. For example, CSP has a *trace semantics*, a *failure semantics* and a *failure divergence semantic* [93]. CCS has mainly an operational semantics. In principle, however, each language can and should have both operational and denotational semantics and their correctness (or consistency) with each other should be proved. Denotational semantics supports the development of verification techniques for specification (or model) refinement and transformation.

Some theories, such as Z, CSP, Action Systems, the B-method, and rCOS have fully formal rules of refinement to support stepwise program derivation. Some other theories have a mathematical definition of the refinement relation, but steps of program derivation are carried out at the semantic level.

CCS and Larch (and CSP too, in addition to its refinement theories based on denotational semantics) provide algebraic reasoning about system model equivalence. However, equivalence is define between high-level models at a high level and those at low level through hiding information, internal interaction, or behaviour.

In purely logical theories such as TLA, UNITY, and dynamic logic (an extension of modal logic), program models are fully specified as logic formulas and specification refinement is directly defined as logic implementation. Then derivations for program development are performed using the deduction rules of the logic.

Lustre, Esterel, and SCADE, are mainly for signals in the control and monitoring of embedded systems. These systems are usually not data-intensive, but their control flow, synchronization, and real-time aspects, are crucial and can be safety-critical. The tools for these frameworks have strong support for correctness-preserving *code generation*. In theory, code generated from a model is a refinement of the model.

Refinement and code generation are, or should be, mostly used in a top-down development process. Decomposition of a large model into submodels and the composition of them are part of the refinement process. Figure 1 from a formal method review paper [104] illustrates the framework of formal refinement.

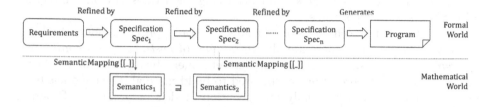

Fig. 1. Process of formal refinement

Verification – Deductive Theorem Proving and Model Checking. Given a model M of software systems and specification *Spec* of a property of the model, as a formula of the logic. The satisfaction of *Spec* by M, denoted as $M \models Spec$ can be proved from a set Γ of em known properties of M. These are made in the *deductive proof system* of the logic. This approach is known as *theorem proving*, rooted in classical *mathematical logic*.

Another method of verification of the satisfaction of a property by a model is using an algorithm that takes as inuts a model M and a specification (i.e., a property) *Spec* and outputs the answer as to whether M satisfies *Spec*. This approach is called *model checking* [22,87]. Model checking can be fully automatic and there are indeed quite a number of software tools for model checking. However, as many satisfaction problems are hard problems in terms of computational complexity, and some are NP-hard problems, the scalability of model checking is still a significant challenge. Therefore, model checking can only effective in some verification problems.

The approach of theorem proving complements model checking by enabling the proof of properties that are not feasible using model checking. Software tools for theorem proving are normally called *theorem provers*. These tools are interactive, rather than being completely automatic. The state of the art of verification tools are those with a combinations of model checking, automatic satisfaction solvers, and interactive deductive proving, although there is still some way to go to become generally effective.

Combination of Formal Techniques for Engineering Formal Methods.
Theories of formal refinement help to provide insight into the understanding
of the relation between development tasks and software correctness, as well as
the validity of links between the techniques used in different development tasks.
However, applying formal rule-based stepwise refinement to large system development is not feasible. Therefore, less formal steps of refinement are often used.
In this case, verification of the correctness such refinement is needed and the
verification can either be done by theorem proving or through model checking of
conditions. Nowadays, interactive theorem provers employ model checking algorithms and SAT/SMT (*satisfiability modulo theories*) solvers. An SMT solver
like Z3 [6] is, differently from model checking, based on decision algorithms for
constraint satisfaction problems. Model-checking algorithms now also integrate
SAT/SMT solving algorithms.

In addition to the techniques of refinement, theorem proving, model checking,
and SAT/SMT solving, there are also techniques of *abstract interpretation* [25]
and *program synthesis* [70]. If we consider refinement being best for top-down
design, abstract interpretation can be used to build more abstract models from
more concrete models, especially for execution models of programs. Program
synthesis is the construction of a program from a specification. This is usually
through constructing proof of the specification (which is a logic formula) to form
a program. Alternatively it may be used to find a model such as an automaton
from a formal logical specification. Abstract interpretation makes use of formal
proof techniques and can have different degrees of automatization.

Through over 50 years research and development, there are now a large number of specification languages, models, and techniques for verification. We have
covered some of the most significant advances in the development of verification
(or proof) tools. Thanks to improving online resources, we refer readers to the
Wikipedia pages for the techniques of theorem proving, model checking, and
SMT solving techniques:

- https://en.wikipedia.org/wiki/Automated_theorem_proving
- https://en.wikipedia.org/wiki/Model_checking
- https://en.wikipedia.org/wiki/Satisfiability_modulo_theories

Each of the above pages contains a reasonably complete list of tools for the
techniques.

The crucial importance of formal specification, design, and verification cannot
be ignored now with the overwhelming increase of software-based safety-critical
applications. For example, aircraft control software systems and car software
systems may be required to be formally specified and verified (e.g., by standards).

However, with the availability of the large body of knowledge of theories,
techniques, and tools, software engineering practitioners, those in industries often
wonder which formal methods are the best. Indeed, we have been asked questions like "which of method X and Y is better?" Considering the complexity
of software development and the large number design problems nowadays, our
answer to this question is a restricted version of the earlier quotes from Brooks,
and Sommerville [99] in Sect. 3, that is:

There is no single formal method or technique that is alone enough for a non-trivial software system development. Rather, a diverse set of formal techniques and tools has to be combined and used with informal engineering methods.

Therefore, in the design and management of a software development process, there is a need to consider which development tasks require what formal techniques and tools, as well as the required expertise in the formal methods to be used. The software architecture should also serve as a knowledge map for the identification of expertise, techniques, and tools. This is the main intention of the notion of engineering formal methods, which we propose in this paper.

6   Domain Modelling

The important aspects of abstraction, development processes, and software architecture, as discussed in Sect. 3 and Sect. 4 have led to empirical modelling and design of software systems. The formal theories and techniques reviewed in Sect. 5 are motivated by and reflect those informal and conceptual ideas and principles.

As claimed in Sect. 5, that a development of a software system cannot be purely formal, it must involve interactions of formal and informal, objective and subjective, and technical and non-technical activities [105]. There is unfortunately an ignorance or lack of understanding of these interactions, in both the academic community and the software industries. This is a crucial factor for the slow adoption or integration of formal methods in industry software development and the lack of enough interest among students to study formal methods.

In traditional model-based system and software engineering, domain modelling and system modelling are in general separated to develop a framework for the combination of informal and formal modelling. We propose to study the relation between modelling the application domain and modelling the requirements of software systems for the domain, and to develop a unification of them into a framework for modelling *Human-Cyber-Physical Systems* (HCPS) in Sect. 8. To this end, we need to understand some core notions, which are important in scientific and engineering modelling, including *concepts, relations among concepts, functionality, processes, components, systems* and *architecture*. These ideas are key to the development of object-oriented, component-based, and service-based modelling frameworks in software engineering from both domain modelling and software systems modelling. We envision that they are important in developing a unification of these modelling frameworks for HCPS.

6.1   Modelling in General

Domain modelling is part of system requirements modelling and analysis, and in general is to clearly and precisely define the functions, operations, services, and processes, together of course with the related concepts and data too. It also relevant to the study of modelling more generally.

In general, a *model* of a *thing* or *object* is an abstraction or a representation of the *essential properties* of that thing or object. What is essential depends on the modeller's interest. In engineering and science, modelling is treated more seriously and systematically. As Lee states, "the act of modeling involves three distinct concepts: the thing being modeled, the model and the modeling paradigm" [57]. There, he gives two examples of modelling. The first is:

> Newtonian model of a mass and a spring (the thing being modeled) consists of an ordinary differential equation (ODE) (the model). The modeling paradigm is the mathematics of calculus and differential equations.

Edward A. Lee 2015

The second is:

> ... a computer program written in C (the model), which models the behavior of an electrical machine (a computer) that transforms binary data stored in electrical memory. Here, the modeling paradigm is the computer science theory of imperative programs.

Edward A. Lee 2015

6.2   Domain Processes, Concepts, and Architecture

Software, and in fact any ICT system, is typically developed for use in an *application domain*, and evolves along with the evolution of the application domain. The first and most common informal activities are in the understanding of the application domain together with the capture and analysis of the requirements of the software system to be designed and maintained.

However, there are different definitions with respect to applications. One commonly used in the community of model-driven development is that the application domain of a software is the segment of reality for which a software system is developed, which can be an organization, a department within an organization, or a single workplace. In fact, a domain in this view is more precisely a concrete *domain scenario*. Another understanding of the domain of a piece of software concerns the *knowledge area* of the application, such as medical and healthcare, enterprise of trading, banking, aerospace, and automotive.

A domain is mainly described in terms of functions, operations, services, and processes in that domain. These are usually called *domain functions*, *domain operations*, *domain services*, and *domain processes*. These are understood at two levels. At the meta level (conceptual level), they define types (or classes) of *instances* of the functions, etc., that are actually executed in the domain. In the meta level, they are described in terms concepts and types of data. At the instance level, executions are defined in terms of instances of concepts (also called *objects*) and data of data types at the meta level. With the view of the domain as a *knowledge area*, the application can be described more generically, but it is then hard to define the stakeholders, and thus scope, boundary of the application, and the concrete performance and properties of the services. Then processes cannot be easily specified. On the other hand, given a concrete application scenario, a domain is always defined with a boundary that demarcates its content. The boundary is often but not necessarily related to a boundary in the physical world, such as a department of a university, a floor of a smart building, or even, say, the heart of a person.

We take the view that a domain always has a boundary that demarcates its content. This *content* comprises the domain functions, domain operations, domain services, domain processes, together with the *concepts* and *types of data* (i.e., data at the conceptual level), which are used in the description of the functions, etc. It is important to understand that the concepts and types of data define the *objects* and *data* which are involved in the execution of the functions, operations, services and processes. Some of these objects are *actors* and some are *resources*. The data is usually used to represent properties of objects, functions, operations, and processes. For domain understanding in general, concerning domain understanding and modelling, analysis at both the meta level and instance level (or execution level) are needed.

Functions, operations, services and processes are all *functionality* or *features*. Their difference is mainly in their granularity and there are applications that are function oriented, operation oriented or interaction oriented, and service oriented or process oriented, depending on their domains. In general, a process-oriented domain often has a layered structure in which processes are formed at a higher layer though coordinating and orchestrating functions, operations, or services in the layer below (sometimes other layers). In this case, processes of a layer can also be abstracted and treated as interface operations or services. These processes can then be used to compose higher-level processes, in order to allow them to collaborate and share resources. For example, the processes related to sales, inventory management processes, and staff management processes in a supermarket are managed and coordinated at the supermarket management level. Furthermore, an enterprise of a supermarket chain comprises the processes that manage, control, and coordinate the processes of the supermarkets within the enterprise.

Thus, a well defined domain forms a *system* and it has a clear horizontally component-based and vertically layered *architecture*, regardless of the level of computerization (or digitization) in the domain. Even with a purely manual system, i.e., with no digital computers used at all, a domain also has an architecture of its organized services and processes in its sub-domains and different layers of abstraction. The architecture also has its executions, which are called the *dynamic behaviour of the domain (architecture)*. Communication for interaction and exchanges of data among the components in a horizontal level and in different layers are involved in a domain execution.

Taking the view of Lee on modelling in Sect. 6.1, the things to be modelled in domain modelling are the domain processing, together with the objects and data involved in the processes. The overall models of these processes form a model of the domain system architecture. There are a few well-known paradigms for domain modelling, including Jackson's *problem frames* [47,48], Parnas' *four-variable* method [81], and the *use-case driven approach* [54,61]. The key idea of these methods is to identify the interface between the environment and (part of) the software system under design (SUD). At this stage, the SUD is actually a model of a domain process or a set of domain processes to be realized by the SUD. These domain processes are, in general, discrete sequences of state changes caused by interactions with their environments. Some domain processes are physical processes and modelled with continuous functions, which are often defined by differential equations. In more general and complex application domains, there are *hybrid processes* of discrete state changes and continuous evolutions between discrete state changes. Obviously, when producing models for processes, the objects and data involved must be modelled. A modelling paradigm provides a theory and techniques for modelling the processes and the architecture at different levels of *abstraction* and from different *view-points*. We give two examples to show these important ideas.

6.3 Discrete Interactive Processes and Physical continuous Processes

Consider a domain $\mathcal{D}$ with it boundary. We are usually (at a moment of time) concerned with a set of processes of the domain that forms a *component* $\mathcal{C}$ of $\mathcal{D}$. The processes in $\mathcal{C}$ can have interactions among themselves, called *internal interactions* or *internal communications*. They also have interactions with the rest of the domain, denoted by $\mathcal{E}$, called the *environment*. These interactions are the *external interactions* or *external communications*. The domain $\mathcal{D}$ can be represented as $\mathcal{D} = \mathcal{C} \parallel \mathcal{E}$, and in this model, $\mathcal{C}$ is modelled with "extensive" details, while the model of $\mathcal{E}$ only focuses on the interactions with $\mathcal{C}$ and abstract assumptions on its behaviour. It can be seen that we can carry out incremental modelling of $\mathcal{C}$ by considering processes one by one.

A Modelling Example of a Discrete Interactive Process. We give an example in which the domain system mainly comprises data or information processes. The argument we make is that different views should modelled in different languages; different domains should be modelled in different languages; even when notations used are syntactically the same, their semantics may be different (at a certain level of abstraction); and the language used should be within the expertise of the modeller. These different modelling notations are known as *domain-specific languages* (DSL).

Example 1 (Point of Sale). We take the problem statement from Larman [54,61]:

> Consider the construction of a software system for Point of Sale to be used in a store to processes sales and manage inventory. The goal is for increased checkout automation to support faster, better and cheaper services and business processes, and [...] quick checkout for the customer fast and accurate sales analysis.

The modelling always starts with informal analysis and description of the domain. For such a data-intensive system (or information system), we propose that in the domain modelling, one needs to identify:

– *domain (business) processes* and represent them as *use cases*;
– *domain concepts* together with their *relations* and model them by a *conceptual class diagram*;
– *business rules* and *constraints* and describe them as *system invariant properties*.

It is important to understand that carrying out each action in a business process involves objects and data. The objects are the main instances or entities of domain concepts. Objects collaboratively involved in an action must be related in some way and this is defined as relations between the domain concepts that define these objects. We can see the understanding of use cases is intrinsically *object-oriented*, although the design and implementation of the software does not have to be object-oriented. When describing a use case, it is important to be clear about the "significant" concepts and objects, giving them definitons that are precise enough for our purposes. The same attention should be paid to relations between concepts.

Figure 2 is an sample description of the use case for checking out a customer, where only cash payments are handled, We give the use case the name "Buy Items with Cash". The description is informal, but tends to be structured and precise.

Note that here we focus on domain processes without even needing a computerized system. Therefore, when we have an interaction of a process with input or triggering actions, we ask what the action will actually have an effect in terms of storing data, checking conditions, doing computation, and making decisions. Specifying what to do is essential, but not what or who does it, or how it is done. In the *Buy Items with Cash* process, we can assume that the Cashier actually takes the computational responsibilities to carry out the actions with tools, even if these are just pen and paper.

We take the use case description as a global behavioural view. It is more concerned with the interactions, but it contains information about domain concepts and data. It also contains an abstract description of the data functionalities of each interaction. However, it is not easy to handle and communicate such an informally described use case. With further analysis, we can create the interaction view model as the sequence diagram in Fig. 3(b) and the conceptual structure view as the *conceptual class diagram* in Fig. 3(a), which we call the *conceptual model* of the use case. These models are more formal with symbolic representations of the process, its concepts, and associations among concepts. We treat a use case as a component of the whole domain system and document use case interaction actions in the component box of Fig. 3(c). These actions in the box are the interface operations of the component with its environment. To study the dynamic flow of control and for application dependency, property verification, such as reachability properties, a state machine model as in Fig. 3(d) is

Use Case: Buy Items with Cash

Typical Course of Events

Actor action	What to do
1. This use case begins when a **Customer** arrives a **Cash Desk** with **items** to purchase.	
2. The **Cashier** obtains and *records* the **identifier** from each **item**.	3. Determines the **item price** and *adds* the **item information** to the **running sale's transaction**. based on the **catalog** The **description** and **price** of the current **item** are presented.
If there is more than one same item, the Cashier can enter the **quantity** as well.	
4. On completion of the item entry, the Cashier indicates to the Cash Desk that item entry is completed.	5. Calculates and presents the *sale total*.
6. Cashier tells the Customer the total.	
7. The Customer gives a **cash payment**, possibly greater than the sale total.	
8. The Cashier *records* the **cash received amount**.	9. Shows the **balance** due back to the Customer. Generate a **receipt**.

Exceptional course

1. Line 2: Identifier is not valid or found.	Exception handling.
2. Line 7: Customer does not have enough money.	Exception handling.

Fig. 2. A use case description

needed. The models in Fig. 3 become fully formalized only when the semantics of the diagrams there are also completely formal. Indeed, their formalization is given in the rCOS method for formal refinement of object-oriented (OO) and component-based systems [19, 21, 41, 65].

Note that we are modelling a domain process and the name of the component *BuyItems-Controoler* represents the *role* or *agent* that carries out what responsibilities of the actions are required to do. In this example, it can be the cashier herself or another agent. Here, the entity *agent* is to provide the separation of the interface events from their effects. We will see in the next section that this separation helps us to identify what can be digitized in a system.

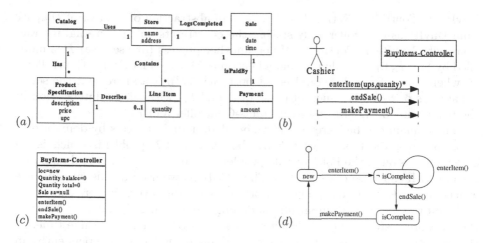

Fig. 3. (a) Class diagram of POST, (b) sequence diagram of use case *BuyItems*, (c) use case controller of *BuyItems*, and (d) state diagram of *BuyItems*

To represent what an action does clearly, we use the notion of a *contract*, which is a *precondition* and *postcondition*. For example, with respect to the action *enterItem(upc, quantity)*, we describe its contract as follows:

- Precondition: *upc* exists and is valid.
- Postcondition:
  - If a new sale, a *Sale* was created.
  - If a new sale, the new *Sale* was associated with the *CashDesk*.
  - A *SalesLineItem* was created.
  - The *SalesLineItem.quantity* was set to *quantity*.
  - The *SalesLineitem* was associated with the *Sale*.
  - The *SalesLineItem* was associated with a *ProductSpecification*, based on *UPC* match.

The precondition assumes what input parameters are allowed for execution and the postcondition specifies what property will be guaranteed after the action if the precondition holds before the action start. Again, the above description of the precondition and postcondition of an action, which form an *contract* of the operation, is informal. The formalization of contracts of use case operations is part of the rCOS method for formal refinement of OO and component-based systems [19, 21, 41, 65].

In rCOS, we have extensively studied ways of creating these view models (see Fig. 3) and defined their formal semantics individually, together with their consistent integration. Now, let us use $\mathcal{D}$, representing the domain of a given supermarket, which has a large number of business processes and objects. Let BuyItems-Controller be the formal integration of the identified *Buy Items with Cash* use case. Then, $\mathcal{D} = \mathcal{E} \parallel$ BuyItems-Controller, where $\mathcal{E}$ represents the environment of BuyItems-Controller in $\mathcal{D}$, i.e., the interactions of actors with

BuyItems-Controller. Notice that here $\mathcal{E}$ is an abstraction of the rest of $\mathcal{D}$ apart from BuyItems-Controller, only stating the constraints on the external interactions with BuyItems-Controller. When another process (or use case) P is modelled by $\mathcal{E}_1 \parallel P$, then the domain model becomes $\mathcal{D} = \mathcal{E}_2 \parallel$ BuyItems-Controller $\parallel$ P, where $\mathcal{E}_2 = (\mathcal{E} \cup \mathcal{E}_1) - (\text{BuyItems-Controller} \cap P)$. Note here that the set of behaviours of $\mathcal{E}_2$ is the union of those of $\mathcal{E}$ and $\mathcal{E}_1$, without the intersection of the behaviours of the use cases BuyItems-Controller and P.

The domain can be incrementally modelled, domain process by domain process. In our project on the CoCoME benchmark [92] problem, which is an extended version of the Point of Sale problem, we used model-driven design of a system with eight use cases [20, 21]. The notations we used in this example are exactly from rCOS. In our previous work on rCOS, however, we were concerned with software system requirements modelling, considering the relation between the software system being modelled and the environment at the same time. In this section, we propose a framework for domain modelling independently, in order to allow us to identify where, what and why software systems are required in the domain.

A Modelling Example of a Continuous Process. This example shows the key ideas of modelling a continuous process. We wish to emphasize that the process of building a model of a thing is a cognitive procedure of analysis, simulation, and reasoning about a sequence of models, involving abstraction, refinement, decomposition, and composition.

Example 2 (Pacemaker). For example, consider the design of an artificial pacemaker, which is a device to maintain an adequate heart rate, for example if the heart's natural pacemaker is not fast enough. For the functioning of a heart, we quote the description from the paper [49]:

> "The Sinoatrial (SA) node, which is a collection of specialized tissue at the top of the right atrium, periodically spontaneously generates electrical pulses that can cause muscle contraction. The SA node is controlled by the nervous system and acts as the natural pacemaker of the heart. The electrical pulses first cause both atria to contract, forcing the blood into the ventricles. The electrical conduction is then delayed at the Atrioventricular (AV) node, allowing the ventricles to fill fully. Finally the fast-conducting His-Pukinje system spreads the electrical activation within both ventricles, causing simultaneous contraction of the ventricular muscles, and pumps the blood out of the heart."

End of Example

Model Refinement: The designer needs to understand a natural heart, both of its structure and behaviour. There can be many models about the rate of a heart, with different levels of accuracy. With each model, the healthiness of the heart can be decided. Therefore, we can have a number of models of a healthy heart.

For example, given a heart, we can use the number of beats per minute (b/m) as its model, and we denote this model as $H_{b/m}$. We define the heart to be healthy if its rate is within [50,90] b/m. Another model of a heart is produced by an electrocardiogram (ECG) test, denoted by H_{ecg}, and the heart is healthy under this model if its ECG test is "normal" (defined according to medical science). For use, there are sophisticated models produced by medical experts, as used for example in the paper [49].

We say that any heart H_{ecg} is a *refinement* of $H_{b/m}$, since there are more details represented in the former than in the latter. More importantly, whether the heart is healthy (or unhealthy) according to H_{ecg} must match this criterion according $H_{b/m}$.

Model Decomposition: Further study on the components of a heart by cardiac electrophysiologists has led to models of hearts as compositions of models of components. For example, a heart has three components, which work together for blood supply. They are the *sinoatrial* (SA) node, the left and right *atria*, and the left and right *ventricles*. The SA node, which is also called the natural pacemaker, regularly generates an electrical pulse; the pulse causes both atria to contract, causing the ventricles to collect and expel blood. We use SA to denote the model of the SA node, LA and RA to denote the models of the left and right atria respectively, and LV and RV the models of the left and right ventricles respectively. Then a component-based model H_c of a heart H is defined to be the composition $SA\|LA\|RA\|LV\|RV$.

The example shows that a model of an object is a representation of the *observation* of the modeller, and the level of details in observations can be incrementally refined top-down or conversely abstracted bottom-up. Refinement by decomposition is to open up an abstract "black box". Abstraction by composition of components is the process of hiding internal details of relations and interaction between components to make a black box.

Multi-views Modelling: When building a model of a complex object, modellers observe the object from a number of different viewpoints [19]. Each view is concerned with certain aspects of the objects. Different views can be orthogonal, but often interrelated, and thus they can be investigated at different times by a single modeller or concurrently by several modellers, with collaboration.

For example, we may start by observing the rate of a heart as its *global behaviour view* and then consider its organization to see its main components of sinoatrial node SA, the left and right atria, LA and RA, and left and right ventricles, LV and RV. For each of these components, we are concerned about the views of their observable functionality in separation, the structure view of their dependency for interaction, and their dynamic interaction view. We now discuss a number of views and show how we can build their models.

Heart Rate: We use a timed function $H_r : Time \mapsto \{0,1\}$ to represent a heart rate as shown in Fig. 4, where $Time$ is the set of non-negative real numbers in this example. We omit the way the rate of a heart is measured here.

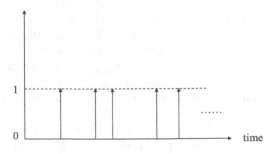

Fig. 4. Heart rate

Interface View of Components: We can use a declarative description for the static functionality view of the components. The following specifications are given using the syntax of rCOS component declarations, but without adhering to the rCOS semantics here however.

```
Component SA {
    provided interface {getSignal()};
    output interface {outPuls()};
}

Component LA {
    provided interface {inSignal()};
    output interface {contract()};
}

Component LV {
    provided interface {inSignal()};
    output interface {bloodIn(), bloodOut()};
}
```

We can have the same models for *RA* and *RV* as for the left counterparts above, respectively, and they can have diagrammatic illustrations similar to UML component diagrams, such as those in Fig. 5.

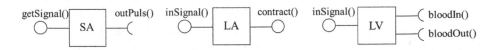

Fig. 5. Components of heart and their interfaces

System Structure View: We build the structural view of the heart by linking the operations (or signals) in the provided and required interfaces of the components. For example, we can use a renaming operation on a component to change the names of operations in order to represent the linkages of the interface operations in different components for interactions. To this end, we rename inSignal() of *LA* and *RA* as outPuls(), to link the output signal of *SA* to the input signal of *LA* and *RA* for their interaction. We denote the versions of *LA* and *RA* after the renaming as *LA[outPuls()/inSignal()]* and *RA[outPuls()/inSignal()]* respectively.

In the same way, we can rename the inSignal() of *LV* and *RV* and have *LV[contract()/inSignal()]* and *RV[contract()/inSignal()]*, to link the output of *LA* and *RA* with *LV* and *RV* for their interactions. Of course, we can rename interface operations with different renaming functions. For example, we can the output signal outPuls() of *SA* as inSignal() of *LV*, instead of renaming inSignal() of *LV* and *RV*. We can have the composite model:

```
Component Heart {
  LA || LA[outPuls()/inSignal()] ||
  RA[outPuls()/inSignal()]|| LV[contract()/inSignal()] ||
  RV[contract()/inSignal()]
}
```

In a formal modelling language, this can be written as an expression of the form $P_1 \parallel P_2 \parallel P_3 \parallel P_4 \parallel P_5$. Figure 6 give a diagrammatic illustration of the structure model. The boundary of the domain system is now clear, formed by the interfaces of *SA*, *LV*, and *RV*, to the outside of the heart.

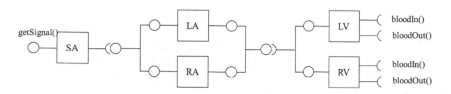

Fig. 6. Structure view of hear

Component Interaction View: The model of the local interface views and the structural view concern static aspects of a heart. To understand how a heart functions, we need to observe the dynamic behaviour of the components and that of the composite heart as a whole.

There are different views of the dynamic behaviour. An important view is how a component interacts with its environment, through its interface operations or signals. Furthermore, there can be different views of interest about interaction behaviours, such as an untimed temporal view and a timed view. We can model both together in one model, but dealing with them separately can be easier when these two aspects are complex. For the temporal order of interactions of a component with its environment, we can use component sequence diagrams [61], as shown in Fig. 7.

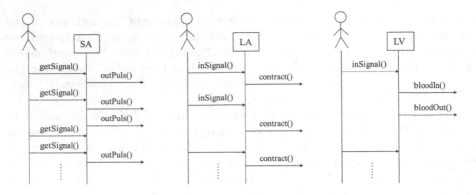

Fig. 7. Component interaction view

System Interaction View: As for the composed whole system, there are two interaction views, the black-box view and a "white box". With the black-box view, as shown in Fig. 8, one can only observe the interactions of the system with its environment without being able to see the internal interaction among the components of the system. Therefore, no other components can interact with the components inside the system through internal interfaces, i.e., those linked pairs of provided and required interface operations. On the other hand, in the white-box view, the interface operations remain visible to the environment and thus they still provide interactions to the outside environment.

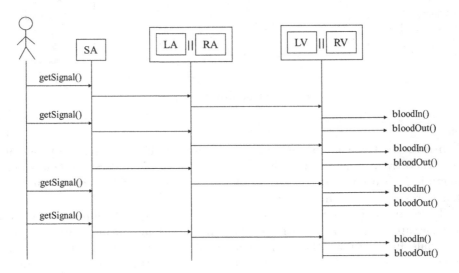

Fig. 8. System interaction view

We notice that it is difficult to use a sequence diagram to show the broadcast signal `outPuls` from SA to both LA and RA, and this is why we make their parallel composition $LA \parallel RA$ a single component.

Timed Interaction View: A model, such as a sequence diagram, for the untimed temporal order of interactions, expresses the causality relation between events, but it may not be expressive enough to define the exact time points of synchronization, depending on the notation used (true concurrency vs. interleaving). However, a model of the timed interactions will present the time information about when exactly an event can or will happen. We can simply use timed functions to represent timed interaction behaviours.

For a component, such as SA, a timed interaction behaviour is a function from time to a set of its interface operations:

$$Ttrace(SA) : Time \mapsto 2^{\{inSignal(),outPuls\}}$$

For any time point $t \in Time$, $Ttrace(SA)(t)$ is a subset of the $2^{\{inSignal(),outPuls\}}$ power set, representing the subset of events in $\{inSignal(), outPuls\}$ occuring at time point $t \in Time$. When $Ttrace(SA)(t)$ is empty, nothing is happening at time t; and when more than one event belongs to $Ttrace(SA)(t)$, these events occur at the same time (with no time delay, even when one causes another). When $Ttrace(SA)(t)$ is a singleton set, we use the element of the set to denote the set for notational convenience.

Obviously, not all functions from the time domain to the interface operations of the component are possible or allowed interaction behaviours. The set of allowed interactions can be constrained by using logic formulas, e.g., stipulating that when an `inSignal()` occurs in SA, an `outPuls()` must occur in a millisecond; and when an `outPuls()` occurs SA, `contract()` must start in half a millisecond.

Another important view can be trajectories of activation, movement (contraction) of the muscle, and the rate of inflow and outflow of blood. Models for these aspects can be defined using differential equations.

Note that in the example above, we only give conceptual discussions about modelling, but we do not claim that the example models in the discussion and figures are necessarily correct models of a heart. Correct models of a heart should be created by or in collaboration with domain experts, in this case cardiac electrophysiologists.

We choose the notations to use from a subset of UML diagrams, which are formally defined in rCOS. However, the semantics we use is intuitive and informal. It is different from the formal semantics, which is defined by rCOS, where interaction is through method invocations. The interactions for the models in Example 1 are signal-based and synchronous broadcasting communication is appropriate. This is more common for systems in which components (processes) are physical objects instead of discrete items of information and data.

7   Traditional Software Requirements Modelling

Different software systems to be developed play different roles in different applications, i.e., domains, or in different parts of domain system. Thus they are modelled, designed, and deployed differently. There are typically two kinds of software:

1. *Software systems to provide digital automation of domain processes.* In this case, a process of the software system is to automate, fully or in part, a domain process. This domain process can be for a computational process, data or information processing, or a control process, that was previously performed manually by *agents* or *roles* in the domain processes. We call this type of software system an *automation software system.* The software system to be developed for the *Point of Sale* system discussed in Example 1, indeed most information systems, are of this kind. Reactive control systems, such as traffic light control system and railway level crossing control systems, are also primarily automation software systems.
2. *Software systems to autonomously monitor and improving the performance of the domain system.* In this case, the processes of the software system are added to interact with processes of the domain systems. They can be seen as redundant components to complement, improve, or correct the behaviour of domain processes. Such software processes are more autonomous, and thus we call them an *autonomous monitoring software system.* The software for an artificial pacemaker is a software system of this kind. The software system for an autonomous room condition monitoring system is also such as system.

We do not claim that there is a clear boundary between these two kinds of software systems. It is usually the case components of both kinds co-exist in a software system. We make this classification because their requirements capture, analysis, and modelling are different Their design of interaction protocols is usually different too.

For a given domain, the requirements modelling of a software system is based on the model of the domain. We consider requirements modelling for automation software systems and autonomous monitoring software systems respectively in the following two subsections and then provide a uniformed notation for their models.

7.1   Requirements Modelling for Automation Software Systems

To design an automation software system, we identify the domain processes (or use cases or tasks) that are to be automated by the software system, together with purposes and added business values. Taking the domain model of each of these use cases, we produce a software model to replace the domain agent (generally called a *use-case controller*), which handle the use case in the domain.

For example, if we are to automate the use case *Buy Items with Cash*, we will build a model of a software component in the following way:

- First, we declare a component with a name, say `Component SalesHandler`, together with its provided and required interface operations (in this case none), where `Component` is a keyword to indicate that this is a software component:

```
Component SalesHandler {
    provided Interface {
        startSale();
        enterItem(upc:UPC, quantity: Quantity);
        ednSale();
        makePayment(amount: Currency)
    }
}
```

This declaration is made based on the `BuyItems-Controller` component box and the sequence diagram in Fig. 2(b). We can also specify the state variables of the component, parameters of the interface operations, and define the types of the variables and parameters.
- Then we make a sequence diagram like the one in Fig. 2(b), but with the agent `BuyItems-Controller` replaced by `<<component>> SalesHandler`.
- Next we identify the concepts and the associations in the conceptual model within the domain model that are involved in the operations of the use case and create a UML class diagram, for example. For this, the contracts of the operations, both informal and formal, are very useful for making sure which objects need to be known (stored, operated on, and transferred through interactions) in the software system, i.e., the "need to know policy" in software modelling. This means the part of the conceptual model of the use in the domain is mirrored in the software model of the use case.
- Now we create the dynamic behaviour model, for example in a UML state machine of the software component.
- We refine the contracts of the operations in the domain use case, or create the contracts if no contract for an operation is given in the domain modelling. We specify the contracts formally when necessary.
- Finally, we define the mapping from the domain elements to the software model and record it as part of the knowledge of the modelling and the modelling elements, for later traceability and other purposes.

It is important to note that developing the models of the software model of the component for a use case is not necessarily a purely mechanical process. Rather, it is a further refinement to the domain use case. Also, in the domain model, the models of a use case do not have to include all the view models, most importantly, the mapping between the modelling elements in the domain use cases and those in models of the corresponding software components.

The modelling elements in the domain and the software components, including sequence class diagrams, sequence diagrams, state machines, contracts of operations, etc., can be defined with formal syntax and semantics for formal analysis, refinement, and verification. If we are only concerned with functionality, each use model consists of the following view model:

1. use case interaction view models – possible modelling notations includes UML sequence diagram, CSP, trace models: rCOS use case sequence diagrams, etc.;
2. conceptual class model (or data model) – possible modelling notations: UML class diagrams, Z notation, VDM, rCOS, etc.;
3. contracts of the case operations – possible modelling notations: rCOS or Hoare Logic;
4. state machine – possible modelling notations: labelled state transition systems (LTS), UML state diagrams, automata, Statecharts, etc.;
5. requirements specifications regarding value-added services, performance, safety, security, fault-tolerance, etc.

With the software components, the use case actors, the *Cashier* (or any other designated agent[2]), interacts with the software component by only passing information into the component and receiving outputs from it, without actually performing any of the functionality of the actions.

Replacing the original agent for actually doing the computational tasks in the domain with the software component requires the design of an interaction mechanism between the software components to realize the interaction between the computer and the actors of the use case. If the actor is human, human-machine interaction technology is used. If the actor is another digital system, appropriate protocols and mechanisms have to be designed. However, at the requirements modelling stage, concrete interaction technologies (or input/output technologies) and protocols are not the main concern.

The philosophical thinking behind this modelling approach is that if we put the model of the software component within the model of the real-world domain, in place of the original agent for the use case, we actually transform the former to a model of a new domain, with the realization and deployment of the software system in the real world transforming the old world to a new world. More precisely speaking, we transform a domain model $\mathcal{D} = \mathcal{E} \parallel \mathcal{C}$ to a model $\mathcal{D}' = \mathcal{E} \parallel \mathcal{S}$, where $\mathcal{S}$ is model of software components to realize the domain component $\mathcal{C}$. With this view, our mindset forms separated views of the real-world domain and the digital system, allowing a view of evolution within the software-defined world. Indeed, we are working in the real world with *software-defined domains*, or actually a software-defined world. This software-defined domain view also provide a model for prototyping and simulation.

Incremental Software Modelling and System Evolution. Sometimes it not possible (due to the state of the art of technology or for financial considerations) or not necessary to automate a whole process. We can model a component that interacts with the original domain agent of the use case. In this scenario, the software component will work in collaboration with the agent to fulfill the use case. For example, we can omit the actions of handling the payment from the automation. Then the software component only needs to inform the agent

---

[2] In old Chinese shops, the Cashier used to send the bill to an accountant sitting in a glass room doing the calculation.

(the *Cashier*) of the total after the `endSale()` to handle the payment. We can also take the domain system with software components that have already been modelled as new domain systems and identify further use cases for automation.

In other situations, we can also extend a use case for which a model of a software component is available. For example, we can extend the *Buy Items with Cash* to a more general *Buy Items* use case that, in addition to cash payments, provides services for credit card payments and cheque payments. In this case, we can extend the model of the software component for *Buy Items with Cash* to a general *Buy Items* use case [63]. This can even be done after the software component for the original use case *Buy Items with Cash* use case has become operational.

Note that new IT developments can enable new use cases too. Also, an automated use case may become outdated by advances in technology, just as a software component can replace a domain agent of a use case. For example, paying by cheque is increasingly rare and even paying by credit card is being replaced by apps on mobile phones.

Component-Based Software Architecture Model. With the view of evolutionary automation, we create evermore models of software components for domain processes and refine existing models of software components. We integrate the software components in ways that allow the interactions among the software components to represent the interaction among the agents who previously handled the use cases in the domain model. This gives us a component-based structure model of the software system. For example, with a number of iterations and refinements, we have created a model for the *Point of Sale* software system. Its component diagram is given in Fig. 9. The interfaces of this integrated software system are use for interactions with the domain system.

Considering the functionality only, we define a model of software architecture as an integrated set of models of software components in which all the five view models of each component as defined earlier in this section, together with their interface operations appropriately (re-)named for the integration. Hence, the architecture is defined syntactically and with a rich semantics.

Requirements Modelling for Autonomous Monitoring Software Systems. Now consider the requirements modelling for an autonomous monitoring software system, such as an artificial pacemaker. A system like this is required in a domain system, where some components may exhibit abnormal or faulty behaviour. The software system is to correct or adjust the behaviour of a faulty behaviour or even to work in its place if the faulty component stops working.

One important characteristic of a faulty component is that faults occur inside the component. The occurrence of a fault may not be observed through the interfaces of the component at the time (or within a certain period of time) of its happening. However, if an error caused by an occurrence of the fault is not corrected or minor abnormal behaviour is not corrected in time, a *failure* of the component can happen, being observed to violate the requirements of the

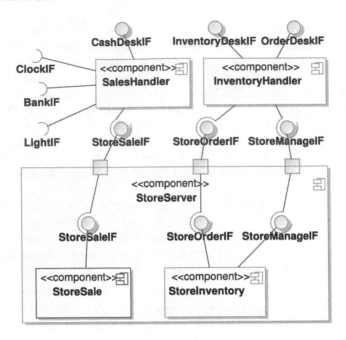

Fig. 9. A software component

component through its interface. Therefore, failures must be avoided to prevent them from spreading to other components and to the environment of the software system. A challenge in the design of a software system for such a domain is to how to detect occurrences of faults or abnormal behaviour where there are no existing interfaces for this.

Consider the design of a pacemaker in Example 2. Here, we have three models $H_{b/m}$, H_{ecg} of a heart H and a component-based model H_c, where we assume that $H_{b/m} \sqsubseteq H_{ecg} \sqsubseteq H_c$. Let us also make the assumption that there is a model for a healthy heart, which is the set of behaviours $HealthyH$.

Let AP be the model of the software system of an artificial pacemaker. We consider a pacemaker to work well if it is compatible with a heart modelled by M, where the model M can be any of $H_{b/m}$, H_{ecg}, and H_c. That is, when the pacemaker works together with the heart, the combined system behaves like a healthy heart. Formally, this means that for the composed model, $(AP \parallel M) \sqsubseteq HealthyH$. By this, we mean that $(AP\parallel M)$ is a *fault-tolerant system* [66,67]. In general, we would like to have the property that if a heart is healthy under a more detailed model, it is also healthy under a coarser model, i.e.:

$$(AP \parallel H_{b/m}) \sqsubseteq (AP \parallel H_{ecg}) \sqsubseteq (AP \parallel H_c)$$

These algebraic properties do not alone provide enough of a specification for designing the software of a pacemaker. We need a model to describe what inputs it receives and the outputs it generates. The requirement for a pacemaker is that it generates a beat (i.e., delivers electrical pulses) when the heart does not beat when it needs to do so. This is the identification of the outputs. In general, the outputs are to correct faults. To identify inputs, however, is to "get" information about occurrences of faults of abnormalities, i.e., to detect problems.

Consider further the case of a pacemaker. We can use a sensor to detect activation of the tissue in the left atrium. When the sensor receives no signal about activation for a given period of time, it generates an electrical pulse and causes contraction of the ventricles. Therefore, the sensor acts as the input interface to the model AP. The interactions of AP with LA and LV are shown in the *component sequence diagram* Fig. 10, where s_1 representing activation of LA is sensed by the sensor. Thus, AP does not generate any output to LV and s_0 representing no activation of LA is sensed.

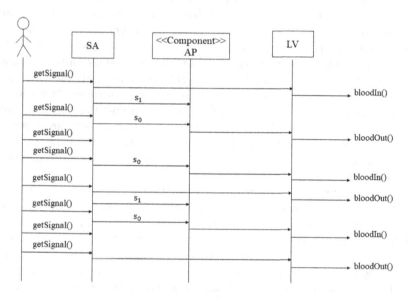

Fig. 10. Interactions between components PA, LA, and LV

Autonomous monitoring software components can also be designed to detect abnormalities of interactions between domain components. In such a case, we can take either of the following approaches:

- We model the protocol as a domain component first with a domain agent to handle the interactions. The monitoring software can then detect abnormalities, such as duplication, losses, corruptions, timing abnormality, etc.
- We take the components involved in the interactions as a composite whole. We then model the internal interfaces needed for detecting and correcting abnormalities as occurrences of internal faults.

Autonomous monitoring software components are usually embedded, physically or logically, within the faulty components in the domain. Therefore, including a software model in the domain, does not change the domain structure: no domain agents are added or removed, but interaction interfaces among the domain agents are changed.

In general, we assume a domain $\mathcal{D}$, a model $\mathcal{C}$ of a part of $\mathcal{D}$ and its environment $\mathcal{E}$. We design a software system $\mathcal{S}$ for monitoring and controlling $\mathcal{C}$, to meet given requirements. Then the software modelling for $\mathcal{S}$ is to transform the domain model $\mathcal{D} = \mathcal{E} \parallel \mathcal{C}$ into a new model $\mathcal{D}' = \mathcal{E} \parallel \mathcal{C} \parallel \mathcal{S}$ that satisfies the requirements. For the artificial pacemaker example, AP is the model $\mathcal{S}$ in the new domain.

7.2   Human-Cyber-Physical Systems – A Unified Architecture View

From the discussion on domain modelling in Sect. 6 and that on software requirements modelling in this section, we can see both are cognitionive processes to obtain incremental and innovative understanding of the domain. For requirements capture and modelling of automation software systems, a use-case driven approach [21,54,63] is more effective and *use-case driven* requirements analysis is similar to, or developed from, Jackson's *problem frames* approach [47,48]. For requirements capture and modelling of autonomous monitoring software systems, it is more a combination a use-case driven approach and Parnas' *four-variable requirements analysis method* [81]. The architecture styles of both are *component-based* or *systems of systems*. Note that in an application domain, both kinds of software systems may be required and thus a combination of requirements analysis methods is needed.

For the development of a software system, either an automation software system or an autonomous monitoring software system, we incrementally transform the application domain by replacing domain processes with software processes or by adding software processes into the domain. These software processes operate with each other and with the domain processes in the transformed domain. It is easy to imagine that there are software processes in the original domain. In this case, software components can be replaced; software component can be monitored, controlled, and enhanced too. Therefore, in such a domain, human individuals, social organizations and systems, cyber-systems (i.e., software systems), and physical processes (such as a heart) interact and collaborate together to perform tasks in the system. Interactions and collaborations are realized through communication networks and interface devices, such as sensors and actuators. Furthermore, communications and interface devices can also be monitored, managed, and controlled by software processes. We thus call such a domain a *Human-Cyber-Physical System* (HCPS), as previously mentioned, and we can see that an HCPS is a continuously evolving system. Modelling an HCPS becomes a uniform modelling framework that combines traditional domain modelling and software requirements modelling.

The term HCPS has evolved from the concept of *Cyber-Physical Systems* (CPS), a type of system that has emerged over several decades [51,97]. We have not seen a reference architecture model for HCPS or any proposal for a systematic modelling framework HCPS architecture. What we propose is that the model of the software systems should be considered in a unified approach to modelling an HCPS. Although there are challenging problems, both in theoretical foundation and in engineering methodology, we are mainly concerned about the interaction mechanisms among cyber-systems, physical processes, and human beings, as well as the impacts of these systems on each other.

8   Towards Architecture Modelling of Evolving HCPS

In general, a *Human-Cyber-Physical System* (HCPS) is a system in a particular domain that consists of human systems, cyber-systems and physical systems (processes). The cyber-systems interact and collaborate with the human systems to undertake living, social, business, and manufacturing tasks by using, controlling, and coordinating the physical systems. Control in an HCPS is dynamically shifted between humans and machines. An HCPS is normally a continuously evolving system where we are concerned with designing software systems for cyber-systems to maintain healthy evolution and to support beneficial evolution of an HCPS.

In this section, we discuss the nature of the component systems, especially the cyber-components required, in a general HCPS, We also argue why an engineering process and technology architecture for using formal methods is required and discuss what we mean by such an engineering process. We discuss why the unifying modelling of domain and software systems that we presented in Sect. 6 and Sect. 7 is desirable for HCPS evolution. Finally we present some research challenges in the design of software systems for HCPS.

8.1   Evolution from CPS to HCPS

The notion of HCPS has resulted due to an evolution from Cyber-Physical Systems (CPS), through integration with techniques of ubiquitous computing (also known as ambient environment), Internet of Things (IoT), big data, cloud computing, and artificial intelligence (AI), with an emphasis on human involvement in the system. CPS was formally proposed in 2006 at a workshop organized by the US National Science Foundation (NSF) [78]. Therefore, an HCPS represents the intersection of the technologies of traditional computation, communication and control, with the new technologies of IoT, big data, cloud computing, and AI. We now briefly discuss the three milestones (or three generations) in the development from CPS, through big data and cloud-based CPS, to HCPS.

Preliminary CPS. CPS was originally defined to refer networked cyber-systems and physical systems, in which:

- the *cyber-world* is formed by systems for computing, control and networking;
- the *physical world* includes mechanical, electrical, and chemical processes, etc.;
- the cyber-systems control the physical side using *sensors* and *actuators*;

- the *network* connects the sensor network, actuator network and the control units, and among the computing systems;
- a *database server* is needed to collect and process events generated in the system, those generated by the sensors, for computation of control decisions.

In such a system architecture, human users of the system are similar to users of traditional computer systems, but without being involved in control decision making. Important related technologies include communication networks, distributed computing and control, and network of sensors. Here, the concept of CPS mainly extends that of *embedded systems* in that the focus of embedded systems is on computational elements hosted in stand-alone devices, while CPS is designed as a network of interacting computational and physical devices. A CPS has many more features, including computations, control, and cooperation that need shared knowledge and information from physical systems to be responsiveness and self-adaptive.

We can see that a joint model of the physical world and the software systems in the cyber-world fits in our modelling framework discussed in Sect. 6 and Sect. 7. However, the challenge lies in the model of interactions and dynamic behaviour of the components in order for the whole system to have the required features. This including difficulties in modelling, such as:

- *communication:* how can the network realize the system-wide properties, such as timeliness,
- *control:* distributed and decentralized control applications are still challenging,
- *hybrid and mobile interactions*: modelling interactions between cyber and physical systems, some of them are mobile, and
- *heterogeneity:* integrated modelling of timing and concurrency of cyber-systems and physical processes, and interoperable composition and integration of models and software components, which are developed by different developers using multiple formalisms and tools.

The focus of a preliminary CPS is very much in collaborative control systems.

Big Data and Cloud-Based CPS. With the technological enabling power of CPS, sizeable and complex applications, such as power grids, industry manufacturing, and traffic control, have kept increasing in multiple dimensions. Different types of networks, including wired and wireless, internet and radio, local and global networks, etc., are used in such a CPS. Therefore, the networks in CPS can encompass the full scope of IoT. Also, a large amount of sensors and actuators, hardware and software components, and physical systems, which are developed and owned by different stakeholders, are managed, monitored, and controlled within the system. During the operation of such a CPS, many events are generated. Collecting and processing the data concerning these events are the basis for effective, reliable, and real-time management and control of the physical processes, hardware, software, and communication networks.

A *data server* is typically responsible for storing and processing the data in a CPS. The control system requests services from the data server according to feedback information or instructions from the users. It then generates control decisions. Data being generated in a complex CPS typically has the properties of extremely large *volume*, high *velocity*, and wide *variety* (i.e., different sources of data). With the huge amount and a large variety of data to be collected in a CPS, storing and processing such a massive amount data requires a technology that is "beyond the ability of typical database software tools to capture, store, manage and analyze" [71]. The solution lies in *big data technology*. However, big data analytics for CPS is not only offline processing of historic data, but more importantly it has to process real-time data and produce responses to events in real-time.

Data processing and analytic for CPS is significantly *valuable* (the fourth "v" of big data after volume, velocity, and variety), which is important in the following aspects:

- First of all, we can design software for data analysis and use AI, based on the large volume of sensors data and system execution data within a CPS, to realize effective, precise and real-time control, and collaboration of physical processes and software components.
- Secondly, the large volume of sensors data and system execution data in a CPS can be used to design and implement software components for monitoring, detecting, and handling abnormalities and faults in the system for fault-tolerance, resilience, and robustness.
- Thirdly, big data analysis is beneficial in designing software components for self-adaption, self-definition for managing the complex dynamic uncertainties in physical environments, and the communication network, and helping to ensure system predictivity, adaptivity, autonomy, reliability, and security.
- With the big data generated in a CPS, more value-added applications and services can be designed and implemented. Consider a lighting system of a city, for example. The data generated by this system can be used to develop services for the city management body, for the police authorities, and for the electricity company's business management.

However, to process and analyse CPS big data effectively, to synthesize information and generate knowledge for smart decision making, and for intelligent and flexible control, we require *cloud computing* and both rule based and machine learning based *artificial intelligence* (AI). The need for cloud computing is also due to the variety of the stakeholders and owners of the data and infrastructures within the CPS. A data server in the cloud becomes the obvious technology solution to providing an open and flexible platform for a variety of users to develop services on the CPS. With such a cloud platform, data analytic models and software can be provided to the control system of the CPS. With a cloud platform, all devices, hardware and software resources, including sensors, actuators, computation resources, data, application software, etc., can be managed, controlled, and shared as services.

A cloud platform is naturally service oriented. Therefore, a big data and cloud-based CPS can effectively leverage *service oriented architecture* (SoA) style to form a CPS of multiple layers from CPSs of different application domains. In the area of industry manufacturing, in particular, there is a clear trend in combinations of customized and personalized design and production, effective coordination of product market analysis and planning, product development, product after-sales services, manufacturing processes, and manufacturing systems management. For example, with marketing analysis systems and after-sales service systems, market information and information about the product quality can be used for product planning, design, quality control and assurance in the production process (including the use of resources, equipment, techniques, and skills of staff), and product testing.

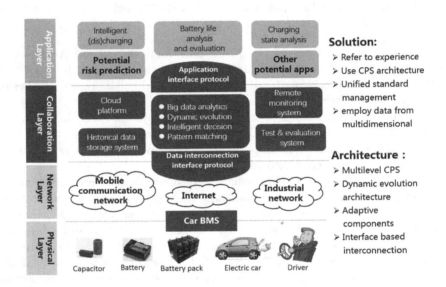

Fig. 11. A proposed architecture of cloud-based battery management CPS

Figure 11 shows a cloud-based CPS that we proposed in a project application for future car battery management. The architecture is organized into four layers. The bottom layer, called the physical layer, consists of car battery management systems and car systems. They are connected by the network layer to form an IoT. The network layer also transfers data collected in the IoT to the cloud computing layer for their storage management, analytics, information synthesis, and knowledge generation. These are to be used for computation, control decision making, and for the development of applications.

In addition to the challenges in modelling a preliminary CPS, there are more difficulties in modelling big data and a cloud-based CPS, among other problems. These includes the following issues:

- A big-data and cloud-based CPS requires software systems developed using different paradigms and architecture styles. These software systems are to interact via heterogenous networks. These pose huge problems of interoperability.
- A CPS is usually safety-critical, and thus its correctness, safety, and the real-time properties of its software components need to be formally provable, and verification of components is required to be compositional. However, there does not yet exists a theory for data-based AI software verification, refinement, and composition.
- Different processes and tasks share data, software services, physical infrastructures, and devices, as well traditional resources for programming execution. For efficient and real-time execution of these tasks concurrently, software abstractions are needed for the management and control of these shared heterogenous resources. Their capabilities and complexity are far beyond those of traditional operational systems. We do not have established models and techniques for these abstractions.

Furthermore, the issue of identifying desired features and quality of service of business, production, and social tasks, and deciding the relevant technologies for their realization. The state-of-the-art requirements modelling and design for CPS does provide full support for such a systematic definition of the technology architecture and process.

Human-Cyber-Physical Systems. The concept of HCPS emerged from two aspects of technology evolution. One is the evolution of integrating human-in-loop control within the control processes of a CPS. The other is the gradual integration of digital social media, social networks in big data technology, cloud computing for knowledge-based intelligent decision making, and the provision of smart services. The integration of these technologies has also been pushing forward with the overwhelming development of deep learning technology.

To consider human factors requires extending the cloud-based CPS architecture, such as the one in Fig. 11, by adding human agents or systems in each layer (except for the network layer). Such an extension then allows, and often requires, extension of the architecture horizontally for a number of HCPSs in different domains to be networked. For example, social systems may need to exchange knowledge about domains. An HCPS for farm machine manufacture, for example, is related to an HCPS for a farm. Extending the architecture horizontally typically leads to extension of the architecture upwards as well. Therefore, we envisage that an HCPS in general has an architecture horizontally and upwards with an open multiple three-layer *system of systems* (Open M3LSOS), as shown in Fig. 12. At the bottom layer are the *unit-level HCPSs* to be connected into the *system-level HCPS*, and the third level is the *system of systems-level HCPS*. Note that an HCPS at a particular level can be used abstractly as a unit to build an HCPS at higher level.

One of the most significant challenges, in addition to those of CPS and cloud-based CPS, is that we need mechanisms for modelling, detecting and possibly

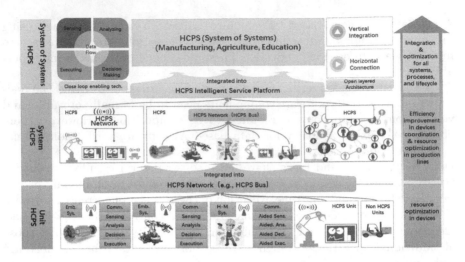

Fig. 12. A cloud-based CPS for battery management

predicting human behaviour, a model of the interactions between humans and cyber-systems, and the possible state changes that can be caused by human actions. We believe that advanced mathematical models and machine learning techniques are needed to help with these issues. Current state-of-the-art techniques are either very coarse and general or too application-specific, such as those of psychological computing, emotional computation, and brain modelling. The development of dynamic human behaviour models that are both accurate and general enough remains an enormous challenge.

8.2   Engineering Formal Methods for HCPS Development

Now we outline a framework for engineering formal methods in software development, software components for HCPSs in particular, in relation to the uniformed framework for domain modelling and software requirements modelling discussed in Sect. 6 and Sect. 7.

A General Model of HCPS. We first briefly summarize the following concepts, principles, and processes in domain modelling in Sect. 6 and software requirements modelling in Sect. 7, respectively:

- For a domain modelling:
  - identify processes and use cases with their actors, noting that some processes are autonomous and do not need an actor to execute;
  - identify the concepts and associations among the processes that involve in the execution of the processes, use cases, and tasks;
  - provide the models of the processes and use cases, their interfaces, together with the model of the domain concepts; and

- integrate the models of the processes and use cases to form the domain model, denoted by $\mathcal{D}$.
- For software requirements modelling in an application domain:
  - identify the use cases that the software system is to automate and the processes that the software system is required to monitor;
  - produce software models for these processes and use cases, together with their conceptual class models (including data structures) and their interfaces with domains, the actors, or processes; and
  - integrate these software models together to form a software model with interfaces to the domain, denoted by $\mathcal{S}$.

We compose $\mathcal{D}$ and $\mathcal{S}$ in a way that replaces the use cases by the models of software components which automate the use cases. Then we add the models of the monitoring software components into the model $\mathcal{D}$. These software components will work together with the processes that are being monitored. We denote the composition as $\mathcal{D} \oplus \mathcal{S}$. Therefore, $\mathcal{D} \oplus \mathcal{S} = (\mathcal{D} - \mathcal{U}) \parallel \mathcal{S}$ if software component $\mathcal{S}$ automates the use cases in $\mathcal{U}$, and $\mathcal{D} \oplus \mathcal{S} = \mathcal{D} \parallel \mathcal{S}$ when software component $\mathcal{S}$ monitors and controls some processes in $\mathcal{D}$. We can see that in $\mathcal{D} \oplus \mathcal{S}$, the automation software component in $\mathcal{S}$ interacts with the actors of the use cases that it automates and the monitoring software in $\mathcal{S}$ interacts with the domain processes that it monitors. Since in general there are humans, cyber-systems, and physical processes interacting through communication networks, we can understand $\mathcal{D} \oplus \mathcal{S}$ as a model of an HCPS.

With model transformations, it is possible to organize $\mathcal{D} \oplus \mathcal{S}$ in a hierarchical component-based and layered architecture, as shown in Fig. 11 and Fig. 12. However, in practice this is only correct conceptually. We still have to solve the challenge of defining the models of humans and interactions between software components and human components before we are actually able to construct a model of an HCPS, as well as specifying and reasoning about its desired functionality and quality of service.

Engineering Formal Methods for HCPS Development. In Sect. 6 and Sect. 7, we discussed the issue that domain modelling and software requirements modelling are both cognitive processes involving informal and formal activities. In fact, a cognitive process cannot be totally formalized. Formal modelling is not necessarily creative or innovative. However, a formal model is beneficial in ensuring correctness and developing deeper insight about the object being modelled. It is the basis for further creative and innovative thinking. Thus, a formal approach is worthwhile in improved modelling for an HCPS.

One of the most significant purpose of formalization is, however, to stabilize the models as milestones in the modelling process. These stabilized formal models are used for formal treatment, such as refinement, integration, verification, simulation, and traceability checking. These formal activities are very important for further informal and creative modelling activities.

Next, we understand that, in general, both domain modelling and software requirements modelling require a variety of expertise and a number of modelling languages. On the other hand, as we have shown in the formal methods review presented in Sect. 5, there is a large number of formal languages and methods. Typically there are several methods that are applicable for the same view or problem. For example, one can use either CSP or CCS for specifying concurrency and communication. Therefore, there is an issue of how to select the languages and methods to be used in the development.

In an HCPS, there is a large variety of software systems within different layers, including the following:

- Unit-level systems: embedded software, device drivers, and operating systems in sensors and devices;
- System level and system of systems (SOS) layer: control and monitoring/ coordinating software, system software for resource management, big data processing and analytics, various kinds of AI software;
- Application layer: apps, web/cloud services, business and workflow management;
- Network layer: communication protocols, network infrastructure and resources management and scheduling, software defined networking (SDN).

Modelling and development of these software systems involves different software architecture styles and technologies, including object-oriented analysis (OOA), service-oriented architecture (SOA), model-driven architecture (MDA), artificial intelligence (AI), etc. These need different formal modelling languages and methods for requirements and design.

The modelling framework we propose is based on the conceptual architecture model in Fig. 12. It starts with software domain and software requirements as follows:

1. apply the domain modelling concepts and principles to build a domain model $\mathcal{D}$, i.e., an HCPS;
2. identify where in the domain model that software systems are required and what kind these will be, following the software requirements modelling concepts and principles;
3. define a process for the software requirements modelling according the nature of the software systems and the interactions with their environments and the expertise of modelling team; the modelling process includes when and what formal models should be produced, by who, and with what methods and tools;
4. build the software model $\mathcal{S}$ for the identified part of the domain in step 2, by the team following the process and using the methods and tools defined in step 3;
5. formalize and carry out verification, validation, and simulation for quality management for the safety-critical models produced in step 4;
6. take the model $\mathcal{D} \oplus \mathcal{S}$ as a new HCPS and repeat this process from step 2.

In each iteration of the above model development process, the HCPS can be extended and different HCPSs for different domains can be composed as a larger

HCPS. These extensions, together with above iterative process, decide the nature of the overall HCPS as it evolves.

With an architecture model of requirements, a process of design, implementation, and deployment, can be defined, either top-down or bottom-up. This demonstrates the importance of the architecture model in defining and managing the development process.

However, significant barriers to the realization of an HCPS development process are still numerous, including in particular modelling human behaviour, human-cyber interaction, composability, controllability and reusability of learning-based software systems.

8.3   Refinement and Evolution of HCPS Model

It is impossible to build a complex HCPS from scratch in one go. Instead, a practical HCPS is continuously evolving. For a given domain, we can think of a model HCPS for the domain at any given time as a result of evolution from the domain developing, incrementally adding an increasing number of software systems.

Given a model built in an iteration of the modelling process, as covered in the previous subsection, software components in this model, as for non-digital processes, can be treated as domain processes and can be:

- replaced by another software component that performs "better" than the original ones;
- monitored, controlled, and coordinated, to ensure that they perform better.

To ensure healthy evolution of an HCPS in this way, we need a notion of *refinement* of HCPS models. For an HCPS component C_1 of an HCPS model $\mathcal{D}$, let P be a (desirable) *property* of $\mathcal{D}$. An HCPS component C_2 is a *refinement* of C_1 in $\mathcal{D}$ with respect to P, denoted by $C_1 \sqsubseteq_P C_2$, if $\mathcal{D}'$ satisfies P, where $\mathcal{D}'$ is obtained from $\mathcal{D}$ by replacing C_1 with C_2.

We do not have such a *partial order* $\sqsubseteq_P$ among HCPS components yet, but the notion of a *contract* [96] in an HCPS is believed to be important for developing such a refinement. With a philosophical intuition, given an HCPS component C, a contract of C means " if the set of behaviours of its environment are assumed to be in the set A, then C guarantees to have it behaviours in G". This contract is written as $A \vdash G$. The meaning of this contract is defined to be $\neg A \cup G$, where $\neg A$ is the complement set of A.

For example, consider the contracts of two pacemakers p_1 and p_2 in the pacemaker example $C_1 = A_1 \vdash G_1$ and $C_2 = A_2 \vdash G_2$. Assume A_1 is the set of behaviours of LA such that the period of time between two contracts is no longer than 3 min; and A_2 is the set of behaviours of LA such that the period of time between two contracts is no longer than 5 min. So A_2 is a weaker assumption than A_1 as $A_1 \subseteq A_2$. If $G_2 \subseteq G_1$, that is G_2 is a stronger commitment than G_1, p_2 is a better pacemaker than p_1. This is because if p_1 works for a heart H, p_2 also works for heart. In general, a contract $C_2 = A_2 \vdash G_2$ is a *refinement* of

$C_1 = A_1 \vdash G_1$, denoted as $C_1 \sqsubseteq C_2$ if $A_1 \subseteq A_2$ and $G_2 \subseteq G_1$, intuitively meaning that latter commits a better service G_2 than G_1 with a weaker assumption (or requirements) A_2 than A_1 on the environment.

There are different definitions of contracts for different systems. For example, a triple $\{pre\}P\{post\}$ of a program P in Hoare Logic is a contract for P, and for a concurrent program P, Jones's *rely-guarantee triple* [24] $\{R\}P\{G\}$ is a contract of P. However, the theory of contracts of this form has yet to develop as a behaviour model of humans; heterogenous components and interactions do not exist.

Even though the formal theory of contracts for HCPSs does not exist, the way of thinking with a notion of a contract is useful in building models and in understanding the evolution of an HCPS. We can see that the following evolution can be applied effectively:

– develop and plug in new components into the HCPS;
– dynamically find and connect components in the HCPS;
– adding more interfaces and/or improving the performance of interfaces, allowing cyber-components to:
  • monitor more and better with respect to its environment;
  • be more autonomous (self-contained);
  • make more intelligent control decisions and provide smarter services;
  • control and coordinate more and better the associated physical components.

Finally, advances of HCPSs also rely on technology development in their application domains and related technologies such production of sensors and actuators. Therefore, rather than designing large HCPSs, it is better to keep evolving an HCPS to improve its optimization, smartness, connectivity, autonomy, and trustworthiness.

8.4 Conceptual Integrity and Domain System Architecture

In Sect. 6, Sect. 7, and this section, we have emphasized multi-view and incremental architecture modelling. Now we can draw the following conclusions:

1. In multi-view modelling, each view model represents certain aspects of the domain system. The *union* of the views gives the whole system.
2. Multi-view modelling is about separation of concern in modelling, dividing the problem of modelling or designing models into problems of modelling from different viewpoints.
3. Refinement of models is about incremental modelling. This can be applied to models of different views and to a group of models or even the models of the whole domain system.
4. Multi-view modelling requires the use of *domain-specific languages*.

We believe multi-view modelling with incremental refinement is helpful and a manageable approach to domain modelling. However, to define and ensure the "integrated unity" of the system architecture from the view models and to maintain this "unity" through the incremental refinement modelling process is known to be a challenging problem in model-driven development [19]. We understand this unity is a major issue in the context of domain modelling[3], the intention of what is called "the conceptual integrity" by Brooks [11]:

> I will contend that conceptual integrity is the most important consideration in system design. It is better to have a system omit certain anomalous features and improvements, but to reflect one set of design ideas, than to have one that contains many good but independent and uncoordinated ideas... a critical need of large projects is that the conceptual integrity can be achieved throughout by chief architects, and implementation is achieved through well-managed effort the architects should develop an idea of what the system should do and make sure that this vision is understood by the rest of the team.

Brooks has not changed his mind. Indeed, he reiterated this in 1995, and again much later at the ICSE 2018 International Conference on Software Engineering [14].

In the context of multi-view and multi-level domain modelling framework, we develop an understanding of conceptual integrity with a domain system architecture view, including the following issues:

1. there is a need for a model of the conceptual view for each component of the system, called the conceptual model of the component;
2. there is a conceptual model of the whole system synthesized from those of the components, in which a concept is related to more than one component;
3. there is a system structure model that defines the partition of the system into subsystems (or components);
4. the subsystem boundaries must be at those places where interfaces between the subsystems are defined rigorously; and this is a defined in a model of each subsystem;
5. models must be defined for the interactions of the subsystems with their environments and their dynamic behaviour models, as well as the interactions of the system as whole and its dynamic behaviour (both black-box and white-box interactions, and behaviour if necessary);
6. the extensions, i.e., the instances (or objects) of the concepts and their relations in the conceptual models, must be clearly defined; and their should be consistency conditions among the concepts and relations across models;
7. the concepts and objects in the conceptual models and their consistency conditions must be consistent with the concepts and objects involved in the interactions and behaviour of the components, and among the components;

---

[3] The word "software" is not meant to be a restriction but in this paper we consider these ideas only within the context of software. Also, the lack of a formal definition for "conceptual integrity" has made it hard to apply this idea systematically and to understand it with better insight.

8. consistency conditions the dynamic models of the subsystems and those of whole system must be defined and ensured;
9. required constraints, both on statics structure models and on dynamic models, should be defined and ensured by the models.

Items 1–4 above model static aspects of the system; item 5 models dynamic aspects; items 6–9 are the required conditions for conceptual integrity, including the requirements in item 9. It is these conditions that are needed to make the models act in "unity".

Therefore, an architecture model of a domain system (e.g., an HCPS) at a given level of abstraction consists of the static structure model of the system described in item 3, the dynamic models described in item 5, and the conceptual models, with the consistency conditions and specification of required constraints.

Apart from the possible path of evolution for an HCPS discussed in Subsect. 8.3, a software architecture in general can be refined and extended in the following ways:

- adding a subsystem that:
  - extends the intention and extension (i.e., the set of instances) of the existing concepts and/or adds new concepts;
  - extends interactions with existing subsystems in the current model, preferably through the system interfaces of the current model; and
  - provides (value-added) interactions with the system environment, including functionalities and services; or improves functionalities and/or performance of the current model.
- refining an existing subsystem, through:
  - decomposing or adding more properties, behaviour, interactions, functionality, etc., according to new knowledge gained; and/or
  - decomposing some of its subcomponents (sub-subsystems).

For component-based design and analysis, we need to treat an architecture model hierarchically. Subsystems are organized in compositions. A subsystem has its own architecture that is the responsibility of its modeller (or architect). In each model refinement step, the conceptual integrity needs to be maintained. For this, traceability of changes and consistency checks are critical. There is a need to develop a framework of architectural modelling in which a set sound methods and tools can be applied in modelling processes. We discuss this in the next section together with software architecture modelling.

9   Concluding Remarks

This tutorial paper is assembled from a number lecture notes, with a mixture of:

- a historical summary about ideas of abstracts,
- a review of formal methods, and

- some thoughts about the relation between domain modelling and software requirements modelling.

The points which we wish to communicate include:

- using a seamless combination of informal and formal modelling, as well as maintaining the domain model as a whole, software system development is modifying the domain model for an HCPS, and then continuing its evolution;
- software system development, for an HCPS in particular, requires the use of multiple formal methods; and normally there is more than one method needed for a particular task;
- the importance of architecture modelling for keeping conceptual integrity as well as for development process definition and management;
- the shift of HCPS system design to system evolution, taking an existing HCPS as an infrastructure for the development new systems and services to extend the original system.

We also discussed the concepts of an HCPS as an integration of a number of recent technologies. The development of an HCPS involves all areas of ICT and its application domain. We have proposed a conceptual architecture model, which has been used to identify some remaining challenges. The architecture defines an HCPS as an open layered system of systems. Finally, we provide a quotation attributed to the pioneer computer scientist David Wheeler FRS (1927–2004), also used by Butler Lampson, on layers of indirection:

All problems in computer science can be solved by another layer of indirection. But that usually will create another problem.

David J. Wheeler [76]

Acknowledgements. Thank you for project support by the National Natural Science Foundation of China (61802318, 61732019, 61672435, 61811530327), the Capacity Development Grant of Southwest University (SWU116007), and the Natural Science Foundation of Chongqing (cstc2017jcyjAX0295). Thank you to Museophile Limited for financial support for Jonathan Bowen.

References

1. Abrial, J.R.: The B-Book: Assigning Programs to Meanings. Cambridge University Press, Cambridge (1996)
2. Ambler, S.: The Agile Unified Process (AUP). http://www.ambysoft.com/unifiedprocess/agileUP.html
3. Back, R.J.: On the correctness of refinement steps in program, development. Ph.D. thesis, University of Helsinki, Finland (1978)
4. Bergstra, J.A., Tucker, V.J.: Expressiveness and the completeness of Hoare's logic. J. Comput. Syst. Sci. **25**(3), 267–284 (1982). https://doi.org/10.1016/0022-0000(82)90013-7

5. Berry, G., Gonthier, G.: The Esterel synchronous programming language: design, semantics, implementation. Sci. Comput. Program. **19**(2), 87–152 (1992). https://doi.org/10.1016/0167-6423(92)90005-V
6. Bjørner, N.: The Z3 theorem prover. GitHub. https://github.com/Z3Prover/z3
7. Boehm, B.W.: A spiral model of software development and enhancement. IEEE Comput. **21**(5), 61–72 (1988). https://doi.org/10.1109/2.59
8. Booch, G.: Object-Oriented Analysis and Design with Applications. Addison-Wesley, Boston (1994)
9. Bowen, J.P.: The Z notation: whence the cause and whither the course? In: Liu, Zhang [68], pp. 103–151. https://doi.org/10.1007/978-3-319-29628-9_3
10. Bowen, J.P., Hinchey, M.G.: Formal methods. In: Gonzalez, T.F., Díaz-Herrera, J., Tucker, A.B. (eds.) Computing Handbook. Computer Science and Software Engineering, 3rd edn, pp. 1–25. Chapman and Hall/CRC Press, Boca Raton (2014). https://doi.org/10.1201/b16812. Section XI, Software Engineering, Part 8, Programming Languages
11. Brooks, F.P.: The Mythical Man-Month: Essays on Software Engineering. Addison-Wesley, Boston (1975)
12. Brooks, F.P.: No silver bullet: essence and accidents of software engineering. IEEE Comput. **20**(4), 10–19 (1987). https://doi.org/10.1109/MC.1987.1663532
13. Brooks, F.P.: The mythical man-month: after 20 years. IEEE Softw. **12**(5), 57–60 (1995). https://doi.org/10.5555/624609.625509
14. Brooks, F.P.: Learn the hard way - a history 1845–1980 of software engineering. In: Keynote at 40th International Conference on Software Engineering (ICSE), Gothenburg, Sweden (2018). https://www.icse2018.org/info/keynotes
15. Broy, M., Stefanescu, G.: The algebra of stream processing functions. Theoret. Comput. Sci. **258**(1–2), 99–129 (2001). https://doi.org/10.1016/S0304-3975(99)00322-9
16. Broy, M., Wirsing, M.: On the algebraic extensions of abstract data types. In: Díaz, J., Ramos, I. (eds.) ICFPC 1981. LNCS, vol. 107, pp. 244–251. Springer, Heidelberg (1981). https://doi.org/10.1007/3-540-10699-5_101
17. Chandy, K.M., Misra, J.: Parallel Program Design: A Foundation. Addison-Wesley, Reading (1988)
18. Chen, L., Babar, M.A., Nuseibeh, B.: Characterizing architecturally significant requirements. IEEE Softw. **30**(2), 38–45 (2013). https://doi.org/10.1109/MS.2012.174
19. Chen, X., Liu, Z., Mencl, V.: Separation of concerns and consistent integration in requirements modelling. In: van Leeuwen, J., Italiano, G.F., van der Hoek, W., Meinel, C., Sack, H., Plášil, F. (eds.) SOFSEM 2007. LNCS, vol. 4362, pp. 819–831. Springer, Heidelberg (2007). https://doi.org/10.1007/978-3-540-69507-3_71
20. Chen, Z., et al.: Modelling with relational calculus of object and component systems - rCOS. In: Rausch, A., Reussner, R., Mirandola, R., Plášil, F. (eds.) The Common Component Modeling Example. LNCS, vol. 5153, pp. 116–145. Springer, Heidelberg (2008). https://doi.org/10.1007/978-3-540-85289-6_6
21. Chen, Z., Liu, Z., Ravn, A.P., Stolz, V., Zhan, N.: Refinement and verification in component-based model driven design. Sci. Comput. Program. **74**(4), 168–196 (2009). https://doi.org/10.1016/j.scico.2008.08.003
22. Clarke, E.M., Emerson, E.A.: Design and synthesis of synchronization skeletons using branching time temporal logic. In: Kozen, D. (ed.) Logic of Programs 1981. LNCS, vol. 131, pp. 52–71. Springer, Heidelberg (1982). https://doi.org/10.1007/BFb0025774

23. Codd, E.F., Lowry, E.S., McDonough, E., Scalzi, C.A.: Multiprogramming STRECH: feasibility consideration. Commun. ACM **2**(11) (1959). https://doi.org/10.1145/368481.368502

24. Collette, P., Jones, C.B.: Enhancing the tractability of rely/guarantee specifications in the development of interfering operations. In: Plotkin, G.D., Stirling, C.P., Tofte, M. (eds.) Proof, Language, and Interaction: Essays in Honour of Robin Milner, pp. 277–308. The MIT Press, Cambridge (2000)

25. Cousot, P., Cousot, R.: Abstract interpretation: a unified lattice model for static analysis of programs by construction or approximation of fixpoints. In: Proceedings of Fourth ACM Symposium on Principles of Programming Languages, pp. 238–252. ACM Press, Los Angeles (1977)

26. Pigott, D.: Online historical encyclopaedia of programming languages (2020). http://hopl.info

27. de Alfaro, L., Henzinger, T.A.: Interface automata. ACM SIGSOFT Softw. Eng. Notes **26**(5) (2001). https://doi.org/10.1145/503271.503226

28. Dijkstra, E.: Guarded commands, non-determinacy and formal derivation of programs. Commun. ACM **18**(8), 453–457 (1975). https://doi.org/10.1145/360933.360975

29. Dijkstra, E.W.: A Discipline of Programming. Prentice Hall, Upper saddle River (1976)

30. Dijkstra, E.W.: The humble programmer. Commun. ACM **15**(10), 859–866 (1972). https://doi.org/10.1145/355604.361591. An ACM Turing Award lecture

31. Floyd, R.W.: Assigning meanings to programs. In: Schwartz, J.T. (ed.) Mathematical Aspects of Computer Science. Proceedings of Symposium on Applied Mathematics, vol. 19, pp. 19–32. American Mathematical Society (1967). https://doi.org/10.1007/978-94-011-1793-7_4. Republished in Program Verification (1993)

32. Forsberg, K., Mooz, H.: The relationship of system engineering to the project cycle. In: Proceedings of the First Annual Symposium of National Council on System Engineering, pp. 57–65, October 1991

33. Giloi, W.K.: Konrad Zuse's Plankalkül: the first high-level, "non von Neumann" programming language. IEEE Ann. Hist. Comput. **19**, 17–24 (1997). https://doi.org/10.1109/85.586068

34. Goguen, J.A.: Higher-order functions considered unnecessary for higher-order programming. In: Research Topics in Functional Programming. Programming Research Group, Oxford University (1987)

35. Grattarola, F.: Margaret Hamilton - coding to the moon. In: A Computer of One's Own, December 2018. https://medium.com/a-computer-of-ones-own/margaret-hamilton-coding-to-the-moon-6ba70b7e6b43

36. Guttag, J.V., Horning, J.J.: Larch: Languages and Tools for Formal Specification. Springer, New York (1993). https://doi.org/10.1007/978-1-4612-2704-5

37. Halbwachs, N., Caspi, P., Raymond, P., Pilaud, D.: The synchronous data flow programming language LUSTRE. Proc. IEEE **79**(9), 1305–1320 (1991). https://doi.org/10.1109/5.97300

38. Hamilton, M.H.: The language as a software engineer. In: keynote at 40th International Conference on Software Engineering (ICSE), Gothenburg, Sweden (2018). https://www.icse2018.org/info/keynotes

39. Harel, D.: Statecharts: a visual formalism for complex systems. Sci. Comput. Program. **8**(3), 231–274 (1987). https://doi.org/10.1016/0167-6423(87)90035-9

40. He, J., Li, X., Liu, Z.: Component-based software engineering. In: Hung, D.V., Wirsing, M. (eds.) Theoretical Aspects of Computing. LNCS, vol. 3722, pp. 70–95. Springer, Hanoi (2005). https://doi.org/10.1007/11560647_5. UNU-IIST TR 330

41. He, J., Liu, Z., Li, X.: rCOS: a refinement calculus of object systems. Theoret. Comput. Sci. **365**(1–2), 109–142 (2006). https://doi.org/10.1016/j.tcs.2006.07.034

42. Hoare, C.A.R.: An axiomatic basis for computer programming. Commun. ACM **12**(10), 576–580 (1969). https://doi.org/10.1145/363235.363259

43. Hoare, C.A.R.: Communicating sequential processes. Commun. ACM **21**(8), 666–677 (1978). https://doi.org/10.1145/359576.359585

44. Hoare, C.A.R., He, J.: Unifying Theories of Programming. International Series in Computer Science. Prentice Hall, Upper Saddle River (1998)

45. IEEE: SWEBOK V3.0: software engineering body of knowledge. IEEE Computer Society (2014). http://www.swebok.org

46. Jackson, M.A.: Principles of Program Design. Academic, Cambridge (1975)

47. Jackson, M.: Software Requirements & Specifications: A Lexicon of Practice, Principles and Prejudices. ACM Press/Addison-Wesley Publishing, Boston (1995)

48. Jackson, M.: Problem Frames: Analysing and Structuring Software Development Problems. Addison-Wesley, Boston (2001)

49. Jiang, Z., Pajic, M., Moarref, S., Alur, R., Mangharam, R.: Modeling and verification of a dual chamber implantable pacemaker. In: Flanagan, C., König, B. (eds.) TACAS 2012. LNCS, vol. 7214, pp. 188–203. Springer, Heidelberg (2012). https://doi.org/10.1007/978-3-642-28756-5_14

50. Jones, C.B.: Systematic Software Development Using VDM. International Series in Computer Science. Prentice Hall, Upper Saddle River (1990)

51. Khaitan, S.K., McCalley, J.D.: Design techniques and applications of cyberphysical systems: a survey. IEEE Syst. J. **9**(2), 350–360 (2014)

52. Kroll, P., Kruchten, P.: The Rational Unified Process Made Easy: A Practitioner's Guide to the RUP. Addison-Wesley, Boston (2003)

53. Lamport, L.: The temporal logic of actions. ACM Trans. Program. Lang. Syst. **16**(3), 872–923 (1994). https://doi.org/10.1145/177492.177726

54. Larman, C.: Applying UML and Patterns: An Introduction to Object-Oriented Analysis and Design and the Unified Process, 2nd edn. Prentice Hall, Upper Saddle River (2001)

55. Laxsen, K.G., Pettersson, P., Yi, W.: Diagnostic model-checking for real-time systems. In: Alur, R., Henzinger, T.A., Sontag, E.D. (eds.) HS 1995. LNCS, vol. 1066, pp. 575–586. Springer, Heidelberg (1996). https://doi.org/10.1007/BFb0020977

56. Leavens, G.T., Baker, A.L.: Enhancing the pre- and postcondition technique for more expressive specifications. In: Wing, J.M., Woodcock, J., Davies, J. (eds.) FM 1999. LNCS, vol. 1709, pp. 1087–1106. Springer, Heidelberg (1999). https://doi.org/10.1007/3-540-48118-4_8

57. Lee, E.A.: The past, present and future of cyber-physical systems: a focus on models. Sensors **1**(3), 4837–4869 (2015). https://doi.org/10.3390/s150304837

58. Leondes, C.T.: Intelligent Systems: Technology and Applications. CRC Press, Boca Raton (2002)

59. Lindsey, C.H., Boom, H.J.: A modules and separate compilation facility for ALGOL 68. ALGOL Bull. **43** (1978). https://doi.org/10.5555/1061719.1061724

60. Liskov, B., Zilles, S.: Programming with abstract data types. SIGPLAN Not. **9**, 50–59 (1974). https://doi.org/10.1145/942572.807045. In: Proceedings of the ACM SIGPLAN Symposium on Very High Level Languages

61. Liu, Z.: Software development with UML. Technical report 259, UNU-IIST: International Institute for Software Technology, United Nations University, Macau (2002)
62. Liu, Z.: Fault-tolerant programming by transformations. Ph.D. thesis, University of Warwick, UK (1991)
63. Liu, Z., Chen, X.: Model-driven design of object and component systems. In: Liu, Zhang [68], pp. 152–255. https://doi.org/10.1007/978-3-319-29628-9_4
64. Liu, Z., Jifeng, H., Li, X.: rCOS: refinement of component and object systems. In: de Boer, F.S., Bonsangue, M.M., Graf, S., de Roever, W.-P. (eds.) FMCO 2004. LNCS, vol. 3657, pp. 183–221. Springer, Heidelberg (2005). https://doi.org/10.1007/11561163_9
65. Liu, Z., Jifeng, H., Li, X., Chen, Y.: A relational model for formal object-oriented requirement analysis in UML. In: Dong, J.S., Woodcock, J. (eds.) ICFEM 2003. LNCS, vol. 2885, pp. 641–664. Springer, Heidelberg (2003). https://doi.org/10.1007/978-3-540-39893-6_36
66. Liu, Z., Joseph, M.: Transformation of programs for fault-tolerance. Formal Aspects Comput. 4(5), 442–469 (1992). https://doi.org/10.1007/BF01211393
67. Liu, Z., Joseph, M.: Specification and verification of fault-tolerance, timing, and scheduling. ACM Trans. Program. Lang. Syst. 21(1), 46–89 (1999). https://doi.org/10.1145/314602.314605
68. Liu, Z., Zhang, Z. (eds.): Engineering Trustworthy Software Systems. LNCS, vol. 9506. Springer, Cham (2016). https://doi.org/10.1007/978-3-319-29628-9
69. Lynch, N.A., Tuttle, M.R.: Hierarchical correctness proofs for distributed algorithms. In: Proceedings of the Sixth Annual ACM Symposium on Principles of Distributed Computing (PODC 1987), pp. 137–151, August 1987. https://doi.org/10.1145/41840.41852
70. Manna, Z., Waldinger, R.: A deductive approach to program synthesis. ACM Trans. Program. Lang. Syst. 2, 90–121 (1980). https://doi.org/10.1145/357084.357090
71. Manyika, J.: Big data: the next frontier for innovation, competition, and productivity (2011). http://www.mckinsey.com/insights/business_technology/big_data_the_next_frontier_for_innovation
72. Mauchly, J.W.: Preparation of problems for EDVAC-type machines (1947). In: Randell, B. (ed.) The Origins of Digital Computers. MCS. Springer, Heidelberg (1982). https://doi.org/10.1007/978-3-642-61812-3_31
73. McCarthy, J.: Towards a mathematical science of computation. In: IFIP Congress, pp. 21–28. IFIP (1962)
74. Mills, H.: Top-down programming in large systems. In: Ruskin, R. (ed.) Debugging Techniques in Large Systems. Prentice Hall, Eaglewood Cliffs (1971)
75. Milner, R.: A Calculus of Communicating Systems. Springer, Heidelberg (1980). https://doi.org/10.1007/3-540-10235-3
76. Murray, D., Fraser, K.: Xen and the beauty of virtualization. In: Spinellis, D., Gousios, G. (eds.) Beautiful Architecture: Leading Thinkers Reveal the Hidden Beauty in Software Design, p. 172. O'Reilly Media, Newton (2009)
77. Naur, P., Randell, B. (eds.): Software Engineering: Report of a Conference Sponsored by the NATO Science Committee, Garmisch, Germany, 7–11 October 1968, Brussels, Scientific Affairs Division, NATO. NATO, January 1969
78. NSF: Workshop on cyber-physical systems, Austin, Texas, 16–17 October 2006. https://cps-vo.org/node/179
79. Nygaard, K., Dahl, O.J.: The development of the SIMULA languages. ACM SIGPLAN Not. 13(8), 439–480 (1978). https://doi.org/10.1145/960118.808391

80. Parnas, D.L.: On the criteria to be used in decomposing systems into modules. Commun. ACM **15**(12), 1053–1058 (1972). https://doi.org/10.1145/361598. 361623
81. Parnas, D.L., Madey, J.: Functional decomposition for computer systems. Sci. Comput. Program. **25**(1), 41–61 (1995). https://doi.org/10.1016/0167-6423(95)96871-J
82. Paul, C., et al.: Documenting Software Architectures: Views and Beyond, 2nd edn. Addison-Wesley, Boston (2010)
83. Perry, D.E., Wolf, A.L.: Foundations for the study of software architecture. ACM SIGSOFT Softw. Eng. Notes **17**(4), 40–52 (1992). https://doi.org/10.1145/141874.141884
84. Petri, C.A., Reisig, W.: Petri net. Scholarpedia **3**(4), 6477 (2008). https://doi.org/10.4249/scholarpedia.6477
85. Plotkin, G.D.: The origins of structural operational semantics. J. Logic Algebraic Program. **60–61**, 3–15 (2004). https://doi.org/10.1016/j.jlap.2004.03.009
86. Pnueli, A.: The temporal logic of programs. In: Proceedings of the 18th Annual Symposium on Foundations of Computer Science SFCS 1977, pp. 46–57. IEEE, September 1977. https://doi.org/10.1109/SFCS.1977.32
87. Queille, J.P., Sifakis, J.: Specification and verification of concurrent systems in CESAR. In: Dezani-Ciancaglini, M., Montanari, U. (eds.) Programming 1982. LNCS, vol. 137, pp. 337–351. Springer, Heidelberg (1982). https://doi.org/10.1007/3-540-11494-7_22
88. Randell, B.: System structure for software fault tolerance. IEEE Trans. Softw. Eng. **22**, 220–232 (1975). https://doi.org/10.1109/TSE.1975.6312842
89. Randell, B.: Position statement: how far have we come? In: Proceedings of the 32nd Annual IEEE International Computer Software and Applications Conference, COMPSAC 2008, 28 July–1 August 2008, Turku, Finland, p. 8. IEEE, IEEE Computer Society (2008). https://doi.org/10.1109/COMPSAC.2008.233
90. Randell, B.: Fifty years of software engineering or the view from Garmisch. In: Keynote at 40th International Conference on Software Engineering (ICSE), Gothenburg, Sweden (2018). https://www.icse2018.org/info/keynotes
91. Randell, B., Buxton, J.N. (eds.): Software engineering: report of a conference sponsored by the NATO science committee, Rome, Italy, 27–31 October 1969, Brussels, Scientific Affairs Division, NATO. NATO (1969)
92. Rausch, A., Reussner, R., Mirandola, R., Plášil, F. (eds.): The Common Component Modeling Example. LNCS, vol. 5153. Springer, Heidelberg (2008). https://doi.org/10.1007/978-3-540-85289-6
93. Roscoe, A.W.: Theory and Practice of Concurrency. International Series in Computer Science. Prentice Hall, Upper Saddle River (1997)
94. Royce, W.W.: Managing the development of large software systems. In: Proceedings of IEEE WESCON, pp. 1–9. IEEE (1970). https://doi.org/10.5555/41765.41801. Reprinted in ICSE (1987)
95. Ryckman, G.F.: 17. The IBM 701 computer at the general motors research laboratories. Ann. History Comput. **5**(12), 210–212 (1983). https://doi.org/10.1109/MAHC.1983.10026
96. Sangiovanni-Vincentelli, A., Damm, W., Passerone, R.: Taming Dr. Frankenstein: contract-based design for cyber-physical systems. Eur. J. Control **18**(3), 217–238 (2012). https://doi.org/10.3166/ejc.18.217-238
97. Schlingloff, B.H.: Cyber-physical systems engineering. In: Liu, Zhang [68], pp. 256–289. https://doi.org/10.1007/978-3-319-29628-9_5

98. Scott, D., Strachey, C.: Toward a mathematical semantics for computer languages. In: Technical Monograph PRG-6, Programming Research Group, Oxford University (1971)
99. Sommerville, I.: Software Engineering, 10th edn. Pearson, Upper Saddle River (2016)
100. Spivey, J.M.: The Z Notation: A Reference Manual. International Series in Computer Science, 2nd edn. Prentice Hall, Upper Saddle River (1992)
101. Stoy, J.E.: Denotational Semantics: The Scott-Strachey Approach to Programming Language Semantics. The MIT Press, Cambridge (1977)
102. Turing, A.M.: Checking a large routine. In: Report of a Conference on High Speed Automatic Calculating Machines, pp. 67–69. Cambridge University Mathematical Laboratory (1949). https://doi.org/10.5555/94938.94952. Reprinted in The Early British Computer Conferences (1989)
103. von Neumann, J.: Introduction to "the first draft report on the edvac". Archive.org. (1945). https://web.archive.org/web/20130314123032/http://qss.stanford.edu/~godfrey/vonNeumann/vnedvac.pdf
104. Wang, J., Zhan, N., Feng, X., Liu, Z.: Overview of formal methods. Ruan Jian Xue Bao/J. Softw. **30**(1), 33–61 (2019). (in Chinese)
105. West, D.: Hermeneutic computer science. Commun. ACM **40**(4) (1997). https://doi.org/10.1145/248448.248467
106. Wheeler, D.J.: The use of sub-routines in programmes. In: Proceedings of the 1952 ACM National Meeting, p. 235. ACM, Pittsburgh, USA (1952). https://doi.org/10.1145/609784.609816
107. Wilkes, M.V., Wheeler, D.J., Gill, S.: Preparation of Programs for an Electronic Digital Computer. Addison-Wesley, Boston (1951)
108. Wirth, N.: Program development by stepwise refinement. Commun. ACM **14**(4), 221–227 (1971). https://doi.org/10.1145/362575.362577
109. Woodcock, J., Larsen, P.G., Bicarregui, J., Fitzgerald, J.: Formal methods: practive and experience. ACM Comput. Surv. **41**(4), 19:1–19:36 (2009). https://doi.org/10.1145/1592434.1592436

Author Index

Printed in the United States
By Bookmasters